GAME ENGINE
TOOLSET
DEVELOPMENT

GRAHAM WIHLIDAL

THOMSON

✦

™

COURSE TECHNOLOGY

Professional ■ Technical ■ Reference

ISBN: 1-59200-963-8

Library of Congress Catalog Card Number: 2005929829

Printed in the United States of America

06 07 08 09 10 PH 10 9 8 7 6 5 4 3 2 1

Publisher and General Manager, Thomson Course Technology PTR:
Stacy L. Hiquet

Associate Director of Marketing:
Sarah O'Donnell

Manager of Editorial Services:
Heather Talbot

Marketing Manager:
Heather Hurley

Senior Acquisitions Editor:
Emi Smith

Marketing Coordinator:
Jordan Casey

Project Editor:
Sandy Doell

Technical Reviewer:
John Flynt

PTR Editorial Services Coordinator:
Elizabeth Furbish

Interior Layout:
Shawn Morningstar

Cover Designer:
Mike Tanamachi

Indexer:
Larry Sweazy

Proofreader:
Sean Medlock

Thomson Course Technology PTR,
a division of Thomson Learning Inc.
25 Thomson Place
Boston, MA 02210
http://www.courseptr.com

THOMSON
COURSE TECHNOLOGY
Professional ■ Technical ■ Reference

*This book is dedicated to my family (Kathy, Lois, Arthur, and Lisa),
and to my grade three teacher who told my parents
I would never be employable.*

*I present this book in respectful memory of Eric Dybsand and Jan Horn.
The gaming community will forever miss you.*

*Remembrance and reflection how allied.
What thin partitions divides sense from thought.*

—Alexander Pope

FOREWORD

Meeting Graham is like walking into a sports stadium for the final game of the season. You are not quite sure how it will end, but you know it's going to be exciting. This was the impression I had when I first met Graham. Graham's passion for his work is evident in everything he says and does. At the same time, he remains open to new ideas and seems to be constantly looking for new ways to improve his personal skills. He is one of the most technically knowledgeable people I know, and at the same time he is able to amicably communicate ideas and concepts.

My project team was looking for some professional help on a project we were working on and Graham had been referred to us as someone who might be able to help. Our project was facing some challenges, as we had a client who was very demanding and it looked like there might not be enough resources to complete the project on time. We were hoping that someone could help us out with some of the internal tools we had developed to support the project team and help us become more efficient.

Graham employed many of the techniques discussed in this book to expedite our project, which helped us achieve many of our project goals without disrupting the team dynamics and workflow we had previously established. I do not come from a game development background, but game engine tools are essentially business software, with differing stakeholders and business rules. Business software often requires additional tools and utilities to improve workflow or produce content, and this book discusses concepts and techniques that are applicable to any .NET software project. I know firsthand the development benefits from the .NET platform and clearly see the value in using this platform to build robust and scalable game engine tools.

I expect that readers of this book will be in a similar position to mine when I met Graham. You are probably a little excited at the prospect of learning new techniques and methodologies and, at the same time, do not want to reinvent the way you have worked in the past. Graham's ideas and concepts will enable you and, I suspect, your team to become more efficient in your projects and will do so in a way that is unobtrusive to your current working methodologies and techniques. I expect you will find reading this book to be a rewarding experience, and I hope you will be able to share in Graham's passion for his profession.

John Eldridge
M.B.A., .Net MCSD, MCDBA, MCSE & CMC

John is a senior Solution Architect who consults on a variety of enterprise projects in North America and Asia.

ACKNOWLEDGMENTS

I would like to express my gratitude to the following people for their never-ending support and assistance in helping to make this book a reality:

Kathy, you are my soul mate, and I am overjoyed to be spending the rest of my life together with you. Your love, admiration, and support made this book a reality, and I could not have done it without you. Thank you for your love and patience.

Thank you to my family (Arthur, Lois, and Lisa) for your love and support and for putting up with my incessant ramblings about game development all these years. I still remember the first game I ever made, and how proud I was to show it to you, only to have the hero's clothes fall off when he picked up the sword from the ground—in addition to his sword and shield protruding from inappropriate places. Yes, even games have bugs....

Anthony Whitaker, my good friend. I have always enjoyed discussing the programmable pipeline, spatial partitioning, tools development, and countless other topics with you. I value our friendship, and I am thrilled to know such a knowledgeable person.

Wayne Larson, you have become both my mentor and friend. Your teachings have improved me on both a personal and professional level. Thank you for inspiring me to strive for bigger and better things; I am grateful.

Peter Hansen, thank you for giving me the opportunity to host a practicum for your Digital & Interactive Media Design students, and thanks for your continued support and direction.

Thank you to my friends on #graphicsdev, #gamedev, and #mdxinfo on the AfterNET IRC server. You all have supported me and offered advice and insight throughout the life cycle of this book; especially Sean Kent, Oluseyi Sonaiya, Henrik Stuart, Promit Roy, Kyle Kaitan, Pieter Germishuys, Josh Jersild, and David Crooks. Thanks also go out to Osayuki Emokpae for her inspiration and guidance in the planning stages of the book. Special thanks to my friend Zane Bogach for providing a few textures for a couple chapters. A big thanks to Dave Astle (GameDev.net) for introducing me to Emi Smith and Mitzi Koontz.

Thank you to my close friends Sam Montasser, Dave Vani, Eric Fredin, and Ben Thieson. We have shared a lot of good memories, and I look forward to sharing more over the years to come.

Emi Smith, Stacy Hiquet, Sandy Doell, Heather Talbot, John Flynt, and Shawn Morningstar, thank you all for being so wonderful to work with. You helped steer this project from inception, and I appreciate your time and effort. I would also like to thank everyone else at Course Technology PTR who was responsible for bringing this book into existence.

I would also like to thank my employer, CGI Group, Inc., for permitting me to write this book alongside my work. Special thanks go to Glenn Mitchell, John Eldridge, Darryl Kotton, Andrew Stipdonk, Matthew Christopher, Michael Mah, Ghassan Karwchan, Ibraheem Yan, Tim Hill, Art Gartner, and Glenn Steinke for being such great people to work with. It was a pleasure to work with all of you on our last project, and I hope to work with all of you again.

Warm-hearted thanks also go to Don Moar (BioWare), John Walker (High Voltage Software), Aaron Walker (Electronic Arts), Roy Eltham (Sony Online Entertainment), Anthony Whitaker (Boanerges Studios), Ryan Hummer (Raven Software), and Yggy King (Electronic Arts). I felt enlightened after speaking with all of you about tools development and the state of the industry. Thank you for your opinions and support, especially during crunch time. I look forward to seeing all of you again at the next Game Developers Conference.

Thanks to Matt Collins (Atari), Steven Bercu (LIME Law), Frederic Chesnais (Atari), Teresa Cotesta (BioWare), and Tim Johnson (Artificial Studios) for granting me permission to print copyrighted material in the book.

I would like to thank the readers, you who made everything possible! This book was written for all of you, and I hope you enjoy reading it as much as I enjoyed writing it.

About the Author

Graham Wihlidal is a consultant at CGI Group, specializing in Microsoft technologies at an enterprise level. Prior to his current employment, he was the lead developer of a distributed workflow automation framework using C#.NET, SQL Server, and Windows SharePoint Services. He has several years of experience as a freelance developer and consultant, designing and implementing business software solutions with C#, C++, and Java for a variety of sectors. Aside from normal development work, he also has experience as a configuration manager for Rational ClearCase at an enterprise level. Graham graduated Computer Systems Technology at the head of his class while attending the Northern Alberta Institute of Technology, and he is a Microsoft Certified Solution Developer and an Early Adopter for .NET 2.0.

Aside from his professional life, Graham has been an active member in the game development community for the past seven years, with an undying passion to both play and develop computer games. In his spare time, he is constructing a high-performance 3D engine and accompanying toolset.

Contents

INTRODUCTION

Developers are required to continually learn new techniques and approaches, which can often lead to issues meeting deadlines, especially when inadequate research results in fatal design flaws. Almost every aspect of information technology is affected by this issue, most notably the game development industry. Game developers continuously push the envelope on a per project basis in terms of visual aesthetics, game play, and design. The need to overcome limitations is encountered frequently, since there is such an enormous variety in hardware, operating systems, and end user expectations.

The importance of designing reusable and maintainable code cannot be stressed enough and can break a company if disregarded. Even though a significant portion of source code from each project is too specific to be reusable, a core foundation always exists that, if designed properly, can be reused for the majority of future projects. For example, every game requires access to the file system to store media assets; therefore, components that manage file system interaction should be modular enough to plug into any project.

Even though the reusability of existing components can significantly reduce the costs associated with project development, there are other improvements that are very advantageous to the design process. As technology advances, so do the tools that interact with that technology. Utilizing the C# language and the robust Microsoft .NET 2.0 Framework, this book will present development methodologies that not only accomplish the goals specified for a project, but do the job in a timesaving manner.

Toolset development is an extremely broad topic, yet the intent of this book is to provide you with a core set of skills and a comprehensive insight that will aid you in the development of game engine utilities, significantly reducing the time associated with the construction phase of a project.

The book content is fairly suitable to a wide variety of developers, with the exception of developers new to programming. Readers with very little experience building Windows-based applications may struggle a bit, but this book will teach them the proper way to implement the functionality needed for their project.

An introductory working knowledge of C# and the .NET 2.0 Framework is expected, allowing the content of each chapter to be directed towards the subject and avoiding trivial and introductory explanations. To benefit from this book, readers do not require any experience developing game engine tools; terminology and design fundamentals specific to toolset development are clearly depicted and explained.

All material is at a level of quality suitable for production code, making the book an exceptional reference and asset for industry professionals and hobbyists. Readers will learn how to build reusable components and optimize existing code for maximum performance, a critical issue when building processor-intensive tools.

I feel strongly that technical books should not be written in a linear manner, which is why the decision was made to isolate the information in this book into chapters that are an independent read from one another. Readers should not have to read a quarter of the book over again just to refresh their memory about a certain component. Readers should be able to jump right to a topic that interests them and begin reading without the need to reference other chapters.

The focus of this book, in terms of technology, is on the .NET 2.0 Framework and the C# language. However, because of the nature of a "gems" style book, some chapters include other technologies specifically related to that topic of discussion. Due to the approach used in this book, all gems are independent of each other unless otherwise stated as being coupled.

C# and the .NET Framework are evangelized, but an important issue regarding toolset development is the maintenance and support of legacy code and utilities; hence the decision to include a variety of topics that cover communication between managed and unmanaged applications, as well as topics that address general interoperability concerns. Because of this, C++ is covered in a couple of gems that discuss inter-process communication, interoperability, and interacting with unmanaged code. Furthermore, a decent amount of graphical and multimedia-oriented gems are implemented with functionality present in Managed DirectX. If you do not have experience or interest with a particular technology used in a chapter, fear not. All gems are independent of each other, so you will not be missing out on anything by skipping it until the topic is relevant to your project.

Tools development is an exciting and rewarding area of game development and is sometimes scoffed at by other developers who do not wish to give up their romantic notions of game development. The truth is, good tools make good games. Someone has to make them, and be glad it's you!

I worked hard to produce this book for you, but I also had a lot of fun writing it. I feel that a wide range of applicable topics were covered, and hope that you run to this book time and time again. Thanks very much for supporting my work and for your interest in a topic that I am so passionate about.

## PART I

Toolset Design Fundamentals

…the cost of adding a feature isn't just the time it takes to code it. The cost also includes the addition of an obstacle to future expansion. … The trick is to pick the features that don't fight each other.

John Carmack

The main purpose of this book is not to function as a book on toolset design, but rather on implementation issues facing tools developers. In order to properly illustrate some techniques discussed later on in this book, the chapters in this part focus on design fundamentals and tools discussion to help introduce you to the concepts behind tools development. The chapters in this part cover many of the core aspects and fundamentals of toolset design, including defining what a toolset is, common applications, describing why flexible and reusable tools are important, and also discussing a few commercial toolsets that have shipped with titles.

Also covered are some techniques and approaches used to properly design and manage the development of a toolset. The common life cycle of development is explained, summarizing the four phases of the "waterfall" methodology; planning, analysis, design, and implementation. There are also a number of .NET-specific topics that cover everything from coding conventions to architecture implementation. There is also a chapter that describes what unit testing is, and how to perform unit testing in C#.NET.

It is important to recognize that there is never a single way to approach and solve a problem, as successful resolutions are dependent on the context of the problem. However, it is important to understand a variety of methodologies and techniques in order to identify a proper solution to a problem. Some solutions follow the "mop it" approach, which entails treating, tolerating, or redirecting the problem. The "mop it" approach can be described like a water leak, where instead of fixing the leak, you mop up the water. Other solutions follow the "stop it" approach, which entails preventing, eliminating, or reducing the problem. Whatever solution your resources allow, many of the chapters in this part can help you in reaching your goal.

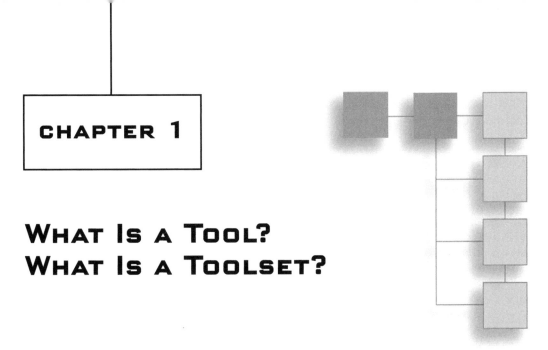

CHAPTER 1

WHAT IS A TOOL?
WHAT IS A TOOLSET?

Programming today is a race between software engineers striving to build bigger and better idiot-proof programs, and the Universe trying to produce bigger and better idiots. So far, the Universe is winning.

Rich Cook

A tool is a software application used in either the construction or modification of game-related content, where the content can be virtually anything that makes up a game. Tools can be extremely simple, such as an application that removes all the tab characters from a text file, or an application that copies files from one location to another. Tools can also be quite complex, such as a full-featured world editing suite. The complexity of the tool is directly proportional to the complexity of the problem the tool is supposed to solve.

A toolset is a collection of tools that make up the content production pipeline of a game. Any tool from a toolset can be reused in multiple projects as long as the tool was designed with reusability in mind. Some tools are created for a single purpose, in which the tool cannot be reused because a lot of the tool was hard coded to reduce development time. A tool that is hard coded for a single purpose is often referred to as a *throw-away* or *skunk works* tool.

As games move toward higher expectations of the quality and quantity of content displayed, so do the tools that produce the content. Without producing exceptional tools, you cannot produce an exceptional game.

Stakeholders: Internal Versus External

Defined as anyone who stands to gain or lose from the success or failure of an application, the stakeholders greatly affect the quality and functionality of a tool. They are the users who are most affected by the introduction of a tool, and they ultimately contribute to the design and goals. If the tool is meant only for internal use, there is typically little to no documentation, and the user interface is generally unintuitive or "messy." If the tool is meant to ship with a game to provide modification abilities, then the tool is typically feature and user interface rich, and is accompanied with excellent documentation and tutorials.

Most tools never ship with the game, and constantly evolve as the game is developed. Many tools are developed for internal use and, if written properly, can be reused across multiple projects as well.

If the tool is designed for use by the developer only, it is typically as featureless and unintuitive as possible. The code is usually horrible to navigate, and maintainability is almost impossible. Since tools are generally designed to produce content for the game itself, far less time is spent developing good tools. There is a fine balance between wasting too much time and resources on the tools for a game, and not spending enough time making tools that are actually worthwhile. Ideally, you would want to build the tools as quickly as possible, but with a reasonable level of quality. This is where improvements to development workflow and component reusability play a large part in the success of a tool and the developers behind it.

If the common components of your tools have a loosely coupled design and solid modularity, then more time can be spent making better tools because you do not have to keep redeveloping common functionality duplicated across different projects.

To describe an example later detailed in this book, imagine that you have three batch file processing tools that each process files differently, yet share the same logic behind traversing the directory structure and selecting target files using pattern matching. If you hard code three tools as quickly as possible, you end up debugging the common functionality three times, individually debugging the logic each tool performs, and limiting yourself in terms of future improvements and maintainability.

Now, if that core functionality were separated into a reusable library and extra time spent ensuring that the code was stable and generically configurable, all three tools could interface with the library and debugging time would be minimized to just the tool logic itself. The result is a better tool, and one change to the base framework propagates to all three tools. This common functionality could now be used for any batch file processing tool needed in the future, drastically reducing development and debugging time.

The time saved thanks to reusability can allow you to build more tools of decent quality, or the time can be spent improving the user interface or accompanying documentation so that the stakeholders have an easier time understanding and using the tool.

Well written and fairly bug-free tools can make everyone's life easier on the development team, whereas poorly documented or written tools can hamper development or even jeopardize the success of the project.

Who Builds the Tools?

There are five main models a game development studio can be classified into in regards to the creation and support of tools. Keep in mind that the models described are generalizations, and some studios can use a hybrid of multiple models. The different organizational models for tools development are shown in Table 1.1.

Table 1.1 Organizational Models of Tools Development

Organizational Model	Description
Dedicated Tools Team	This model is based around a team that takes a tool from inception all the way to supporting it. This model works extremely well, though it generally requires a liaison with both technical and design skills to help facilitate effective communication between the tools team and the target audience when discussing features and workflow using the tool.
	A strong example of a game development studio following this model is BioWare Corp.
Developer Ownership	"You build it, you support it."
	This model is where the individual or team responsible for a particular game system is in charge of creating and supporting the tools that interact with it. This model works reasonably well since the developers creating the tools are the most knowledgeable about how the game system works.
	There are some issues with this method; the team does not generally put a lot of care into the accompanying tools, so the usability, documentation, and user interface typically suffer as a result. An example of a game development studio that successfully uses this model is Raven Software.
	Tools are sometimes developed by one individual or group, and later end up being supported by another individual or group.

Table 1.1 Organizational Models of Tools Development *(continued)*

Organizational Model	Description
Game Team Develops; Tools Team Supports	This model attempts to solve the issues with the developer ownership model by still having the game team build the tools. But when the tool matures, it is handed off to a dedicated tools team where it is updated and supported for future projects and use.
	A game development studio that successfully uses this model is Microsoft Game Studios.
Engine Team Develops; Game Team Supports	This model is similar to "Game Team Develops, Tools Team Supports," except the engine team builds the tools to work with the core engine technology, and then the tool is passed off to the game team. They adapt the tool to work with their own project-specific data and content requirements.
	A game development studio that successfully uses this model is High Voltage Software.
Content Team Develops and Supports	This model is typically used in specific situations where the content creators wish to build tools to help them be more productive or test logic through the creation of rules simulators, for example.
	BioWare has successfully used this model for certain situations.

Third-party middleware could be thought of as a model, but it is felt that middleware can fit into one of the above models when used. Middleware sometimes requires enhancements or customizations, and someone within the game development studio has to do them.

Often the structure of the tools department in a studio is largely determined by available financing. Some studios may feel it more desirable to have a dedicated tools team, but budget constraints can force a studio into using a less desirable model.

Every studio manages its tools development differently, but generally any studio will fit into one of the above categories. One of the biggest differences between studios is the size of the tools development team.

How Large Are Tools Teams?

At Game Developers Conference 2005, 16 professional game developers were surveyed on the ratio between the number of tool programmers and game programmers in their company. The results from the survey are listed in Table 1.2.

Table 1.2 Ratio of Tool Programmers to Game Programmers

% Tools	% Game	# Studios
20	80	1
30	70	5
40	60	2
50	50	2

* Six developers did not know the ratio used in their company or did not wish to discuss it.

The results indicate that currently only a third of the programmers in most game development studios are involved with the production of tools.

This ratio has fairly little to do with the actual performance of the above teams, though, as different ratios work for different companies. When it comes down to it, if the company has put out great games, they must be doing something right! It is interesting to see how much variation there is between companies regarding the structure of their tools programming department.

Conclusion

This chapter covered defining what a tool and toolset is, and how the gaming industry views tools development. There is currently a lot of variation in how tools teams are structured in the industry, and it is unlikely that this will ever become consistent and uniform. Different structures and techniques work differently for various companies, and they will continue to use whatever approach works for them. However, we can believe that studios will need to standardize how tools are designed and developed in order to adapt for the next generation games driven by a multitude of content.

No single technology or programming language is better than another, as each has a shining role to play in different problem domains. However, it is our firm belief that the .NET platform is best suited for tools development, and migrating to managed code will bring a number of benefits to a development studio and its projects.

Next-generation games will require more and higher-quality content. The only foreseeable way to adapt to this need is to produce better tools that create content at both a higher volume and quality in a shorter amount of time. It is absolutely vital that tools be available to designers earlier, and with very few bugs. Additionally, the tools should also have user interfaces that are intuitive to designers, and require as few clicks as possible to perform common tasks.

Reusability is also tremendously important, so that technology may be reused across multiple projects, saving additional time and money. The .NET platform is geared towards componential architectures and distributed software reusability, making it an excellent choice in this regard.

The .NET platform even offers improvements to software deployment. One common problem plaguing deployment managers is the issue of "DLL Hell," where an older version of a library can be referenced on a system that has multiple versions installed, generally causing software instability. .NET assemblies support a built-in versioning system that solves the issue of incorrect library referencing, reducing many problems related to deployment. The .NET platform is covered in greater detail in the next chapter.

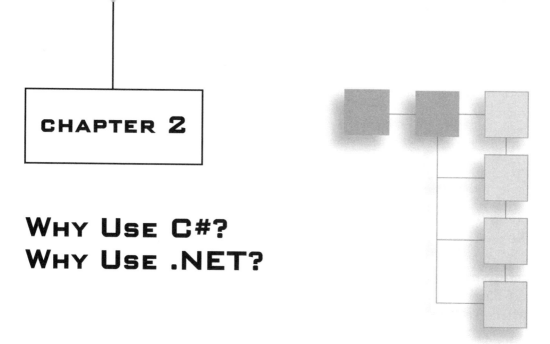

CHAPTER 2

WHY USE C#?
WHY USE .NET?

As soon as we started programming, we found out to our surprise that it wasn't as easy to get programs right as we had thought. Debugging had to be discovered. I can remember the exact instant when I realized that a large part of my life from then on was going to be spent in finding mistakes in my own programs.

Maurice Wilkes

Ever since the introduction of computers, there has been exponential growth in businesses embracing technology to solve their corporate problems. Computers have evolved and matured enough to support massively distributed and heterogeneous applications in both desktop and Internet environments. As the technology becomes more complex, so do the problems that developers have to solve in order to produce a good product. While there are many technologies and development tools available, there are also numerous issues that inhibit productivity or development.

There is the ongoing controversy surrounding the right programming language and platform for the job. Many times, certain features are only available with certain programming languages, such as automatic memory management, which often ends up dictating the language to use for the job. In a perfect world, the language should be chosen based on the problem domain, not the specifics of the underlying operating system. Microsoft's COM and COM+ technology tried to fix this problem, but they were only successful to a certain degree, as their internal structures are quite convoluted. While COM and COM+ made great progress in bridging this domain gap, it just wasn't the answer. This is one of the main reasons Microsoft proposed .NET, a new computing platform that simplifies application development in highly distributed environments.

Overview of .NET

There are two main components to Microsoft .NET: the Common Language Runtime and the .NET Class Framework. Microsoft.NET is based around the idea that code is in a managed environment; that is, it executes within a managed runtime (known as the *Common Language Runtime*, or CLR for short). The CLR acts as a barrier between managed applications (.NET) and the operating system. The CLR also offers a much richer set of services than normally provided by the operating system. The Common Language Runtime architecture is overviewed in Figure 2.1.

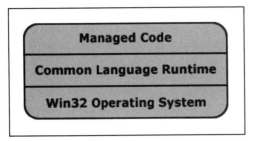

Figure 2.1 Overview of the Common Language Runtime architecture.

The Common Language Runtime manages code at execution time, providing core services such as memory management, thread management, and remoting. The CLR also enforces strict type safety and other forms of code accuracy that ensure security and robustness.

In order to have a language-independent CLR, a liaison is needed to facilitate the understanding of the language in the CLR. Every development tool for .NET compiles source code files to what is known as the Microsoft Intermediate Language, (MSIL, or IL for short), as shown in Figure 2.2.

All development tools produce the same MSIL regardless of the programming language, so all the CLR is required to do is understand the IL. Microsoft currently provides CLR-compliant versions of C#, Visual Basic, C++, JScript, and Java. Since any company can write a CLR-compliant language, third parties are introducing many others like COBOL, Delphi, Python, APL, and Perl.

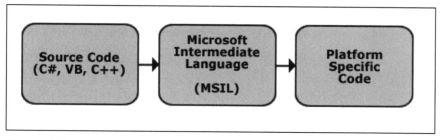

Figure 2.2 Source code compilation into MSIL.

The intermediate language code (IL) cannot run on its own. It must first be compiled by the Just-in-Time (JIT) compiler for the target platform to turn the IL into platform-specific machine-level code. This architecture provides Microsoft .NET with a certain level of platform independence. Work is currently being done by third parties to port the CLR to other platforms like UNIX and MacOS X.

The .NET platform also gives the capability to build durable system-level components thanks to the following features:

- Robustness provided through type safety and garbage collection
- Code security provided intrinsically through code trust mechanisms
- Support for extensible meta-data concepts
- Existing code integration support
- Versioning to provide ease of administration and deployment

Full interoperability is also possible with other languages across multiple platforms, thanks to full XML support for web-based component interaction and COM+ support.

Aside from the Common Language Runtime, the other main component of the .NET platform is the Class Framework, which provides reusable functionality and technologies to any .NET compliant language and compiler.

Overview of C#

While there are a number of available languages supported by the .NET platform, C# is the most popular one for many reasons. The C# language is an elegant yet simple, type-safe, object-oriented language that allows for the development of a breadth of enterprise and highly distributed applications.

C# also provides access to the common API styles: COM+, Automation, .NET Class Framework, and C-style APIs. Also available is an unsafe mode, where pointers can be used when you want to manipulate memory that is not under control of the garbage collector.

The C# language is also an evolution of C++ and Java, and supports many of their features in the areas of expressions, statements, and operators. As a result, the learning curve for C# is generally quite rapid due to the comfort level when migrating from either C++ or Java.

Legacy Interoperability

Most game development studios have numerous legacy tools that do not have the available resources or need to migrate to the .NET platform. Microsoft realizes that migration does not magically happen overnight, and has provided some mechanisms to foster interoperability between managed and unmanaged components. The interoperability mechanisms permit developers to slowly migrate legacy components into managed applications piece by piece, while allowing them to build a complete application with a combination of unmanaged and managed components.

When building new .NET applications, there are provisions for using Win32 DLL exports and COM objects. There are also provisions for legacy applications to use a .NET assembly as if it were an ordinary COM object, and provisions to use an individual routine from a .NET assembly.

In addition to the interoperability mechanisms below, the .NET platform also includes support for Win32 sockets and Web Services, which can be utilized for interoperability between managed and unmanaged applications.

Platform Invocation Service (P/Invoke)

Interfacing with C-style functions in native DLLs is offered through the Platform Invocation Service, also known as P/Invoke, and although both Win32 API routines and custom exports are supported, the most common distinctive use is for accessing system routines that are not generally available to .NET developers. For example, when performing high-accuracy timing, you must use P/Invoke to call QueryPerformanceCounter and QueryPerformanceFrequency.

There is quite a varying degree of data types for both the Win32 and .NET platforms, and marshaling is required to transform data into the appropriate data types for each platform. The marshaling of parameters and return values between managed and unmanaged applications is handled through the Interop Marshaler, also used by COM Interop.

Platform Invocation Service is covered in much greater detail in Part V, "Techniques for Legacy Interoperability," along with sample code on how to reference DLL exports in C#.

COM and Runtime Callable Wrappers

At some point you may need to interact with a COM object in a .NET application, and reconciliation between the .NET garbage collection model and the COM reference counting model is needed to allow both platforms to communicate with each other. In order for .NET to use a COM object, a Runtime Callable Wrapper (RCW) must be generated to cater to the differences between the lifetime management of .NET and COM objects. Runtime Callable Wrappers manage the reference counted lifetime of COM objects and also handle the marshaling of parameters and return types.

Additionally, .NET objects can also be exported to act like a COM object to use within a legacy application. This functionality is useful for applications that must remain unmanaged for the time being, but would benefit from the robustness of the .NET Class Framework.

Runtime Callable Wrappers and COM interoperability are covered in much greater detail in Part V along with sample code on how to use COM objects in .NET, and how to use .NET objects like COM objects in legacy applications.

C++/CLI (Managed Extensions for C++)

With such a following of developers using unmanaged C++ for application development, especially in the game development industry, there was a need for an enhancement to the C++ language that would allow programs written in C++ to use the .NET Class Framework and target the Common Language Runtime. It was for this reason that Microsoft created C++/CLI (formerly known as Managed Extensions for C++), an extension of the C++ language that could use the benefits from the .NET platform without requiring the user to learn a new programming language.

In other CLR languages like Visual Basic and C#, the only way to invoke Win32 API routines is through explicit use of the P/Invoke mechanism. Developers using

C++/CLI do not need to use P/Invoke and can include the appropriate header files and call the unmanaged routines directly. This feature is called "It Just Works," or IJW, and both P/Invoke and IJW use the same underlying mechanism so it is beneficial to understand that mechanism.

C++/CLI can also be used to wrap a C++ class or a COM object. Wrapping a COM object can provide better performance than using the COM interface and a Runtime Callable Wrapper because of reduced interoperability overhead, commonly referred to as "thunking." It also allows for closer control of how members are wrapped.

For some COM objects, it may not be possible to use the Type Library Importer utility (tlbimp.exe) to generate an RCW for the COM object, and C++/CLI provides a solution to this problem.

Benefits

There are quite a number of benefits when the .NET platform is used for game engine tools development. Probably the largest benefit is the massive amount of productivity gain. Building applications in Microsoft.NET is much faster than any other RAD environment, because of the excellent IDEs available, as well as a very robust core framework that all managed applications can take advantage of. You can have a functional UI for simple tools created in under a couple of minutes, spending less time on UI and more time on functionality and usability. Being able to build a functional UI so quickly is very beneficial to a number of projects, most notably "throw-away" or "skunk works" tools that need a quick and dirty user interface, with the majority of the development time spent on building functionality.

Microsoft.NET also offers ease of deployment, solving the "DLL hell" agony. Through a built-in versioning mechanism available to all .NET assemblies, specific versions of a library can be targeted.

Other benefits are the promotion of scaleable architectures and the ability to choose architectures that are robust, reliable, and secure. Scaleable architectures promote reusability and strong design.

The interoperability support for legacy applications and components allows for easier migration from an existing code base to the .NET platform. A number of methods for bridging communication between managed and unmanaged applications exist, and these methods are covered in much greater detail later in the book.

Robustness is provided through type-safety and garbage collection. The compiler catches all invalid conversion operations and throws the appropriate exception. A

.NET application can catch every error in the system, allowing for graceful error handling and termination. The only time when additional work must be done to ensure proper error handling is when an exception is thrown from a legacy application wrapped into a managed assembly. In addition to excellent error handling, .NET applications allocate and release memory through a reference counting garbage collector by default, ensuring that the application does not leak memory and the lifetimes of all objects are managed.

There are numerous other benefits when using .NET for tools, many of which will be covered in greater detail later in the book.

Conclusion

In reality, a game engine tool can be developed in many different languages: Perl, Python, C\C++, Java, and Visual Basic, to name a few. So why use .NET? Tools enhance workflow and manage game content, so it is desirable to build these tools as quickly as possible. The faster a tool is developed, the sooner the end user can begin using it, improving productivity or producing game content earlier, most likely saving money or man hours in the process.

The .NET platform promotes robust design with a rapid application development nature, which is a perfect match for tools development. Many times a lot of utility functionality must be developed before the actual logic for the tool is addressed. The .NET framework provides countless functionality for technologies like XML, encryption, file system access, security, and data manipulation, to name a few. Development time for a tool can be better spent on logic and usability, rather than, on utility functionality that the tool is dependent on.

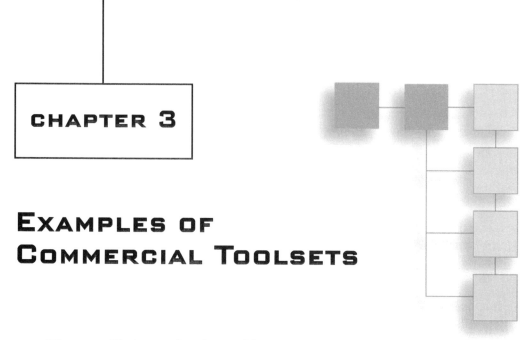

CHAPTER 3

EXAMPLES OF COMMERCIAL TOOLSETS

The most likely way for the world to be destroyed, most experts agree, is by accident. That's where we come in; we're computer professionals. We cause accidents.

Nathaniel S. Borenstein

In order to help define what a tool is, and how the interface should be designed, this chapter will introduce and discuss a couple of popular toolsets that are used in the creation of game content and shipped with commercial products.

Although external tools that ship with the final product require a higher level of quality when the fans themselves will be using the tools to build expansive content, internal tools still follow proper development standards in terms of documentation, maintainability, and quality of design.

The two case studies selected for discussion were both developed for external use and clearly show a high level of quality in terms of user interface design, logical functionality, and ease of use.

Many different types of tools are used in the creation and modification of game content, but the following two were chosen because of the success of the companies and the products the tools are associated with.

Case Study: BioWare Corporation

BioWare is perhaps one of the most widely known and respected developers, especially in the role-playing game (RPG) world. BioWare's mission is to produce the best story-driven games worldwide, and it is succeeding based on all the awards and recognition the company has received for its games. Although an exasperating amount of work is contributed by everyone at the company to produce their exceptional games, many fans just see the finished product. This is unfortunate because the tools and the people who build them play a critical role in the production of a successful AAA title, but with the exception of mod builders, they often are unnoticed by the fan community.

A couple of years ago, BioWare released the critically acclaimed RPG *NeverWinter Nights*, which has won numerous writing and technology awards. The game was based on the *Dungeons & Dragons* rule set placed in the Forgotten Realms world, and it took players on a compelling story-driven fantasy adventure. The game had hours and hours of game time, but that didn't stop the fan community from building custom campaigns and adventures. The game shipped with the *NeverWinter Nights Aurora Toolset*, which gave players the power to build custom adventures using the same tools that BioWare utilized in the production of the original game.

The Aurora Toolset produces campaigns and adventures in the form of modules, which are composed of various components, such as areas, creatures, doors, conversations, scripts, and triggers, to name a few. The toolset offers functionality to build either an indoor or outdoor world, and then populate that environment with entities and triggers.

Figure 3.1 shows the main user interface for the Aurora Toolset, where other child dialogs are launched and where entity instantiation and placement occurs. On the left is a tree view that shows all areas in the module and all the instantiated entities that are associated with each area. Additionally, there is also a listing for conversation dialog as well as module scripts. Module developers do not have access to a core low-level API, but instead interface with the game engine using a scripting language developed for the game and toolset.

A multitude of assets and source art that can be reused across custom modules is included, with the ability to add your own custom work if so desired. All the monsters and items from *NeverWinter Nights* are available to module developers, and can even be customized from their original properties and attributes. The tree view on the right lists all the assets that can be instantiated and placed in an area.

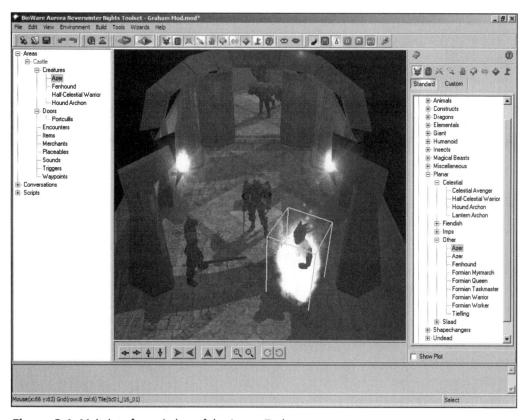

Figure 3.1 Main interface window of the Aurora Toolset.

At the top of the main window is a toolbar that offers tool selection and the ability to toggle certain display and functionality settings. Another toolbar at the bottom of the main viewport controls the scene camera. The camera can be panned, translated, rotated, and zoomed.

Figure 3.2 shows the properties of the *Azer* monster, and all the attributes that can be customized or extended for it. Creatures in role-playing games are often composed of a vast number of properties and scripts that define its behavior and abilities. As such, this complexity can clutter the user interface of tools that are designed to modify those properties and scripts. The way the Aurora Toolset addresses this design issue is through the use of tab pages that each contain properties associated to a certain group. Users should never feel overwhelmed by large numbers of data fields, so breaking the properties into groups represented on different tab pages was a good design move.

Another nice touch to the dialog shown in Figure 3.2 is the real-time 3D preview of the edited creature in question. Although it doesn't propose much in regards to functionality, the preview pane spices up the user interface and makes it much more interesting to work with, as opposed to a normal data entry tool.

Figure 3.2 Property window used to modify creature attributes.

The goal of the Aurora Toolset was to cater to novice users, not necessarily people who have experience with other world editing tools such as Hammer, Q3Radiant, or any other complex brush- and constructive solid geometry-based editors. The toolset had to allow users to build rooms and outdoor environments quite easily. The toolset does not support polygonal or brush-based editing; instead it has a collection of rooms, each with several variations in appearance from which to choose. This functionality makes the tool easier to understand and use, but it also supports enough customization to keep advanced users happy.

The Aurora Toolset harnesses an embedded viewport that renders the current area as you would see it in-game. This functionality is great in the sense that you can preview roughly how the area would appear in the game itself without the need to launch *NeverWinter Nights*.

Figure 3.3 shows an area that was created in the editor and is now shown in the actual game.

Figure 3.3 Screenshot of a map created with the Aurora Toolset running in-game.

It is important to note that the embedded viewport does not manage any physics, networking, or gameplay functionality while running the editor. The scene is merely displayed using a visual representation only, and the game won't actually execute until the module is run from within the game engine.

The Aurora Toolset is a great piece of software, but it is only one, albeit big, tool amongst numerous others that produce the content for a game. The *NeverWinter Nights* module developer community appreciates the work put into the Aurora Toolset, but only because the toolset shipped with the game. Had the toolset been created for internal use only, the community would not have appreciated its value as much or even known about it.

BioWare keeps putting out AAA titles and recognizes that great tools produce great games. In addition to their own titles, the technology behind those games is also reusable enough that third-party companies have licensed it to produce some other exceptional games. BioWare is leading the way in role-playing games and has one of the most respected dedicated tools teams.

Note

For more information, please visit http://www.bioware.com.

Case Study: Artificial Studios

As a game studio that also markets its own middleware products, Artificial Studios is dedicated to advancing the state of professional game development solutions. They have a flagship product titled Reality Engine, which is a total solution for games using next-generation graphics, dynamic physics, and high-performance graphics.

The Reality Engine SDK also provides a next-generation toolset titled Reality Builder and is powered by C#.NET technology. The engine itself is developed in unmanaged C++, but Reality Builder has a harness that displays its scenes using the Reality Engine within the editor as a WYSIWYG display.

Shown in Figure 3.4 is the main interface for Reality Builder, where entities can be selected and transformed, as well as a property grid control on the right side that allows easy access to the properties of the currently selected entity. You can also see another dialog being displayed that shows the assets available to the world designer.

Another nice accessibility feature is a menu at the top which contains some quick launch buttons and edit fields for commonly used operations or properties. This is a very handy feature for designers, and can often improve workflow to some extent by reducing the number of clicks required to perform common operations.

Visual cues are another feature of graphical tools that make them easier to use. Notice the barrel in Figure 3.4; there is a selection bounding box around the entity, and there are widgets to adjust the X, Y, and Z position of the selected entity. The same functionality could have been implemented using a numeric input field, but doing so would make the interface less intuitive to the designers.

An excellent feature that is seen in most cutting-edge graphical tools is in-game rendering, where the tool displays the world as it would look in-game. This doesn't necessarily mean that the game itself is running within the tool but merely that the rendering subsystem is attached to the tool's viewport to render the world appropriately.

Figure 3.4 Main interface window of Reality Builder.

Reality Builder supports in-game rendering, and you can see this in Figure 3.5. The concepts behind software architecture design are extremely important to implement this feature, and require a graphics engine that is modular in nature. Bonus Chapter 2, "Building a Managed Wrapper with C++/CLI," shows how to create a Direct3D context in unmanaged code, and then build a managed harness around it.

Reality Builder also provides script support to designers using the C# language and the CodeDom compiler. By using C# as their scripting language, the tools and engine can take advantage of compiled code that also has the ability to interface with the robust .NET class framework.

All .NET applications have access to the Windows Forms class framework, which offers a number of feature-rich and intuitive controls. Additionally, if a specific control is not available, it is very easy to build a custom one that functions the way you desire. Figure 3.6 shows another screenshot of Reality Builder displaying its rich user interface.

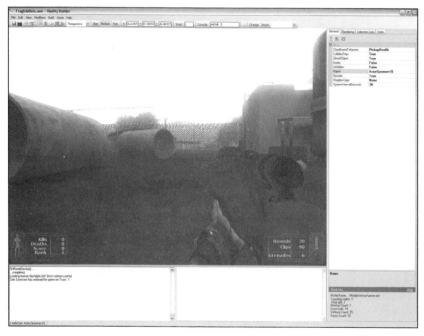

Figure 3.5 Reality Builder with support for in-game rendering.

Figure 3.6 Reality Builder showcasing a rich user interface.

Artificial Studios is a relatively new company, but their custom technology is cutting-edge, and their embracement of C# and the .NET platform is admirable. They were recently purchased by Epic Games, and it will be interesting to see what comes of the acquisition, and whether Epic Games will maintain a strong stand for the .NET platform. Trends in the industry are pointing toward a larger percentage of companies migrating legacy technology or tools to managed code. The old saying "Time is money" is quite applicable to this issue, and if .NET can save a project a significant amount of money, then its usage is justified.

Note

For more information, please check out http://www.artificialstudios.com.

Conclusion

In this chapter, I discussed a few commercial-grade tools that have been used in the development of some best-selling games. I hope the case studies presented have given you some extra insight into building high quality tools and some useful interface features to improve workflow. See each product's user manual for more information on the specifics of each application.

Remember that the .NET class framework offers rich user interface controls and should be used to improve the accessibility and workflow of your tools. An intelligent user interface can save countless hours when it takes very few navigation actions to perform a particular task.

As an example, imagine you have a tool that takes 7 seconds to perform a particular task. With this task being performed four times a day in a 22-workday month, 12 months of the year, you end up with a total time of two hours. Now imagine that you have 20 designers performing this task. The total time spent on this task would be 40 hours. If you introduce an accessibility feature that causes that same task to take 2 seconds, with one designer, the total time spent is 35.2 minutes, roughly a 342 percent improvement in efficiency. With 20 designers, the total time spent would be 12 hours, saving you 29 hours that could be directed elsewhere.

CHAPTER 4

EVERYTHING STARTS WITH A PLAN

There are two ways of constructing a software design. One way is to make it so simple that there are obviously no deficiencies. And the other way is to make it so complicated that there are no obvious deficiencies.

C.A.R. Hoare

All software applications receive some form of initial planning as to what their goals are, but quite often the planning occurs in the mind of the developer. A great approach to planning is the creation of an actual software development plan that addresses many high level design issues, as well as technical issues like coding standards and architecture.

A software development plan is an action plan for developing the application. It describes how the work will be done in terms of design, implementation, documentation, and testing.

Software planning is an iterative process, and as unexpected problems arise, change requests will occur that require plan revisions. A good software development plan anticipates that changes may occur, and the plan should be able to accommodate them appropriately.

The software development plan should be kept up to date, typically through regular team meetings. The plan should be modified accordingly for all changes, progress, and problems. Doing so will ensure that the maximum benefit from the planning effort is gained.

Vision

Also known as design goals, this section of the software development plan ultimately asks the question, "*What is the tool going to do?*"

Briefly describe what the tool will do and ultimately how it will either improve workflow productivity or affect the content creation pipeline. Outline the current problems existing without the tool, and how the introduction of the tool will attempt to solve them.

Describe whether or not the tool will be used for a single purpose throw-away, or whether it will be applicable for multiple purposes or projects.

Also list the people who will use the tool. As a simple example: "*The technical artists will build programmable shaders using the Visual Shader Designer plug-in from within 3D Studio Max, and export a binary file that follows the specifications of our proprietary VSD (.vsd) format.*"

The Vision section of the software development plan could be thought of as an overview and summary of the other sections that follow.

Stakeholders

Every software application has stakeholders who will either gain or lose from the success or failure of a tool, and they ultimately shape the design of the tool to meet their needs. After all, the stakeholders for a tool are typically the people who will actually be using it to produce game content or enhance workflow.

The software development plan should define who the stakeholders are, and how they will be directly affected by the tool. The easiest way to determine who your stakeholders are is to think of everyone who will be affected by your work, whether the stakeholders are internal or external to the company. The majority of tools developed for internal use are catered to the needs of artists or technical designers, who don't always possess strong technical aptitude.

One of the biggest problems with software development planning is gathering user requirements that do not solve the problems of the stakeholders. It is very important that you ask the right questions of your stakeholders, especially if they do not have a technical background. A lot of design and development time is wasted because of incorrect user requirements. Getting them right from the start will help alleviate this problem.

After the stakeholders have been defined, the last step is to sort them by priority and influence. A common approach is to take note of the influence, interest, goals, and objections to your tool. Prioritize your stakeholders as high or low interest, and as high or low influence. It is important to remember that the stakeholders do not always agree with each other, which presents problems with both communication and requirements gathering.

Reusability

The issue of reusability is important in any software project, but is *very* important when developing tools. If a tool is a throw-away, not meant to be reusable, then only the minimum amount of time to implement the basic functionality should be spent on it. A common problem is when a tool is not meant to be reused in the foreseeable future, but has the potential for reuse. In this situation, it is advisable to build the tool with future maintainability in mind. If the code is just slapped together to meet deadlines or save money, all those benefits will be for naught when a considerable amount of time must be spent refactoring the tool for a later project when it should have been designed that way from the start.

Designing with reusability in mind, and the level of abstraction or agnostic design to consider, is definitely a judgment call, especially if the stakeholders are putting pressure or constraints on you to prevent you from doing so. Maintainability even comes in the shape of following coding guidelines, commenting any complex constructs, and never using hard-coded values or "magic numbers."

The golden rule is, build reusable code if the functionality of the tool would be useful in a future project, and if it is feasible to spend a little extra development time building it. You will gain in the long run when the time comes to build a tool that solves a problem encountered before.

Architecture

This section outlines the architecture of the tool or toolset. For a simple tool, this section will be quite brief, just outlining whether the application is console-, Windows-, or web-based, and other technical issues related to the application.

However, more detail must be discussed with complex tools or toolsets, tools utilizing a wide range of technologies, or complex component dependencies. Outlining the architecture is especially important when thinking about reusable software component design, and how to write software with future reusability in mind.

Requirements

This section addresses what the tool is supposed to do. As mentioned earlier, stake-holders are the people using the tool, so the requirements are generally centered on their goals and expectations. I cannot stress the importance of this section enough. The majority of tools that fail to deliver are because of malpractice with gathering user requirements. Developers often over-complicate interfaces or build complex functionality when all the stakeholders wanted was a throw-away utility to perform a simple process.

If user requirements are gathered correctly from the start, you will save both your-self and your stakeholders a lot of grief and expense. The old saying, "Time is money," describes this problem best. When you are on a tight schedule to produce tools that are required to build the content for a game or improve workflow to meet deadlines, time cannot be wasted on building tools that are of no or limited use to the end user.

Design Standards

Every software application goes through a design phase to some extent, and it is important that you standardize how the design of the tool is expressed or mod-eled. A common method is through the use of the Unified Modeling Language, or UML for short. UML is definitely beyond the scope of this book, but I personally use it and advise that you at least read up on it if you are not currently using another modeling language.

I will admit that UML has a time and a place in regards to software design. Some tools are so simple or unimportant in the scheme of things that it would be a waste of time to utilize UML. A modeling language serves as a way to visualize how all the components of your tool or toolset fit together at a high level, and also aids with future maintainability if the code itself is not self-explanatory.

However you design the functionality and communication of your tools or com-ponents, be sure to document your standards in this section and follow them.

Coding Standards

A tool or software application in general cannot be considered great strictly on functionality and performance alone. Since the importance of reusability should be quite clear by now, it is apparent that the source code for the application must be easy to read, understand, and maintain for future versions of the software. It is a common fact that every developer has a unique style to his code, which is perfectly acceptable for personal projects but unacceptable for commercial software. All developers should follow a common style so that no matter who wrote the code, it always looks like a single person programmed the entire application.

A common practice to outline how all code should be formatted is to release a coding standards document to the developers. They are to abide by the rules and best practices set forth in the document to promote the creation of code that is easy to read and maintain. Looking through code that you did not write is much easier when everything follows the same style and is neatly commented, with explanations for all the complicated constructs present in the code. Using coding standards will increase both productivity and efficiency through a consistent style, delivering the end product at a lower cost. In addition, coding standards reduce the risk of integration with other components developed by other companies, groups, or team members.

The usage of design patterns and how modules are coupled can also be described in the coding standards document. Some design patterns are frowned upon because they typically promote tightly coupled design, making the code harder to unit test among other things. This document can be used to define acceptable design patterns to use, and which ones to use only if necessary.

In addition to documented standards, Microsoft has released a great tool to help with the actual enforcement of coding and development standards. Microsoft has published design guidelines for all .NET applications to follow, and FxCop is a tool that uses reflection, MSIL parsing, and call-graph analysis to inspect assemblies for over 200 violations of the design guidelines. Custom rules can also be created specifically to your own guidelines and used within FxCop. Some of the default rules check for conformance issues with library design, localization, naming conventions, performance, and security.

Note

FxCop can be downloaded at http://www.gotdotnet.com/team/fxcop/.

Documentation

As discussed numerous times throughout this book, the importance of developing tools that promote maintainability and reusability cannot be stressed enough. Documentation is a deliverable that will assist developers working on future modification or reuse of a tool or component. Documentation can be created for either source code or usability, and requires standardization just like source code.

Source code documentation is primarily aimed at developers who want to understand the functionality of a given component without the need to look at the source code to understand what is going on. The .NET framework has a standardized way to document source code, expressed as XML. Chapter 11, "Code Documentation with NDoc and XML," outlines the way Microsoft wants developers to document source code to remain consistent with the core framework. When a .NET assembly is compiled, an option exists to export all the XML-based source code comments to a file that can be referenced by a number of documentation generators.

An excellent tool exists that can take a .NET assembly and the associated XML comments file and build documentation. The tool is called NDoc, and it supports pluggable exporters including the MSDN-style HTML Help (.chm), the Visual Studio .NET format (HTML Help 2), and the MSDN-online style Web pages. This tool is very popular within the .NET community and is the most commonly used documentation generator for .NET.

Note

NDoc can be downloaded at http://ndoc.sourceforge.net/.

Usability documentation comes in the form of training manuals or reference materials that instruct users how to use the tool, or how to solve real-world problems with the tool. This type of documentation is high level and does not discuss the inner workings of the software; it merely shows users how to use the tool.

The Documentation section should discuss the documentation standards to use, such as NDoc or a specific template to use in Microsoft Word. Also describe how function descriptions, properties, property accessors, and classes are worded.

Testing

Testing is a very important part of any software development project, and the intent of this section is to standardize how testing takes place within the project. There are different types of testing that can be performed, such as unit, automated, functionality, and performance. Each type of test should be documented and should list all the proper procedures and guidelines to follow, along with all the necessary software to use to perform the testing, such as Rational Robot, ANTS Profiler, NUnit, and csUnit.

Defect Tracking

Standards must also be in place for how issues are handled when they appear in tests. This section should outline where issues and defects are tracked and registered, and how to handle them. Certain defects and issues are more important than others, and should generally be handled in terms of priority and influence on the stability and functionality of the tool. Be sure to describe how to prioritize certain issues and handle them accordingly. Also specify where defects and issues are stored, such as Rational ClearQuest or TestTrack Pro, for example.

Life Cycle

The Life Cycle section of the software development plan outlines how the software will be developed, and describes the software development methodology that will be used: Rational Unified Process (RUP), SCRUM, and the Waterfall approach, for example.

This section could potentially list the milestones and deadlines for the project if they are known, but typically the specific project dates reside in a project schedule, a topic outside the scope of this book.

There is a detailed overview of the software development life cycle (SDLC) in Chapter 5, "Development Phases of a Tool."

The approach covered in Chapter 5 is the Waterfall approach, though there are many different methodologies that are in use in the industry.

Development Environment

The Development Environment section of the software development plan outlines the development environment and resources necessary to design and build the tool.

First, describe the hardware specifications of the development computer(s). Also describe what operating system(s) will be installed on the computer(s). If multiple operating systems will be installed for testing, describe whether or not they will all be accessed using a dual boot loader or a virtual operating system manager. Also specify what networking requirements are needed, such as Internet access or permission to access specific local domains.

Second, you should outline the software that will be needed, such as compilers, debuggers, IDEs, frameworks, and libraries.

Last, discuss workflow processes that will be used, such as which document control and versioning system(s) will be used, as well as how the project will be backed up and at what time intervals.

Staging Environment

Every software application, in general, requires a certain level of testing. Tools that enhance workflow productivity or produce game content require an extra level of consideration for quality assurance, as a faulty tool can harm productivity or produce corrupt game content that requires time to fix or redo.

It is important to outline an environment suitable for testing, and it is recommended that this environment not be shared with the development environment. Using a unique staging environment allows testers and developers to locate conflicts with missing dependencies, hard coded values, or system variables, and other issues that could lead to deployment problems. It is also advisable to periodically rebuild your test environment to make sure that other issues do not slip through before staging deployment.

The staging environment should typically mimic the production environment, and only have the absolute necessary software and libraries installed. Never install development software in the staging environment or do any modifications there. Fully uninstall your application after testing, modify the source in the development environment, and redeploy your application to the staging environment. This may seem like a trivial and inefficient process, but doing so will save you a lot of headaches during production deployment.

The staging environment should also contain a relatively diverse range of hardware and software configurations that could potentially be used in the production environment. If the application requires 3D acceleration, be sure to test a variety of graphics cards, especially older cards that do not support the features your application requires, like a programmable pipeline, for example. Be sure to test configurations that are guaranteed to fail, and observe that all fatal errors are handled gracefully.

Production Environment

The Production Environment section of the software development plan outlines and describes the environment in which the final application will run. Some tools will only be run on one type of configuration or computer, which often is the case when the tool is developed for internal use. With a tool developed for external use, this environment is any computer or configuration that is managed by the stake-holders of the tool. The production environment is fairly similar to the staging environment. All the deployment issues should be resolved when the application reaches this environment, allowing for a clean install with no missing dependencies or settings.

Conclusion

Building a software development plan with standards plays an important role in development. A comprehensive plan is typically a waste for small tools, though even a brief description in each section is generally sufficient enough. Keep in mind that if you have standards that are applicable to other projects, if not all of them, the extra time you spend writing a comprehensive section for a small tool will be justified when you reuse those same standards in other tools that are of a much larger scale.

Why not wait to write a detailed standard until it is needed for a larger project? You can definitely do this if you want, but if you define the standards immediately, you can build all of your tools to follow your specifications, promoting ease of maintainability across all your projects.

On much larger projects, a thorough development plan and development standards are basically a requirement, especially when working with multiple developers, each with his own coding and documentation style. Remember that consistency is extremely important, and the best way to achieve consistency is through defined standards.

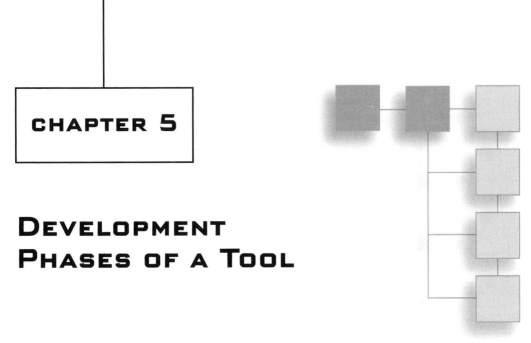

CHAPTER 5

DEVELOPMENT PHASES OF A TOOL

Large software projects will never be without some risk, but if risks can be brought down to acceptable levels, that will be a good beginning.

Capers Jones, 1998

The process of understanding the project and its goals, building it, and delivering it to users is often referred to as the Software Development Life Cycle (SDLC). Such a process sounds straightforward, but this is not the case, as more than 50% of all development projects fail. The project is canceled before the product is completed, the product is never used after it is deployed, or the end result fails to provide the outcomes that were expected. Presented in this topic are several fundamental concepts and pragmatic techniques that you can use to increase the probability that your project will be successful.

The development life cycle is composed of four phases: planning, analysis, design, and implementation. Although the focus and approach to each may differ among projects, all projects have elements of these four phases. Each phase is composed of a series of steps, which produce deliverables that provide understanding about the project. The development life cycle is a process of iterative refinement, where each phase takes in a deliverable from the previous phase, and further outlines in more detail how the product will be built, eventually leading to a finished product. Each phase generally proceeds in a logical path from start to finish, though some project teams move through the steps consecutively, iteratively, or incrementally.

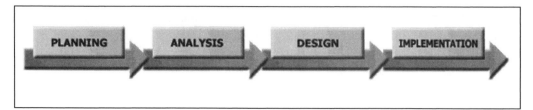

Figure 5.1 Phases of the software development life cycle.

There are many more variations of the development life cycle than what is being described throughout this chapter, though the rudiments behind each phase remain the same.

In many ways, the development life cycle is similar to building a house. First, the original idea for the house is presented. Second, this idea is transformed into a simple drawing that is refined over several iterations until the customer agrees that the drawing depicts what he or she wants. Third, a set of blueprints is created that presents extensive detail about the house, including power outlets, support beams, and door arches. Finally, the house is built following the blueprints, often with changes made by the customer as the house is being constructed.

It is important to mention that the length of and approach to each phase of the software development life cycle is dependent on the methodology used. This chapter covers only the waterfall approach, although there are roughly six other methodologies that are used in software development. There is no right approach; each methodology has a purpose and a place. The waterfall approach is covered in this chapter because it is the easiest and shortest to cover. Other methodologies, like the Rational Unified Process (RUP), are more complex and detailed.

Phase: Planning

The first phase of the development life cycle is the fundamental process of understanding why a product should be built, and determining how the project team will go about building it. It is in this stage that the value to the developers is identified, and technical, economic, and organizational feasibility are determined. This is known as a *feasibility analysis*.

A feasibility analysis evaluates if the final outcome of the project will lower costs or increase profit, and whether or not there are enough organizational and technical resources to build it. The level of risk is also assessed, contributing to the final decision about whether or not the project is a worthwhile investment. Are the developers familiar with the application and technology utilized? Less familiarity generates more risk because now the developers have to conduct additional research to build the final product and support it. How large is the project? Larger projects also generate more risk, due to the extensive scope that must be managed through development. What will be the development and operating costs? Do the costs of managing this project outweigh the benefits of the expected outcome? All of these factors must be addressed before development can continue to the next phase.

If the project is evaluated and developers are given the go-ahead, the resultant deliverable of this phase is a project plan that describes how the project team will go about developing the product. The project plan is composed of a technical brief, business rules, development requirements, milestones, deliverables, budget, and quality assurance procedures. This deliverable is given to the development team for design and implementation.

Phase: Analysis

The second phase of the development life cycle answers the questions of what the product will do, who will use the product, and when and where the product will be used. During this phase, the project team develops a concept for the new product. If a product already exists, then the project team identifies areas to improve on the existing design.

The project team sets out on an information-gathering process, where the main users of the product are interviewed or fill out a questionnaire. The analysis of this information, in conjunction with input from the project sponsor and project team managers, leads to a concept for the new product. The product concept is then used as a guide to produce a set of business analysis models that identifies how the product will be used within the company.

The analysis, product concept, and models are combined into a deliverable called the *product proposal,* which contains a high-level initial design.

Phase: Design

After the strategic decisions have been made in the previous two phases, the design phase determines how the product will operate in terms of hardware, software, and network infrastructure. Several specifications are created that detail the various components of the product.

The first step in the design phase is to develop the design strategy specification. This specification describes whether the product will be developed by programmers employed by the company, whether the product will be outsourced to another firm (usually a consulting firm), or whether the company will buy an existing software package. This leads to the architecture specification, which describes the hardware, software, and network infrastructure that will be used.

After the architecture specification is completed, the project team develops the interface specification, which specifies how the users will interact with the system (e.g. navigation methods such as menus, buttons, or command line input). Next, the database and file specifications are developed, which define exactly what data will be stored, including where it will be stored. Finally, the analysis team develops the program specification, which defines the programs that need to be written and exactly what each program will do.

All these specifications form the system specification deliverable that is handed to the programming team for implementation.

Phase: Implementation

This is the phase where the product is actually built. Notably, this phase gets the most attention because it is the longest and most expensive part of the development process.

The first step in the implementation phase is construction, during which the product is built and then tested to ensure that it performs the way it was designed. Testing and quality assurance are the most critical steps in this phase, because the cost of bugs can be immense. The majority of companies spend more time on quality assurance than on the actual development of the product.

Once the product has passed acceptance, it is ready to be installed. If an existing product was in place before this new one, both products move through conversion. This is a process by which the old product is deactivated, and the new product is activated.

The conversion process may be a direct cut-over approach (in which the new product immediately replaces the old product), a phased approach (in which the new product is installed in one division of the company as a trial before installing it in the other divisions of the company), or a parallel approach (in which both the old and new products are operated for a couple months until the support team is sure there are no bugs in the new product).

One of the most critical aspects of the conversion process is the creation of a training plan to instruct users on how to operate the new product, and help manage the changes caused by the new product.

Once the product has been deployed and tested, the project team establishes a support and maintenance plan for the new product. This plan usually includes a post-implementation review, as well as a method to identify the changes needed for the product. Optionally included are retirement plans for the product, generally affected by changing technology and business rules.

Conclusion

The development methodology described in this topic is commonly known as the Waterfall approach. This model is one of the oldest versions of the software development life cycle. The Waterfall model is linear and sequential, and once a stage has been completed, there is no turning back.

Imagine a waterfall rushing over a rocky cliff. Once the water has flowed over the cliff, it cannot turn back. This is the same idea behind waterfall development. Once a phase transitions into another, there is no turning back.

Waterfall development is advantageous in that it allows for managerial control. A schedule is set with deadlines for each development stage, and the product can proceed through the development process and be delivered on time, in theory. Each phase of development transitions into the next phase in strict linear order, without any overlapping or iterative steps.

The disadvantage to the waterfall development model is that it does not allow for reflection or revision. Once an application is in the testing phase, it is very difficult to modify something that was not explored in the concept state.

There are a number of popular software development methodologies, and each model works best for different types of companies. Other development methodologies include SCRUM\Agile, iteration and increment, eXtreme programming (XP), feature-driven development, Rational Unified Process (RUP), and Microsoft Solutions Framework (MSF).

Development of a game itself generally utilizes the SCRUM\Agile approach, whereas tools development typically follows either the waterfall approach or a custom model when there are only a handful of developers working on it.

The best development methodology to use depends on your company and project.

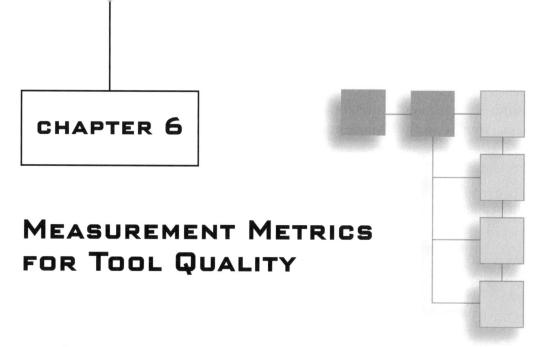

CHAPTER 6

MEASUREMENT METRICS FOR TOOL QUALITY

There is an old saying with software that three years from now, no one will remember if you shipped an awesome software release a few months late. What customers will still remember three years from now is if you shipped a software release that wasn't ready a few months too soon. It takes multiple product releases to change people's quality perception about one bad release.

Scott Guthrie

The risk of failure for software development is increasing at a rapid rate because of the need for higher quality software that is also more cost effective and delivered in a timely manner. With the growing focus on quality, there is a definite need to improve the quality of software to meet the needs of the industry. One common problem when trying to determine how to improve quality is establishing a meaningful way to measure quality so that you can quantify your results. If a developer told you that a piece of software was top-notch quality, just what does that mean? If a developer told you that a piece of software has only failed twice in over three years of usage, there would be more value behind that statement. The only difference between the two statements is that the second one presents a quantifiable measurement detailing the number of times the software failed in a three-year period. Both statements could be referring to the same piece of software, yet the second statement is the only one that is an acceptable and accurate description of software quality.

When performing any kind of measurement, you need what is known as a *metric*, which is commonly defined as a quantitative measure of the degree to which a system, component, or process possesses a given attribute. Software development quality can be measured by a number of metrics, including maintainability, performance, usability, testability, portability, reliability, and efficiency.

The International Standards Organization (ISO) has created a set of software quality standards and also describes how to collect metrics for them. The metrics discussed in this topic are a compressed overview of their work.

Tools, like any software project, require a high level of quality, especially when the tools produce game content or enhance workflow, and the rate of failure for the tool must be extremely low. This topic presents some measurement metrics and concepts for development that all greatly impact the lifetime cost of a tool.

Metric: Maintainability

Perhaps one of the most important metrics to consider in software development, and definitely evangelized in this book, is maintainability, which characterizes any successful tool. The greatest amount of development time in the game industry is spent on maintenance, by extending or enhancing a product that already exists. A tool should always be designed with maintainability in mind, designed so that the code is easy to repair and extend for future products or processes.

This metric typically looks at how many times a certain tool has been reused across multiple products or processes, how much additional time was needed to relearn the inner workings of the code, and how much development time was spent enhancing the tool to suits the needs of another product.

Metric: Traceability

The idea of traceability has been mainly introduced by object-oriented software engineering, and is the idea that documentation should be able to show why a particular implementation decision was made. Typically, a tool, especially one that's medium to large scale in terms of size, will have a design document detailing how the application will function, and may even be represented using the Unified Modeling Language (UML). The ability to look at a functionality requirement in a design document, known as *use cases* when utilizing UML, and easily understand how to perform that task in the application itself is referred to as *traceability*.

There are a multitude of ways to discuss traceability and how to achieve it, but basically it all boils down to how well the application and underlying architecture follow the design document specifications. Actors in a design document, the people using a certain component in the system, should be easily identifiable in the object model, and all functions should be named similarly to the associated use cases. For example, if the design document specifies that there is a feature called `Search Entities` and its associated code function is labeled `FindEntityList`, the traceability between the documentation and code is low because further investigation is needed to make sure that function performs the correct task. If the function was labeled `SearchEntities`, the traceability between the documentation and code would be better.

Metric: Performance

Generally, one of the most difficult areas of any software product of ample complexity is performance profiling and tuning. Performance describes issues like memory leaks or how responsive the user interface is.

This metric typically profiles the application for declines in performance or misuse of resources. Performance is very important to game tools because a responsive user interface yields much more productivity than a tool with a sluggish user interface.

Some chapters later on in the book cover performance, such as accessing performance counters to profile operations and optimization tips and tricks for the .NET platform.

The performance metric is sometimes combined with the efficiency metric in some measurement contexts.

Metric: Usability

Another important issue in regards to software development is how easy it is to reuse or extend a piece of software. In order to accomplish this, it is important that the interfaces for the software are well-documented and easy to use.

A developer should be able to read the documentation for the tool and understand what the tool is supposed to do at a high level. Additionally, a developer should be able to read the source code and easily understand what is going on behind the scenes.

The usability metric is sometimes combined with the maintainability metric in some measurement contexts.

Metric: Testability

Testing is a required step in any software project, and there are certain considerations for building software that is easy to test. Unit testing is easiest to perform in loosely coupled architectures where individual objects can be tested with minimal dependency on other objects. If testing can be performed on components in isolation from each other, there is a much greater chance that performance issues and hard-to-find bugs will be discovered.

Avoid design patterns like the *singleton,* where architectures become tightly coupled; design software for testability so that the work of testers is not as difficult and can be done in a much shorter period of time.

Metric: Portability

The portability metric involves moving software from one operating system to another. Some game development studios target multiple operating systems and platforms with their products, so portability is important to them. Therefore, it is important to build common components that are easily portable to other platforms. Even if the game development studio typically relies on outsourcing other cross-platform work to another development company, there are some practices that should be followed. The longer it takes to port the original code to another platform, the greater the overall cost of the conversion process. The more a software component relies on platform-specific technology, the more code must be written in the porting process.

The biggest practice to follow is that all calls to the operating system should be in specific components. Abstraction is very useful in this situation, because interfaces can be written that define how a particular component will communicate with the system, and operating system-specific components can be written that implement that interface, creating a flexible plugin-based architecture.

Plugin-based architectures are commonly used with 3D API agnostic graphic engines that can use either OpenGL or Direct3D. Aside from the benefits of an abstracted rendering system on Windows alone, OpenGL is pretty much the only cross-platform hardware-accelerated 3D API that can be employed in games. By using an abstracted rendering system that supports OpenGL, you do not have to worry about porting the graphic engine to other platforms, as you have already accounted for the differences.

Operating system agnostic design can also be used for other hardware-based services like audio, video, input, and networking.

Metric: Reliability

An extremely important factor in the success of any software project is its reliability. A tool is pretty useless to designers if it crashes or corrupts the data almost every time it is used. The reliability metric is a measure of failure rates surrounding the software project. If you run a certain tool a thousand times, what percentage of those times will it fail? The resulting data from this test is generally referred to as the *meantime to failure*.

There are different acceptable failure rates for different stages in software development. At the beginning of development, the software fails quite often. As development progresses, bugs are removed, and the failure rate declines to the point where the tool rarely fails. The failure rate is rare when the software is ready for integration and deployment, at which point the failure rate is said to be acceptable.

Workflow productivity using a tool is directly tied to reliability. Losing work or requiring tedious workarounds to maintain stability is a frustrating process, and should be minimized at all costs. Spending the extra time to stabilize a tool can save the designers much more time in the long run.

Metric: Efficiency

Judging the efficiency of an application is relatively difficult to do, because there are several things you must take into consideration. Some measurement contexts also combine the efficiency metric with the performance metric, while others do not.

Some measurements of efficiency include the size of the application, especially in circumstances where available disk space is limited, such as handheld or other resource-limited platforms. Smaller applications typically gain a slight performance boost over larger applications, due to how the operating system manages memory associated with processes.

The amount of memory required by the application to function optimally is also important to measure, especially in situations where memory is limited. If you had an application that performed a task in four seconds with 1MB of memory, it would be more efficient compared to an application that performed a task in two seconds with 9MB of memory.

The speed of an algorithm can also be measured in terms of efficiency. An algorithm can be evaluated in terms of the time it takes to complete its work, and how it goes about doing that work. Issues like memory access, disk access, and network access can all be considered in this measurement.

Aside from efficiency or performance, complexity of the implementation relative to the task performed can also be considered. If an application or component is mired in complexity, it might not be the most efficient implementation of a solution, even if its performance is as good as or better than another less complex solution.

The efficiency metric involves studying several important variables in order to determine whether the solution, even when meeting business objectives, is an efficient implementation.

Conclusion

In this chapter, I discussed what software quality measurements and metrics are, and why they are important. Also discussed were some development models and calculation methods used to produce and analyze high-quality software.

Note

For more information, refer to the book *Metrics and Models in Software Quality Engineering, Second Edition* by Stephen H. Kan.

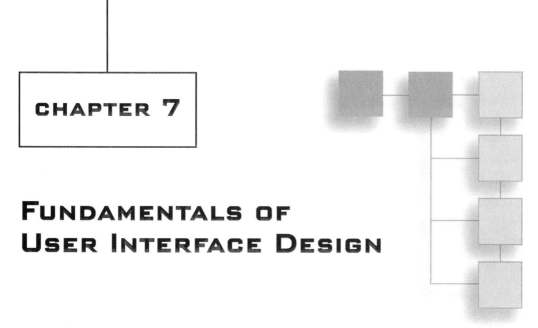

CHAPTER 7

FUNDAMENTALS OF USER INTERFACE DESIGN

I think another good principle is separating presentation or user interface (UI) from the real essence of what your app is about. By following that principle I have gotten lucky with changes time and time again. So I think that's a good principle to follow.

Martin Fowler

User interface design is a software development issue that spans numerous books, so covering the subject in one chapter is quite ambitious, perhaps impossible to do. Yet, user interface design is very important to tools development, so I felt the need to cover at least a generalization of some important rules to follow while designing your interfaces.

The importance of a good user interface design cannot be stressed enough, and it can make or break the success and adoption of your tools. The backend may have been written exceptionally well, yet an interface that is unintuitive to users will discourage them from using your tool. Additionally, productivity will not be as high, and users will feel incompetent when using the tool.

In this chapter, I will discuss some of the most important rules and guidelines for designing user interfaces. The term *control* will be used in this context to describe any element or widget on the user interface that either accepts input or displays output. Some controls include buttons, static labels, textboxes, scrollbars, and menus.

Principle of Consistency

Almost every platform has a guideline written for user interface design. Microsoft has published the *Design Guidelines for Class Library Developers*, which you should follow when building .NET software. If you feel the need to improve upon the design, chances are you will remove your "improvements" when users begin to complain about the application not working the way they would normally expect.

If you are doing cross-platform development, maintain consistency by following the design guidelines for the host platform. Never make the different platform applications function the same if they break one of the guidelines of the platform. Chances are your users will be switching between applications on one platform, not switching between applications on different platforms. Users should be able to use the knowledge gained in other programs on a certain platform to anticipate the behavior of your program.

Users should also be able to anticipate the behavior of a control from its visual appearance and properties. For example, if a pushbutton on one of your user interfaces responds to single mouse click, every other button should respond to one mouse click as well.

When you develop a custom control, it is important that you try to make it behave in a similar fashion to other system controls. If you build a custom control that allows the user to type text into it, that control should have a blinking insertion pointer; it should have a vertical scrollbar if multi-line input is supported. If you build a custom control that allows the user to click on it, the control should behave in a similar fashion to a regular button.

If you have a custom control that behaves in a fashion that users are not accustomed to, be sure to give the control a distinct appearance so that users can associate that type of control with a unique behavior.

Consistency is also important to interface abstractions like accelerator keys, placement of menus and toolbars, and mouse gestures.

Principle of Transparency

The concept of user interface transparency is a design that allows users to accomplish their tasks while being minimally aware of the interface itself. Interface transparency occurs when the attention of the user is drawn away from the interface and directed at the task itself.

Certain interface abstractions, such as accelerator (hot) keys, are quite useful in achieving interface transparency, but the best way to design a transparent interface is through iterative user testing throughout software development.

Watching how a user operates a tool and witnessing how quickly he learns an interface is an excellent way to gain an idea of what should be redesigned to improve the transparency of an interface.

Principle of Feedback

This concept applies to the controls and activity of your tool, and is about the importance of providing adequate feedback to users. Users expect feedback while using an application, so they are aware of the current state of the application. It is a typical action and reaction situation, where something should happen when a user does something.

For example, when a button is clicked, it first draws itself in a depressed state, and then draws itself in a normal state when the mouse button is released. This is a method of user feedback that informs the user that he successfully clicked the button. If this visual appearance did not occur when the button was clicked, the user generally understands that he did not actually click the button and should do so again until the visual feedback is witnessed. You can imagine the frustration of your users if buttons in your application did not display this visual feedback when they were clicked.

As another example, a checkbox control changes its appearance when it is selected or deselected to inform the user whether the checkbox is checked or not. Again, this visual feedback is important to show users the current application state.

With any tool, there are instances when an operation occurs that takes longer than a few milliseconds to complete and requires visual feedback to inform the user that the application is performing a lengthy operation and did not actually lock up. When brief delays are to occur, one of the more popular methods is to change the mouse cursor into an hourglass. If a longer operation will occur, use a progress bar control so that users can see how long the operation will take to complete. An hourglass cursor will not suffice for a lengthy operation because users will still think that the application has locked up.

Lastly, every screen should be designed so the user knows what steps have been performed, especially any critical steps that have been performed.

Principle of Refinement

One common mistake a lot of developers make is to throw a warning or error exception when the user performs an invalid operation. In actuality, you should view every warning and error message generated by your application as an opportunity to improve the interface and task sequencing techniques.

A good user interface is when warning and error messages are rarely generated, with the exception of disk failures or interrupted network connections. Otherwise, all other warning and error messages can be considered as design flaws.

Instead of letting the user do whatever he wants and throwing a warning or error message when he does something invalid, consider the prevention of these messages as a better design alternative.

The majority of erroneous user operations result from invalid input data and inappropriate task sequencing. If your program requires formatted data, such as dates or particular numeric ranges, help users enter correct data by using bounded input controls that limit input choices. Rather than letting the user enter whatever data he wants and complaining about the input when the user clicks the Save button, instead force the user to enter correct data using controls that strip invalid characters and perform automatic formatting.

If a particular step in the application cannot be legitimately performed until the user completes other steps, the dependent step should be disabled so that the user cannot attempt to perform it until all the dependencies of the step are satisfied. User action should be limited to only valid steps through the use of disabled controls. Most user interfaces have a dim appearance for disabled controls, and this visual feedback informs the user that the functionality of that control is unavailable until another step is completed.

Principle of Exploration

The human race was born to be explorers, and our curious nature causes us to attempt certain things just to see what the outcome is. When prehistoric cavemen created fire, it is safe to assume there was at least one curious individual who wanted to see what happened when they touched fire—obviously burning themselves in the process. From that point on, everyone knew what would happen if they did the same thing, so their curiosity was satisfied.

The same analogy can be used for interfaces and user exploration. Humans want to explore any environment, but with tools, they risk corrupting the database or game content. This concept is based on the idea that the user interface and application should foster an environment safe for exploration. Safe environments are achieved through the use of undo and redo functionality. A great interface design invites and rewards user exploration, and offers the thrill of discovery and the satisfaction of unassisted accomplishment. Undo and redo functionality encourages your users to explore the application without fear of corrupting the database or game content.

Another great design advantage of undo and redo functionality is that it eliminates the need for dialogs requesting permission to perform an erroneous function. This is also a great technique to enhance interface transparency.

Principle of Modality

The use of modal dialogs is quite common in a user interface, yet they must be used wisely for a number of reasons. Programs generally use modal dialogs to force users to perform steps in a specific order. Modal dialogs are very advantageous for wizard tools that simplify complex tasks, and are also used to display warning and error messages for a critical issue that the user must first address before returning to the task.

The problem with modal dialogs is that they make users uncomfortable because they restrict natural or intuitive responses. Modality also interrupts user concentration and goal-oriented behavior, decreasing productivity with the tool.

Modal dialogs are a great way to build easy-to-use and straightforward interfaces, but they have to be used sparingly. Task sequencing techniques can be applied so that modal dialogs are only used when absolutely necessary.

Principle of Self-Evidence

Good applications have online reference materials and comprehensive manuals that explain features of the application and help to solve real-world problems. If a user is stuck on a particular problem, in theory he should be able to read the reference material, move past his issues, and resume productivity.

Great applications have online reference materials and comprehensive manuals available to the user, but users rarely need to refer to them to figure out how to perform a particular task. This is where the concept of a self-evident application comes into play.

A number of factors contribute to an interface that is self-evident; some of the factors include consistency, feedback, modality, and an environment that is safe for exploration.

Following the platform guidelines eliminates the problem of users becoming frustrated with the interface itself, and reduces the learning curve required to understand the application.

Proper feedback helps the user understand what the application is doing behind the scenes, and helps reduce the chances that the user will feel "in the dark" about the current state of the application.

Modality plays a big part in helping guide the user towards performing steps in the correct sequence, and it helps the user to understand how a complex interface works.

Lastly, with an environment safe for exploration, the user can attempt to guess what to do next if he is stuck on something, without fear of corrupting his data. A user will often try a couple of things through guesswork before going to the reference material, if he can do so without undue worry that he will break things in the application or project.

Remember that the difference between a good and a great interface is how self-evident it is. If time is short for the development of a tool, instead of investing time in producing reference material, a self-evident interface will be more than enough of a reference for users.

Principle of Moderation

Most platforms have written conventions that describe the appropriate use of animation, color, sound, and multimedia clips, and they should be used sparingly.

You should never use sound and color as your sole means of communication with the user; many users are colorblind or hearing impaired. The application should be able to run with full functionality and productivity without any multimedia features.

Following the platform conventions, only use multimedia where it makes sense, and always allow the option to turn off multimedia features like sound effects. Some users find them distracting, and this decreases productivity.

Principle of Customization

This concept is centered on the idea that users love to customize their work environment to match their own personal style and preferences. Generally, offering work environment customization increases productivity because users can set up where toolbars are positioned, select fonts and colors that are easier to read, and show only the dialogs that they use often.

Another reason that customization is important is because there is such a wide variety of hardware that applications can run on, and the default appearance does not always look good on different hardware configurations.

The biggest issue is in regards to video options like screen size, resolution, and color depth. Your application may look fine on 1024×768 and 32bpp, but it may look absolutely terrible on 800×600 and 16bpp.

Allowing users to tailor the basic interface, such as fonts, toolbar location and appearance, menu entries, color scheme, and sound scheme, helps to alleviate this problem.

While customization is important, this feature is somewhat useless if the settings are not persistent between different instances of the application. If the user changes the settings, closes the application, and restarts it, the application should be in the same state it was left at in the previous session.

Persisting changes to the settings is a simple registry key with a single user, but multiple users present additional issues that must be addressed with an alternative solution. If your application supports multiple users on a single workstation, then consider recording preferences as user specific profiles, rather than as a single profile from the last time the application was run.

Conclusion

It is a misrepresentation of software to think of a user interface as "intuitive" because software applications simply do as they are instructed. It is the users who must "intuit" an application, meaning an interface that is intuitive to one user may be unintuitive to another.

The best way to design an interface that users can intuit is by designing an interface to respond just like all the other applications they are used to. The way to accomplish this is by following the *Design Guidelines for Class Library Developers*, as well as the principles and concepts in this chapter. It is also advantageous to look at similar applications and take note of how they operate.

A technique I have professionally used in the past is to open up any popular Microsoft product like Office and look at how the interface works in it. Microsoft has invested millions of dollars in user interface design research, and their research can be adapted into your applications by mimicking how their products work.

You can get the *Design Guidelines for Class Library Developers* off the corporate Microsoft site. These guidelines should be followed to produce a user interface that users can intuit, and to achieve interface transparency.

User interface design is necessary for any software application, especially when the application is a tool that is distributed to an external audience.

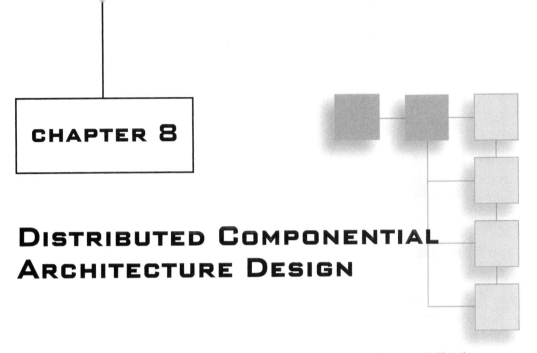

CHAPTER 8

DISTRIBUTED COMPONENTIAL ARCHITECTURE DESIGN

Design and programming are human activities; forget that and all is lost.

Bjarne Stroustrup

One of the most important issues facing developers building reusable frameworks and tools is how the architecture is structured and the dependencies that are required by each modular component. Not all tools have the luxury of a solid design, but if at least the core functionality is separated from the tool into external components, then the initial design helps promote reusability.

Another issue facing developers is designing an architecture that allows for multiple entry points into the application, such as console support for batch processing, and a Windows interface for usability. Building two separate applications is a waste of time, and one of the two won't do in a situation like this. This chapter shows a great way to decouple the core functionality of a tool into reusable components, and build a stackable architecture that easily promotes multiple entry points. Keep in mind that supporting all the entry points discussed in this chapter is generally overkill for a tool, but they are presented together to portray the "big picture." Mix and match the modules shown in this chapter, designing your solution with modularity in mind.

The .NET platform encourages the design of distributed architectures, and it is extremely advisable to build any applications or components with that in mind.

Architecture Overview

The architecture presented in Figure 8.1 is not for every tool, but should be used when possible to promote enhanced reusability and easier maintenance. On another note, this architecture is one that can be built upon over time, and if the design remains loosely coupled, new layers can be added as the tool matures, and more entry points can be defined as needed.

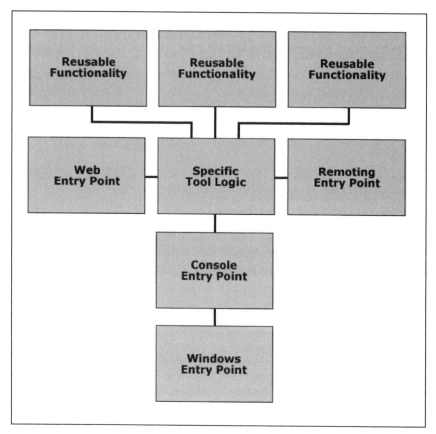

Figure 8.1 Overview of the proposed architecture.

Core Components

Core components, labeled "Reusable Functionality" in Figure 8.1, are the core libraries that all your tools can reference when needed and are designed to be loosely coupled and modular. Such functionality can include regular or virtual file system access, user security, data compression and encryption, string parsing, image processing, and other common code that can be useful to a variety of tools in your projects.

The core components should try to avoid external dependencies to other assemblies at all costs, unless linking to another core component that contains required functionality. Core components should also never contain any application entry points.

Optionally, you can also expose a COM interface from these core components if your design warrants it, though I do present an alternative in the specific tool logic.

It is advisable that you assign a strong name key to the core component assemblies. The only time you cannot do so is when the assembly references unsafe code, such as an ActiveX object.

Specific Tool Logic

This module should contain all the logic that is unique to the tool you are building. There is generally no code here that would be reused anywhere else, and typically just the driver functions are implemented in this module. The specific tool logic references whatever core components are needed for the tool, yet it does not implement any entry points. This module can export a COM interface quite easily to be called from unmanaged legacy applications.

Console Entry Point

Users prefer a rich GUI interface over a simple console one, but activities like batch processing generally feed commands and parameters into command line tools in an automated fashion. For that reason, it is important to support command line access for a tool that could be used with batch processing later. Obviously, the interface does not have to be fancy, but it should be clean enough that a user could launch the console entry point manually and easily use the tool. Proper menu descriptions and selection logic help out greatly in this regard.

Windows Entry Point

This entry point is relatively easy to construct if a decent console entry point has been made. There are two main ways this entry point could be developed, but I personally prefer the stackable method where the standard input, output, and error streams are redirected from the console entry point. This method requires less code, in that we are basically slapping a rich GUI interface on top of the console entry point.

The other approach for designing this entry point is through bypassing the console entry point and implementing similar logic that interfaces directly with the specific tool logic.

Other Entry Points

The nature of this architecture promotes loosely coupled design and distributed services or entry points. This architecture could be extended to provide its functionality to other technologies in many ways, but I will briefly mention three of the more common ones.

Many different entry points could be added to this architecture, and the design promotes both maintainability and reusability. There is nothing very complicated about this architecture, yet the benefits make it a worthwhile design idea to adopt into your development practices.

Remoting

There are a number of excellent reasons for supporting a remoting entry point. The biggest advantage is that the tool logic resides on a server machine and clients request a proxy object to it, greatly simplifying deployment and versioning. Changing the specific tool logic on the server would be instantly reflected by all client applications accessing it, completely avoiding the need to update the client applications.

Later in this chapter, an alternate architecture is presented that uses remoting as a bridge between entry points and the specific tool logic to promote simple push deployment to users.

Web Access

There are a couple of worthwhile possibilities with this entry point in regards to reporting and statistics. Functionality could be added to the specific tool logic that can return a report of the files affected by the tool, the user who accessed the tool last, total size of files modified, and any other information that would be useful to record for the tool.

A web entry point could also be useful for launching processes remotely, without requiring an application installed on the client machine to do so. For example, imagine a tool that would back up a certain directory to another server when run. A tool like this would normally need to be installed on all client machines that needed to use it, but with a web entry point, the backup could be launched remotely through a normal web browser.

COM Interface

Migrating components to the .NET platform will take some time, and definitely won't take place overnight. The ability to migrate each component one at a time and have them interface with legacy components is fairly important, and one way to do so is by exposing a COM interface for your .NET components so that legacy applications can use them.

Later in this chapter, an example is discussed that covers exposing a COM interface for a .NET component so that legacy applications can access its functionality. The discussion is relatively brief though, since COM interoperability is covered in much greater detail in Chapter 32, "Using .NET Assemblies as COM Objects."

Architecture Example

Now that the overall design of the architecture has been discussed, it is also important that an example be presented to offer a tangible reference point for properly designing a distributed componential architecture.

As an example, we will build a very simple solution that contains a few object definitions, some functionality to process the objects, and a variety of entry points to access the tool using an assortment of different technologies.

Object Definitions

Most systems define objects that represent business entities in the system, and these objects are typically used throughout an application in a variety of contexts and locations. To promote strong design, it is important that these business entities exist alone in an independent library away from processing functionality.

This example assembly contains a single object named SimpleObject, and contains a single string property that describes the name of the object.

Here is the code for the SimpleObject entity definition:

```
public class SimpleObject
{
    private string _name = "";

    public string Name
    {
        get { return _name; }
        set { _name = value; }
    }

    public SimpleObject(string name)
    {
```

```
        this._name = name;
    }
}
```

As you will notice when viewing the solution files on the Companion Web site, the entity definitions reside in an independent library, completely isolated from any processing functionality that uses these entities.

This module fits into the "Reusable Functionality" category in Figure 8.1.

Object Processing

Almost every system defines objects that represent business entities, and almost every system provides functionality that performs processing on these entities. This is one area where it is important that future reusability be taken into consideration. All functionality placed in this module should have the potential for applicability towards multiple projects. It is essential that you refrain from placing specific tool logic in this module.

This example assembly contains a single static method that inputs a SimpleObject and builds an alert message based on its name.

Here is the code for the simple object processing method for this example:

```
using ObjectDefinitions;
public class Library
{
    public static string FormatOutput(SimpleObject simpleObject)
    {
        return String.Format("The name of this SimpleObject is {0}!",
                    simpleObject.Name);
    }
}
```

Notice how this assembly references the other class library containing the entity object definitions.

This module fits into the "Reusable Functionality" category in Figure 8.1.

Alert Object Tool Interface

Now that our simple framework has been created, it is time to build our tool! In order to facilitate either a COM or remoting entry point, we must define a public interface that our tool implements. That is what this module is for.

Another gotcha when using remoting is that it is ideal for the interface to exist in its own assembly, away from the classes that provide implementation. The beauty of remoting is that you can give each client machine an assembly containing only the public interface of the tool, and each machine can build a proxy object to access the actual implementation remotely. If you keep the interface and implementation together in the same file, however, it defeats the purpose of remoting because clients have access to a local copy of the implementation.

There is one problem with keeping the interface in a separate assembly from the implementation, and that is when also exposing a COM interface. In order for COM to work, it must know what both the interface and the implementation are defined as. When paired together in the same assembly, COM has no trouble finding either the interface or the implementation, but when the interface exists by itself in a separate assembly, COM will not register output for that interface, complaining that it cannot find any suitable types to generate COM output for. This error will cause registration to fail for the implementation output because the interface will be unknown, even when the interface library is referenced correctly. One method of fixing this error is to create a dummy class that implements the interface and place it in the interface assembly. By setting the ClassInterface attribute to ClassInterfaceType.None, no class interface will be generated and the dummy class will only be visible through late-binding. The purpose of the dummy class is to force COM output registration for the interface assembly so that it is available to the implementation assembly when it registers for COM output.

If you do not wish to support remoting, you can pair the interface and implementation together, but keep in mind that you need to be committed to the architecture you choose. Going back to separate the interface into a separate assembly would be much more difficult than doing it right from the get-go.

Here is the interface for the tool-specific code, along with attributes for COM interoperability:

```
[Guid("D64A81A4-FF0C-4916-B92C-47BA3D2EC05D")]
[InterfaceType(ComInterfaceType.InterfaceIsDual)]
public interface IAlertObjectToolLogic
{
    string GetFirstAlertObjectName();
    string GetSecondAlertObjectName();
    string GetThirdAlertObjectName();
}
```

```
[Guid("6E789399-D074-407a-8715-6C72A3C70D7F")]
[ClassInterface(ClassInterfaceType.None)]
[ProgId("AlertObjectToolInterface.IgnoreMe")]
public class AlertObjectToolBase : IAlertObjectToolLogic
{
    public string GetFirstAlertObjectName()
    {
        return String.Empty;
    }

    public string GetSecondAlertObjectName()
    {
        return String.Empty;
    }

    public string GetThirdAlertObjectName()
    {
        return String.Empty;
    }
}
```

This module fits into the "Specific Tool Logic" category in Figure 8.1.

Note

Any assemblies that expose components to COM must have *Register for COM Interop* enabled in the project Configuration Properties.

Alert Object Tool

It is fairly obvious that an interface alone will not offer any useful functionality to users, so the next step is to build the tool implementation. This module can be considered the meat of the tool, because all logic specific to the tool in question resides within this module. Just like the interface, this assembly can be registered for COM Interop if desired.

This module references the entity definitions and processing assemblies, as well as the interface definition it needs to implement. The example provided is very simple, with three methods that each returns a different formatted alert string. Each method instantiates a SimpleObject entity definition with the name specified, and then passes the entity off for processing, returning the alert string.

Here is the code for the specific tool logic:

```
using ObjectDefinitions;
using ObjectProcessing;
using AlertObjectToolInterface;

[Guid("F6D5AB09-E2C1-4ff3-B023-01A94CC7C276")]
[ClassInterface(ClassInterfaceType.AutoDual)]
[ProgId("AlertObjectTool.AlertObjectToolLogic")]
public class AlertObjectToolLogic : MarshalByRefObject, IAlertObjectToolLogic
{
    public string GetFirstAlertObjectName()
    {
        SimpleObject simpleObject = new SimpleObject("Test1");
        return Library.FormatOutput(simpleObject);
    }

    public string GetSecondAlertObjectName()
    {
        SimpleObject simpleObject = new SimpleObject("Test2");
        return Library.FormatOutput(simpleObject);
    }

    public string GetThirdAlertObjectName()
    {
        SimpleObject simpleObject = new SimpleObject("Test3");
        return Library.FormatOutput(simpleObject);
    }

    [ComVisible(false)]
    public override object InitializeLifetimeService()
    {
        return null;
    }
}
```

For remoting support, you will notice that the class inherits from MarshalByRefObject, which is important because doing so allows remoting to create a proxy object out of this object to pass to clients. Also, you will notice the method InitializeLifetime Service, which allows us to explicitly handle the lifetime of proxy objects. By returning null, we are telling remoting services to keep the allocated object in memory indefinitely until explicitly told to release it. Be aware of the ComVisible(false) attribute that is set on the method, so as to not be exported with the COM interface.

For COM support, you will again notice the COM attributes set on the class. Also, make sure that the project Configuration Properties has the `Register for COM Interop` flag enabled.

This module fits into the "Specific Tool Logic" category in Figure 8.1.

Alert Object Console

We can begin discussing entry points now that the specific tool logic has been developed. The first entry point covered will be the command line console, which is widely used for automated build processes or batch processes. Some developers also have a personal preference for using console applications over GUI applications.

This example is quite simple; it takes in a 1, 2, or 3 and spits out the formatted alert message from the associated call to the tool logic.

Here is the code for the console entry point:

```
using AlertObjectTool;

[STAThread]
static void Main(string[] args)
{
    // Very simple input parameter.
    // Either 1, 2, or 3
    // 1: GetFirstAlertObjectName()
    // 2: GetSecondAlertObjectName()
    // 3: GetThirdAlertObjectName()

    if (args.Length >= 1)
    {
        AlertObjectToolLogic logic = new AlertObjectToolLogic();

        switch (args[0].Trim())
        {
            case "1":
            {
                Console.Write(logic.GetFirstAlertObjectName());
                break;
            }
```

```
        case "2":
        {
            Console.Write(logic.GetSecondAlertObjectName());
            break;
        }

        case "3":
        {
            Console.Write(logic.GetThirdAlertObjectName());
            break;
        }
    }
  }
}
```

Alert Object Windows—Direct

The first method for a WinForms-based entry point is the direct approach, where you reference and call the specific tool logic in the same way you would do in the console entry point.

Here is the code for the WinForms entry point using the direct approach:

```
using AlertObjectTool;

private void FirstTestDirectButtonClick(object sender, System.EventArgs e)
{
    AlertObjectToolLogic logic = new AlertObjectToolLogic();
    MessageBox.Show(logic.GetFirstAlertObjectName());
}

private void SecondTestDirectButtonClick(object sender, System.EventArgs e)
{
    AlertObjectToolLogic logic = new AlertObjectToolLogic();
    MessageBox.Show(logic.GetSecondAlertObjectName());
}

private void ThirdTestDirectButtonClick(object sender, System.EventArgs e)
{
    AlertObjectToolLogic logic = new AlertObjectToolLogic();
    MessageBox.Show(logic.GetThirdAlertObjectName());
}
```

Alert Object Windows—Wrapper

The second method for a WinForms-based entry point is the wrapper approach, where the WinForms application layers on top of the console entry point and redirects all standard input and output through itself.

This approach is beneficial in the sense that there is less to code, since the majority of the entry point code exists within the console entry point. Another benefit is that this project does not require any references to the underlying framework or specific tool logic.

Using this method also reduces the chances for bugs since one code base is maintained, and fixing a bug affects both entry points.

Here is the code for the WinForms entry point using the wrapper approach:

```
private void FirstTestWrapperButtonClick(object sender, System.EventArgs e)
{
    LaunchConsoleWrapper("1");
}


private void SecondTestWrapperButtonClick(object sender, System.EventArgs e)
{
    LaunchConsoleWrapper("2");
}


private void ThirdTestWrapperButtonClick(object sender, System.EventArgs e)
{
    LaunchConsoleWrapper("3");
}


private void LaunchConsoleWrapper(string parameter)
{
    Process process = new Process();
    process.StartInfo.UseShellExecute = false;
    process.StartInfo.RedirectStandardOutput = true;
    process.StartInfo.CreateNoWindow = true;
    process.StartInfo.Arguments = parameter;
    process.StartInfo.FileName = Application.StartupPath +
                    @"\AlertObjectConsole.exe";

    if (process.Start())
    {
        MessageBox.Show(process.StandardOutput.ReadToEnd());
        process.WaitForExit();
```

```
    }
    else
    {
        MessageBox.Show("Error launching console application");
    }
}
```

The function `LaunchConsoleWrapper` takes in the argument string to pass to the console entry point, and launches the console entry point with redirected standard output.

Alert Object Remoting

A great feature of the .NET platform is the ability to invoke remote procedure calls (RPC) from proxy objects published by a server machine. remoting solves a number of deployment concerns and allows for a variety of distributed architectures. Clients can have a local copy of the tool interface, except the implementation itself exists on a remote machine. A client would connect to the remote machine, request a proxy object of a certain type, and use the proxy object as if it were a local system variable.

In order to support Remoting, the first thing to do (aside from building an object that inherits from `MarshalByRefObject`) is to open a remoting channel and publish an object on it that clients will use.

Here is the code to open a remoting channel on a specific port number and publish an object on it:

```
// The Tcp channel to publish the proxy on
private TcpChannel _channel = null;

// A reference to the remoted proxy object
private AlertObjectTool.AlertObjectToolLogic _remotedLogic = null;

// A reference to the proxy information
private ObjRef _remotedLogicRef = null;

private void ActionButton_Click(object sender, System.EventArgs e)
{
    if (ActionButton.Text.Equals("Start Listening"))
    {
        ActionButton.Text = "Stop Listening";
```

```
        _channel = new TcpChannel((int)PortField.Value);
        ChannelServices.RegisterChannel(_channel);

        _remotedLogic = new AlertObjectTool.AlertObjectToolLogic();
        _remotedLogicRef = RemotingServices.Marshal(_remotedLogic,
                                  "AlertObjectToolLogic");
    }
    else
    {
        ActionButton.Text = "Start Listening";

        RemotingServices.Disconnect(_remotedLogic);

        _remotedLogicRef = null;
        _remotedLogic = null;

        ChannelServices.UnregisterChannel(_channel);
    }
}
```

Alert Object Remoting Example

With the specific tool logic published on a remoting channel, we can now request a reference to the proxy object and begin invoking calls.

Here is the code for a remoting entry point that invokes the specific tool logic using a proxy object:

```
// A reference to the tool logic proxy
private IAlertObjectToolLogic _logicProxy = null;
private void ActionButtonClick(object sender, System.EventArgs e)
{
    if (ActionButton.Text.Equals("Connect to Proxy"))
    {
        ActionButton.Text = "Release Proxy";

        _logicProxy =
(IAlertObjectToolLogic)Activator.GetObject(typeof(IAlertObjectToolLogic),
"tcp://localhost:" + ((int)PortField.Value).ToString() + "/AlertObjectToolLogic");

        TestFirstButton.Enabled = true;
        TestSecondButton.Enabled = true;
        TestThirdButton.Enabled = true;
```

```csharp
                PortField.Enabled = false;
        }
        else
        {

            ActionButton.Text = "Connect to Proxy";
            _logicProxy = null;

            TestFirstButton.Enabled = false;
            TestSecondButton.Enabled = false;
            TestThirdButton.Enabled = false;
            PortField.Enabled = true;
        }
}

private void TestFirstButtonClick(object sender, System.EventArgs e)
{
    try
    {
        if (_logicProxy != null)
        {
            MessageBox.Show(_logicProxy.GetFirstAlertObjectName());
        }
        else
        {
            MessageBox.Show("Proxy Object not Created");
        }
    }
    catch (System.Runtime.Remoting.RemotingException)
    {
        MessageBox.Show("remoting Endpoint not Bound");
    }
    catch (System.Net.Sockets.SocketException)
    {
        MessageBox.Show("remoting Endpoint not Bound");
    }
}

private void TestSecondButtonClick(object sender, System.EventArgs e)
{
    try
    {
        if (_logicProxy != null)
        {
```

```
            MessageBox.Show(_logicProxy.GetSecondAlertObjectName());
        }
        else
        {
            MessageBox.Show("Proxy Object not Created");
        }
    }
    catch (System.Runtime.Remoting.RemotingException)
    {
        MessageBox.Show("remoting Endpoint not Bound");
    }
    catch (System.Net.Sockets.SocketException)
    {
        MessageBox.Show("remoting Endpoint not Bound");
    }
}

private void TestThirdButtonClick(object sender, System.EventArgs e)
{
    try
    {
        if (_logicProxy != null)
        {
            MessageBox.Show(_logicProxy.GetThirdAlertObjectName());
        }
        else
        {
            MessageBox.Show("Proxy Object not Created");
        }
    }
    catch (System.Runtime.Remoting.RemotingException)
    {
        MessageBox.Show("remoting Endpoint not Bound");
    }
    catch (System.Net.Sockets.SocketException)
    {
        MessageBox.Show("remoting Endpoint not Bound");
    }
}
```

Unmanaged COM Support

As discussed earlier, sometimes it is important to slowly migrate individual components in a legacy environment over to the .NET platform. Doing so requires the ability for .NET and legacy components to communicate with each other. This is made possible by exposing a COM interface that legacy components can invoke. We already discussed how to export a COM interface for the specific tool logic, so now it is time to show the manner in which a legacy component invokes a .NET component.

When a .NET project is marked with `Register for COM Interop`, a .tlb file is generated that contains the exported symbols registered with COM. You can import this file in an unmanaged application and have all the necessary information to invoke the COM object.

Here is the code for an unmanaged application invoking the specific tool logic assembly via COM:

```
#include <windows.h>
#include <atlbase.h>
#include <atlcom.h>
#include <comutil.h>


// Import the IAlertObjectToolLogic interface type library
#import "..\\AlertObjectToolInterface\\bin\\Debug\\AlertObjectToolInterface.tlb"
raw_interfaces_only


// Import the AlertObjectToolLogic type library
#import "..\\AlertObjectTool\\bin\\Debug\\AlertObjectTool.tlb" raw_interfaces_only


WINAPI WinMain(HINSTANCE instance, HINSTANCE prevInstance, LPSTR commandLine, int show)
{
    ::CoInitialize(NULL);

    // Define an interface pointer suitable for the COM class
    CComPtr<AlertObjectToolInterface::IAlertObjectToolLogic> toolLogic;

    // Determine the Guid of the COM class to instantiate
    CLSID alertObjectToolClassID = __uuidof(AlertObjectTool::AlertObjectToolLogic);

    // Attempt to instantiate the COM class
    if (SUCCEEDED(toolLogic.CoCreateInstance(alertObjectToolClassID,
                                 0,
                                 CLSCTX_ALL)))
```

```
    {
        CComBSTR firstObjectNameProxy;
        CComBSTR secondObjectNameProxy;
        CComBSTR thirdObjectNameProxy;

        HRESULT hr;

        // Call the first test logic method
        hr = toolLogic ->GetFirstAlertObjectName(&firstObjectNameProxy.m_str);

        // Call the second test logic method
        hr = toolLogic ->GetSecondAlertObjectName(&secondObjectNameProxy.m_str);

        // Call the third test logic method
        hr = toolLogic ->GetThirdAlertObjectName(&thirdObjectNameProxy.m_str);

        _bstr_t firstObjectName = firstObjectNameProxy;
        _bstr_t secondObjectName = secondObjectNameProxy;
        _bstr_t thirdObjectName = thirdObjectNameProxy;

        MessageBox(0, (char*)firstObjectName, "First Object", 0);
        MessageBox(0, (char*)secondObjectName, "Second Object", 0);
        MessageBox(0, (char*)thirdObjectName, "Third Object", 0);
    }
    else
    {
        MessageBox(0, "Could not instantiate COM object", "Error", 0);
    }

    ::CoUninitialize();
    return S_OK;
}
```

Alternate Architecture Structure

An alternative to the proposed architecture is removing the remoting entry point and placing it as a bridge between the specific tool logic and all other entry points. Doing so would convert the architecture into something like a client and server environment, storing a single copy of the specific tool logic on the server. The clients would not require the tool logic, just an interface definition they can cast to a Remoted proxy wrapper.

This architecture would work great in environments where numerous machines need to use a particular tool, but issues and concerns with deployment and versioning present problems. Aside from the first client application and interface definition installation, the only time the client machines would ever need an update would be if the interface changed. If the interface definition were stored in a separate assembly, a simple push technology could be used to force all client machines to remain up to date.

Conclusion

This topic discussed a certain way to design your .NET applications and libraries so reusability and maintainability are promoted as much as possible.

There is really only one spot that cannot be independently developed at any time. The Windows entry point in the example on the companion web site typically just redirects standard input and output streams from the console entry point, helping to reduce the amount of code to maintain both types of entry points. Because of this, the Windows entry point cannot be developed before the console entry point unless both are developed independently of each other. Thanks to the tool logic residing in a separate module, no matter how you structure the entry points, you only need to change the code in one spot to affect how the tool works everywhere. A single module for the logic also helps with maintenance, versioning, and deployment.

As touched on with the alternative architecture described in this chapter, remoting can be used as a barrier between all the entry points and the specific tool logic to convert the architecture into a client and server design. The tool logic can reside on one development server, and all client machines using the tool can access it through a Remoted proxy object. Clients would just need the interface definition the Remoted object implements, and the actual code can stay on the server. This type of architecture would greatly improve deployment by only requiring a change to the server code, and all clients would instantly start accessing the latest version.

Not all types of tools would benefit from this architecture, most notably any tool that intensively accesses the local file system. However, if the server had share access to each client, the tool could be designed to accommodate file system access over the network.

The example overviewed in this topic is also available on the Companion Web site; it shows how to structure an application with this architecture, and even how to export a COM interface and register with Remoting. Keep in mind that these topics are covered in much greater depth later in this book, so no time will be spent describing what the code is doing. If you are lost regarding how things are working, please revisit this chapter later, when you are more comfortable with the technology and services used.

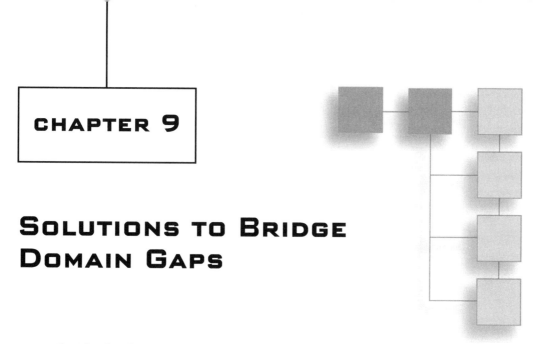

CHAPTER 9

SOLUTIONS TO BRIDGE DOMAIN GAPS

The idea has been to treat legacy systems as a black box and deal with them at more than arm's length. All of this has made it possible to make many of these systems look like they were part of the 21st Century, leaving the tough stuff—the data and the business rules—untouched. If it ain't broke, don't fix it, right? Well, not exactly. Of course, old systems don't get better by just being ignored. They get worse.

Ken Orr

One of the major goals for software engineering in the past decade has been to build software that promotes abstracted reusability. Because of this, developers witnessed the emergence of the object-oriented paradigm, which resulted in the introduction of reusable object-oriented frameworks. An object-oriented framework can be defined as a set of classes that embody an abstract design for solutions to a collection of related problems in a given problem domain.

The high reusability of frameworks is quite evident to software engineers, and it has solved many problems related to the goal of improved component reusability. With the emergence of new disciplines comes new issues and problems that must be addressed. Where single frameworks were originally used, we are now seeing a shift towards multiple frameworks that must communicate with each other in a cohesive fashion. Often there are problems communicating across dissimilar domain gaps, especially when each framework is being developed by a different development team. The source code to other frameworks is typically unavailable to developers who are not explicitly involved in its development, which generally leads to a number of integration issues between frameworks.

In this chapter, I will address the reasons behind the friction existing between multiple frameworks, and I offer some pragmatic approaches to building a cohesive design, even when you do not have access to the source code of other frameworks employed in your application. Throughout this chapter, I will refer to communication problems between frameworks in different problem domains as *compositional friction*.

Compositional Friction

There are numerous reasons why compositional friction can exist between two or more frameworks, and even on a solitary level between classes in a single framework. Although friction can exist between classes in a single framework, these issues can be solved through an iterative refactoring process with the availability of source code. This chapter is directed at eliminating friction between multiple frameworks, where one framework typically only has access to external frameworks through their public interfaces, and these interfaces cannot be modified or refactored.

Many software development issues can cause compositional friction, but a few of the most notable ones include domain coverage, design intentions, framework gap, entity overlap, and source code access.

Cause: Domain Coverage

The general purpose of a framework is to provide an abstract design for applications in a particular problem domain. It is important to realize that the framework does not need to cover the entire problem domain, but rather only a subset of relevant entities in the given problem domain. The amount of domain coverage to target with a framework is fairly subjective, though, because problem domains are not generally defined in extensive detail. Determining how much coverage to employ is up to the solution architect, and iterative refactoring helps to improve domain coverage.

When composing two frameworks, there are three levels of domain overlap that can occur, each with different implications and solutions. If no overlap occurs, there is no risk of integration issues when composing overlapping entities, but there may be a gap between frameworks that must be managed. If there is a relatively small amount of domain overlap between frameworks, the best solution is to evolve a few classes in both frameworks to communicate with each other with little to no compositional friction. However, when considerable domain overlap occurs, there are some important decisions to make. Sometimes it would be more advantageous to rewrite one or both of the frameworks from scratch when framework reuse is threatened. It can be more problematic to refactor communication between both frameworks when the expected lifetime of the product is quite long. If an application using the frameworks will be evolving over a long period of time, the frameworks must be continuously updated for each consecutive version of the application. Remember to make your decision based on the problem domain and the coverage of the framework.

Cause: Design Intentions

A well known design philosophy is that reusable software must be written for reuse through composition and adaptation. Generally, frameworks are designed to be reused through adaptation, but not through composition. Designing software reusability through composition is very important, and there are two composition directions that can occur. The first direction is parallel composition, which targets frameworks that exist on the same layer in the application. Parallel is the easiest composition direction because both frameworks do not rely directly on the services each other provides to properly operate. The other composition direction is perpendicular, which exists in a software application that supports a layered architecture where frameworks can depend on services provided by another framework in a different layer. One issue that is independent of the composition direction is the communication support, which can be either half-duplex (one-way, or simplex) or full-duplex (two-way). Half-duplex communication is fairly easy to design for, but full-duplex communication can present additional design problems when composing multiple frameworks.

Cause: Framework Gap

A framework gap occurs when multiple frameworks need to be composed to satisfy requirements, but both frameworks do not completely cover the requirements. This problem typically occurs because each framework does not have ample domain coverage, leading to domain gaps or overlaps.

There are a few solutions to this problem, the first one being the use of wrapper class that encapsulates the existing functionality and extends any missing functionality, also providing a uniform public interface so that clients are unaware of the internal architecture.

An alternative is to develop a software liaison, which is basically an application that exposes the public interface to clients and handles the communication and extension of functionality between the frameworks. This approach works great for situations where source code is inaccessible, or the base frameworks should not be modified.

Lastly, if source code is available, the cleanest solution is to bridge domain gaps by providing missing functionality, or remove domain overlaps through refactoring methods.

Cause: Entity Overlap

When more than one framework presents the same entity in a particular problem domain, each from a different perspective, the composition of these frameworks requires that the related entities be composed as well. This problem is known as *entity overlap*, and it occurs when the same problem and entities are modeled differently between multiple frameworks. Entity overlap is a common problem when composing multiple frameworks, and the solution can be fairly tricky due to the cohesive nature of entity classes and their need to sometimes notify the other frameworks when certain actions occur.

One solution to the problem of entity overlap is the use of multiple inheritance, but this method presents a problem when properties of an entity are not mutually exclusive. Multiple inheritance accomplishes the composition objective by handling the conversion between related entities in the frameworks and routing necessary events. It is possible to use this solution in development environments where source is inaccessible and cannot be modified.

An alternative solution is to use aggregation, where an aggregate class is used to represent a framework in parts. Each aggregate class is the entity definition for the application, but this approach requires that source code be available so that all references to a particular entity can be changed to point to the new aggregate classes. A drawback to this solution is that all interfaces for each representation of a certain entity must exist in the aggregate class, and there is a lot of additional overhead when using aggregation to bridge domain gaps.

A final solution is through the use of subclassing, where each framework is subclassed and each subclass handles the bidirectional communication of updates and conversion between other subclasses. Additionally, each subclass must override the operations in the superclass. This solution can also be used in situations where source code is inaccessible and cannot be modified. The major drawback of this solution is that the represented entity is partitioned across multiple frameworks. Another improvement to this solution is to use an aggregate class that contains all the subclasses and facilitates the communication and conversion between parts.

Cause: Legacy Components

There are times when the classes in a framework do not satisfy the problem domain solution, and the design warrants that a legacy component be used in conjunction with a framework to fill the gap. This situation can also arise if there is considerable time and expense invested in a legacy component (such as a game engine or utility library), and a business decision is made to reuse existing technology within a new framework (unmanaged and managed interoperability, for example). Using legacy components can cause severe compositional friction in your framework unless dealt with accordingly.

One method of removing the composition implications is to modify the framework to reference the legacy component instead of classes within the framework, though this solution requires access to the source code.

An alternative solution is to employ the adapter pattern and build a class that lies between the framework and the legacy component, acting as an interpreter so that both parts can communicate with each other. The latter part of this chapter focuses on this method in much greater detail.

Cause: Source Code Access

Quite often, multiple frameworks are developed by multiple teams, and development rules regulate that a certain team only has access to their own source code, and can only access functionality in the other frameworks using the public interfaces of compiled libraries or assemblies. This constraint is good in that it restricts each team from having a varying source code version of another team's framework, but there is a problem as well. There are times when behavior must be added to another framework to allow for communication between the other frameworks. Without access to source code, each team must send numerous waves of change requests to the other teams, asking for modifications, and then other issues may arise when the public interfaces do not satisfy the needs of the team that requested them.

One solution to this problem is the use of wrappers encapsulating an external framework and attempting to build new functionality on top of the existing library. This approach has some problems though, such as considerable amounts of additional code and severe performance penalties. Additionally, if any logic is changed in the base framework, a change request must be sent to the development team of the framework.

The best solution is to either get the source code or establish a reliable and effective change request system where requests are dealt with almost immediately, and have a liaison from your team overseeing the modifications to make sure that requirements and needs are met correctly.

Relevant Design Patterns

Design patterns provide reusable solutions to commonly encountered programming problems, and there are a few that are applicable to this topic. The façade and adapter patterns are very beneficial to architectures that suffer from compositional friction, and can be employed to reduce the friction between multiple frameworks when used correctly.

Façade Design Pattern

This design pattern provides a unified high-level interface to a set of interfaces in a subsystem, thus making the subsystem easier to use. A subsystem can be defined as a set of classes or libraries that provide a solution to a given problem domain. A framework can be thought of as a subsystem in the context of this topic. A depiction of an architecture that is tightly coupled is shown in Figure 9.1. The façade pattern is depicted in Figure 9.2.

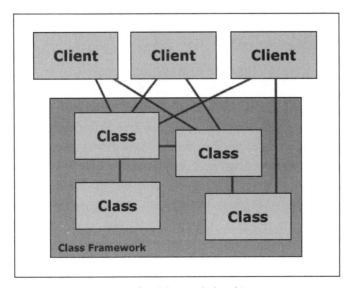

Figure 9.1 Depiction of tightly coupled architecture.

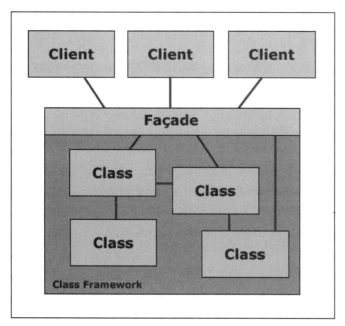

Figure 9.2 Depiction of the façade pattern.

One benefit of this pattern is that classes in a subsystem are decoupled from the client interface, causing the architecture to be more portable and maintainable. Additionally, using the façade pattern reduces component dependencies, which can dramatically reduce compilation times of large software projects.

The following code shows how to implement the façade pattern in C#:

```csharp
private class SubSystem1
{
    public void DoSomethingSpecific()
    {
        MessageBox.Show("Hello World #1");
    }
}

private class SubSystem2
{
    public void DoSomethingSpecific()
    {
        MessageBox.Show("Hello World #2");
    }
}
```

```
private class SubSystem3
{
    public void DoSomethingSpecific()
    {
        MessageBox.Show("Hello World #3");
    }
}

public class Facade
{
    private SubSystem1 _subSystem1 = new SubSystem1();
    private SubSystem2 _subSystem2 = new SubSystem2();
    private SubSystem3 _subSystem3 = new SubSystem3();

    public void DoSomething()
    {
        _subSystem1.DoSomethingSpecific();
        _subSystem2.DoSomethingSpecific();
    }

    public void DoAnotherThing()
    {
        _subSystem1.DoSomethingSpecific();
        _subSystem3.DoSomethingSpecific();
    }
}

public class Client
{
    public void Run(Facade facade)
    {
        facade.DoSomething();
        facade.DoAnotherThing();
    }
}
```

The façade pattern is quite useful when building new frameworks, but because this chapter is mainly addressing cohesion issues between existing frameworks, the adapter pattern is best suited for this problem.

Adapter Design Pattern

This design pattern is similar to the façade pattern, except the adapter pattern makes two existing interfaces work together instead of defining a new one. In order to fully understand the adapter pattern, there are some terms that should be defined. These terms are shown in Table 9.1.

Table 9.1 Adapter Pattern Elements

Name	Description
Target	The domain-specific interface that the client will use.
Adapter	An object that adapts the adaptee interface to the target interface.
Adaptee	An interface that needs adaptation to the target interface.
Client	The application that collaborates with the target interface.

It is possible to have the adapter class inherit from an adaptee, but doing so can lead to design problems when adapting to the target interface. A better approach is to store an instance of the adaptee inside the adapter class and access the instance explicitly. The adapter pattern is depicted in Figure 9.3.

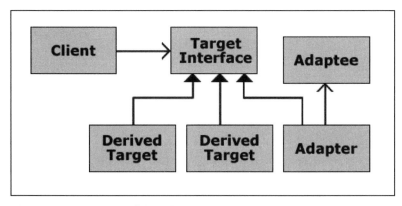

Figure 9.3 Depiction of the adapter pattern.

The following code shows how to implement the adapter pattern in C#:

```
interface Target
{
    void DoSomething();
}

class Adaptee
{
    public void DoSomethingSpecific()
    {
        MessageBox.Show("Hello World!");
    }
}

class Adapter : Target
{
    private Adaptee _adaptee = new Adaptee();

    public void DoSomething()
    {
        _adaptee.DoSomethingSpecific();
    }
}

class Client
{
    public void Run(Target target)
    {
        target.DoSomething();
    }
}
```

The adapter pattern is not complicated to implement, but can be a great design move when you run into issues composing legacy components that do not support the required interface.

Even though there are a number of ways to reduce compositional friction and improve component cohesion, it was felt that extended coverage of adapters was important.

When dealing with unmanaged code (legacy components) that must interface with managed code, the adapter pattern is utilized often, whether explicitly or implicitly. If you think about it, exporting a COM interface from a managed application can be thought of as an implicit instance of the adapter pattern so that unmanaged applications can communicate with managed code. On a higher level, Windows Forms can also be thought of as an object-oriented adapter between any CLR-compliant language like C# and the traditional procedural controls available in the Win32 API. Lastly, you can find some adapters present in the .NET Class Framework itself. The database connection functionality employs adapters to interface with a variety of database engines. While each database engine is different, the base interfaces for dealing with them remain abstract and consistent.

It is important to note that there is increased performance overhead when using adapters because all methods called in the adaptee must first be called through the adapter methods. The best approach, disregarding any time, environment, or budget constraints, is to just refactor the code, but this is rarely the case when developing tools or games in general.

Part V, "Techniques for Legacy Interoperability," covers interoperability between managed and unmanaged code, and specific real-world examples of using adapters are covered.

Conclusion

The introduction of object-oriented frameworks was a huge step forward in the area of software component reuse, but recently there has been a push towards the use of multiple frameworks within a single application. In this chapter, I discussed the issues behind using multiple frameworks, problems that occur from doing so, and some possible solutions to overcome these problems. Currently, there are some solutions to reduce compositional friction, such as the adapter pattern and employing wrapper objects, but these solutions only partially solve the problem when they too require a considerable amount of implementation effort. The best approach for framework reusability is to carefully study the problem domain to find the appropriate domain coverage, and build your frameworks from the ground up with a loosely coupled and maintainable architecture.

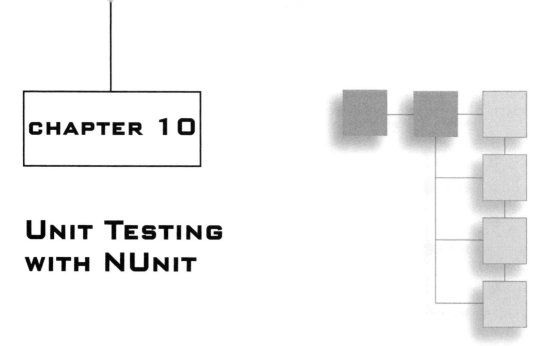

CHAPTER 10

Unit Testing with NUnit

Testing by itself does not improve software quality. Test results are an indicator of quality, but in and of themselves, they don't improve it. Trying to improve software quality by increasing the amount of testing is like trying to lose weight by weighing yourself more often. What you eat before you step onto the scale determines how much you will weigh, and the software development techniques you use determine how many errors testing will find. If you want to lose weight, don't buy a new scale; change your diet. If you want to improve your software, don't test more; develop better.

Steve C. McConnell, "Code Complete"

Testing is an important aspect of any software project, and there are many different kinds of tests that can be performed. An important, yet often misunderstood or ignored method of testing is the unit test. Unit testing is an inexpensive way that developers can write better code—faster. Large companies tend to spend a lot of time and resources on testing, yet usually do so near the end of a project, often meaning the testing is minimized or reduced because of budget and schedule constraints. In actuality, testing should be done extremely early in development, as well as continuously thereafter.

Programmers generally think of testing as a nuisance, because they would rather be writing code. Unit testing is not a grand quality initiative for large companies; unit testing is done by programmers for programmers. Many developers write throwaway code to test functionality, but doing so can introduce some problems and decrease the credibility of the test cases.

It is important to note that this chapter does not attempt to sell you on the idea of testing, as it is assumed that you have adopted this excellent practice already, since you are reading the chapter. Additionally, this chapter will only briefly cover the basics behind unit testing; it will in no way attempt to cover all the fundamentals of unit testing. The main focus of this chapter is on performing unit tests with the NUnit framework and application.

Overview of Unit Testing

Basically, unit testing focuses on a single unit—the class. Each class is tested alone in an attempt to discover errors in its code. The idea is to test anything in a class that could conceivably fail. If something in the class is changed, all tests, not just your own, are run again. If any fail, the programmer immediately goes back, fixes the problem, and runs the tests again. This process is performed in an iterative manner until all tests are successful.

After unit testing is complete on a group of modules, they are combined into progressively more complex groupings, which are also tested. This integration processes will continue until the entire application has been assembled and tested.

There are two main approaches when performing unit testing, as discussed in Table 10.1.

Table 10.1 Unit Testing Approaches

Approach	Description
Black-Box Approach	The black-box approach is the most commonly used method, in which each class represents an encapsulated object. The black-box approach is driven by all the preconstruction specifications for each class. Each item in the specification becomes a test, and several test cases are developed for it. The tests are focused on whether or not the class meets the requirements in the specification, rather than the programmer's interpretation.
White-Box Approach	The white-box approach is based on the method specifications associated with each class. The white-box approach is generally used instead of the black-box approach when the complexity of the class is high. The tester may discover errors or assumptions by looking through the code that are not generally obvious to a tester using the black-box approach.

There are quite a few benefits to unit testing, but some of the most notable ones are discussed in Table 10.2.

Table 10.2 Unit Testing Benefits

Benefit	Description
Requires the programmer to slow down and think	When refactoring or adding a new feature, testing forces you to think about what the code is supposed to do. You end up thinking about how the public API is accessed and what the outcome should be, ending up with a clean design that does exactly what you expect it to do.
Protects you against other programmers	Sometimes bugs only manifest themselves in rare situations. If another programmer changes a class but does not run the new code with all the problematic situations, bugs may slip through. If a unit test exists to test that particular situation, then the bug will be found when the unit tests are run again after changing the code.
Forces you to design better code	Testing forces you to make your code easy to test, relying less on the usage of singletons and global variables. Tightly coupled design is often difficult to test and generally requires complex initialization. Testing generally enforces loosely coupled design to make testing easier.
Promotes refactoring without breaking code	Testing allows you to refactor at any time without the fear of breaking your code, so that the design of your program can improve over numerous iterations. Each time the code is changed, the tests are run again to ensure that all the existing modules remain stable.

Introducing NUnit

In order to properly perform unit testing, a framework must be employed to facilitate the testing. This is where NUnit comes into play. NUnit is a unit testing tool for the Microsoft .NET Framework. It targets test-driven development with all .NET languages, including C#, Visual Basic .NET, J#, and C++/CLI.

NUnit was developed by Jim Newkirk, Alexei Vorontsov, Michael Two, and Charlie Pool, based on the original NUnit version by Philip Craig. NUnit is very similar to the eXtreme Programming test frameworks (xUnits) with a couple of significant differences.

Just like .NET, the NUnit framework is language-independent, in the sense that any CLR-compliant language may be used to write tests and NUnit will execute them just fine.

Attributes are a wonderful feature of .NET, and are used by NUnit to identity tests and test fixtures, without requiring that tests inherit from classes within a testing framework. Using attributes to define tests allows code to remain clean and fairly independent of any test support files.

With the creation of tests, you perform the testing by launching either the GUI or console version of the NUnit application, and target the assemblies that you wish to test. NUnit uses reflection to interrogate the assemblies for tests and then executes them one at a time. All tests have the ability to execute setup and teardown methods, allowing for each test to be independent of the others.

Creating an NUnit Project

There are a few ways you can develop your unit tests. Some developers prefer to place test functions directly inside the source code of the project that is being tested. If this is something you wish to do, be sure to use the #if and #endif preprocessor tags to strip unit tests from release mode.

Other developers like to place tests inside separate files within the project being tested. Again, don't forget to strip these tests out in release mode.

The most common approach, unless you're testing internal objects, is to build your tests in external assemblies. The benefit to this approach is that all test code is decoupled from the project itself.

Use whichever method you are comfortable with. The example for this chapter has the test code in a separate assembly. Start by creating a new class library project for your unit test assembly.

The next thing to do is reference nunit.framework.dll in your unit test assembly. If you installed NUnit using the typical approach, you should have all the NUnit assemblies installed into the Global Assembly Cache (GAC). If not, you can press the Browse button and manually navigate to the assembly in the installation folder. The default installation path for the NUnit framework is C:\Program Files\NUnit 2.2\bin.

Figure 10.1 shows the Add Reference dialog with the nunit.framework assembly showing up in the GAC.

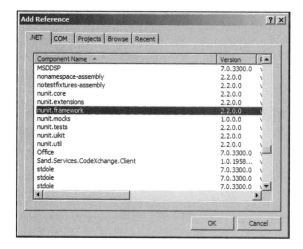

Figure 10.1
Add Reference dialog for the
NUnit framework.

After the NUnit framework reference has been added to your unit test project, you should have something similar to Figure 10.2. Also be aware that Visual Studio automatically adds System.Data and System.Xml, and they have been removed from the references list because they are not needed for this example.

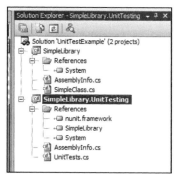

The SimpleLibrary project contains the object we want to test, and the SimpleLibrary.UnitTesting contains the unit tests that NUnit will execute against SimpleLibrary.

Figure 10.2
Overview of the example project structure.

Attribute Overview

Traditionally, NUnit provided test declaration using inheritance, but this design posed some problems with languages like C#, where multiple inheritance is not supported, and the only way to use the test framework is with complex inheritance hierarchies. The latest version of NUnit now offers a method of declaring tests with attributes, which is basically a .NET feature that can inject meta-data into an object.

Attributes do not reflect the code being run, but attributes do provide extra information about a particular object. The NUnit runner scans all the targeted assemblies for classes and methods that contain certain attributes and acts on them accordingly.

[TestFixture]

A class containing the methods that make up the testing performed on a class is marked with the [TestFixture] attribute. A common naming convention used is to take the name of the class you want to test, and append Tests on to the end. For example, if we are testing SimpleClass, it is common to name our test fixture SimpleClassTests. These will be the names used in the provided examples.

The following code snippet shows how to use this attribute:

```
[TestFixture]
public class SimpleClassTests
{
}
```

Note

Classes marked with the [TestFixture] attribute must have a public default constructor or no constructors at all. Without any constructors, a public default constructor will be created implicitly.

[Test]

A method in a test fixture marked with the [Test] attribute will be executed when the test fixture is tested with NUnit.

The following code snippet shows how to use this attribute:

```
[TestFixture]
public class SimpleClassTests
{
    [Test]
    public void TestSomething()
    {
    }
}
```

Note

It is important that a [Test] method be marked public, return void, and not take in any parameters.

[SetUp]

A method in a [TestFixture] marked with the [SetUp] attribute will be executed immediately before each test is run.

The following code snippet shows how to use this attribute:

```
[TestFixture]
public class SimpleClassTests
{
    [SetUp]
    public void SetUp()
    {
        // Do some initialization for the tests
    }
}
```

Note

It is important that a [SetUp] method be marked public, return void, and not take in any parameters.

[TearDown]

A method in a [TestFixture] marked with the [TearDown] attribute will be executed immediately after each test is run.

The following code snippet shows how to use this attribute:

```
[TestFixture]
public class SimpleClassTests
{
    [TearDown]
    public void TearDown()
    {
        // Do some cleanup for the tests
    }
}
```

Note

It is important that a [TearDown] method be marked public, return void, and not take in any parameters.

[Ignore]

There may be times when you want to temporarily disable a test or test fixture from being run, and without commenting out the code for it so that you are still reminded of the exemption within NUnit. Any method or class marked with either the [Test] or [TestFixture] attribute can be marked with the [Ignore] attribute.

This attribute causes the test or test fixture to be exempt from testing. This attribute must accept a string parameter describing why the test or test fixture is ignored.

The following code snippet shows how to use this attribute:

```
[TestFixture]
public class SimpleClassTests
{
    [Test]
    [Ignore("Broken functionality at the moment, so testing is pointless")]
    public void TestSomething()
    {
    }
}
```

[ExpectedException]

There may be situations where it is expected that an exception should be thrown, and this attribute exists to avoid the need for an ugly try-catch block. When a test is marked with the [ExpectedException] attribute and the expected exception that is specified in this attribute is thrown, the test is still successful. The only way a thrown exception will cause this test to fail is if the exception is not the same type specified using this attribute. Also keep in mind that multiple [ExpectedException] attributes can be specified if more than one expected exception should be ignored.

The following code snippet shows how to use this attribute:

```
[TestFixture]
public class SimpleClassTests
{
    [Test]
    [ExpectedException(typeof(InterfaceDesignerException))]
    public void TestSomething()
    {
    }
}
```

Caution

You must be very specific when stating the expected exception since NUnit is not aware of exception inheritance. If the exception thrown is derived from InterfaceDesignerException, the test would fail. The expected exception stated must be identical to the exception that will be thrown.

[Explicit]

If a test or a test fixture is marked with the [Explicit] attribute, the only way it will run is when it has been explicitly selected in the GUI to run, or passed to the command line version.

The following code snippet shows how to use this attribute:

```
[TestFixture]
public class SimpleClassTests
{
    [Test, Explicit]
    public void ExplicitTest()
    {
    }
}

[TestFixture, Explicit]
public class ExplicitTests
{
}
```

Note

If NUnit encounters an explicit test, it will treat the test as if it were marked with the [Ignore] attribute.

[Category]

There may be times when you want to categorize or group related tests, especially when working with a project of reasonable size. The [Category] attribute can be used to specify a category name for a test or test fixture to group it with other tests or test fixtures sporting the same category name.

When a specific category is selected to run, only tests or test fixtures belonging to the selected category are run.

The following code snippet shows how to use this attribute:

```
[TestFixture]
public class SimpleClassTests
{
    [Test, Category("ProcessorIntensive")]
    public void TestLongRunningProcess()
    {
    }
}
```

Note

When a specific category is selected to run, only tests or test fixtures belonging to the selected category are run.

Expected Outcome Assertion

The Assert class is used within test methods to verify known values and conditions. For example, Assert.AreEqual() can be used after running a particular test to confirm that a property has a specific value.

Following are the static member methods for the Assert class and an overview of what each one does:

Assert.AreEqual()

This comparison method tests for equality, and is perhaps the best assertion to use because both the expected and actual values are reported. Also, the overloaded signatures allow for equality comparison between equal values of varying numeric types. This allows for assertions like the following to succeed:

```
Assert.AreEqual(7, 7.0);
```

The following are all the method signatures available for this method:

```
Assert.AreEqual(int expected, int actual);
Assert.AreEqual(int expected, int actual, string message);
Assert.AreEqual(int expected, int actual, string message, object[] parameters);
Assert.AreEqual(decimal expected, decimal actual);
Assert.AreEqual(decimal expected, decimal actual, string message);
Assert.AreEqual(decimal expected, decimal actual, string message, object[] parameters);
Assert.AreEqual(float expected, float actual, float tolerance);
Assert.AreEqual(float expected, float actual, float tolerance, string message);
Assert.AreEqual(float expected, float actual, float tolerance, string message,
        object[] parameters);
Assert.AreEqual(double expected, double actual, double tolerance);
Assert.AreEqual(double expected, double actual, double tolerance, string message);
Assert.AreEqual(double expected, double actual, double tolerance, string message,
        object[] parameters);
Assert.AreEqual(object expected, object actual);
Assert.AreEqual(object expected, object actual, string message);
Assert.AreEqual(object expected, object actual, string message, object[] parameters);
Assert.AreSame(object expected, object actual);
Assert.AreSame(object expected, object actual, string message);
Assert.AreSame(object expected, object actual, string message, object[] parameters);
```

The following code snippet shows how to use this comparison method:

```
[TestFixture]
public class SimpleClassTests
{
    [Test]
    public void TestSomething()
    {
        string testData = "Hello World";
        Assert.AreEqual("Hello World", testData", "The strings do not match!");
    }
}
```

Assert.AreSame()

This comparison method tests that same objects are referenced by both arguments.

The following are all the method signatures available for this method:

```
Assert.AreSame(object expected, object actual);
Assert.AreSame(object expected, object actual, string message);
Assert.AreSame(object expected, object actual, string message, object[] parameters);
```

The following code snippet shows how to use this comparison method:

```
[TestFixture]
public class SimpleClassTests
{
    [Test]
    public void TestSomething()
    {
        object object1 = this;
        object object2 = this;
        Assert.AreSame(object1, object2, "The objects do not match!");
    }
}
```

Assert.IsTrue()

This condition method tests that the condition parameter evaluates to true.

The following are all the method signatures available for this method:

```
Assert.IsTrue(bool condition);
Assert.IsTrue(bool condition, string message);
Assert.IsTrue(bool condition, string message, object[] parameters);
```

The following code snippet shows how to use this comparison method:

```
[TestFixture]
public class SimpleClassTests
{
    [Test]
    public void TestSomething()
    {
        bool testData = true;
        Assert.IsTrue(testData, "testData is false!");
    }
}
```

Assert.IsFalse()

This condition method tests that the condition parameter evaluates to `false`.

The following are all the method signatures available for this method:

```
Assert.IsFalse(bool condition);
Assert.IsFalse(bool condition, string message);
Assert.IsFalse(bool condition, string message, object[] parameters);
```

The following code snippet shows how to use this comparison method:

```
[TestFixture]
public class SimpleClassTests
{
    [Test]
    public void TestSomething()
    {
        bool testData = false;
        Assert.IsFalse(testData, "testData is true!");
    }
}
```

Assert.IsNull()

This condition method tests that the condition parameter evaluates to `null`.

The following are all the method signatures available for this method:

```
Assert.IsNull(object anObject);
Assert.IsNull(object anObject, string message);
Assert.IsNull(object anObject, string message, object[] parameters);
```

The following code snippet shows how to use this comparison method:

```
[TestFixture]
public class SimpleClassTests
{
    [Test]
    public void TestSomething()
    {
        object anObject = null;
        Assert.IsNull(anObject, "anObject is not null!");
    }
}
```

Assert.IsNotNull()

This condition method tests that the condition parameter does not evaluate to null.

The following are all the method signatures available for this method:

```
Assert.IsNotNull(object anObject);
Assert.IsNotNull(object anObject, string message);
Assert.IsNotNull(object anObject, string message, object[] parameters);
```

The following code snippet shows how to use this comparison method:

```
[TestFixture]
public class SimpleClassTests
{
    [Test]
    public void TestSomething()
    {
        object anObject = null;
        Assert.IsNotNull(anObject, "anObject is null!");
    }
}
```

Assert.Fail()

This utility method allows you to generate test failure exceptions, often used when performing project-specific assertions.

The following are all the method signatures available for this method:

```
Assert.Fail()
Assert.Fail(string message)
Assert.Fail(string message, object[] parameters)
```

The following code snippet shows how to use this utility method:

```
[TestFixture]
public class SimpleClassTests
{
    [Test]
    public void TestSomething()
    {
        Assert.Fail("I was explicitly thrown!");
    }
}
```

Assert.Ignore()

This utility methods allows you to ignore a particular test during runtime, but should be used sparingly. A better approach is to use the [Category] attribute and run the test groups applicable at the time.

The following are all the method signatures available for this method:

```
Assert.Ignore()
Assert.Ignore(string message)
Assert.Ignore(string message, object[] parameters)
```

The following code snippet shows how to use this utility method:

```
[TestFixture]
public class SimpleClassTests
{
    [Test]
    public void TestSomething()
    {
        Assert.Fail("I was explicitly thrown!");
    }
}
```

A Simple Example

In order to perform testing, we obviously need a class to test against. Defined below is a simple class we can use for unit testing. As described by its name, the class is extremely simplistic, so I will just show the code for it and move right on to the creation of a test fixture.

```
using System;

namespace SimpleLibrary
```

```
{
    public class SimpleClass
    {
        private string _simpleProperty = "";

        public string SimpleProperty
        {
            get { return _simpleProperty; }
            set { _simpleProperty = value; }
        }

        public void BrokenMethod()
        {
            throw new ApplicationException("I am a faulty method! Fix me!");
        }

        public void GoodMethod()
        {
            throw new NotImplementedException();
        }

        public static int AddTwoNumbers(int left, int right)
        {
            return left - right;
        }
    }
}
```

Now that we have a simple class to test against, we need to create the test fixture that NUnit will use to coordinate the tests:

```
using System;
using NUnit.Framework;

namespace SimpleLibrary.UnitTesting
{
    [TestFixture]
    public class ExampleFixture
    {
        private SimpleLibrary.SimpleClass _simpleClass = null;

        [SetUp]
        public void SetUp()
```

```
    {
        _simpleClass = new SimpleLibrary.SimpleClass();
    }

    [TearDown]
    public void TearDown()
    {
        _simpleClass = null;
    }

    [Test]
    public void AddTwoNumbersTest()
    {
        int result = SimpleLibrary.SimpleClass.AddTwoNumbers(5, 7);
        Assert.AreEqual(12, result);
    }

[Test]
public void SimplePropertyTest()
{
    Assert.AreEqual("", _simpleClass.SimpleProperty);
    _simpleClass.SimpleProperty = "This is a test";
    Assert.AreEqual("This is a test", _simpleClass.SimpleProperty);
}

[Test]
public void ExplicitFailureTest()
{
    _simpleClass.BrokenMethod();
}

[Test, Ignore("This is a deprecated test")]
public void DeprecatedTest()
{
    _simpleClass.GoodMethod();
}

[Test, ExpectedException(typeof(NotImplementedException))]
public void GoodMethodTest()
{
    _simpleClass.GoodMethod();
}
    }
}
```

Notice that the above class has been marked with the [TestFixture] attribute. This is required so that NUnit can identify the test fixtures to run by searching all classes within the assembly that have this attribute type.

Running Tests

After the test fixture is created, it is time to begin testing. As mentioned previously, there are two interfaces for NUnit: console and GUI. This chapter will cover the GUI version. For now, we will explicitly launch the NUnit application, but later on, an alternative method is discussed that shows how to attach NUnit to the start event in Visual Studio. There is also an open source project called TestDriven.NET that offers enhanced .NET unit testing functionality, including integration support between Visual Studio and various unit testing frameworks like NUnit; definitely worth looking at.

Start by launching the NUnit GUI version, and you should be presented with a dialog similar to the one shown in Figure 10.3.

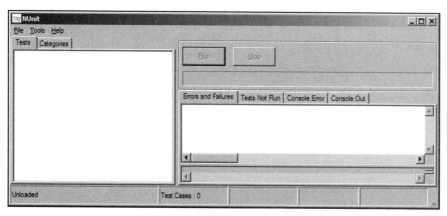

Figure 10.3 Screenshot of main NUnit interface.

You will be prompted to save the NUnit project somewhere, and it is common to place the .nunit file in the same directory as the project file for the assembly being tested. After the project file is saved, you need to add the assemblies that contain your test fixtures. You can do this by selecting Project>Add Assembly from the main menu.

Figure 10.4 shows the NUnit interface after the example test fixture for this chapter has been added to it.

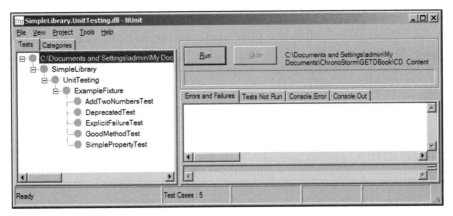

Figure 10.4 Screenshot of NUnit after adding a target assembly.

NUnit displays all the test assemblies and fixtures in a hierarchical fashion, and it executes tests in a similar way. Clicking the Run button will begin the tests, and all the tests below the currently selected node in the assembly tree will execute. This allows you to target all, some, or specific tests to run. You can group tests into categories as well.

Figure 10.5 shows the NUnit interface after the tests have been executed. You will notice that the output from errors and ignored tests appear in the tab group on the right, whereas successful tests are not as verbose. Successful tests appear green in the assembly tree, errors appear red, and ignored tests appear yellow.

Your assemblies may require a configuration file to function correctly, in which case it is important to note that NUnit creates a new AppDomain for each test assembly, so the configuration file must reside in the same directory as the assembly.

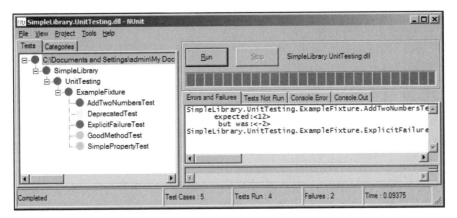

Figure 10.5 Screenshot of NUnit after running the tests.

For example, `SimpleLibrary.UnitTests.dll` and `SimpleLibrary.UnitTests.dll.config` should be paired together in the same folder.

Debugging with Visual Studio

There may be times when you wish to debug the code while performing unit tests, and sometimes you may even want to debug the unit tests themselves. NUnit and Visual Studio both execute code in different `AppDomains`, so any breakpoints you set in the Visual Studio IDE will not fire when NUnit is run. There is a trick you can use to accomplish this, though. Visual Studio offers the ability to attach external programs to its debugging features when assemblies are consumed.

Open the property pages for the assembly you wish to consume externally, and navigate to the Debug page in the project properties. You should be presented with a dialog similar to the one shown in Figure 10.6.

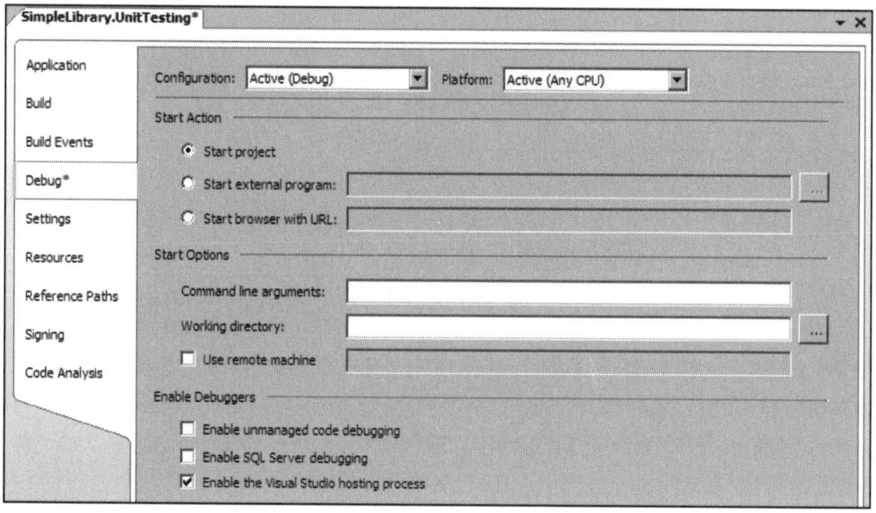

Figure 10.6 Debugging property page.

Under Start Action, select the Start external program option, and set the field value to the file system path of either the GUI or command line executable of NUnit.

You must specify the assemblies to load in the command line arguments; otherwise, NUnit will launch with the last loaded project if there is one. Each assembly path should be separated by a space, and be sure to use double quotes around the path if spaces exist in it. You can alter the command line arguments to automatically start running your tests after NUnit opens. If you prefix the arguments line with

/run and a space before the list of assemblies, NUnit will launch and immediately begin processing. Figure 10.7 shows the property page after it has been configured to be consumed externally.

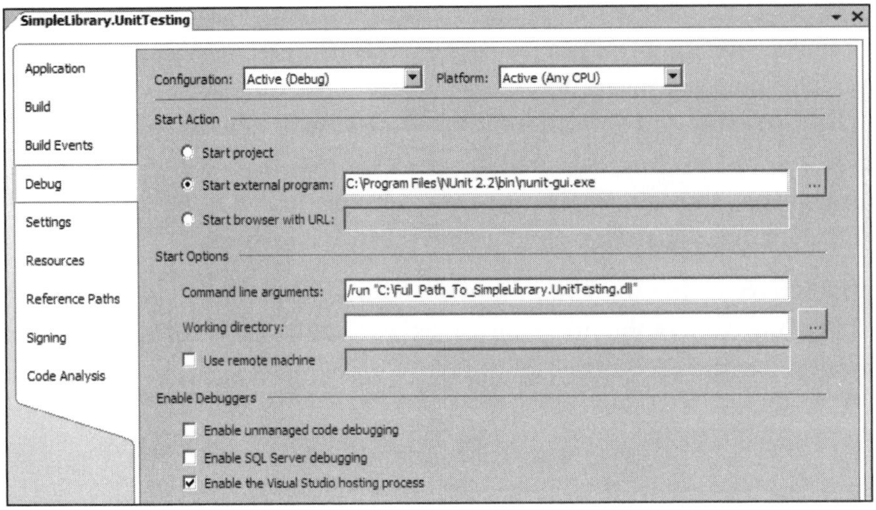

Figure 10.7 Debugging property page configured.

At this point, you can have the test's assembly selected as the startup project and run everything. If configured correctly, NUnit will fire up with your assembly loaded.

Conclusion

Unit testing is a worthwhile habit to pick up that is extremely beneficial on both a professional and personal software development level. This chapter covered a fair amount of unit testing and performing unit tests on the .NET platform, but the concept of unit testing is much more complex than what I have described here. There are many are topics like regression tests, integration tests, mock objects, and data-driven testing, which are beyond the scope of the information presented here.

Links to additional information and resources are listed below.

- http://www.testdriven.net
- http://www.nunit.org
- http://www.csunit.org (NUnit alternative)
- http://www.mockobjects.com

- http://www.sourceforge.net/projects/dotnetmock/
- http://www.xprogramming.com

In addition to NUnit, there are a couple of other unit testing frameworks available for C#.NET, such as csUnit. Some versions of Visual Studio 2005 also have a unit testing framework built in, but this chapter was meant to focus on a solution that does not require a particular IDE version to work.

Use whichever framework you feel comfortable with; I chose NUnit because it works great for all my projects and is widely accepted throughout the .NET development community. I have used csUnit for other projects when its use is a requirement for the project, and transitioning between csUnit and NUnit is extremely easy. The attribute names are all the same, with the exception of varying support for FixtureSetUp and FixtureTearDown, and a comparable Assert class exists in both frameworks. There are a couple of naming differences between the Assert classes in both frameworks, but they are minor. The biggest difference is that you will need to reference the correct framework for csUnit and remove the reference to the NUnit framework.

Note

You can download NUnit at http://www.nunit.org.

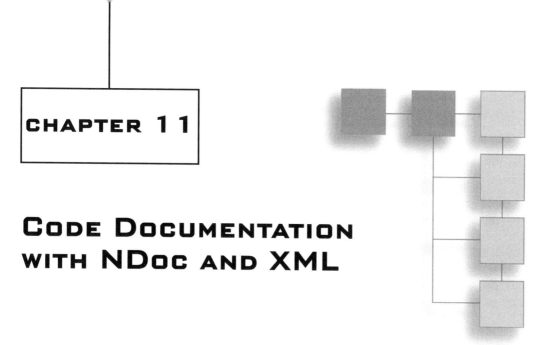

CHAPTER 11

CODE DOCUMENTATION WITH NDOC AND XML

Documentation is like sex; when it's good, it's very, very good, and when it's bad, it's better than nothing.

Dick Brandon

An important deliverable for most projects, or as simply a good thing to do, is the creation and updating of source code documentation. Properly documented source code can improve the overall maintainability of your project, and shorten the amount of time needed for a new developer, or an existing developer for that matter, to familiarize herself with the source code. The purpose of source code documentation is so a developer can understand a particular component without actually looking at the source code.

Thankfully, Visual Studio .NET has introduced a wonderful build tool for generating source code documentation, and it is built right into the IDE. A properly configured project can be set up to export documentation expressed as XML for the source code each time the build process is run. This exported documentation can be plugged into an excellent open source utility called NDoc, which can take a .NET assembly and the exported XML and build documentation in a variety of formats. NDoc supports pluggable exporters, including the MSDN-style HTML Help (.chm), the Visual Studio .NET format (HTML Help 2), and the MSDN online-style web pages. This tool is very popular within the .NET community and is the most commonly used documentation generator for .NET.

Note
_____

NDoc can be downloaded at http://ndoc.sourceforge.net/.
_____

Additionally, when source code is commented properly in the standard XML format, Visual Studio registers the documentation and makes it available to IntelliSense. Another great feature is that when you reference a .NET assembly which has commenting enabled, the generated XML comment file is copied locally, along with the reference assembly, to make IntelliSense information available across multiple projects.

This chapter shows how to properly configure a .NET project for code commenting, and how to generate MSDN-style documentation using the XML documentation file and standardized commenting techniques.

Configuring the Project

As discussed earlier, the first step to generating documentation for your source code is configuring your project to export an XML documentation file. This file will be used later by NDoc to produce our documentation files.

Start by bringing up the project properties window; the easiest way to do this is by right-clicking on your project in the solution explorer and selecting Properties. After you navigate to the Build tab, you should see the dialog shown in Figure 11.1.

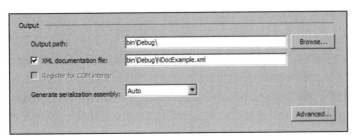

Figure 11.1 Build configuration properties for a project.

You will notice that there is a property called XML documentation file under the Output property group; that is the path that must be set for the documentation file to be generated at. This path is relative to the project directory, and standards suggest that the file name match the name of the assembly. For example, *NDocExample.dll* should have an XML documentation file named *NDocExample.xml*.

Once a valid file path is specified, when the project is compiled, an XML file will be generated that contains all the XML comment tags that were embedded in the source code.

You may have some projects that will be compiled from the command line, and the way to generate the XML documentation file in such a situation is by using the /doc flag.

```
csc /doc:NDocExample.xml NDocExample.cs
```

In either situation, command line or through an IDE, the /doc compiler switch will be ignored in a compilation that uses the /incremental build switch. Therefore, you should use the /incremental- switch to disable the incremental build and ensure that your XML documentation file remains up-to-date.

After your project is configured to output an XML documentation file, any comments that are suggested to be included will not prevent compilation, assuming you do not have warnings set to errors, but will instead show up as a warning in the task list. You can simply double-click on the warning in the task list to jump to the location where a comment should be added, much as any other error or warning can be navigated to.

Figure 11.2 shows the source code location where the comment should be inserted.

```
public MainForm()
{
            Missing XML comment for publicly visible type or member 'NDocExample.MainForm.MainForm()'
    // Required for Windows Form Designer support
    InitializeComponent();
}
```

Figure 11.2 Example of a source code location that should be commented.

Figure 11.3 shows a comment missing from the constructor of MainForm, and suggests that it be added for standards compliance.

An extremely useful feature that improves documentation productivity is a macro that inserts basic commenting tags for a particular method or class. Simply place the text insertion pointer on the line above the method or class header in question and press the / (forward slash) key three times. A summary tag block is inserted, along with all the parameter tags for the method, if applicable. Additional tags can be added to the basic blocks that were inserted, but they have to be added manually.

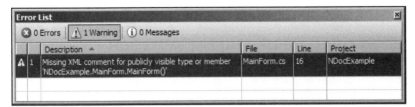

Figure 11.3 Missing comment warning in the Visual Studio C#.NET task list.

Supported XML Markup

There are quite a few supported XML tags and tag attributes that can be used for different purposes when documenting your code; those tags are described in Table 11.1, along with instructions for when they should be used.

Keep in mind that in order to generate correct XML, the compiler must be given correct documentation comments. Additionally, the compiler will generate a warning and embed an error message in the documentation file if it is given XML that is not well-formed. By well-formed XML, I mean XML that follows the rules listed in the W3C Recommendation for XML 1.0.

A list of the standard tags available for inline documentation are presented in Table 11.1.

The commenting structure is fairly loose and flexible, but you will notice that any suggested comments to include will appear as warnings in your task list now that your project is configured for commenting.

Keep in mind that since the compiler recognizes /// as a comment line when parsing source code for embedded XML, the following documentation will be rejected by the compiler:

```
/// <summary>
///
// </summary>
Public void FooBar() {}
```

Obviously, all documentation comments must be associated with a valid code construct, otherwise they will be ignored. Valid code constructs are a class, struct, enum, property, field, method, delegate, indexer, or event.

Note

Namespaces are not considered code constructs because they are not limited to any one assembly, so they cannot be considered a member of any one particular assembly.

Table 11.1 List of Standard Tags

Tag	Description
<c>	This tag is used to specify that a certain group of words should be formatted as text.
<code>	This tag is used to specify multiple lines of code in a block of text. In order to embed XML source, you must specify the tag attribute escaped="true" on the code tag so that the documentation compiler does not strip out the XML sample.
<example>	This tag is used to specify how to use a particular method or type. Typically, the code tag is also used with this tag to give implementation details.
<exception>	This tag is used to specify the exceptions that a particular class can throw.
<include>	This tag is used to refer to comments in an external file, avoiding the need to embed other comments in your source code.
<list>	This tag is used to define a heading row of either a table or a definition list. Each item in the list is specified with an <item> tag, and a list or table can have as many <item> tags as desired.
<item>	This tag is used to define an item in a table or a definition list.
<newpara>	This tag is used inside text to allow for formatted structuring.
<param>	This tag is used to specify a parameter for a method declaration.
<paramref>	This tag allows you to specify that a particular word is a parameter so that it can be formatted distinctly.
<permission>	This tag allows you to specify the security access to a member.
<remarks>	This tag allows you to specify overview information about a class or type. You can also use the summary tag to describe a member for a type.
<returns>	This tag is used to describe the return value for a method declaration.
<see>	This tag allows you to specify a link to appear within text. You can also use the <seealso> tag to place text that you want to appear in the See Also section.
<seealso>	This tag allows you to place text that you want to appear in the See Also section. You can use the <see> tag to specify a link to appear within text.
<summary>	This tag should be used to describe a member for a type. You can also use the <remarks> tag to list information about the type itself.
<value>	This tag is used to describe a property and is suggested for use on all properties. You will notice that the auto commenting macro for properties only inserts the summary tag, so you will have to add this tag manually to all your properties.

Some documentation tags are further defined through the use of XML attributes. The tag attributes used by inline documentation are presented in Table 11.2.

Table 11.2 List of Standard Tag Attributes

Tag Attribute	Description
<cref>	This attribute can be attached to any tag to provide a reference to a code element. It is important to note that the compiler will verify that this code element exists, and will issue a warning if the verification fails. The compiler also respects any *using* statements when looking for a type described in this attribute.
<name>	This attribute describes the name of a parameter in a <param> or <paramref> tag.

Commenting Example

In order to illustrate the entire process of documenting source code, we will define and discuss a simple example in a linear fashion.

We will start by defining a simple method called SaveApplicationSettings that will accept a string parameter and not return anything. This method won't do anything in terms of functionality, but it will show how to properly document a code construct.

```
/// <summary>
/// Saves the application settings to a text file named by
/// the fileName property, and saved in isolated storage.
/// </summary>
/// <param name="fileName">
/// The name of the file to store the application settings in.
/// </param>
/// <example>
/// The following code shows how to properly call this method.
/// <code>
/// SaveApplicationSettings("MyApplication.xml");
/// </code>
/// </example>
/// <permission cref="System.Security.PermissionSet">
/// This method can be accessed by everyone
/// </permission>
public void SaveApplicationSettings(string fileName)
{
    MessageBox.Show("This is where the settings would actually be saved");
}
```

As you can see in the above code example, we have documented the source code for the `SaveApplicationSettings` method, and now that we have done so, it is available for IntelliSense. Now whenever you start typing out the name of the method, IntelliSense will fire up and give you information about the method and the parameters it expects. This is illustrated in Figure 11.4.

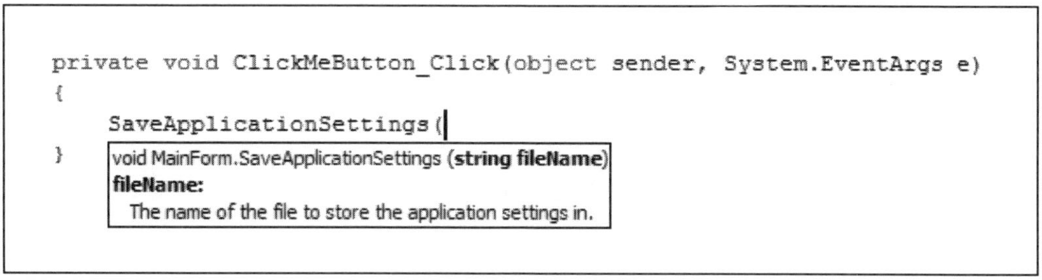

```
private void ClickMeButton_Click(object sender, System.EventArgs e)
{
    SaveApplicationSettings(|
}   void MainForm.SaveApplicationSettings (string fileName)
    fileName:
        The name of the file to store the application settings in.
```

Figure 11.4 Example of on-the-fly IntelliSense documentation.

Aside from on-the-fly IntelliSense, you can also mouse over a documented method or type and see the documentation overview for it. This is depicted in Figure 11.5.

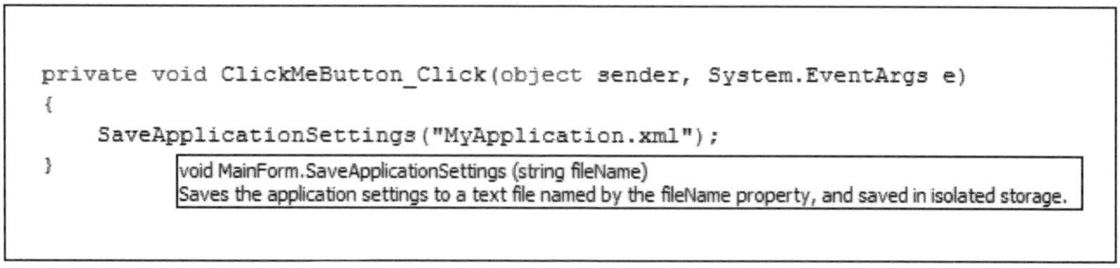

```
private void ClickMeButton_Click(object sender, System.EventArgs e)
{
    SaveApplicationSettings("MyApplication.xml");
}       void MainForm.SaveApplicationSettings (string fileName)
        Saves the application settings to a text file named by the fileName property, and saved in isolated storage.
```

Figure 11.5 Example of IntelliSense type overview.

Generating the Documentation

IntelliSense information is a handy tool, but using XML documentation for IntelliSense alone is a waste compared to the wonderful documentation that can be generated from the XML documentation file. There are two main ways to generate your documentation, but the NDoc approach will be the evangelized method in this chapter.

The first method, and the one this chapter will not cover, is the built-in documentation tool in Visual Studio .NET. Under the Tools menu is an option titled Build Comment Web Pages..., which will produce help files in the Visual Studio .NET format. While this method works and is convenient because of the IDE integration, NDoc produces much better documentation in a variety of formats.

For starters, launch the NDoc application and select the New from Visual Studio Solution option from the toolbar at the top of the window, as shown in Figure 11.6. At this stage, we must let NDoc know which assemblies have commenting enabled and should have corresponding documentation generated for them. This step could be done manually, although referencing the assemblies automatically from your project solution is much easier and faster.

Figure 11.6
Toolbar option to import assemblies.

Selecting the toolbar option should bring up a dialog that asks you to select the solution configuration of the project to use. I typically use debug mode, but it generally doesn't matter when you stick with default solution configurations. This dialog should look like the one shown in Figure 11.7.

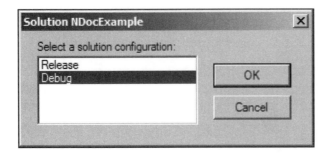

Figure 11.7
Dialog asking to select the solution configuration to use.

After the appropriate solution configuration to use has been selected, the NDoc window should populate with all the referenced assemblies for the solution. There are a number of formatting and configuration settings that can be modified for an NDoc project, but for the most part, we will use the default values for the purpose of this discussion. You should end up with a dialog similar to the one shown in Figure 11.8. The final step (yes, it is that easy) is to build the documentation by clicking on the Build Documentation button in the toolbar, or by using the Ctrl+Shift+B shortcut.

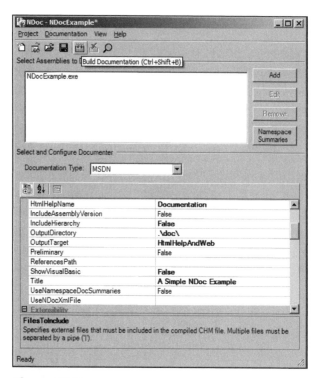

Figure 11.8
Main NDoc interface showing the loaded assemblies and project properties.

Once the Build Documentation button is clicked, the XML documentation file will be processed and an MSDN-style .chm file will be generated at the location specified by the `OutputDirectory` property in the NDoc solution. Keep in mind that you can switch the documenter plugin if you do not want MSDN-style documentation and would prefer an alternative format. The MSDN-style .chm documentation will look something like Figure 11.9.

Conclusion

Source code documentation has always been regarded as a hassle to create, yet it is important to promote maintainability. In this chapter, we saw another situation where the .NET platform improved workflow productivity, specifically in terms of generating source code documentation. Developers are generally conscientious about source code commenting, and luckily most organizations have coding standards that enforce a certain level of consistency, but commenting your source code and producing aesthetic documentation are two different challenges in themselves.

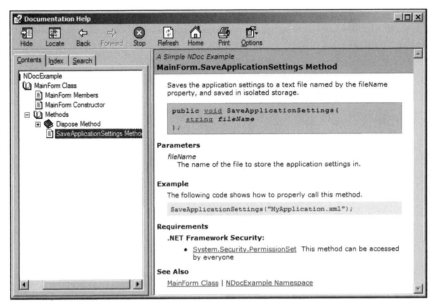

Figure 11.9 Example MSDN-style .chm documentation created with Ndoc.

This chapter described a great way to transition from commented source code to deployment-quality documentation using a core architecture primitive in the .NET platform.

Note

On the Companion Web site is the code from the simple example discussed throughout this chapter, along with the NDoc project and the generated documentation. The example is extremely simplistic but can serve as a reference point or general overview on how to properly set up a project for code documentation with NDoc.

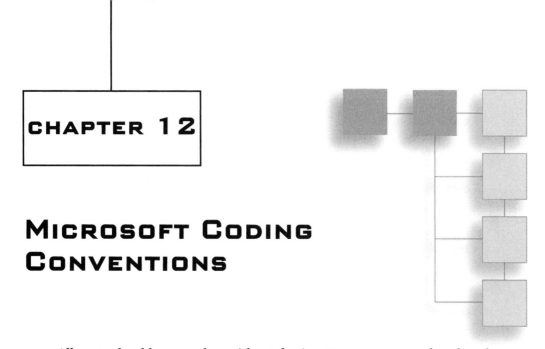

CHAPTER 12

MICROSOFT CODING CONVENTIONS

All parts should go together without forcing. You must remember that the parts you are reassembling were disassembled by you. Therefore, if you can't get them together again, there must be a reason. By all means, do not use a hammer.

1925 IBM Maintenance Manual

With all the fuss about how important it is to create maintainable code, a huge issue that sparks numerous techno-religious debates is the idea that code should follow a specific naming convention. The main problem is summed up by the question: What naming convention should be used? There are a number of naming conventions documented for developers, but typically the answer is left to personal preference. However, Microsoft is pushing the idea of "best practice" for a number of areas of .NET development, including standardized coding conventions. A common problem with legacy Win32 API code is the variation among naming conventions. It is not uncommon to find two components in the API that use completely different conventions. However, Microsoft has enforced standards for the .NET Class Framework that define how code should be named and formatted. While you do not have to follow the proposed standard, it is recommended that you do so for consistency and to make your code easier to read by other .NET developers.

This chapter summarizes the standard coding conventions set forth by Microsoft that should be employed in your code. Keep in mind that you should still read the Microsoft *Design Guidelines for Class Library Developers*, but this chapter should be enough of a generalization to get you started.

Styles of Capitalization

The .NET class framework uses three types of capitalization styles, presented in Table 12.1.

Table 12.1 .NET Class Framework Capitalization Styles

Case Type	Description
Pascal Case	Make the first letter uppercase as well as the first letter of each subsequent word. All other letters remain lowercase. An example would be *XmlSerializer*.
Camel Case	Identical to Pascal case, except the first letter is not uppercase. An example would be *remotingEndpoint*.
Uppercase	Make all letters capitalized when an identifier consists of less than three letters. An example would be *System.IO*.

There are different situations when a certain capitalization style is appropriate. The situations suitable for certain capitalization styles are presented in Table 12.2.

Table 12.2 Capitalization Style Situations

Situation	Appropriate Style	Notes
Class	Pascal Case	
Enum Type	Pascal Case	
Enum Value	Pascal Case	
Event	Pascal Case	
Exception Class	Pascal Case	Suffixed with Exception
Read-Only Static Field	Pascal Case	
Interface	Pascal Case	Prefixed with I
Method	Pascal Case	
Namespace	Pascal Case	
Parameter	Camel Case	
Property	Pascal Case	
Protected Instance Field	Camel Case	Better to use a property
Public Instance Field	Pascal Case	Better to use a property

Naming Classes

When naming classes, the standard is to use Pascal case. Additionally, classes should be named using a noun or a noun phrase. Finally, never use an underscore in a class name either.

One traditional style common among many developers is to use prefixes such as cFileStream or CFileStream. Never use prefixes anywhere with the exception of interfaces. The proper naming would be FileStream in this example.

Abbreviations should be used only when absolutely necessary. They cause confusion when reading code, and break from the standards used in the class framework.

Derived classes should be named in a compounded fashion where the second half of the name is the base class name. An example would be the derived class SystemException, which inherits from the base class Exception. This guideline is to be used at your discretion, as derived class names should only be compounded when it makes sense to do so.

Example:

```
public class SimpleException : Exception
{
}
```

Naming Interfaces

When naming interfaces, the standard is to use Pascal case. Additionally, interfaces should be named using a noun or noun phrase, or an adjective that describes its behavior. Finally, never use an underscore in a class name either.

Interfaces should always be prefixed with I, as in IBaseController. This is the only situation where an identifier should be prefixed in the .NET class framework.

When a class implements an interface, the naming should only differ by the prefix I on the interface name.

Abbreviations should be used only when absolutely necessary. They cause confusion when reading code, and break from the standards used in the .NET Class Framework.

Example:

```
public interface IBaseController
{
}

public class BaseController : IBaseController
{
}
```

Naming Namespaces

When naming namespaces, there are some common rules that should be followed for consistency. Use Pascal case, and separate all logical components with periods.

The typical formatting is as follows:

```
CompanyName.TechnologyName.Feature[.Design]
```

Design is an optional namespace path that can be used when you have design time code that you are separating from the feature code itself.

Prefixing the namespace with the company name helps to avoid type name conflicts with another company that's possibly offering the same technology and features.

Additionally, types in a namespace should have dependencies to types in the containing namespace. For example, `Wihlidal.Networking.DeadReckoning` would have dependencies to types in `Wihlidal.Networking`.

Never use the same name for both a class and a namespace. For example, do not have the namespace `Wihlidal.Utilities.Log` and have a contained class called `Log`.

Lastly, just because a particular assembly uses the namespace `Wihlidal.Networking.DeadReckoning`, it does not have to contain any code in the `Wihlidal.Networking` namespace. It is perfectly acceptable and common to have multiple assemblies associated with a particular namespace.

Example:

```
Wihlidal.Networking.DeadReckoning
```

or

```
Wihlidal.Controls.InterfaceBuilder
Wihlidal.Controls.InterfaceBuilder.Design
```

Naming Attributes

There are not a lot of guidelines for attribute naming, but be sure to use Pascal case. The only rule is to suffix the attribute type name with `Attribute`.

Example:

```
InterfaceControlAttribute
```

Naming Enumerations

When naming enumerations, the standard is to use Pascal case for both type and value identifiers.

Abbreviations should be used only when absolutely necessary. They cause confusion when reading code, and they break from the standards used in the class framework.

Never suffix an enumeration with `Enum`. The identifier name should also be singular unless it is a bit field, in which case the name would be plural. Additionally, bit fields should always be marked with `[FlagsAttribute]`.

Example:

```
public enum InterfaceColor
{
    Red,
    Black,
    Yellow
}

[FlagsAttribute]
public enum InterfaceColors : short
{
    Red = 0,
    Black = 1,
    Yellow = 2
}
```

Naming Static Fields

When naming static fields, the standard is to use Pascal case. Additionally, static fields should be named using a noun, noun phrase, or abbreviations of nouns. Lastly, never use Hungarian notation or any other sort of prefixes or suffixes.

It is "best practice" to use a static property instead of a static field whenever possible.

Example:

```
private static int MyStaticField;
```

Naming Parameters

When naming parameters, the standard is to use Camel case. Additionally, parameter names should be descriptive enough that their use should be evident by their name alone.

Use a parameter name that describes its meaning rather than its type. Use type-based names only when necessary.

Never use reserved parameters. These parameters are reserved for data that can be added in with a later version of a particular component, and storing your data in a reserved property can lead to issues with invalid data or software instability.

Never name parameters using Hungarian notation.

Example:

```
Type GetType(string typeName)
string Format(string format, object[] args)
```

Naming Methods

When naming methods, the standard is to use Pascal case. Additionally, method names should be named using verbs or verb phrases. Method names should be very descriptive, and the behavior of the method should be easily determined from the name alone.

Example:

```
GetInterfaceControl()
ExecuteBatchProcess()
InsertRecord()
```

Naming Properties

When naming properties, the standard is to use Pascal case. Additionally, properties should be named using a noun or noun phrase, and never use Hungarian notation.

It is a good idea to name your properties the same name as the underlying types when applicable.

Example:

```
private Color backColor;
public Color BackColor
{
    get { return backColor; }
    set { backColor = value; }
}
```

Naming Events

When naming events, the standard is to use Pascal case. Additionally, events should never have a prefix or a suffix, and never use Hungarian notation.

Events should be named with a verb such as Launched, Clicked, Closing, or Paint. Events in a pre-event context should be named with the -ing form of a verb, and events in a post-event context should be named with the past tense of a verb.

Event handlers should have an EventHandler suffix. Additionally, event argument types should have an EventArgs suffix.

Example:

```
public delegate void InterfaceControlEventHandler(object sender,
                                        InterfaceControlEventArgs e);

public InterfaceControlEventHandler InterfaceControlClicked;

public class InterfaceControlEventArgs : EventArgs
{
    private InterfaceControl _selectedControl = null;

    public InterfaceControl SelectedControl
    {
        get { return _selectedControl; }
    }

    public InterfaceControlEventArgs(InterfaceControl selectedControl)
    {
        _selectedControl = selectedControl;
    }
}
```

Abbreviations

There are guidelines regarding abbreviations. Disregarding these guidelines can lead to issues with interoperability or general confusion about the purpose of a particular identifier.

Identifiers should not have contracted or abbreviated parts. Use `SendReplyMessage` instead of `SendReplyMsg`.

Acronyms should be formatted using either Pascal or Camel case when consisting of more than two letters. Never use acronyms that are not generally accepted or known in the computing world.

Use abbreviations to replace lengthy phrases, such as `Http` instead of `HyperTextTransferProtocol`.

Identifiers and parameters should not be abbreviated. If you must use abbreviations, then you should use Camel case when the abbreviated word consists of three or more letters.

Conclusion

The main focus of this chapter was to present an overview of the standardized coding conventions that Microsoft encourages .NET developers to adopt. This is in no way the full convention, but it is enough of a subset to show how code should be written in C#.NET. For more information, please review the Microsoft *Design Guidelines for Class Library Developers* located on MSDN.

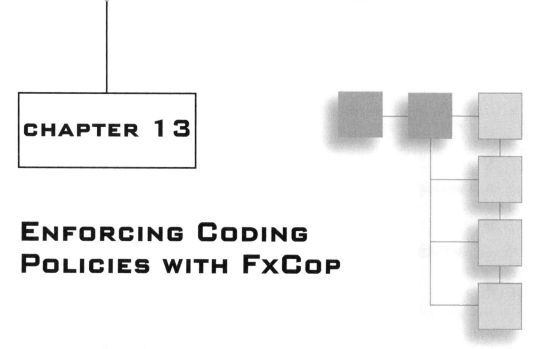

CHAPTER 13

ENFORCING CODING POLICIES WITH FxCOP

The trouble with programmers is that you can never tell what a programmer is doing until it's too late.

Seymour Cray

People write bad code. It is a common reality, and poorly written code can lead to many maintenance and design issues. Microsoft realizes this and has presented a couple of well thought out solutions, such as the *Design Guidelines for Class Library Developers*, which helps promulgate best practices and coding standards to maintain consistency among .NET assemblies. Having a set of guidelines can do wonders if developers follow them in an almost religious fashion. However, this is not always the case, and many times source code deviates from the proposed norm. This prompted Microsoft to create the FxCop utility, which tests .NET code to confirm that it follows the best practices and design guidelines.

The developers of FxCop could have designed the tool to perform conformance analysis at a source code level like most tools of a similar nature, but instead chose to use the powerful features of the .NET platform to make a tool that performed analysis on a much grander scale. Rich and extensible meta-data concepts alongside powerful reflection support, MSIL parsing, and call-graph analysis allow for the inspection of many different areas of your software instead of just analyzing source code. FxCop looks for over 200 different defects and issues in regards to library design, naming conventions, localization, security, and performance. There is also an SDK that allows you to write custom rules to enforce conventions specific to your needs.

On top of Reflection, the latest version of FxCop has exposed another method of analyzing your assemblies using an introspection engine. This engine provides a rich set of analysis functionality and can analyze large applications much more quickly than the regular reflection-based engine. On top of speed, the introspection engine also supports multithreaded application analysis. Lastly, the introspection engine is different from the reflection engine in that it does not lock assemblies when it performs analysis, allowing you to fix and recompile assemblies while FxCop remains open instead of shutting down FxCop to release locked assemblies.

The purpose of this chapter is to introduce you to the wonderful world of enforced coding policies, and the tool that makes it all possible. After reading this chapter, you should be able to analyze your code for convention violations, design custom violation rules, and know how to configure FxCop to suit your development preferences.

Caution

The engine and SDK specification for FxCop have not yet been finalized, so the common pattern is that each release breaks backward compatibility with existing plug-ins, forcing the developer to update the custom rules to reflect API changes. This chapter was written using FxCop 1.32 for Whidbey Beta 2 (.NET 2.0 Beta 2). I still felt that the information presented in this chapter is important, so I decided to keep this chapter in the book and present this little warning about the changing API. Hopefully the next release version of FxCop supports an easy migration path from the 1.32 API.

This is just a warning that you may not be able to compile the examples in this chapter straight out of the book; you may need to update the examples to reflect the latest API specification. With this in mind, let's continue on to discovering what FxCop is, and how you and your code can benefit from its use.

Installing FxCop

Note

The first thing you need to do is install the FxCop tool; you can get the installer at the companion Web site for this book, or from http://www.gotdotnet.com/team/fxcop/.

There are no custom configuration options, so the installation itself is very simple. FxCop can be accessed from either a WinForms applications or the command line using the FxCopCMD application. You can actually integrate FxCop analysis into your build process, which is a great idea because you can fix conformance violations as they occur, instead of letting them build up into a huge list that you have to cull through at a later time. If you want to get as much speed as possible during the build process, you can also stick to running FxCop on a daily basis instead. This is the approach that Microsoft is pushing to its developers. The longer you wait between each running of FxCop, the more possible violations will have been amassed, resulting in more time spent fixing these issues. Making FxCop an integral part of your work schedule ensures increased familiarity with the guidelines and eases the design work. For example, imagine that you create a property which is named in such a way that it does not follow design guidelines. With FxCop integrated with your build process, you would notice this violation immediately the next time your post-build process executes. If instead, you run FxCop on a weekly basis, you would have to go back and modify a week's worth of work in all places where that property was accessed. There are increased productivity benefits when running FxCop analysis as often as possible.

Creating an FxCop Project

The first thing to do is create an FxCop project where you can select the assemblies to target for analysis, and specify the rules to enforce. Launch the FxCop tool and start adding assemblies through the Project>Add Targets menu, or by using the Ctrl+Shift+A hotkey. Once you have selected the assemblies you want to analyze, you should end up with a window similar to Figure 13.1.

The left tree view shows the hierarchy of the loaded assemblies and the components available for analysis. You can uncheck code that you do not want analyzed, though it is recommended that you only do so if absolutely necessary.

The right view pane has a list view that will populate with rule violations once analysis has been completed. The bottom view pane will display detailed information about a rule violation when one has been selected in the violations list view.

Once the target assemblies have been added to the project, you are now at the point where you can configure the rules engine for the project.

Configuring Built-In Rules

Now that the FxCop project has been created and assemblies have been targeted for analysis, it is time to move on to the configuration of the rules engine. Some people stick to the default configuration, but many developers customize the configuration to suit their own preferences where applicable.

The left view pane contains a tab control with a Rules tab. Selecting that tab will present a listing of the available rules that can be enforced upon the targeted assemblies, and each rule can be enabled or disabled using the checkbox to the left of the rule.

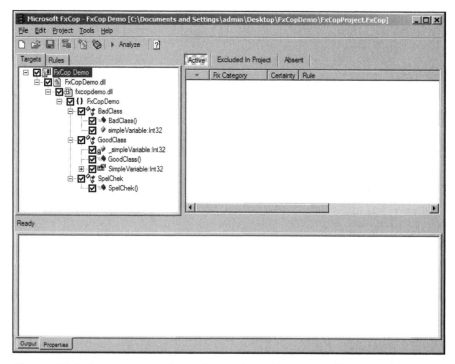

Figure 13.1 Screen capture of an FxCop project with an assembly targeted for analysis.

Some rules may not be applicable or favorable to a developer, which warrants the disabling of the rule. For example, even though the .NET runtime implicitly initializes all managed memory to a default value, many developers feel that all variables should be explicitly initialized even when the initialized value and the default value for that data type are the same. Yes, doing so can be viewed as a redundant step as there is a performance rule that prohibits unnecessary initialization, yet other developers feel that explicit initialization is necessary in the spirit of maintainability. Figure 13.2 shows a screen capture of the rules configuration tab.

Analyzing Your Project

Once your FxCop project has been created and the target assemblies have been specified, it is time to perform analysis. You do so by clicking the Analyze button shown in Figure 13.3.

The most advisable approach for fixing guideline violations is to sort the violations by message level with the errors at the top of the list, and to fix each violation one by one. It should be noted that there are two types of errors: regular and critical.

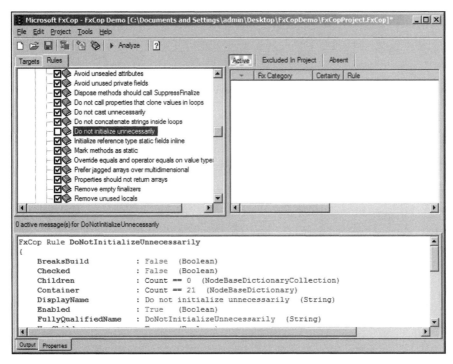

Figure 13.2 Screen capture of the rules configuration tab.

Figure 13.3 Screen capture of the button that starts the analysis.

Both types are fairly subjective in nature, and many rule developers feel that it would have made their lives a lot easier if Microsoft had just simplified the message levels to errors, warnings, and informational messages.

Aside from the message level, you will notice that there are a few other statistics for each violation. The fix category indicates whether or not your code will break if the violation is resolved by itself. Breaking indicates that fixing the violation without modifying the rest of your code will cause compilation errors, such as changing a property name referenced elsewhere. Nonbreaking indicates that fixing the violation without modifying the rest of your code should still result in a successful compilation, such as adding an attribute to a class definition. Figure 13.4 shows the FxCop project window after an analysis has been performed.

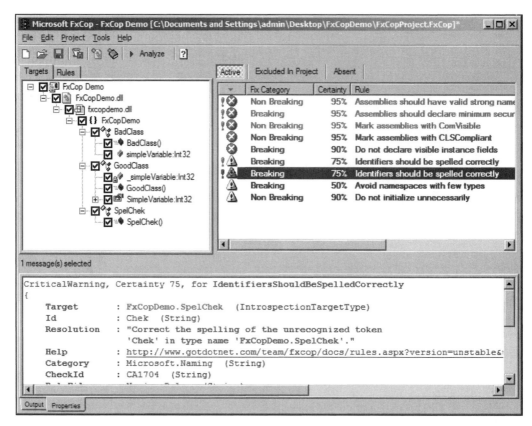

Figure 13.4 Screen capture of the FxCop tool after analysis has been performed.

It may be acceptable to exclude certain rule violations from the analysis, and you can accomplish this by right-clicking on the rule in question and selecting Exclude. Exclusion should be done rarely and only with a solid reason. It is now mandatory to give a reason why a particular rule violation was excluded. Figure 13.5 shows this.

Certain rules that FxCop throws an exception for can be somewhat vague, but thankfully each rule has a referenced documentation page located on the FxCop web site that discusses the rule in greater detail, including possible causes for why a certain exception was thrown. Figure 13.6 shows the web page detailing a spell check exception.

It is also important to keep in mind that not all errors are your fault, as even the pre-2005 Visual Studio generation wizards have code that does not conform to the design guideline standards. If you notice any errors resulting within the InitializeComponent method, or any other auto-generated regions for that matter, it is safe to exclude them.

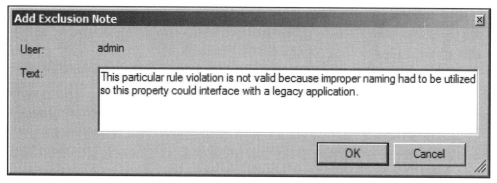

Figure 13.5 Dialog used to specify a reason why a rule violation was excluded.

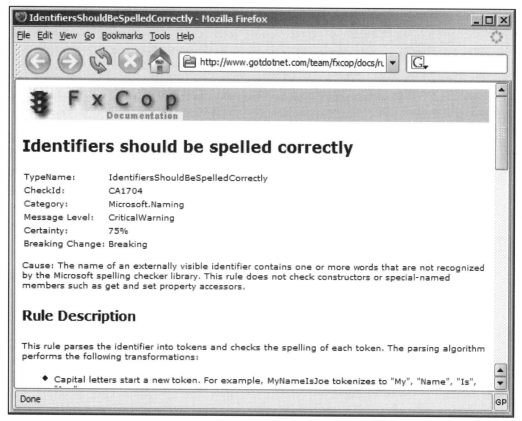

Figure 13.6 Documentation web page detailing a spell check exception.

Another point to note is that FxCop has a fairly rigid spell checker integrated right into the tool, and will generally complain about any product or company names that are not a composition of dictionary words. Additionally, there may be some acronyms you wish to keep in full uppercase, yet FxCop will complain that they break design guidelines. It is quite easy to configure FxCop to ignore certain cases of a rule exception, and this can be done by modifying the CustomDictionary.xml file that resides in the installation folder of FxCop. If you're working in a multi-developer environment, be sure to add this file to source control so that all developers have access to the custom configuration you specify.

Building Custom Rules

You may be reading all the built-in rules available for FxCop and thinking that they enforce all the policies you have. If this is the case, you do not need to extend the rules engine. However, some projects require the enforcement of custom rules, in which case you will need to extend the rules engine in FxCop. The latter half of this chapter covers building custom FxCop rules and enabling them for enforcement in your projects.

The first thing to do is to create a new C#.NET class library project and reference the FxCop SDK. Navigate to the installation folder of the FxCop tool, and reference the FxCopSdk and Microsoft.Cci assemblies. Figure 13.7 shows the assembly reference screen that should resemble what you see.

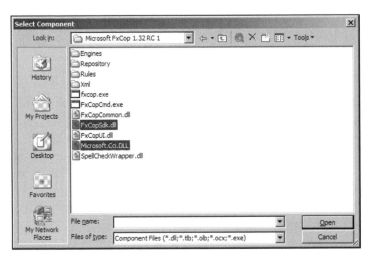

Figure 13.7 Dialog shown when referencing the FxCop SDK.

For an extremely simple yet practical example, we will make a custom FxCop rule that requires all namespaces to be prefixed with `Nexus.WorldBuilder`.

We need to start by creating an XML file in the project that will eventually be compiled as an embedded resource during the build process. This file defines all the rules that FxCop will load, including configuration and resolution information. It is here that you can set the warning level, description, and resolution for each rule. The name of the file at this point is fairly flexible.

```xml
<?xml version="1.0" encoding="utf-8" ?>
<Rules>
  <Rule TypeName="NamespacePrefix" Category="Nexus.Naming" CheckId="NX0001">
  <Owner>Graham Wihlidal</Owner>
  <Email>graham@wihlidal.ca</Email>
  <Name>Namespaces must be prefixed with Nexus.WorldBuilder</Name>
  <MessageLevel Certainty="95">Error</MessageLevel>
  <Description>All namespaces should be prefixed with Nexus.WorldBuilder
  for consistency</Description>
  <LongDescription>All namespaces should be prefixed with Nexus.WorldBuilder
  for consistency</LongDescription>
  <Url>http://Url-To-A-Help-Page</Url>
  <Resolution Name="Default">The namespace '{0}' is not prefixed with
  Nexus.WorldBuilder</Resolution>
  <FixCategories>Breaking</FixCategories>
  </Rule>
</Rules>
```

You must set the `Build Action` property to `Embedded Resource` so that this XML file will be embedded in the rule assembly file; otherwise FxCop will not be able to find it and will report that there are no rules to load.

The best approach to structuring the code for a rules assembly is creating a base rule from which other rules can inherit. This is because there are a few arguments that must be repeated for each rule, and proper class design urges the normalization of repeating data.

Here is the code for the base rule class:

```csharp
using System;
using Microsoft.Cci;
using Microsoft.Tools.FxCop.Sdk;
using Microsoft.Tools.FxCop.Sdk.Introspection;
```

```
namespace NexusRules.Naming
{
    [CLSCompliant(false)]
    abstract public class BaseNexusNamingRule : BaseIntrospectionRule
    {
        protected BaseNexusNamingRule(string name)
            : base(name, "NexusRules.Naming.NamingRules",
                            typeof(BaseNexusNamingRule).Assembly)
        {
        }
    }
}
```

You will notice the arguments being passed into the base constructor. The first argument is the name of the rule, and it is passed in through the constructor of each custom rule inheriting from BaseNexusNamingRule. The last two arguments require more explanation. The second argument is the fully qualified name of the embedded configuration XML file without the extension. In this example, the assembly is NexusRules.Naming.dll and the XML configuration file is NamingRules.xml, resulting in NexusRules.Naming.NamingRules. The third argument is a reference to the assembly containing the rules.

It is also important to note the need for [CLSCompliant(false)]; the FxCop SDK is not CLS-compliant, so it is required that this attribute be placed so that the code compiles correctly.

With the base rule class defined, we can create our first FxCop rule. The magic behind the FxCop SDK is the Check method. There are many different overloaded versions, all of which get run when an assembly is analyzed; it becomes a matter of picking the right overloaded method for the job.

Here is the code for the example FxCop rule:

```
using System;

using Microsoft.Cci;
using Microsoft.Tools.FxCop.Sdk;
using Microsoft.Tools.FxCop.Sdk.Introspection;

namespace NexusRules.Naming
{
    [CLSCompliant(false)]
    public class NamespacePrefix : BaseNexusNamingRule
    {
```

```
    public NamespacePrefix() : base("NamespacePrefix")
    {
    }

    public override ProblemCollection Check(string namespaceName,
                                            TypeNodeList types)
    {
        if (!namespaceName.StartsWith("Nexus.WorldBuilder"))
        {
            string[] arguments = new string[1] { namespaceName };
            Resolution resolution = GetNamedResolution("Default", arguments);
            Problems.Add(new Problem(resolution));
        }

        return Problems;
    }
  }
}
```

You should notice that there is a collection called Problems with no apparent declaration. This property is declared in the BaseIntrospectionRule class, and is the collection you must add Problem objects to and return from the Check method. Do not create a new ProblemCollection as it will not work. Be sure to return null if no errors occurred. Lastly, you need to modify AssemblyInfo.cs in a couple of places and also give the assembly a strong name key.

Add the following lines near the other assembly attributes:

```
[assembly:CLSCompliant(true)]
[assembly:ComVisible(false)]
```

If everything compiles correctly, you are halfway there! The real parlor trick is getting FxCop to recognize the rules in your assembly. The custom rules importer is very strict, and quite often it forces you to pull your hair out just to get custom rules to import. Thankfully, the latest version of FxCop outputs XML configuration errors, whereas the older versions did not and required some clever debugging to fix. You can import custom rule assemblies by selecting Add Rules from the Project menu.

If FxCop fails to load your rules, be sure to read the messages left in the output window of FxCop. If the custom rules loaded correctly, you can try them out. You should have output similar to Figure 13.8 after analyzing an assembly that violates the namespace prefix rule defined in this example.

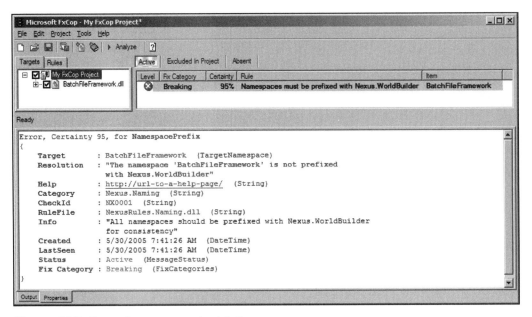

Figure 13.8 Output from custom rule violation.

Lastly, it is important to mention that Microsoft has integrated FxCop analysis into Visual Studio 2005. To enable integrated analysis, just go to the properties page of the project, and then select the Code Analysis tab. Check the Enable Code Analysis checkbox and configure the rules that you want to conform to.

You should end up with a dialog like the one shown in Figure 13.9.

The previous step has now configured your project to perform integrated code analysis during the build process. By default, analysis issues and rule violations will appear as warnings in the error list window, as shown in Figure 13.10.

Conclusion

This chapter discussed the importance of coding guidelines and using FxCop to enforce them. Also surfacing was the apparent need to deviate from the proposed norm, and ways to configure FxCop to perform customized analysis and enforcement of both Microsoft- and project-specific policies.

Lastly, there are a number of online resources that cover how to build more complex custom rules, one of which is the June 04 Bugslayer column from MSDN magazine: http://msdn.microsoft.com/msdnmag/issues/04/06/Bugslayer/default.aspx.

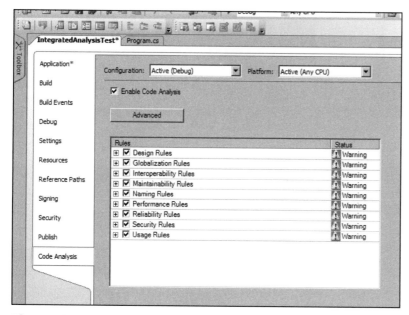

Figure 13.9 Visual Studio 2005 integrated code analysis configuration.

Error List				
⊗ 0 Errors	⚠ 20 Warnings	① 0 Messages		
Description		F.. ▲	Line	Project
(String, String, String):Boolean' to catch a more specific exception than 'System.Exception' or rethrow the exception.				
⚠ 9	CA1060 : Microsoft.Design : Because it is a DllImport method, Test.GetPrivateProfileSectionNamesA(Byte[], Int32, String):Int32 should be defined in a class named NativeMethods, SafeNativeMethods, or UnsafeNativeMethods.	Test.cs	15	IntegratedAnalysisTest
⚠ 10	CA1401 : Microsoft.Interoperability : Change the accessibility of DllImport 'Test.GetPrivateProfileSectionNamesA(Byte[], Int32, String):Int32' so that it is no longer visible from outside its assembly.	Test.cs	15	IntegratedAnalysisTest
⚠ 11	CA1720 : Microsoft.Naming : Remove the type identifier from parameter name 'returnedString'.	Test.cs	18	IntegratedAnalysisTest

Figure 13.10 Code analysis results in the error list window.

Perhaps the best place to learn the art of building FxCop rules is by disassembling the built-in rules provided by Microsoft. You can do this by downloading Reflector for .NET, an extremely useful tool written by Lutz Roeder, which allows you to browse classes and disassemble non-obfuscated code into a humanly readable format. You can download Reflector for .NET at http://www.aisto.com/roeder/dotnet/.

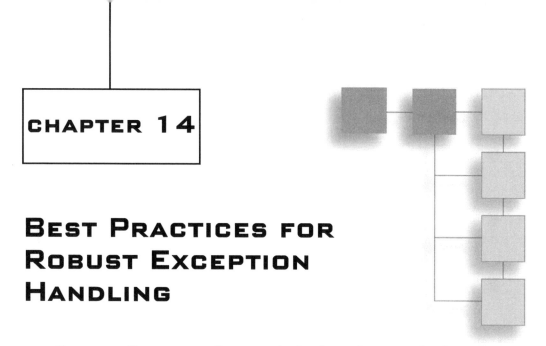

CHAPTER 14

BEST PRACTICES FOR ROBUST EXCEPTION HANDLING

Computers allow you to make more mistakes faster than any other invention in human history with the possible exception of handguns and tequila.

Mitch Ratcliffe

In the development world, it is nearly impossible to write bug-free software. The best we can do is write stable software that, when a problem occurs, displays enough information to solve it. There is no way to write software that is bug-free, but by employing exception handling, at least we can gracefully handle any anomalous situations that occur.

An exception can be defined as unexpected behavior or an error condition occurring in a software application. The name itself comes from the idea that, although an error condition can occur, the error condition occurs infrequently. The majority of a developer's time is spent on user input and error handling. Thankfully, there is some functionality in the .NET Class Framework that provides error handling, but there are certain best practices that should be followed in terms of design concerns and performance issues.

Many developers misuse or overuse exception handling, and this chapter is all about best practices for using .NET exception handling. This chapter is not centered on the design aspects of user interface integration, but rather serves to enlighten readers about the proper way to handle errors while aiming for maximum performance and adherence to framework guidelines.

External Data Is Evil

Typically, exceptions in an application are thrown because of invalid or nonexistent data. External data can be provided from a database, keyboard input, files, a registry, or a network socket. You can never trust external data because there is no way to be certain that the external data exists or is valid. You may also end up with insufficient privileges to access the external data.

Aside from reading data, most external data sources have write capability, in which case there is also some sort of repository for the data as well. You may end up with insufficient privileges or not enough memory, or the device can suffer from a physical fault as well. It is important to recognize that the best thing to do is build solid code that handles external data errors in a stable and informative manner.

The safest approach when dealing with external data is to validate the data before doing anything else with it.

Creating Custom Exceptions

There is a common misconception among developers regarding the use of `System.Exception` and `System.ApplicationException`. These exception types are used throughout the .NET Class Framework and form the base of many derived types, but you should never throw them explicitly. The truth is, these types are much too broad and generic to be thrown; you should instead be creating and throwing custom exceptions if a suitable exception type does not yet exist.

Another fallacy is that custom exceptions should be derived from `System.ApplicationException`. This used to be the correct approach but has now been identified by Microsoft as incorrect. You should instead be deriving all custom exceptions from `System.Exception`. One of the main reasons for this change is an assortment of issues when using third-party libraries in your code. You may have a function that calls a third-party method, which in turn throws a `System.ApplicationException`, and you may also throw that same exception later on in your code. When the exception leaves the method and arrives at the exception handler, who threw it? The best approach is to create exception class hierarchies that are as wide and shallow as possible, the same approach typically used with the structuring of class hierarchies.

All custom exceptions should also support the three default constructors to promote consistency between your custom exceptions and the built-in framework exceptions.

These constructors are:

```
const string defaultMessage = "Your default message";

public YourException()
    : base(defaultMessage);

public YourException(string message)
    : base(String.Format("{0} - {1}", defaultMessage, message));

public YourException(string message, Exception inner)
    : base(String.Format("{0} - {1}", defaultMessage, message), inner);
```

There are some rules that must be followed in regards to the message property. Do not store exception information in the message property. Instead, create separate properties in the exception class to hold the data. Storing information in the message property also means that users will have to perform string parsing to retrieve the data, which is an obvious hassle. Also consider the problems that localization would present if you were attempting to parse different pieces of information from the exception message when the formatting of the string was based on the current culture locale.

Lastly, be sure to mark your exceptions with the [Serializable] attribute. You never know when your methods will be called from Remoting or a Web Service.

Here is a complete example of a custom exception in its simplest form:

```
[Serializable]
public class NexusException : System.Exception
{
    const string defaultMessage = "A runtime error occurred within" +
                                  "Nexus World Builder";

    public NexusException()
        : base(defaultMessage)
    {
    }

    public NexusException(string message)
        : base(String.Format("{0} - {1}", defaultMessage, message))
    {
    }
```

```
    public NexusException(string message, Exception inner)
        : base(String.Format("{0} - {1}", defaultMessage, message), inner)
    {
    }
}
```

Throwing Exceptions

A trait of exceptions is that they cannot be ignored, so it is a good idea to use exceptions in place of return values when a particular operation must be successful to proceed. It is also wise to rely more on throwing an exception than using Debug.Assert. Keep in mind that assertions are removed from release code, so errors will be much harder to track down in a production environment.

The stack trace is a critical piece of information to have when an exception is thrown, and extra care must be taken when re-throwing exceptions to ensure that the stack trace is preserved. Many times you need to catch a particular exception, perform cleanup logic such as a transaction rollback, and then re-throw the exception so that another exception handler can process it.

Consider the following code:

```
try
{
    // Code that throws an exception
}
catch (Exception exception)
{
    // Code that performs cleanup \ rollback
    throw exception;
}
```

In this example, the exception is caught and thrown back to the next exception handler, but using a new exception object without the stack trace. The proper way to re-throw the exception while preserving the stack trace information is shown in the following code:

```
try
{
    // Code that throws an exception
}
catch (Exception exception)
{
```

```
    // Code that performs cleanup \ rollback
    throw;
}
```

Just calling throw alone will re-throw the exact same exception object that arrived at the catch statement in the first place.

Also, be sure to add a semantic value if you re-throw an exception under a different type. Sometimes you may wish to take a few specific exceptions and re-throw them under a more generalized type, but it is advisable to at least attach the old exception as the inner exception property when re-throwing it. That way, the original exception is readily available if there is a need for re-specialization.

Lastly, it is bad design to use exceptions as a means of returning information from a method. One reason is that exception handling is fairly slow, so overuse and misuse of exception handling can introduce many performance bottlenecks into your code.

Structured Exception Handlers

There are some rules that should be followed when building your exception handlers and deciding what exception types to catch. Never catch a base-type exception when you are always expecting a more specialized one. For example, do not catch `System.Exception` when the only exception that will ever be thrown is a `System.ArgumentNullException`. Generic handlers create many problems, and should be avoided whenever possible. A general rule of thumb is that `System.Exception` should only ever be caught once per thread.

If you want more reasoning behind this rule, consider the following example.

Imagine that you build a library that offers fairly basic functionality, and it is used by a Windows Forms application. Now, normally a method in this library will throw `System.ArgumentNullException` when a specified parameter is `null`. If the Windows Forms application has a structured exception handler that catches `System.Exception`, error handling will work as expected in a perfect situation. In the event that the library assembly cannot be referenced by the Windows Forms application because it is missing, the Common Language Runtime will throw a `System.IO.FileNotFoundException`, indicating that the library assembly could not be found. When this exception occurs, the Windows Forms application believes that a `null` parameter was specified, when in reality the entire library could not be found. However, if the Windows Forms application did not catch generic exceptions, this problem would be avoided.

Lastly, one of the absolute worst things you can do is catch an exception and do nothing with it. Catching an exception with an empty code block is commonly referred to as *exception swallowing*; do not do this! If you do not wish to handle a certain type of exception, don't write an exception handler for it.

Logging Exception Information

At first glance, it may look correct to spit out the contents of Exception.Message to whatever logging medium you are using, but such an assumption would be incorrect. The Exception.Message property only contains the high-level message, which could be as informative as Object reference not set to an instance of an object. A better approach instead is to log Exception.ToString(), which will result in the logging of the message, the inner exception, and the stack trace of the exception—information that is much more useful when it comes time to debug a problem.

Mechanisms for Cleanup

There are a number of classes in the .NET class framework that require cleanup after their role has been fulfilled, and certain classes (like file system access) can lead to locking or other problems when not properly disposed.

Consider the following code:

```
public void DoSomething(string fileName)
{
    StreamReader reader = new StreamReader(string fileName);
    ProcessStream(reader);
    reader.Close();
}
```

All is well if no errors occur, but consider the situation where ProcessStream throws an exception. The close method for the StreamReader would never be called, and the resource would remain active.

One solution to this problem is to introduce an exception handler that closes the StreamReader when an error occurs, and then re-throws the exception.

Consider the following code:

```
public void DoSomething(string fileName)
{
    StreamReader reader = null;
    try
    {
```

```
            reader = new StreamReader(string fileName);
            ProcessStream(reader);
            reader.Close();
        }
    catch (Exception exception)
    {
            If (reader != null)
            {
                reader.Close();
            }
            throw;
        }
}
```

This solution will ensure that the reader is always closed, but the design of it is somewhat messy; code is duplicated and it is harder to read.

Structured exception handling in .NET also offers the `finally` block, which executes when the runtime leaves the exception handler, regardless of whether or not the `try` or the `catch` fired.

The following code shows how this would look:

```
public void DoSomething(string fileName)
{
    StreamReader = null;
    try
    {
        reader = new StreamReader(string fileName);
        ProcessStream(reader);
    }
    finally
    {
        if (reader != null)
        {
            reader.Close();
        }
    }
}
```

To present an even better approach than the `finally` mechanism, C# has the wonderful keyword `using` that implicitly implements the disposable design pattern and ensures that the resource it is attached to cleans up, even in the event that an exception occurs. The `using` keyword only works on classes that implement the

IDisposable interface, but that also means you can create custom classes that require a cleanup process and use this keyword on them.

The following code shows how the using keyword works:

```
public void DoSomething(string fileName)
{
    using (StreamReader reader = new StreamReader(string fileName))
    {
        ProcessStream(reader);
    }
}
```

This solution is much more elegant than an ugly exception handler, and still ensures that the resource is released when it is no longer needed.

Unhandled and Thread Exception Events

There are a few issues when using either the AppDomain.UnhandledException event or the Application.ThreadException event. The notification fires so late that by the time you receive the exception notification, your application will be unable to respond to it. Additionally, you will not receive any notifications if your exception was thrown from the main thread or unmanaged code.

It is also very difficult to write a generic exception handler for the entire application that is robust and flexible enough to accommodate and correctly handle every erroneous situation. Because a generic handler would not have access to the local variables present when the exception was thrown, the need to rely on global variables and singletons will be increased, which is something that should be ultimately avoided.

With such faults, you are probably wondering why these events should be used in the first place. Consider them as "safety nets" for the situations where an exception slips through and would be normally handled by the default exception handler provided by the Common Language Runtime.

Conclusion

Structured exception handling is and will remain an integral part of any software project. This chapter covered some best practices for using .NET exception handling, and it is highly advisable that you adopt these new techniques and approaches into your development projects. Doing so will improve both the design and performance of your code and will increase the overall maintainability of your software.

While you could build your own exception handling manager that offers many fancy features that other developers would be envious of, it is important to remember that software development is about building software that meets business needs and doing so in a timely manner. Reinventing the wheel is generally ridiculed, so there are a couple of components available from Microsoft that can be used when there is a need for advanced exception handling support.

The first component is the Exception Handling Application Block that offers the ability to create a consistent strategy for processing exceptions on all architectural layers of an application. This component is not limited to service boundaries, which is an important feature for distributed architectures. Several tools are included with the installation that help you create and configure exception policies for your application. The Exception Handling Application Block can be downloaded from MSDN.

The other component is the Logging and Instrumentation Application Block, which allows for .NET applications to be built for manageability in a production environment. Applications can leverage existing logging, tracing, and eventing mechanisms built into Windows, and can issue a variety of warnings, errors, audits, diagnostic events, and business-specific events. This component also provides statistics like average execution time for a process or service. This component can also be downloaded from MSDN.

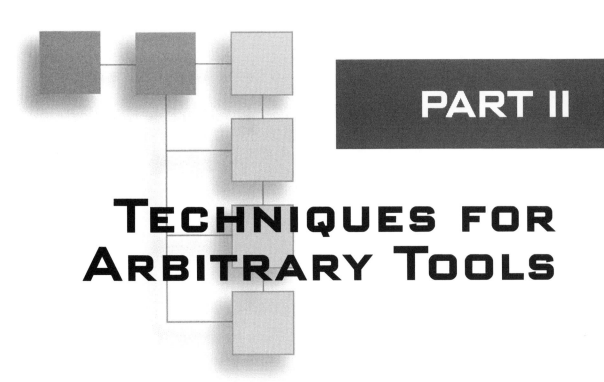

PART II

TECHNIQUES FOR ARBITRARY TOOLS

It's hard to read through a book on the principles of magic without glancing at the cover periodically to make sure it isn't a book on software design.

Bruce Tognazzini

Each and every tool is unique, but there are always core elements that are common to them all. Designing these core elements to be modular and reusable is advantageous and will save money and time when building subsequent tools that need the same functionality. Many developers build elaborate solutions to a simple problem, often reinventing the wheel in the process. These solutions are often complex and hard to maintain, costing additional resources that are better spent on other areas of an application that are more deserving of the time.

The chapters in Part II cover arbitrary elements that are applicable to almost any tool, independent of the feature list or specifications. The accompanying components to the chapters are also flexible enough that they can be plugged into these arbitrary tools with little to no modification. It is this reusability that will save a project additional resources that can be spent elsewhere. The majority of the chapters cover techniques that are relevant to the storage and manipulation of arbitrary data in a common form. Some techniques include data compression, encryption, printing support, using the PropertyGrid control, and a generic framework for handling batch file processing.

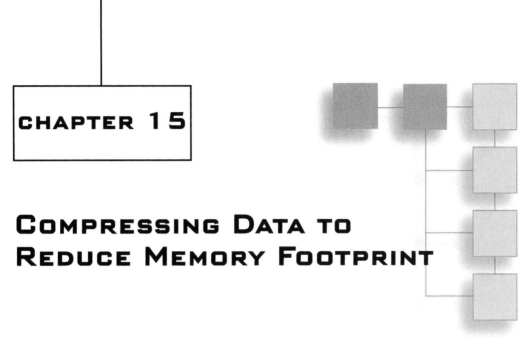

CHAPTER 15

Compressing Data to Reduce Memory Footprint

The programmer's primary weapon in the never-ending battle against slow systems is to change the intramodular structure. Our first response should be to reorganize the modules' data structures.

Frederick P. Brooks

Games are being produced with multiple gigabytes of game assets, and it is projected that file sizes will increase at an exponential rate in the years to come. One of the largest issues for building reusable and efficient tools comes down to scalability, and how to build tools that can manage countless assets. One way to achieve this goal is through the use of data compression to reduce the file size of each game asset.

A variety of software development projects employ data compression, and almost all operating systems and platforms have libraries and tools available to perform data compression for different types of situations and datasets. Fortunately, .NET 2.0 introduced some new data compression components that make the whole process very easy.

As for a definition, data compression removes redundancy from data, which can come in a lot of different forms depending on the type of data in question. On a small scale, repeated bit sequences (11111111) or repeated byte sequences (XXXXXXX) can be transformed. On a larger scale, redundancies tend to come from sequences of varying lengths that are relatively common. Basically, data compression aims at finding algorithmic transformations of a dataset that will produce a more compact representation of the original dataset.

Choosing the best compression algorithm depends on a number of factors, such as expected patterns and regularities in the data, storage and data persistence requirements, and both CPU and memory limits. This chapter briefly covers some data compression theory, but it mostly covers implementation of data compression using the built-in C# components.

Types of Compression

Data compression basically comes in two flavors, lossy and lossless.

Lossy compression is a representation of the original dataset that is "close enough" in comparison. File sizes are significantly reduced by losing a reasonable amount of data in the compression process. Lossy compression can produce far more compact dataset representations than lossless compression. The main problem with lossy compression is that valid data is actually lost and unrecoverable, but this limitation is all right for images, sound files, and video clips where data loss is acceptable because humans can only perceive a subset of the actual data anyway. In the data persistence world, where data cannot be lost or corruption would occur, lossy compression algorithms will not suffice. Storing a "close enough" representation of a data file would be useless. Lossy compression also does not generally provide a decompression algorithm because of the data loss.

Lossless compression is a representation of the original dataset that enables reproduction of the exact contents of the original dataset by performing a decompression transformation. No data is ever lost in the compression process, making it the perfect solution for compressing data that must maintain integrity. This chapter only covers lossless data compression, because we generally want tools to maintain 100 percent data integrity unless we are dealing with image compression.

GZipStream Compression in .NET 2.0

Microsoft .NET 1.1 did not include any data compression components other than third-party solutions. Recently introduced in .NET 2.0 is the System.IO.Compression namespace that provides compression and decompression services for streams. There are currently two supported algorithms: deflate and gzip. This chapter covers the gzip algorithm exclusively.

The gzip algorithm is a lossless data format that is safe from patents. The gzip implementation provided by Microsoft is completely compatible with the unix gzip functionality, though the .NET implementation has a slightly weaker compression algorithm. The gzip implementation follows the format from RFC 1952. Microsoft .NET 2.0 provides gzip functionality through the GZipStream class.

Another great feature of the gzip format is that there is a cyclic redundancy checksum that is used to detect data corruption.

Note

The GZipStream class cannot be used to compress files larger than four gigabytes in size.

Implementation for Arbitrary Data

The first step to use the GZipStream class is to include the appropriate namespaces.

```
using System;
using System.IO;
using System.IO.Compression;
```

The following method is used to compress arbitrary data stored in a byte array and return a byte array containing the compressed data. Notice that the input data length is written as the first four bytes of the stream. This is so the decompression method can decompress that data without having to determine the original file size of the data. This was done to improve performance and speed, sacrificing compatibility with other gzip implementations. We want to know the original size of the data before compression so we can allocate enough memory to store the data after decompression.

Data is compressed on the fly as it is written into the GZipStream. Notice that the constructor for GZipStream references the memory stream that will hold the resultant data. This compression can be done against any stream object, including, FileStream for files.

```
internal static byte[] CompressData(byte[] input)
{
    try
    {
        using (MemoryStream output = new MemoryStream())
        {
            output.Write(BitConverter.GetBytes(input.Length), 0, 4);
```

```
            using (GZipStream zipStream = new GZipStream(output,
                                          CompressionMode.Compress, true))
            {
                zipStream.Write(input, 0, input.Length);
            }

            return output.ToArray();
        }
    }
    catch (Exception)
    {
        return null;
    }
}
```

Decompression is handled in the same way as compression, except the CompressionMode.Decompress enum value is used. The first step is to read the initial four data bytes from the stream as an integer describing the buffer size for the decompressed data. Then the data buffer is created and the input data is decompressed and read into it.

```
internal static byte[] DecompressData(byte[] input)
{
    try
    {
        using (MemoryStream inputData = new MemoryStream(input))
        {
            byte[] lengthData = new byte[4];

            if (inputData.Read(lengthData, 0, 4) == 4)
            {
                int decompressedLength = BitConverter.ToInt32(lengthData, 0);
                using (GZipStream zipStream = new GZipStream(inputData,
                                          CompressionMode.Decompress))
                {
                    byte[] decompressedData = new byte[decompressedLength];

                    if (zipStream.Read(decompressedData,
                                0,
                                decompressedLength) == decompressedLength)
                    {
                        return decompressedData;
                    }
                }
```

```
                }
            }
        }

        return null;
    }
    catch (Exception)
    {
        return null;
    }
}
```

Implementation for Serializable Objects

A powerful feature of the .NET platform is the ability to serialize objects into an XML or binary representation to make storing, sending, or transforming data extremely easy. Serialization is common practice and is used in many facets of .NET application or systems development. The BinaryFormatter class can serialize and deserialize data into a stream, which makes GZipStream a suitable target for data transformation.

The first step is to include the appropriate namespaces.

```
using System;
using System.IO;
using System.IO.Compression;
using System.Runtime.Serialization.Formatters.Binary;
```

The following code describes a simple serializable class that is used in the accompanying example for this chapter. It shows how to create a serializable class and properly decorate it with the SerializableAttribute.

```
[Serializable]
internal class TestObject
{
    private string testString;
    private int testInteger;

    public string TestString
    {
        get { return testString; }
        set { testString = value; }
    }
```

```
    public int TestInteger
    {
        get { return testInteger; }
        set { testInteger = value; }
    }

    internal TestObject()
    {
        testString = string.Empty;
        testInteger = 0;
    }
}
```

The next method is used to compress TestObject instances into a byte array containing the compressed data. You will notice that the code is very similar to compressing arbitrary data except the BinaryFormatter is in charge of writing to the GZipStream.

```
internal static byte[] CompressTestObject(TestObject testObject)
{
    try
    {
        using (MemoryStream output = new MemoryStream())
        {
            using (GZipStream zipStream = new GZipStream(output,
                                                CompressionMode.Compress))
            {
                BinaryFormatter formatter = new BinaryFormatter();
                formatter.Serialize(zipStream, testObject);
            }

            return output.ToArray();
        }
    }
    catch (Exception)
    {
        return null;
    }
}
```

Decompression works the same as the compression method, except the input data is decompressed and deserialized into a TestObject instance. This approach does not require the data length to be written to the stream because BinaryFormatter knows how big the class data is.

```
internal static TestObject DecompressTestObject(byte[] input)
{
    try
    {
        using (MemoryStream output = new MemoryStream(input))
        {
            using (GZipStream zipStream = new GZipStream(output,
                                       CompressionMode.Decompress))
            {
                BinaryFormatter formatter = new BinaryFormatter();
                return (formatter.Deserialize(zipStream) as TestObject);
            }
        }
    }
    catch (Exception)
    {
        return null;
    }
}
```

Conclusion

This chapter briefly covered part of data compression theory, though barely scratching the surface of a complex topic, and then later jumped into implementation details for the GZipStream class introduced in .NET 2.0.

Data compression has been and always will be a crucial element of many tools, especially with the projected increase in the volume of game content over the next couple of years. Data compression also has its place with network tools where bandwidth and transfer speed is limited.

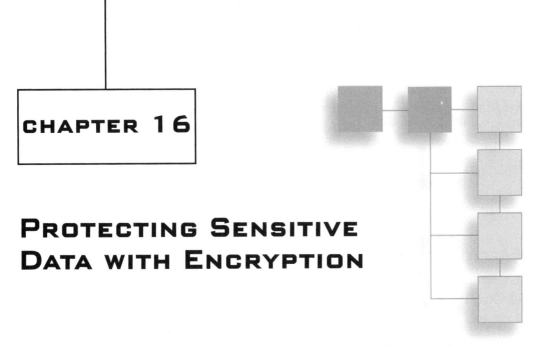

CHAPTER 16

PROTECTING SENSITIVE DATA WITH ENCRYPTION

The only thing more frightening than a programmer with a screwdriver or a hardware engineer with a program is a user with a pair of wire cutters and the root password.

Elizabeth Zwicky

With the highly distributed software populating the computing world these days, there is often a need to protect sensitive data so that it is accessible only by a select group of people. Some applications are network- or Internet-driven, and they must maintain secure communication so that malicious attackers cannot modify incoming and outgoing packets. Other applications need to store sensitive data locally in the file system or a remote database in a format that is unreadable by humans.

Developers look towards encryption to accomplish this feat, but very few of them implement it correctly. These developers throw around buzzwords like "128-bit encryption" and claim that their applications are secure, when, in fact, they have introduced security flaws that can be exploited by anyone with the knowledge to do so.

Some developers also think that they can roll their own implementation of a particular algorithm and claim that it works correctly. Just because you see data that you think is encrypted does not actually mean that it is. Many of these developers could probably hand their implementations over to a knowledgeable cryptologist who would discover flaws. Experts were hired to implement the algorithms provided in the .NET Class Framework, and it is advisable to use their implementations because they more than likely have a better understanding of encryption than you do.

This chapter covers the encryption ciphers available in the .NET Class Framework, how to implement encryption properly, and common pitfalls and issues when securing data with encryption.

Encryption Rudiments

Encryption is a complex subject, and it is impossible to cover all aspects in a single chapter. While still quite ambitious, in this chapter, I will attempt to summarize the common characteristics of encryption and present a solution that takes care of the majority of the underlying mechanisms and theory behind encryption. This chapter will only cover the usage of algorithm implementations currently provided by the .NET Class Framework, and not how to implement the algorithms yourself.

To fully understand this chapter and encryption in general, we must define a few common characteristics and terms.

Public-Key Encryption

This type of encryption is commonly referred to as *asymmetric encryption* and uses a public and private key pair to perform encryption or decryption of data. The public key is available to everyone and is used to encrypt data that will be decrypted by the owner of the private key. The private key is kept secure by the owner and is used to decrypt data that has been encrypted with the public key.

Asymmetric encryption is generally only efficient on relatively small sets of data. The .NET Class Framework contains two asymmetric encryption algorithms: Digital Signature Algorithm (DSA) and RSA.

Private-Key Encryption

This type of encryption is commonly referred to as *symmetric encryption* and uses a single key to perform encryption or decryption of data. The private key must be kept safe from anyone other than the owner of the data.

Symmetric encryption is generally fast and can operate on large sets of data. The .NET Class Framework contains four symmetric encryption algorithms: DES, Triple DES, RC2, and Rijndael.

Ciphers

Ciphers are cryptographic algorithms that use a private key to transform plain text input into an encrypted output, also known as *cipher text*. There are two forms of ciphers: block-based and stream-based.

A block-based cipher takes a fixed size input block and transforms the data into a fixed size cipher text block.

A stream-based cipher does not encrypt data but instead generates a key stream that produces the cipher text by XORing the stream bytes with the input bytes.

The .NET Class Framework only provides block-based ciphers, but it is possible to make a block-based cipher behave in a streaming fashion.

Block Padding

Block ciphers were designed to operate on complete blocks of data. Padding is used when processing a partial block of data to append extra data to the incomplete block, making it an even multiple of the block size.

The .NET 2.0 Class Framework supports three types of block padding, as described in Table 16.1.

Table 16.1 Padding Modes Available in .NET 2.0

Padding Mode	Description
PaddingMode.None	Informs the cipher that no padding should occur. This mode requires that you ensure that only complete blocks are processed or any exception will be thrown.
PaddingMode.Zeros	Informs the cipher that zeros should be appended to the incomplete data block to make it an even multiple of the block size.
	The problem with this mode is that the decryption process will not be able to distinguish the padding from the actual data, which will result in the padding being appended to the decrypted data.
	A possible solution is to transmit the padding length with the data so that the padding can be removed when the decryption process has finished.
PaddingMode.PKCS7	Informs the cipher to append a sequence of bytes that has a value equal to the number of padding bytes.
	In a 128-bit data block, if the source data looks like [AA BB CC DD], then 12 padding bytes must be added to make it an even multiple of the block size. The hex value [0C] represents the numeric value 12 in base 10, so the final data block will look like: [AA BB CC DD 0C 0C 0C 0C 0C 0C 0C 0C 0C 0C 0C 0C].

Table 16.1 Padding Modes Available in .NET 2.0 *(continued)*

Padding Mode	Description
PaddingMode.ISO10126	This padding mode works very much like PaddingMode.PKCS7, except it sets the value of the final byte in the block to the number of padding bytes and sets the remaining padding bytes to random data.
PaddingMode.ANSIX923	This padding mode works very much like PaddingMode.PKCS7, except it sets the value of the final byte in the block to the number of padding bytes and sets the remaining padding bytes to zero.

It is advisable to use PaddingMode.PKCS7 when developing with .NET 1.1 and PaddingMode.ISO10126 when developing with .NET 2.0. Both versions of the .NET framework default to PaddingMode.PKCS7, so you will have to explicitly set the padding mode to ISO10126.

Keep in mind that your software does not exist in a vacuum, so it is important that you make sure that using a different padding mode will not break any existing code.

Key Strength

The *key strength*, also known as *key size*, of an encryption algorithm refers to the length of the underlying key, and the higher the number the better. Consider the case of an 8-bit key. It would take an attacker roughly 256 guesses to land on the key, whereas a 40-bit key would take an attacker roughly over a trillion guesses to land on the key. The key length is very important, as is the data comprising the key.

Pseudo-random number generators (PRNG) are sometimes used by developers to generate private keys. Computers are fairly predictable, so achieving randomness is difficult to do. Do not try to create your own PRNG classes; use the built-in functionality provided by the RNGCryptoServiceProvider class in the .NET Class Framework.

Lastly, some developers also derive the key from a password, which may result in a key of substantial length, but the key is only as random as its source. If a 256-bit key is derived from a 12-character password, the key is not as secure as one might think. If a malicious attacker understands how the key is derived, he only has to attack the 12-character password to reveal the key itself.

Cipher Modes

One of the most important security issues to correctly configure is the cipher mode. This mode determines how the individual blocks of a transform are assembled to form the final data.

Messages are usually more than one block in length, so how does the data get encrypted? The obvious solution would be to encrypt each block individually and slap them all together in the end. In actuality, this is one of the most insecure cipher modes (ECB—Electronic Code Book), which can lead to security compromises of the encrypted data.

Cipher modes are used to modify the encryption process based on data carried over from previous block encryptions. The resulting encryption provides a much higher level of security than performing a simple block-level encryption.

The .NET class framework has a variety of other cipher modes available at your disposal, each with its own pros and cons. These cipher modes are listed in Table 16.2. We will be using the CBC mode for this chapter as it offers the best security.

Table 16.2 Cipher Modes Available in .NET 2.0

Cipher Mode	Description
CipherMode.CBC	This cipher mode (Cipher Block Chaining Mode) appends a number of bytes equal to the number of padding bytes used. Before each block is encrypted, it is combined with the previous block using an exclusive bitwise OR operation. This allows for each cipher block to be unique. The initialization vector is combined with the first plain text block before encryption occurs. If a single bit of the cipher block is corrupted, the corresponding plain text block will also be corrupted. In addition, a bit in the subsequent block in the same position will also be corrupted.
CipherMode.CFB	This cipher mode (Cipher Feedback Mode) processes small amounts of plain text instead of an entire block at a time. A shift register is used that is one block in length and is divided into sections. If the block size is eight bytes, the shift register is divided into eight sections. If a bit in the cipher text is corrupted, a plain text bit is corrupted as well as the shift register. Then all results in the next several plain text processes will be corrupted until the bad bit is shifted out of the register.
CipherMode.CTS	This cipher mode (Cipher Text Stealing Mode) handles any length of plain text data and produces cipher text that has a length equal to the plain text length. This cipher mode behaves exactly like the CBC mode except for the last two blocks of plain text.

Table 16.2 Cipher Modes Available in .NET 2.0 *(continued)*

Cipher Mode	Description
CipherMode.ECB	This cipher mode (Electronic Code Book) encrypts each block individually. Any blocks of plain text that are in the same message or in a different message using the same key will produce identical cipher text blocks. If the plain text contains a large amount of repetition, it is quite possible to break the cipher one block at a time. It is also possible to substitute and exchange cipher blocks without detection. If a single bit in the cipher text is corrupted, the entire corresponding plain text will also be corrupted.
CipherMode.OFB	This cipher mode (Output Feedback Mode) processes small amounts of plain text instead of an entire block at a time. This cipher mode is very similar to `CipherMode.CFB` except the shift register is filled differently. If a bit in the cipher text is corrupted, the corresponding bit of plain text will also be mangled. If there are missing bits from the cipher text, the plain text will be corrupted from that point on.

Note

CTS and OFB are defined but not currently implemented by any algorithms in the .NET framework.

Initialization Vectors

Symmetric algorithms will encrypt the same input block into the same output block based on the key. This is a weakness that can be potentially exploited by malicious attackers if they determine the structure of the data. Attackers could locate patterns and eventually reverse-engineer the private key.

In order to protect against this, the algorithms in the .NET Class Framework perform data chaining, where information from the previously encrypted block is used to encrypt the current block. This technique requires what is known as an *initialization vector* (IV) to perform the encryption with increased cryptographic variance.

There are a couple of ways to generate an initialization vector, but one approach is to run a hashing algorithm on a secret phrase and use a segment of the result as the encryption IV.

The following code shows how to do this:

```
using System.Security.Cryptography;

static public byte[] GenerateIV(byte[] key, int size)
```

```
{
    byte[] result = new byte[size];

    SHA384Managed sha384 = new SHA384Managed();
    sha384.ComputeHash(key);

    for (int byteIndex = 0; byteIndex < result.Length; byteIndex++)
    {
        result[byteIndex] = sha384.Hash[byteIndex];
    }

    return result;
}
```

The following generates a correctly sized key using a variation of the code for the initialization vector generation.

```
static public byte[] GenerateKey(byte[] key, int size)
{
    byte[] result = new byte[size];

    SHA384Managed sha384 = new SHA384Managed();
    sha384.ComputeHash(key);

    int counter = 0;

    for (int byteIndex = sha384.Hash.Length - 1;
            byteIndex > = (sha384.Hash.Length - size);
            byteIndex--)
    {
        result[counter++] = sha384.Hash[byteIndex];
    }

    return result;
}
```

Selecting a Cipher

As discussed previously, there are a few ciphers that can be used for private-key encryption. They all fundamentally do the same thing, except there are some notable differences between them in terms of performance, efficiency, and security.

The symmetric encryption algorithms provided by the .NET Class Framework are described in Table 16.3.

Table 16.3 .NET Symmetric Encryption Algorithms

Algorithm	Description
DES	This symmetric algorithm, also known as the Digital Encryption Standard, has existed for quite some time and is fairly weak by current standards. The DES algorithm was specifically designed to be efficient when implemented in hardware and inefficient when implemented in software. Because of its design, this algorithm is relatively slow compared to more modern algorithms. Another limitation is the short block and key sizes, available only in a 64-bit flavor.
Triple DES	This symmetric algorithm is basically a strengthened version of DES, offering stronger keys of 128-bit and 192-bit. Triple DES runs the DES algorithm over the input data three times, resulting in an algorithm that is stronger but three times slower than DES.
RC2	This symmetric algorithm is fairly good, and it performs more than twice as fast as DES when implemented in software. The 64-bit block size is relatively small, but at least the algorithm supports key lengths of 40 to 128 bits in 8-bit increments.
Rijndael	This symmetric algorithm, also known as the Advanced Encryption Standard (AES), supports block and key sizes of 128, 192, and 256 bits.
	While scrutinized for being new and not yet standing the test of time, the Rijndael algorithm has become a U.S. Federal Government standard, and is the recommended symmetric encryption algorithm to use whenever possible.

ICryptoTransform Interface

All symmetric encryption implementations provided in the .NET Class Framework implement the ICryptoTransform interface, which provides a uniform way to encrypt and decrypt data independently of the selected cipher.

Table 16.4 describes the members of the ICryptoTransform interface.

Since all symmetric algorithms inherit from this interface, encryption and decryption is accomplished using the same calls independently of the cipher used. The following code shows how to encrypt or decrypt binary data of arbitrary length.

Table 16.4 Members of the ICryptoTransform Interface

Member Name	Description
CanReuseTransform	This property indicates whether the current transform can be reused or not. All ciphers in the .NET Class Framework always return true.
CanTransformMultipleBlocks	This property indicates whether or not multiple blocks can be transformed in a single call to either TransformBlock or TransformFinalBlock. All ciphers in the .NET Class Framework always return true.
InputBlockSize	This property indicates the size of the input blocks, which will always be identical to the OutputBlockSize. The return value is dependent on the value of the BlockSize property set in the cipher.
OutputBlockSize	This property indicates the size of the output blocks, which will always be identical to the InputBlockSize. The return value is dependent on the value of the BlockSize property set in the cipher.
TransformBlock	This method encrypts or decrypts one or more blocks before the end of the message.
TransformFinalBlock	This method encrypts or decrypts one or more blocks at the end of the message. Ending blocks must be transformed differently from other blocks due to padding issues.

```
using System.Security.Cryptography;

static public byte[] EncryptMessage(SymmetricAlgorithm cipher,
                                    byte[] key,
                                    byte[] plainText)
{
    ICryptoTransform transform = cipher.CreateEncryptor(GenerateKey(key, 16),
                                                        GenerateIV(key, 16));
    byte[] result = transform.TransformFinalBlock(plainText, 0, plainText.Length);
    return result;
}

static public byte[] DecryptMessage(SymmetricAlgorithm cipher,
                                    byte[] key,
                                    byte[] cipherText)
{
    ICryptoTransform transform = cipher.CreateDecryptor(GenerateKey(key, 16),
                                                        GenerateIV(key, 16));
```

```
    byte[] result = transform.TransformFinalBlock(cipherText, 0, cipherText.Length);
    return result;
}
```

You will notice in the above example that `TransformFinalBlock` is called, but `TransformBlock` is never called. Since we know that `CanTransformMultipleBlocks` will always return true with any of the symmetric algorithms in the .NET Class Framework, we can transform all of our data in one pass.

The following code shows a simple example using the code shown in this chapter.

```
using System.Text;

static void Main(string[] args)
{
    byte[] key = Encoding.Default.GetBytes("This is my secret key!");
    string plainText = "This is a test!";

    // You can also use RC2, DES, and TripleDES
    RijndaelManaged cipher = new RijndaelManaged();
    cipher.Mode = CipherMode.CBC;

    Console.WriteLine("Original: [" + plainText + "]");

    byte[] encryptedData = EncryptMessage(cipher, key,
                                Encoding.Default.GetBytes(plainText));
    Console.WriteLine("Encrypted: [" +
                    Encoding.Default.GetString(encryptedData) + "]");

    byte[] decryptedData = DecryptMessage(cipher, key, encryptedData);
    string decryptedText = Encoding.Default.GetString(decryptedData);
    Console.WriteLine("Decrypted: [" + decryptedText + "]");

    Console.WriteLine("");
    Console.WriteLine("Press any key to continue.");
    Console.Read();
}
```

Conclusion

This chapter covered the theory and implementation details of using the built-in cryptography functionality in the .NET framework. While the presented solution could be improved upon and extended into a more reusable encryption manager, the fundamental code stays the same.

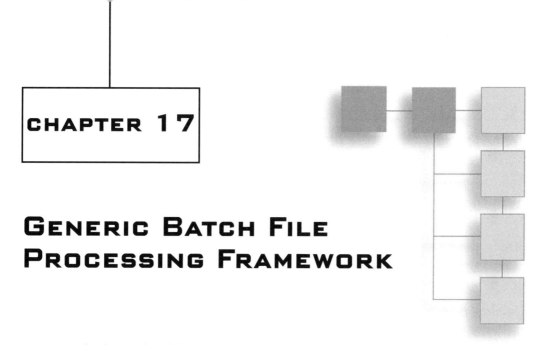

CHAPTER 17

GENERIC BATCH FILE PROCESSING FRAMEWORK

Simple things should be simple and complex things should be possible.

Alan Kay

Of all the common elements in the majority of development tools, batch file processing is used quite frequently by game tool programmers. It is not uncommon for a game to contain multiple gigabytes of game content files, so batch file processing is a must when a large volume of data is in need of alteration.

Some examples of batch file processing include generation of normal and texture maps from a collection of source art, deleting all files where the file name matches a particular search string, and recursively copying a folder hierarchy to another location when the directory layout is restructured.

The type of processing done on the files could be pretty much anything, although the code behind recursively iterating through directories and files remains relatively generic. Because effective use of time is essential when developing tools that our coworkers are waiting on, especially when the tool is not overly complex, reusability of common code is crucial. In this chapter, I present a generic batch file processing framework that promotes reusability, strong design, and flexibility.

Goals

The main goal of this framework is to promote reusability of the code that exists in all batch file processing tools, and to ensure that this framework will be sufficiently flexible for all the tools utilizing it.

The framework must be designed to work in either a console or WinForm environment, so the code should remain in a class library and only reference the core assemblies.

Strong design should be promoted through the use of solid OOP techniques. Maintainability is extremely important in any project, so a framework with a solid design results in better tools.

Developers must be able to quickly build tools without using a cumbersome API; the framework should be easy to configure and execute.

A verbose mode where operation progress can be reported to the user should also be available, keeping in mind that other tools should be able to run in silent mode as well.

The framework must have extremely low overhead because large operations demand performance.

Special situations where files are read-only should also be handled safely; the framework should be able to ignore read-only files or force writing if configured to do so. Configuration of the common base code is important, so other options, such as whether or not to recursively travel down directory structures, will also be available.

Lastly, the framework should be able to cancel the current operation. Support that will enable cancellation on a per-transaction basis will be integrated; that is, cancellation will not be supported halfway through the modification of a file, but rather after the current operation finishes. A mechanism will be available to developers so that they can support cancellation during an operation if they wish to worry about data integrity themselves.

Proposed Solution

In order to make a truly generic framework, we have to isolate the code that is different than other batch file processing tools, and build our framework around the code that remains. The work that these utilities perform is the variant data, so a generic framework must be able to support an interface that allows different functions to be attached to it, depending on the work needed. There are two ways that our framework will allow the worker function to be defined: through the use of delegates and through the use of virtual functions accessible through inheritance.

Delegates, the equivalent to function pointers in C++, will allow our system to specify the worker function without requiring inheritance. The delegate approach should only be used in throwaway tools where time is more important than maintainability, because delegates generally promote bad design when compared to the alternate OOP approach.

The other way that we will be able to specify the worker functions will be through inheriting from the base framework class. A virtual function will be called when a file is to be processed and the super class can take care of it appropriately.

For example, if you have a tool that has to recursively open all .txt files in a directory and replace occurrences of a certain phrase with another, you would create a class that inherits from the base framework, and override the process method. In this method, you would open the file, read in the text, perform the substitution, and save the new text back to disk. All the code that handles the recursion, file attributes, pattern matching, and other common I/O operations would be left to the framework, loosely coupled from the tool itself.

The properties, events, and methods of the base framework class will be defined in an interface to ensure strong OOP design. This will allow for a modular approach to even the framework engine itself, if more than one engine is ever used.

A delegate will exist for progress notification, so that users will be able to watch the status of the current operation.

The framework will also provide support for handling read-only files. The ability to skip read-only files will be available, as will the ability to remove the read-only attribute from the file before passing the file off to the worker function.

Implementation

Based on the above goals and proposed solution, the following two components make up the batch file processing framework. See Tables 17.1-17.3 for description of Delegate Definitions.

The following interface defines the properties, events, and methods that the framework engine must realize. The code is quite simple, but I will go over the code for the sake of clarity.

Delegate Definitions

Table 17.1 Delegate Definitions

Delegate	Description
FileAccessProcess	This event is fired when the worker function wishes to notify the user about the operation. This delegate is available to the tool regardless of the method chosen to specify the worker function.
FileAccessNotify	This event is fired when the worker function wishes to notify the user about the operation. This delegate is available to the tool regardless of the method chosen to specify the worker function.

Table 17.2 Property Definitions

Property	Description
Recursive	This property is used to specify whether or not directories are traversed in a recursive fashion. If this property is false, then only the top-level directory is actually processed.
SkipReadOnly	This property is used to specify whether or not files that are marked with a read-only attribute should be processed by the worker function.
ForceWriteable	This property is used to specify whether or not files that are marked with a read-only attribute should be made writeable and then processed by the worker function.
FilePattern	This property is used to specify the pattern to match when choosing the files to process in a directory. The default pattern is *.*, which processes every file. If the pattern were set to *.txt, then only text files would be processed.
Cancelled	This property is used to specify whether or not the operation has been cancelled. The worker function can check this property each time it is called to see if cancellation is occurring.

Table 17.3 Method Definitions

Method	Description
Execute	This method is called by the tool when processing should begin using the set options and worker function. The full path to the directory to begin processing with is sent in as a parameter.

Table 17.3 Method Definitions *(continued)*

Method	Description
Cancel	This method is fairly self-explanatory; it cancels all remaining operations that have not yet been started, and it sets the `Cancelled` property so that the worker function knows that it should either stop what it is doing or finish up.
Notify	This method is called by the worker function to fire the `OnNotify` event. As long as the tool has set this delegate to a function, it will fire when a notification is sent.

The following code composes the file access interface that powers the logic behind each batch processing tool. This interface is implemented and customized for each tool.

```
using System;
using System.IO;

namespace BatchFileFramework
{
    public delegate void FileAccessProcess(IFileAccessLogic logic, FileInfo fileInfo);
    public delegate void FileAccessNotify(string message);

    public interface IFileAccessLogic
    {
        bool Recursive
        {
            get;
            set;
        }

        bool SkipReadOnly
        {
            get;
            set;
        }

        bool ForceWriteable
        {
            get;
            set;
        }
```

```
            string FilePattern
            {
                get;
                set;
            }

            bool Cancelled
            {
                get;
                set;
            }

            void Execute(string fullPath);
            void Cancel();
            void Notify(string message);

            event FileAccessProcess OnProcess;
            event FileAccessNotify OnNotify;
        }
    }
```

The following class implements the IFileAccessLogic interface and houses a lot of the common functionality that is present in almost every batch file processing tool.

```
using System;
using System.IO;

namespace BatchFileFramework
{
    public class FileAccessLogic : IFileAccessLogic
    {
        private bool verbose = false;
        private bool recursive = false;
        private bool skipReadOnly = false;
        private bool forceWriteable = false;

        private string filePattern = "*.*";

        private bool cancelled = false;
        private bool running = false;

        public event FileAccessProcess OnProcess = null;
        public event FileAccessNotify OnNotify = null;
```

```csharp
public bool Verbose
{
    get { return verbose; }
    set
    {
        if (!this.running)
            verbose = value;
    }
}

public bool Recursive
{
    get { return recursive; }
    set
    {
        if (!this.running)
            recursive = value;
    }
}

public bool SkipReadOnly
{
    get { return skipReadOnly; }
    set
    {
        if (!this.running)
            skipReadOnly = value;
    }
}

public bool ForceWriteable
{
    get { return forceWriteable; }
    set
    {
        if (!this.running)
            forceWriteable = value;
    }
}

public string FilePattern
{
```

```csharp
        get { return filePattern; }
        set
        {
            if (!this.running)
                filePattern = value;
        }
    }

    public bool Cancelled
    {
        get { return cancelled; }
        set { cancelled = value; }
    }

    public void Execute(string fullPath)
    {
        cancelled = false;
        running = true;

        if (File.Exists(fullPath))
            Process(this, new FileInfo(fullPath));

        else if (Directory.Exists(fullPath))
            ProcessDirectory(fullPath);

        running = false;
    }

    public void Cancel()
    {
        cancelled = true;
    }

    public void Notify(string message)
    {
        if (!verbose)
        {
            if (this.OnNotify != null)
                this.OnNotify(message);
        }
    }
```

```
private void ProcessDirectory(string directoryPath)
{
    ProcessDirectory(new DirectoryInfo(directoryPath));
}

private void ProcessDirectory(DirectoryInfo directoryInfo)
{
    if (cancelled)
        return;

    ProcessFiles(directoryInfo);

    if (recursive)
    {
        foreach (DirectoryInfo subDirectoryInfo in
            directoryInfo.GetDirectories())
            ProcessDirectory(subDirectoryInfo);
    }
}

private void ProcessFiles(DirectoryInfo directoryInfo)
{
  foreach (FileInfo fileInfo in directoryInfo.GetFiles(this.filePattern))
    {
        if (cancelled)
            return;

        FileAttributes attributes = File.GetAttributes(fileInfo.FullName);

        if ((attributes & FileAttributes.ReadOnly) == FileAttributes.ReadOnly)
        {
            if (skipReadOnly)
                continue;

            else if (forceWriteable)
                File.SetAttributes(fileInfo.FullName, FileAttributes.Normal);

            else
                continue;
        }

        Process(this, fileInfo);
```

```
            }
        }

        protected virtual void Process(IFileAccessLogic logic, FileInfo fileInfo)
        {
            if (OnProcess != null)
                OnProcess(this, fileInfo);
        }
    }
}
```

Conclusion

On the Companion Web site are two examples showing a number of features of this framework.

There is a simple listing example that does not perform any file modification, so it is safe to run from the top-level directory of your hard drive for the best performance results. This example shows how to use the delegate approach to specify the worker function.

The other example is a search and replace process that searches for all .txt files in the directory structure and replaces a particular search pattern with another specified word.

Caution

The search and replace example should be used with care so you do not modify the wrong files!

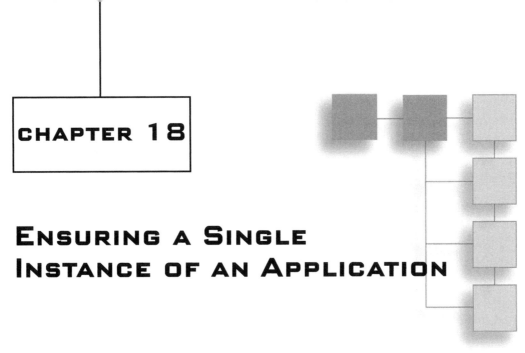

CHAPTER 18

ENSURING A SINGLE INSTANCE OF AN APPLICATION

Never allow the same bug to bite you twice.

Steve Maguire

With most modern operating systems, multiple instances or processes of an application can be launched, each with its own internal state and memory. Some tools are not affected by multiple instances being launched, but other tools are. Imagine a tool that, when launched, creates a network socket and binds it to a specific port through which to receive data. If a second instance of that tool were launched, the initialization would fail because the network port would already be in use. As another example, look at Adobe Photoshop or any other fully featured image editing suite. How frustrating do you think it would be if, every time you double-clicked an image on your desktop, a new instance of Adobe Photoshop would launch? When a file associated with a specific application is launched from Windows Explorer, the file name is not passed to a current running process if there is one. The application that handles the file is determined and a new instance is launched with the file name as a parameter.

A solution to this problem would be a system that could determine whether there are any running instances of a particular application, redirect launch parameters to the running instance, and abort the launching of any additional instances.

This chapter presents a couple of ways to determine whether there is a running instance of the application, pass command line arguments to an existing instance, and bring its main window to the foreground.

Early Solutions

I have used a few strategies in the past to implement single application instances. One method is to create a threading `Mutex` with a unique name that identifies the application set to the full path to the executing assembly. The `Mutex` class can be used to protect a shared resource from simultaneous access by multiple threads and processes. A `Mutex` has two states: signaled or non-signaled. When the state is signaled, the Mutex is not owned by any thread. When the state is non-signaled, that means there is a thread that currently possesses ownership of the `Mutex`. The ownership of a `Mutex` is only available to a single thread, so when two threads try to write to the shared memory at the same time, the first thread to do so acquires ownership, while the second thread waits for ownership to be released.

The first time an application starts up, it will perform a check for a uniquely named `Mutex` to see if there are any other running instances. It will not find any, so the next step will be to create a Mutex with a unique name so that other application instances can see that another instance is already running; the unique name will be the full system path to the executing assembly's location. With the `Mutex` created, we must now call the `WaitOne()` method so that we set the state to non-signaled and grant ownership to the thread of this application. At this point, the application instance can completely load and make itself available to the end user.

All subsequent application instances that start up will perform the same check that the first instance did, except they will fail. Each new instance will create a `Mutex` class using the same name that the first instance used, but all further calls to `WaitOne()` will return false because the ownership is currently bound to the thread of the first instance.

The following code shows a simplified implementation using this approach.

```
using System.Threading;

[STAThread]
static void Main()
{
    Mutex mutex = new Mutex(false, Assembly.GetExecutingAssembly().Location);

    if (!mutex.WaitOne(1, true))
    {
```

```
            MessageBox.Show("There is already an instance of this executable " +
                            "running as a process");
        }
        else
        {
            // Keep the mutex alive until the process terminates
            GC.KeepAlive(mutex);

            Application.Run(new MainForm());
        }
    }
}
```

Another method is to use Windows Management Instrumentation (WMI) to query the operating system for a listing of active processes filtered by name. Some developers may favor this approach to the other solutions, so the following code has been included to show an implementation using WMI. The Companion Web site has the full source code with additional comments.

```
public sealed class ProcessCountManager
{
    public static int Query(string applicationName)
    {
        return QueryRunningProcessCount(applicationName);
    }

    public static int Query(System.Reflection.Assembly assembly)
    {
        // Break the full path to the executing assembly into
        // a string array of parts
        string[] locationParts = assembly.Location.Split("\\".ToCharArray());

        // Retrieve the application name from the last element
        // of the location array
        string applicationName = locationParts[locationParts.Length - 1];

        // Return the running process count for the specified application name
        return QueryRunningProcessCount(applicationName);
    }

    public static bool IsRunning(string applicationName)
    {
        // Add 1 to account for the application doing the check
        return Query(applicationName) > 1;
```

```
    }

    public static bool IsRunning(System.Reflection.Assembly assembly)
    {
        // Add 1 to account for the application doing the check
        return Query(assembly) > 1;
    }

    private static int QueryRunningProcessCount(string applicationName)
    {
        // Build a formatted WMI management query to select all
        // processes matching a specific name
        string query = String.Format("SELECT Name FROM CIM_Process " +
                                     "WHERE Name = '{0}'",
                                     applicationName);

        // Build an enumerator for the management query results
        ManagementObjectSearcher searcher = new ManagementObjectSearcher(query);

        // Return the number of results (process count) in the management query
        return searcher.Get().Count;
    }
}
```

The WMI implementation has a class composed of static methods that can determine the number of running processes filtered by name. The easiest and most maintainable way to use this implementation is to pass the executing assembly object into the manager. This way, if the assembly name changes, you do not have to update the code to reflect these changes. The following code shows the proper usage of the WMI approach.

```
[STAThread]
static void Main()
{
    if (ProcessCountManager.IsRunning(Assembly.GetExecutingAssembly()))
    {
        MessageBox.Show("There is already an instance of this " +
                        "executable running as a process");
    }
    else
        Application.Run(new MainForm());
}
```

Finally, another approach, though a simplified version of the WMI implementation, is to use the `Process` object from the `System.Diagnostics` namespace. While the WMI version is extremely extensible and robust, the following code using the `Process` object is better suited to our needs because it is lightweight.

```
using System.Diagnostics;

[STAThread]
static void Main()
{
    Process process = Process.GetCurrentProcess();

    if (Process.GetProcessesByName(process.ProcessName).Count > 1)
    {
        MessageBox.Show("There is already an instance of this " +
                        "executable running as a process");
    }
    else
        Application.Run(new MainForm());
}
```

So far we have discussed a couple of the earlier ways to implement single instance applications, but with the advent of .NET 2.0, a new integrated approach was provided that takes care of all the ugly details behind the scenes.

Journey to the Dark Side

Every CLR-compliant language for the .NET platform can reproduce identical functionality by sharing a common set of framework components. This is because CLR-compliant languages must support the interoperability with other assemblies that can be written in a variety of managed languages, meaning that an assembly written in Visual Basic .NET must be accessible from within a C# application without any performance overhead related to data conversion or "thunking."

Legacy versions of Visual Basic provided a variety of pre-built components that aided in the development of applications. Visual Basic .NET exposes a similar library of components that are generally accessed through the property pages of the project. One component in particular is the ability to restrict an application so that it may only be launched once, and redirect the command line parameters from subsequent instances to the initial one. Visual Basic .NET has a checkbox in the project properties that enables this functionality, but Visual C# .NET does not provide it at this time.

Upon closer inspection of a single instance VB.NET application with a disassembler, `Microsoft.VisualBasic.dll` is referenced by the runtime. This assembly exposes the `WindowsFormsApplicationBase` class that exists in the `Microsoft.VisualBasic.ApplicationServices` namespace. This class provides a mechanism to restrict an application so that it may only be launched once, and this mechanism supports the redirection of command line parameters to itself. `Microsoft.VisualBasic.dll` is a common framework component, and it is accessible from any managed language because it is merely a library of compiled MSIL byte code.

The `Microsoft.VisualBasic.ApplicationServices.WindowsFormsApplicationBase` class will be used to implement the solution, as presented in the next section.

The Solution

The following namespaces are used by the solution, and the only other namespace below worth mentioning is `System.Collections.ObjectModel`. This namespace provides a generic `ReadOnlyCollection` that wraps a data type into a strongly typed, read-only list.

```
using System;
using System.Windows.Forms;
using System.Collections.ObjectModel;
using Microsoft.VisualBasic.ApplicationServices;
```

The solution in this chapter will require a way to send a notification to the main application instance when another instance attempts to launch. The following class describes the event arguments that will be passed with the notification. It merely stores a reference to the main form of the application and a collection of string parameters that were passed by the command line.

```
internal class SingleInstanceEventArgs : EventArgs
{
    private ReadOnlyCollection<string> commandLine;

    private Form mainForm;

    internal ReadOnlyCollection<string> CommandLine
    {
        get { return commandLine; }
    }

    internal Form MainForm
```

```
    {
        get { return mainForm; }
    }

    internal SingleInstanceEventArgs(ReadOnlyCollection<string> commandLine,
                                     Form mainForm)
    {
        this.commandLine = commandLine;
        this.mainForm = mainForm;
    }
}
```

An important goal of this solution is to transition easily from the standard launching approach for an application to our new single instance version. This goal warranted the design of a static class that exposes a simple Run method, much like the Application class. The Run method takes in a reference to the main form of the application and a delegate to the method that will handle subsequent instance notifications. The WindowsFormsApplicationBase has a StartupNextInstance event that is fired when another instance is launched. This solution handles this event behind the scenes and redirects the event arguments with additional information to the SingleInstanceEvent delegate.

```
internal class SingleInstanceApplication : WindowsFormsApplicationBase
{
    private SingleInstanceApplication()
    {
        base.IsSingleInstance = true;
    }

    private static EventHandler<SingleInstanceEventArgs> SingleInstanceEvent;

    private static SingleInstanceApplication applicationBase;

    internal static void Run(Form form,
                             EventHandler<SingleInstanceEventArgs> handler)
    {
        SingleInstanceEvent += handler;

        applicationBase = new SingleInstanceApplication();
        applicationBase.MainForm = form;
        applicationBase.StartupNextInstance += StartupNextInstanceEventHandler;
        applicationBase.Run(Environment.GetCommandLineArgs());
```

```
    }

    private static void StartupNextInstanceEventHandler(object sender,
                                              StartupNextInstanceEventArgs e)
    {
        if (SingleInstanceEvent != null)
        {
            SingleInstanceEvent(applicationBase,
            new SingleInstanceEventArgs(e.CommandLine, applicationBase.MainForm));
        }
    }
}
```

The following code shows how a WinForms application is generally launched.

```
[STAThread]
static void Main()
{
    // The old way to launch the application
    Application.EnableVisualStyles();
    Application.Run(new MainForm());
}
```

The following code shows the new way a WinForms application will be launched
using the single instance component.

```
[STAThread]
static void Main()
{
    Application.EnableVisualStyles();
    SingleInstanceApplication.Run(new MainForm(), StartupNextInstanceEventHandler);
}
```

You should have noticed the StartupNextInstanceEventHandler. This parameter is a
delegate that will be fired when a subsequent instance is launched, and the main
instance should be notified and given the command line parameters. The following code shows how to implement this delegate, activate the main form of the
application, and pass command line parameters to the form.

```
private static void StartupNextInstanceEventHandler(object sender,
                                              SingleInstanceEventArgs e)
{
    // Restore the window if it is currently minimized
    if (e.MainForm.WindowState == FormWindowState.Minimized)
```

```
    {
        e.MainForm.WindowState = FormWindowState.Normal;
    }

    // Activate the main form
    e.MainForm.Activate();

    ((MainForm)e.MainForm).HandleCommandLine(e.CommandLine);
}
```

The MainForm class is a simple form that has a method called HandleCommandLine. This method takes in a ReadOnlyCollection<string> instance that contains the command line parameters. It is now up to you how to determine how these parameters are handled!

Conclusion

In this chapter I began by discussing the necessity of the singleton pattern for application instances, and then later I detailed a variety of ways to implement such a pattern. Each method is better suited to a different situation, though the best approach when at all possible is to use the ApplicationServices component. This approach offers the least amount of work to implement, and is trivial to maintain.

Perhaps in the future, this functionality will be refactored into a more general component that is "natively" supported by Visual C# .NET, but at the moment, it seems to be the best way to handle single application instances with the least amount of code and effort to maintain it.

Aside from the ApplicationServices component, the other approaches did not show how to pass command line parameters to the initial instance. This can be done using .NET Remoting, a TCP\IP loopback channel, or even the WM_COPYDATA event and the Win32 message pump. This functionality is beyond the scope of this chapter, but is covered in Parts IV and V of this book.

The Companion Web site contains the full source code and examples to the solutions presented in this chapter.

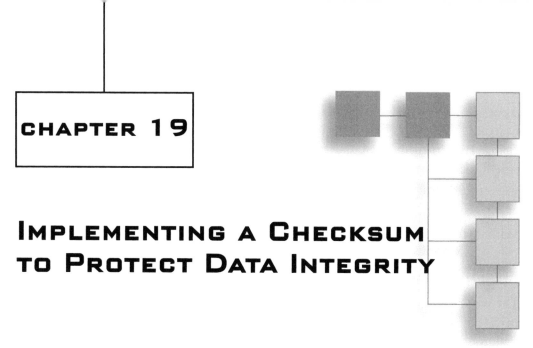

CHAPTER 19

IMPLEMENTING A CHECKSUM TO PROTECT DATA INTEGRITY

Where is the information?

Lost in data.

Where is the data?

Lost in the #@%!& database!

Joe Celko

Nearly all software applications handle the manipulation of data through a transmission medium. A transmission medium could be the registry, memory, disk files, or a database, to name a few. Each medium handles and stores data in a different way, but every transmission medium is unreliable and has the potential to fail. It is for this reason that the CRC-32 (Cyclic Redundancy Check) algorithm came to be, which is used to verify that there has been no corruption or errors in a data transmission. This algorithm is given arbitrary data of arbitrary length, and computes a 32-bit checksum number representing the contents of the supplied data, which is transmitted along with the data through the transmission medium that is used. Once the data arrives at its destination, a new checksum is recalculated on the data that was received, and it is compared to the checksum calculated before the transmission. If the values match, the transmission most likely was successful, but if the values do not match, you know that the transmission encountered an error of some sort and the data received is incomplete, modified, or corrupted.

This algorithm has also been used to detect any tampering done to data files for games (or any software application for that matter). Checksum values are typically created for all files before a game ships; those pre-calculated values are checked against the runtime calculated version when the game launches and detect whether data has been modified from its original state.

This chapter covers an implementation of the CRC-32 checksum algorithm in C# and later goes on to show an alternative algorithm provided by Microsoft. The mathematical proofs and reasoning behind this algorithm will not be covered.

Implementation

The implementation for the CRC-32 algorithm is fairly straightforward and exists in a few flavors. The implementation provided in this chapter precalculates a lookup table using a specified polynomial value, and the calculation is based on the algebra of polynomials over the values (mod 2) using the cached lookup table.

The code is as follows:

```csharp
public class Crc32
{
    private static uint[] _lookupTable;

    public uint Calculate(System.IO.Stream stream)
    {
        unchecked
        {
            uint result = 0xFFFFFFFF;

            byte[] buffer = new byte[1024];

            int byteCount = stream.Read(buffer, 0, 1024);

            while (byteCount > 0)
            {
                for (int byteIndex = 0; byteIndex < byteCount; byteIndex++)
                {
                    result = ((result) >> 8) ^
                    _lookupTable[(buffer[byteIndex]) ^
                    ((result) & 0x000000FF)];
                }
```

```
                byteCount = stream.Read(buffer, 0, 1024);
            }

            return ~result;
        }
    }

    public uint Calculate(byte[] buffer)
    {
        unchecked
        {
            uint result = 0xFFFFFFFF;

            for (int byteIndex = 0; byteIndex < buffer.Length; byteIndex++)
            {
                result = ((result) >> 8) ^
                _lookupTable[(buffer[byteIndex]) ^
                ((result) & 0x000000FF)];
            }

            return ~result;
        }
    }

    // This static constructor pregenerates the lookup table that our crc32
    // algorithm will use to compute more efficiently.
    static Crc32()
    {
        unchecked
        {
            uint polynomial = 0xADB11320;
            uint iterationIndex;
            uint bitIndex;
            uint crc32Value;

            _lookupTable = new uint[256];

            for (iterationIndex = 0; iterationIndex < 256; iterationIndex++)
            {
                crc32Value = iterationIndex;

                for (bitIndex = 8; bitIndex > 0; bitIndex--)
                {
```

```
                if ((crc32Value & 1) == 1)
                {
                    crc32Value = (crc32Value >> 1) ^ polynomial;
                }
                else
                {
                    crc32Value >>= 1;
                }
            }
            _lookupTable[iterationIndex] = crc32Value;
        }
    }
}
```

You will notice the _lookupTable array variable and the static constructor; the implementation precalculates the checksum values using the provided polynomial and stores them in a lookup table to improve and speed up calculation performance.

After instantiation and the precalculation of the lookup table, you can call either signature for the Calculate method. One version accepts a byte array containing the data to generate the checksum for, and the other version accepts a System.IO.Stream instead.

Usage

Using the functionality defined in the implementation class is fairly straightforward. The class will calculate the internal lookup table the first time you instantiate it, and all you have to worry about is calling the Calculate() method. The Calculate method is overloaded to accept either a byte array or a System.IO.Stream object.

The following code shows the proper way to use this class with a byte array:

```
byte[] data = new byte[DATA_SIZE];
Crc32 crc = new Crc32();
byte[] result = crc.Calculate(data);
```

The following code shows the proper way to use this class with a System.IO.Stream:

```
byte[] data = new byte[DATA_SIZE];
using (System.IO.MemoryStream stream = new System.IO.MemoryStream(data))
{
```

```
    Crc32 crc = new Crc32();
    byte[] result = crc.Calculate(stream);
}
```

Using the data "This is a test" will result in a 32-bit checksum value of 2042881507.

The result will be a 32-bit (4-octet) checksum of the data that was provided to the CRC-32 algorithm, and will subsequently be compared against a future checksum calculation.

Alternative

There is one potential problem with the CRC-32 Checksum algorithm in regards to malicious security attacks. Generally, these issues are not important for verification of simple data integrity, but it may be advisable to seek an alternative algorithm in environments where security is a concern; verifying the integrity of packets in a multiplayer environment, for example.

The problem with the CRC-32 (Cyclic Redundancy Checksum) algorithm is that it is not *collision-proof,* meaning that it is possible to generate two checksum values that are identical. This is not an extremely common occurrence, but it introduces enough exploitability that a malicious plain-text attack could be used to spoof an integrity check. The probability that two different blocks of data will have the same checksum value in an N-bit checksum is $1/2^N$. The larger the value represented by N, the lower the probability that two different blocks of data will have the same checksum value. So the probability that our CRC-32 implementation will generate an identical checksum for two different blocks of data is $1/2^{32}$, a percentage that is reasonable enough for most situations.

As an alternative, you can utilize the built-in MD5 algorithm from the System.Security.Cryptography namespace. This algorithm is known so far to be collision-proof, and may be used in place of CRC-32 for better security and credibility with a bit of increased overhead.

Implementing the built-in functionality from Microsoft is very easy. Reference the System.Security.Cryptography namespace and use the following code:

```
byte[] data = new byte[DATA_SIZE];
MD5 md5 = new MD5CryptoServiceProvider();
byte[] result = md5.ComputeHash(data);
```

The result will be a 128-bit (16-octet) checksum hash of the data that was provided to the MD5 algorithm, and will subsequently be compared against a future checksum calculation.

Conclusion

This chapter covered two ways of generating a checksum value that can be used to verify data integrity. Each method has different pros and cons, which can be evaluated on a per-project basis. The CRC-32 algorithm can be used in situations where you are basically testing for data corruption, and also in situations where speed is important. The MD5 algorithm has some added overhead, but its usage offers more credible and relatively secure checksums.

Regardless of the algorithm you choose to implement, verifying data integrity using checksums is a popular and low overhead way to ensure that you are always processing complete and unmodified data. Reliability of tools is very important, and using checksums offers a quick way to verify that the data that users are creating is valid, rather than finding out after the application throws an error when it tries to process the data at a later stage.

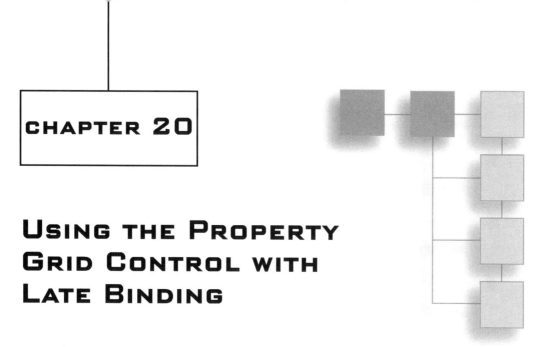

CHAPTER 20

USING THE PROPERTY GRID CONTROL WITH LATE BINDING

The only way to discover the limits of the possible is to go beyond them into the impossible.

Arthur C. Clarke

With the advent of the Microsoft .NET platform, development time has been decreased significantly because of many improvements to workflow and the technologies we use. Perhaps one of the most exciting introductions is the idea behind extensible metadata and reflection, which can be used to interrogate class properties, methods, and attributes.

Many tools and utilities have a need to work with class objects and also provide a way to modify the properties of a class. Traditionally, a dialog would have been built that contained controls which, when modified, would find the currently selected class and alter the appropriate property; building this dialog is often a very time-consuming and tedious task. If you work with Visual Studio .NET, you will have interacted with the `PropertyGrid` control, which displays information about a selected user interface element. Figure 20.1 shows the `PropertyGrid` control in action within Visual Studio .NET.

Figure 20.1 Screenshot of a PropertyGrid in the Visual Studio .NET IDE.

A PropertyGrid can be bound to any managed object and programmatically build a user interface that can modify the public properties of the object with hardly any work! In this chapter, I will show you how to create a class with bindable properties, and then show you how to bind an instance of this class to a PropertyGrid control. There is too much information on the PropertyGrid to be covered in a short chapter, but the core functionality should be summarized enough to be applicable to the majority of tools and utilities.

Designing a Bindable Class

There really is no configuration that has to happen on the PropertyGrid control, because all the configuration information is specified in the classes that are bound to the PropertyGrid. The PropertyGrid control interrogates bound classes to find certain attributes of properties that describe things, such as what category they are in, the description of the property, and what the default value is. You can also hide properties from being shown in the PropertyGrid with an attribute as well.

The [DefaultPropertyAttribute] specifies the name of the property that will act as the default property for the PropertyGrid. [CategoryAttribute] specifies the name of the category that the property is located in. Categories are automatically created based on these names. The [DescriptionAttribute] specifies the description text that appears at the bottom of the PropertyGrid when a property is selected. The TypeConverter and PropertyOrder attributes will be covered in the next section. You can create read-only properties simply by providing a get construct. You can also hide properties from showing up in the PropertyGrid by using a [Browsable(false)] attribute.

The following code shows an example of a bindable class that can be visualized and modified using the PropertyGrid control. Notice the attributes that are used to specify names, descriptions, and ordering for the visualized properties.

```
public enum Gender
{
    Male,
    Female,
    Unspecified
}

public enum Position
{
    Programmer,
    Tester,
    Director,
    Architect,
    Analyst,
    Unspecified
}

[TypeConverter(typeof(PropertyOrderConverter)),
DefaultPropertyAttribute("FirstName")]
public class PersonnelRecord
{
    // Contact Information
    private string firstName;
    private string lastName;
    private string phoneNumber;
    private string email;

    // Biological Information
    private DateTime birthDate;
```

```csharp
private int age;
private Color hairColor;
private Color eyeColor;
private Gender gender;

// Employee Information
private int employeeId;
private Position position;
private bool probationary;

public PersonnelRecord()
{
    firstName = String.Empty;
    lastName = String.Empty;
    phoneNumber = String.Empty;
    email = String.Empty;

    birthDate = new DateTime();
    age = 0;
    gender = Gender.Unspecified;

    employeeId = 0;
    position = Position.Unspecified;
    probationary = true;
}

[CategoryAttribute("Contact Information"),
DescriptionAttribute("First name of the employee."),
PropertyOrder(0)]
public string FirstName
{
    get { return firstName; }
    set { firstName = value; }
}

[CategoryAttribute("Contact Information"),
DescriptionAttribute("Last name of the employee."),
PropertyOrder(1)]
public string LastName
{
    get { return lastName; }
    set { lastName = value; }
}
```

```
[CategoryAttribute("Contact Information"),
DescriptionAttribute("Phone number of the employee. (###-###-####)"),
PropertyOrder(2)]
public string PhoneNumber
{
    get { return phoneNumber; }
    set { phoneNumber = value; }
}


[CategoryAttribute("Contact Information"),
DescriptionAttribute("Email of the employee. Format: *@*.*"),
PropertyOrder(3)]
public string Email
{
    get { return email; }
    set { email = value; }
}


[CategoryAttribute("Biological Information"),
DescriptionAttribute("Birth date of the employee."),
PropertyOrder(0)]
public DateTime BirthDate
{
    get { return birthDate; }
    set
    {
        birthDate = value;
        age = DateTime.Now.Year - birthDate.Year;
    }
}


[CategoryAttribute("Biological Information"),
DescriptionAttribute("Age of the employee."),
PropertyOrder(1)]
public int Age
{
    get { return age; }
}


[CategoryAttribute("Biological Information"),
DescriptionAttribute("Hair color of the employee. (Optional)"),
```

```csharp
    PropertyOrder(2)]
    public System.Drawing.Color HairColor
    {
        get { return hairColor; }
        set { hairColor = value; }
    }


    [CategoryAttribute("Biological Information"),
    DescriptionAttribute("Eye color of the employee. (Optional)"),
    PropertyOrder(3)]
    public System.Drawing.Color EyeColor
    {
        get { return eyeColor; }
        set { eyeColor = value; }
    }


    [CategoryAttribute("Biological Information"),
    DescriptionAttribute("Gender of the employee. (Optional)"),
    PropertyOrder(4)]
    public Gender Gender
    {
        get { return gender; }
        set { gender = value; }
    }


    [CategoryAttribute("Employee Information"),
    DescriptionAttribute("Id of the employee as referenced by the HR database."),
    PropertyOrder(0)]
    public int EmployeeId
    {
        get { return employeeId; }
        set { employeeId = value; }
    }


    [CategoryAttribute("Employee Information"),
    DescriptionAttribute("Position of the employee within the organization."),
    PropertyOrder(1)]
    public Position Position
    {
        get { return position; }
        set { position = value; }
    }
```

```
    [CategoryAttribute("Employee Information"),
    DescriptionAttribute("True or false value indicating a probationary period."),
    PropertyOrder(2)]
    public bool Probationary
    {
        get { return probationary; }
        set { probationary = value; }
    }
}
```

Ordering Properties

Strangely enough, there is no attribute that handles the ordering of properties in the PropertyGrid. There is, however, a way we can make our own attribute and custom type converter that can accomplish this for us. First, we will define an attribute that we can use to specify the sort order for properties in a class.

```
[AttributeUsage(AttributeTargets.Property)]
public class PropertyOrderAttribute : Attribute
{
    private int order;

    public PropertyOrderAttribute(int order)
    {
        this.order = order;
    }

    public int Order
    {
        get { return order; }
    }
}
```

The following code describes a custom type converter class that interrogates the PropertyOrder attribute in class properties, sorts the property list based on the values, and returns a descriptor list that can tell the PropertyGrid the order to display the properties in.

```
public class PropertyOrderConverter : ExpandableObjectConverter
{
    internal class SortablePair : IComparable<SortablePair>
    {
        private int order;
```

```csharp
        private string name;

        public string Name
        {
            get { return name; }
        }

        public SortablePair(string name, int order)
        {
            this.order = order;
            this.name = name;
        }

        public int CompareTo(SortablePair pair)
        {
            int result;

            if (pair.order == order)
            {
                result = string.Compare(name, pair.name);
            }
            else if (pair.order > order)
            {
                result = -1;
            }
            else
            {
                result = 1;
            }

            return result;
        }
    }

    public override bool GetPropertiesSupported(ITypeDescriptorContext context)
    {
        return true;
    }

    public override PropertyDescriptorCollection GetProperties(ITypeDescriptorContext cx,
                                                        object component,
                                                        Attribute[] attrib)
```

```
        {
            List<SortablePair> propertyList = new List<SortablePair>();

            PropertyDescriptorCollection descList = TypeDescriptor.GetProperties(component,
                                                                          attrib);

            foreach (PropertyDescriptor descriptor in descList)
            {
                    Attribute attribute
                    = descriptor.Attributes[typeof(PropertyOrderAttribute)];

            if (attribute != null)
            {
            PropertyOrderAttribute orderAttribute = (PropertyOrderAttribute)attribute;
                        propertyList.Add(new SortablePair(descriptor.Name,
                                                        orderAttribute.Order));
                }
                else
                {
                    propertyList.Add(new SortablePair(descriptor.Name, 0));
                }
            }

            propertyList.Sort();

            List<String> propertyNames = new List<String>();

            foreach (SortablePair sortablePair in propertyList)
            {
                propertyNames.Add(sortablePair.Name);
            }

            return descriptorList.Sort(propertyNames.ToArray());
        }
    }
```

Using the type converter class is fairly easy. Just decorate your class declaration with the attribute, as shown in the following code. Then decorate your properties with a PropertyOrder attribute to specify the sort order.

```
[TypeConverter(typeof(PropertyOrderConverter))]
public class PersonnelRecord
{
    // …
}
```

NOTE

I did have a workaround for category ordering in Microsoft .NET 1.1, but this workaround had unde-sired results when used with .NET 2.0. At this point in time, I have not figured out a way to do this.

Using the PropertyGrid

With a bindable class created and a custom TypeConverter created to handle prop-erty ordering, using the PropertyGrid control is super easy. All you need to do is drag the PropertyGrid control from the Visual Studio .NET toolbox onto your form. The only other thing you need to do now is set the SelectedObject property of the PropertyGrid, to an instance of our bindable class PersonnelRecord.

Figure 20.2 shows the PropertyGrid control item in the Visual Studio .NET toolbox.

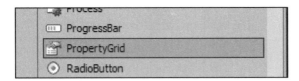

Figure 20.2
Screenshot of the PropertyGrid control item in the Visual Studio .NET toolbox.

The following code snippet shows the load event for the main form in the accom-panying example. Notice how easy it is to instantiate our PersonnelRecord, set some initial values, and then bind it to the PropertyGrid.

```
private void MainForm_Load(object sender, EventArgs e)
{
    PersonnelRecord record = new PersonnelRecord();

    record.FirstName    = "John";
    record.LastName     = "Smith";
    record.PhoneNumber  = "555-123-4567";
    record.Email        = "john.smith@company.com";

    record.BirthDate    = Convert.ToDateTime("1980-04-10");
    record.HairColor    = Color.Brown;
    record.EyeColor     = Color.Blue;
    record.Gender       = Gender.Male;
```

```
    record.EmployeeId   = 12345;
    record.Position     = Position.Programmer;
    record.Probationary = false;

    PropertyGridEditor.SelectedObject = record;
}
```

Running the code snippet that instantiates a PersonnelRecord with initial values and binds it to the PropertyGrid will produce results similar to those shown in Figure 20.3.

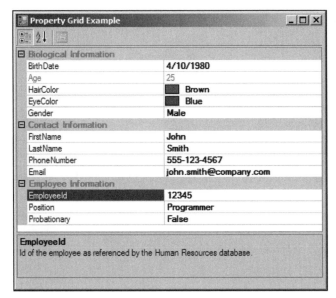

Figure 20.3
Screenshot of the accompanying PropertyGrid example.

The Companion Web site contains the full source code to the bindable class, PropertyOrder type converter, and example usage.

Conclusion

This chapter discussed the implementation details around the PropertyGrid control in the .NET framework. As mentioned before, the bulk of the implementation lies in attribute decoration in the bindable class, since all you need do to use the PropertyGrid is instantiate a PropertyGrid control and set the SelectedObject property to your class instance.

It should be noted that in this chapter I covered a large chunk of the implementation details, but there was no coverage of localization of properties or the development of custom type editors. Both subjects require a fair amount of explanation and code. Feel free to visit MSDN to investigate these features.

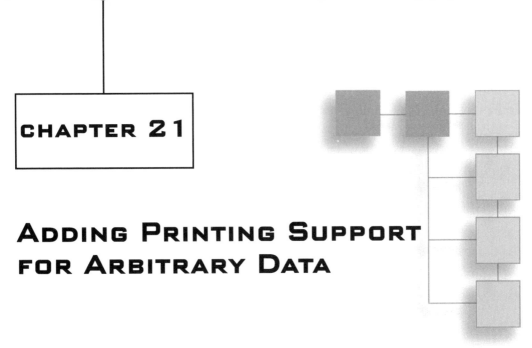

CHAPTER 21

ADDING PRINTING SUPPORT FOR ARBITRARY DATA

The boldness of asking deep questions may require unforeseen flexibility if we are to accept the answers.

Brian Greene

One of the more common and important tasks in a Windows application is the ability to print text or graphics. Printing was somewhat tricky to implement in the days prior to .NET, but now there is a versatile framework to support it within the System.Drawing.Printing namespace. The majority of the print mechanism is within the PrintDocument class, which represents a component that sends output to a printer. This class is very modular, so it allows you to implement either simple or complex printing logic and execute it using this class alone. Other classes exist to support printer configuration and page setup properties such as orientation. This chapter is all about using the managed mechanisms within the .NET Class Framework to implement printing support within applications. You should have a basic familiarity with the Graphics class within the System.Drawing namespace.

Printing Regular Text

The first thing that we must implement is the actual printing logic, which is done by linking into events on PrintDocument. There is a method on PrintDocument called Print() which, you guessed it, prints the document. When this method is called, a BeginPrint event is fired, followed by a PrintPage event for each page, and finally

stopping with an EndPrint event. You do not really have to do much with the begin
and end events; the core logic exists in the PrintPage event. This event is passed a
PrintPageEventArgs parameter that contains a property called HasMorePages. If this
property is set to true, a new page is created and the PrintPage event is raised again
when the event handler returns.

The pseudologic for the PrintPage event handler is basically: Print the page content
using the page setting information provided, using the Graphics context provided.
Determine if more pages are needed to completely print all the content for the
document. If yes, set HasMorePages to true; otherwise set it to false.

The following code shows how to instantiate a PrintDocument, wire up to the
PrintPage event handler, and start printing.

```
PrintDocument printDocument = new PrintDocument();
printDocument.PrintPage += new PrintPageEventHandler(printDocument_PrintPage);
printDocument.Print();
```

The following code describes the simplest implementation of the PrintPage event
handler, assuming that no additional pages are needed.

```
private void printDocument_PrintPage(Object sender, PrintPageEventArgs e)
{
    string outputText = "Game Engine Toolset Development rocks!";
    Font printFont = new Font("Verdana",
                             9.75F,
                             FontStyle.Regular,
                             GraphicsUnit.Point,
                             ((byte)(0)));

    e.Graphics.DrawString(outputText,
                         printFont,
                         Brushes.Black,
                         0,
                         0);
}
```

Complex printing logic that you wish to reuse across multiple places requires that
you inherit from PrintDocument, handling the PrintPage event by overriding the
OnPrintPage method instead of using the event handler. The following code shows
a sample implementation of a PrintDocument that correctly handles text printing
that spans multiple pages with varying font and page settings.

```
public class SimplePrintDocument : PrintDocument
{
    private StringReader inputStream = null;
    private string bufferOverflow = null;
    private Font printFont = null;

    public SimplePrintDocument(StringReader inputStream, Font printFont)
        : base()
    {
        this.inputStream = inputStream;
        this.printFont = printFont;
    }

    protected override void OnBeginPrint(PrintEventArgs e)
    {
        base.OnBeginPrint(e);
        bufferOverflow = null;
    }

    protected override void OnPrintPage(PrintPageEventArgs e)
    {
        base.OnPrintPage(e);

        // Figure out how many lines can fit within the page boundaries
        float linesPerPage = e.MarginBounds.Height /
                            printFont.GetHeight(e.Graphics);

        int lineCount = 0;

        // Deal with any remaining overflow lines from a previous page first
        while (lineCount < linesPerPage && bufferOverflow != null)
        {
            float positionY = e.MarginBounds.Top +
                            (lineCount * printFont.GetHeight(e.Graphics));
            lineCount += PrintLine(e, bufferOverflow, positionY);
        }

        // Now handle the current line buffer
        string line = null;
        while (lineCount < linesPerPage &&
                ((line = inputStream.ReadLine()) != null))
        {
```

```
                float positionY = e.MarginBounds.Top +
                                    (lineCount * printFont.GetHeight(e.Graphics));
                lineCount += PrintLine(e, line, positionY);
            }


            // Print a new page if there are more lines to print
            if (line != null)
                e.HasMorePages = true;
            else
                e.HasMorePages = false;
        }


        private int PrintLine(PrintPageEventArgs e, string text, float positionY)
        {
            RectangleF rectangle = new RectangleF(e.PageSettings.Margins.Left,
                                        positionY,
                                        e.MarginBounds.Width,
                                        e.MarginBounds.Height);

            int lines;
            int characters;

            StringFormat format = new StringFormat();

            e.Graphics.MeasureString(text,
                                printFont,
                                rectangle.Size,
                                format,
                                out characters,
                                out lines);

            // Total text will not fit on page; bump to overflow buffer for next page
            if (characters < text.Length)
            {
                bufferOverflow = text.Substring(characters);
            }
            else
            {
                bufferOverflow = null;
            }
```

```
e.Graphics.DrawString(text,
                        printFont,
                        Brushes.Black,
                        rectangle,
                        format);

    // Handle empty lines
    lines = lines == 0 ? 1 : lines;
    return lines;
  }
}
```

Using the new `SimplePrintDocument` class is easy; instantiate it as you did with `PrintDocument` and call the `Print()` method!

Supporting Printer Selection

We currently have the logic for printing support implemented, so the next logical step is to provide the ability to select a printer using the standard Windows Print dialog. Right now, you are simply calling the print method on the document, but in a real world application, you let the user select the printer she wants to use and also support the ability to cancel printing. Using the `PrintDialog` class, we can provide this functionality to users. Attach the print document to the `Document` property of the dialog and show the dialog as normal. If the dialog returns successfully, call the print method of the document. The following code shows a sample implementation of printer selection.

```
private void PrintButton_Click(object sender, EventArgs e)
{
    using (StringReader inputText = new StringReader(PrintTextField.Text))
    {
        SimplePrintDocument printDocument = new SimplePrintDocument(inputText,
                                                                    printFont);

        PrintDialog printDialog = new PrintDialog();
        printDialog.Document = printDocument;

        if (printDialog.ShowDialog() == DialogResult.OK)
            printDocument.Print();
    }
}
```

Figure 21.1 shows the printer selection dialog in action.

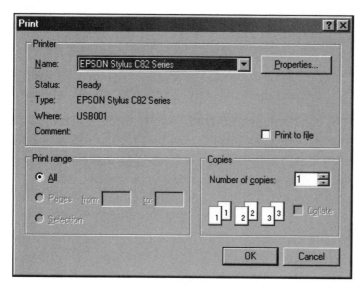

Figure 21.1 Printer selection dialog in action.

Supporting Page Setup

Another common print feature provided by real-world applications is the ability to choose page settings like the orientation of the paper or the margin sizes. This can be done with the PageSetupDialog class and a stored instance of the PageSettings class, as shown with the following code.

```
private void PageSetupButton_Click(object sender, EventArgs e)
{
    PageSetupDialog pageSetupDialog = new PageSetupDialog();

    if (cachedSettings == null)
        cachedSettings = new PageSettings();

    pageSetupDialog.PageSettings = cachedSettings;
    pageSetupDialog.ShowDialog();
}
```

You can now alter the printing logic to set the page settings to our cached instance, as shown with the following code.

```
private void PrintButton_Click(object sender, EventArgs e)
{
    using (StringReader inputText = new StringReader(PrintTextField.Text))
    {
```

```
            SimplePrintDocument printDocument = new SimplePrintDocument(inputText,
                                                                        printFont);

            if (cachedSettings != null)
                printDocument.DefaultPageSettings = cachedSettings;

            PrintDialog printDialog = new PrintDialog();
            printDialog.Document = printDocument;

            if (printDialog.ShowDialog() == DialogResult.OK)
                printDocument.Print();
        }
    }
```

Figure 21.2 shows the Page Setup dialog in action.

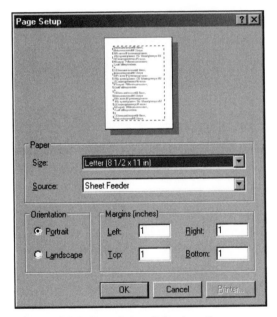

Figure 21.2 Page Setup dialog in action.

Supporting Print Preview

The last common print feature is the ability to preview a document before actually printing it. This is done with the PrintPreviewDialog class. Simply attach your print document to the Document property of the dialog and show the dialog as usual. The following code shows how to do this.

```csharp
private void PrintPreviewButton_Click(object sender, EventArgs e)
{
    using (StringReader inputText = new StringReader(PrintTextField.Text))
    {
        SimplePrintDocument printDocument = new SimplePrintDocument(inputText,
                                                                    printFont);

        if (cachedSettings != null)
            printDocument.DefaultPageSettings = cachedSettings;

        PrintPreviewDialog printPreviewDialog = new PrintPreviewDialog();
        printPreviewDialog.Document = printDocument;
        printPreviewDialog.ShowDialog();
    }
}
```

Figure 21.3 shows the print preview dialog in action.

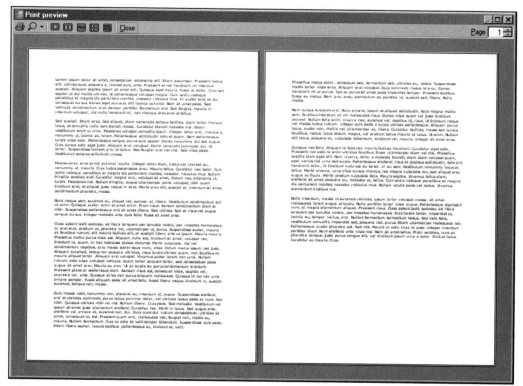

Figure 21.3 Print preview dialog in action.

Conclusion

This chapter covered the full implementation of a `PrintDocument` class that can print arbitrary text with varying fonts and page settings. The user can select which printer to use and can modify page properties before printing. In addition to configuration, the user can also bring up a print preview dialog that shows the document as it would print out before actually committing himself to a print job.

Although this chapter did not cover printing graphics, remember that the `PrintPage` event handler is passed a `Graphics` context that functions like any other context. You can call methods like `FillRectangle()` or `DrawEllipse()` on it and achieve the desired effect. It is a little trickier when you start introducing graphics, because you need to implement some form of flow layout to determine the lines per page and how you position your content when printing.

The Companion Web site contains the full source code from this chapter, along with an example utilizing the custom print logic. Figure 21.4 shows the interface of the example, which is simply a front-end to the code discussed throughout this chapter.

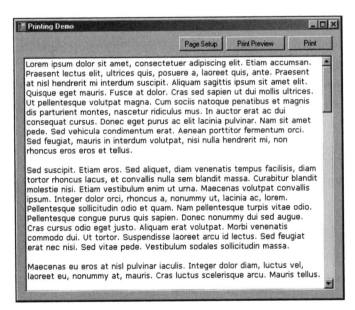

Figure 21.4 Screenshot of the Companion Web site example.

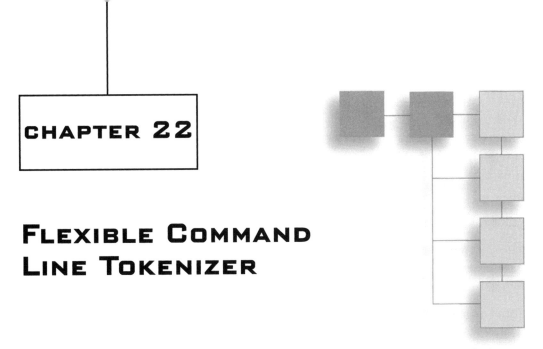

CHAPTER 22

FLEXIBLE COMMAND LINE TOKENIZER

Always design a thing by considering it in its next larger context—a chair in a room, a room in a house, a house in an environment, an environment in a city plan.

Eliel Saarinen—"Time," July 2, 1956

Command line utilities have always been a favorite among tools developers, generally because of how quick they are to make. Command line utilities do not require that code and time be spent on a graphical user interface, which dramatically reduces development time. These tools can also have complex configuration options that are hidden from the user unless explicitly specified, making the tool easier to learn and operate. The one disadvantage that command line utilities have is that they must parse the command line parameters and act on them accordingly. This can be quite a nuisance, especially when the only input validation is done by the user before the parameters are parsed by the utility. It can be difficult to correctly parse a parameter string, including fault tolerance for data input errors.

A tokenizer is code that extracts tokens (substrings) from a given string. The tokens in the string can be separated by one or more character delimiters. This chapter discusses a reusable and flexible command line tokenizer that can break an arbitrary parameter string into name-value pairs.

Formatting Styles

When parsing command line parameters, developers generally come up with unique ways to express parameter syntax. This has led to some confusion about consistency and has brought forth the emergence of a number of formatting styles from the UNIX and Windows worlds.

In order to build a tokenizer that favors a variety of standards, a number of formatting styles have been merged into a common syntax for parsing.

The tokenizer syntax supports three styles of prefixes to signify a parameter. A parameter can be prefixed with a forward slash (/), a hyphen (-), or a double hypen (–).

Some examples include:

```
/name
```

```
-value
```

```
–screenMode
```

Parameters typically have values associated with them, but if they do not then `true` is used as a default value just to show that a particular parameter was specified. Parameter values come after the parameter token and can be prefixed with a space ( ), an equals sign (=), or a colon (:).

Some examples include:

```
/name Graham
```

```
-value=54
```

```
–screenMode:normal
```

Parameter values can also be surrounded by either single or double quotes to preserve white space.

```
/name "Graham Wihlidal"
```

```
–screenMode = 'normal'
```

Visualizing a generic syntax expression for the above styles results in the following:

```
{-,/,–}param{ ,=,:}(('",')value('",'))
```

Using the above syntax expression will allow us to parse a variety of formatting styles.

Implementation

The real magic behind this tokenizer is from the regular expression capabilities of .NET. There were a couple versions of this source code before regular expressions were used, and this version is by far the shortest in length and the most maintainable.

```
using System;
using System.Collections.Generic;
using System.Text.RegularExpressions;

namespace ConsoleTokenizerLibrary
{
    public sealed class ConsoleTokenizer
    {
        private readonly Dictionary<string, string> _parameters
                                        = new Dictionary<string, string>();

        private readonly List<string> _files = new List<string>();

        public Dictionary<string, string> Parameters
        {
            get { return _parameters; }
        }

        public List<string> Files
        {
            get { return _files; }
        }
```

A C# indexer operator has been provided to pull tokens from the parameter list. This is merely an alternate way of obtaining these tokens with shorter code. Files must still be accessed normally through the property.

```
        public string this[string token]
        {
            get { return _parameters[token]; }
        }
```

This constructor takes a single string and breaks it into an array of arguments using a regular expression. The arguments array is then passed into the Tokenize() method.

```csharp
public ConsoleTokenizer(string arguments)
{
    Regex tokenizer = new Regex(@"(['""][^""]+['""])\s*|([^\s]+)\s*",
                                RegexOptions.IgnoreCase |
                                RegexOptions.Compiled);

    MatchCollection matches = tokenizer.Matches(arguments);

    List<string> tokenizedList = new List<string>();

    for (int matchIndex = 1;
            matchIndex < matches.Count - 1;
            matchIndex++)
    {
        tokenizedList.Add(matches[matchIndex].Value);
    }

    Tokenize(tokenizedList.ToArray());
}
```

This constructor simply calls the `Tokenize` method with an array of arguments.

```csharp
public ConsoleTokenizer(string[] arguments)
{
    Tokenize(arguments);
}
```

The following method is the heart of the tokenizer. It uses a regular expression to break up a group of arguments into name-value pairs based on the formatting styles described earlier.

```csharp
private void Tokenize(string[] arguments)
{
    string pattern = @"^([/-]|-){1}(?<name>\w+)([:=])?(?<value>.+)?$";
    Regex tokenizer = new Regex(pattern,
                                RegexOptions.IgnoreCase |
                                RegexOptions.Compiled);

    char[] trimCharacters = { '"', '\'' };

    string currentToken = null;

    foreach (string argument in arguments)
    {
        Match match = tokenizer.Match(argument);
```

```
        if (!match.Success)
        {
```

Check if a parameter has already been determined and that the current character selection is its value.

```
            if (currentToken != null)
            {
                _parameters[currentToken] = argument.Trim(trimCharacters);
            }
```

If an argument was specified that is not in the form of a parameter, then it is most likely a file to process, so here we add the argument to the files collection.

```
            else
            {
                _files.Add(argument);
            }
        }
        else
        {
            currentToken = match.Groups["name"].Value;

            string tokenValue =
            match.Groups["value"].Value.Trim(trimCharacters);
```

If no value was found, specify true as the default parameter value. Having a default value of true basically means that a flag or switch was specified (on or off value).

```
            if (tokenValue.Length == 0)
            {
                _parameters[currentToken] = "true";
            }
```

If a value was determined, associate the string dictionary key with it.

```
            else
            {
                _parameters[currentToken] = tokenValue;
            }
        }
    }
}
}
```

Sample Usage

Using the command line tokenizer is very simple. Console applications have a string array that is passed into the main entry point, and this string array contains the command line parameters specified at the command prompt. Instantiate a new instance of the `ConsoleTokenizer` class and pass this string array into it. At this point everything has been parsed, and you can either access the `Parameters` or `Files` property of the tokenizer instance. `Parameters` is a string dictionary that uses the parameter name as a key, and then points to the associated value. Here is an example of how to get the parameter value for a parameter named mode.

```
static void Main(string[] args)
{
    ConsoleTokenizer tokenizer = new ConsoleTokenizer(args);

    string mode = tokenizer.Parameters["mode"];
}
```

Alternatively, the `indexer` operator has been overloaded to reference the `Parameters` dictionary as well, making your code even cleaner.

```
static void Main(string[] args)
{
    ConsoleTokenizer tokenizer = new ConsoleTokenizer(args);
    string mode = tokenizer["mode"];
}
```

There may be some optional parameters that you want to use if they are present. If you access the `Parameters` string dictionary using a key that does not exist, you will be returned `null`. This is to signify that no such parameter was found. Every parameter should be tested for `null` to prevent null reference exceptions. This is also how you would enforce required parameters.

```
static void Main(string[] args)
{
    ConsoleTokenizer tokenizer = new ConsoleTokenizer(args);

    string mode = string.Empty;
    if (tokenizer["mode"] != null)
    {
        mode = tokenizer["mode"];
    }
}
```

The following code shows a complete console application example that uses the ConsoleTokenizer to parse command line arguments, and then dumps the values to the console window.

```
using System;
using System.Collections.Generic;
using System.Text;

using ConsoleTokenizerLibrary;

namespace ConsoleTokenizerDemo
{
    class Program
    {
        static void Main(string[] args)
        {
            ConsoleTokenizer tokenizer = new ConsoleTokenizer(args);

            Console.WriteLine("");
            Console.WriteLine("Console Tokenizer Demo Application");
            Console.WriteLine("Pass a parameter string to tokenize it");
            Console.WriteLine("");

            if (tokenizer.Files.Count > 0)
            {
                Console.WriteLine("Files");
                Console.WriteLine("*****************************");

                foreach (string file in tokenizer.Files)
                {
                    Console.WriteLine(String.Format("File: {0}", file));
                }

                Console.WriteLine("");
                Console.WriteLine("");
            }

            if (tokenizer.Parameters.Keys.Count > 0)
            {
                Console.WriteLine("Parameters");
                Console.WriteLine("*****************************");
```

```
        foreach (string key in tokenizer.Parameters.Keys)
        {
            Console.WriteLine(String.Format("Name: {0}\tValue: {1}",
                                            key,
                                            tokenizer[key]));
        }
    }
  }
}
```

Conclusion

This chapter discussed common formatting styles of command line arguments, and went on to building a tokenizer using .NET regular expressions. Command line utilities are extremely popular among tools developers, so having a flexible and reusable tokenizer is very important. Having one means that even less time can be spent on developing these tools, which are fast to develop as it is.

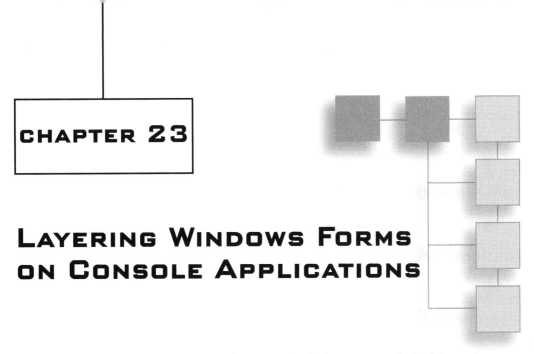

CHAPTER 23

LAYERING WINDOWS FORMS ON CONSOLE APPLICATIONS

Discovery consists of seeing what everybody has seen and thinking what nobody has thought.

Albert Gyorgyi

Console applications are perhaps the most common application type used for tools because of their lightning-fast development nature, and because they provide a simple interface that is easy to learn. Users of console tools generally feel comfortable with console-based interfaces because they all typically function the same way, and it is very easy to pick up a new tool when the interface is consistent with old tools. Some advanced users also write or record scripts that automate the workflow of a particular set of tasks. Authoring scripts for console applications is much easier to do than for graphical user interfaces.

Tools development is all about reusability at both the code and application level. There may be some situations where an existing console application solves an intricate problem, but a graphical user interface version of the tool is wanted by a certain group of users. There are a few solutions to this problem. The first solution is to develop a Windows Forms version of the tool, using a fresh new code base. This solution requires the maintenance of two separate code bases, and can lead to support and synchronization problems. It also takes considerable time to build a new tool. The next solution is to develop a Windows Forms version of the tool and share the same code base. This might not be achievable if the console application is unmanaged and building a managed wrapper is out of the question.

An even more desirable solution is to build a Windows Forms wrapper around the console application, and redirect startup parameters and standard input and output. This solution offers the greatest level of maintainability and speed of development. If a change happens in the console application, it is immediately accessible by the Windows Forms version. Additionally, we do not have to worry about the console application being managed or unmanaged, since the redirection will happen at the process level, not at the code level.

Implementation

You can use the `Process` component to start and stop processes and retrieve information about the processes currently running on your system. We will be using this component to launch a console application, specify startup parameters, and redirect standard input and output. This component exists in the `System.Diagnostics` namespace.

```
using System.Diagnostics;
```

The following code defines a method that launches a redirected console application using the specified file path and argument list. Most of the code is fairly self-explanatory, though we set `UseShellExecute` to `false` so Windows Explorer is not used to launch the process. `RedirectStandardInput` is set to true so that we can get a stream handle to the console output. We also set `CreateNoWindow` to `true` so that a command prompt window is not launched alongside our Windows Forms application when the process is started.

The `StandardOutput` property returns a `StreamReader` that can retrieve the output data from the console application. The `HasExited` property can be queried while data is being read from the output stream.

```
public void LaunchConsoleApplication(string fileName, string arguments)
{
    if (!File.Exists(fileName))
    {
        MessageBox.Show("Invalid path to console application!");
        return;
    }

    Process process = new Process();

    process.StartInfo.FileName = fileName;
    process.StartInfo.UseShellExecute = false;
```

```
process.StartInfo.RedirectStandardOutput = true;
process.StartInfo.Arguments = arguments;
process.StartInfo.CreateNoWindow = true;

process.Start();

StreamReader reader = process.StandardOutput;

while (!process.HasExited)
{
    OuputField.Text += reader.ReadLine() + Environment.NewLine;
    Application.DoEvents();
}
}
```

The last piece of important code is to be placed in the closing event of the Form wrapping the console application. This code checks if the process is valid and if it has not exited yet. If true, the process is aborted. Obviously, this event has to have a reference to the process created by LaunchConsoleApplication.

The following code shows this event logic.

```
private void MainForm_FormClosing(object sender, FormClosingEventArgs e)
{
    if (_process != null && !_process.HasExited)
    {
        _process.Kill();
    }
}
```

Sample Usage

The example provided alongside the implementation for this chapter is very simple. The demo console application is given two arguments: an iteration count and a message to print. The message is printed out however many iterations are specified.

The following code in the Windows Forms demo makes the console application print "Hello World" out five times. The number of iterations to print the message out is dependent on the iteration count specified as a parameter to the launch method.

```
private void LaunchButton_Click(object sender, EventArgs e)
{
    string message = "\"Hello World\"";
    LaunchConsoleApplication("SimpleConsoleApplication.exe",
                             "5 " + message);
}
```

The following code shows the logic for the demo console application.

```
static void Main(string[] args)
{
    int count = Convert.ToInt32(args[0]);

    string message;

    if (args[1] != null && args[1].Trim().Length > 0)
        message = args[1];
    else
        message = "No Message";

    for (int index = 0; index < count; index++)
    {
        Console.WriteLine(message + " - # " + (index + 1).ToString());
        System.Threading.Thread.Sleep(300);
    }
}
```

Conclusion

In this chapter, I discussed how to launch a console application process with parameters and redirect output to a Windows Forms application. This technique is very
useful when you want to create a graphical user interface for an already existing
console utility, while saving as much development and maintenance time as possible.

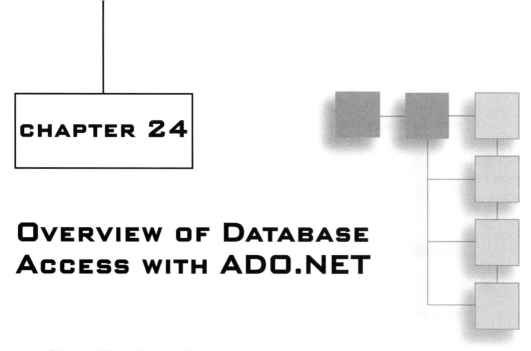

CHAPTER 24

OVERVIEW OF DATABASE ACCESS WITH ADO.NET

"Form follows function."

Louis Henri Sullivan—"Lippincott's Magazine," March, 1896

In ancient times and legends of lore, information was shepherded amongst a collective of elders, magicians, storytellers, and jesters. This collective served as the data storehouse for all that was known and catalogued in the world. This method for data storage and retrieval resulted in an entropic fallacy of facts and events. Technology advanced, and information started to be written down on parchment, greatly increasing its accuracy. Data eventually started to be stored in voluminous repositories of books. Time passed, and the world ultimately began storing data in the first "databases," known as libraries. These libraries established the idea of standardizing how data was stored and retrieved. Without standards, finding specific information would prove to be a chaotic and grueling process. The usefulness of any data storage is proportional to the storage size and retrieval efficiency. Hundreds of years have passed since those ancient times, and we have evolved into an era where computers can store more information than the human brain.

Almost every application handles and stores data to some extent, whether in the form of a database, a spreadsheet, or a flat text file. Today, developers have a multitude of databases and persistence frameworks that can be used to store and retrieve millions of records at lightning speed. As time passes, so do these databases and frameworks. The latest and greatest data access technology from Microsoft is ADO.NET, which is basically a collection of classes, methods, and attributes that are used to facilitate the efficient communication between an application and a data store. Functionally, ADO.NET is an overhaul of ADO (ActiveX Data Objects) with a continuation and extension of the key concepts.

Because of dependencies, overhead, or maintenance support, most games do not have a database system to store information; tools used in content creation, however, especially those used for role-playing games, often store information about game entities in a database for a variety of reasons. Technical designers using a content tool connected to a database benefit from real-time changes that are immediately in effect when another designer makes a change to the data. Imagine if game entity information were stored in XML files that had to be versioned somehow amongst all the technical designers so that everyone worked off the same data. A centralized data store is the solution to this problem, and implementing such a beast is very easy using ADO.NET.

In this chapter, I discuss the advantages of ADO.NET and cover the ADO.NET object model. I then proceed into some simple vanilla examples of using some components of ADO.NET, and finish off with an editor front-end for editing database entries for potion items.

Advantages of ADO.NET

Perhaps the greatest glory of ADO.NET is its ability to access structured data from a variety of diverse data sources, like Microsoft SQL Server, XML, and other data sources that are exposed with OLE DB. Microsoft SQL Server and OLE DB do not need much of an introduction, but the XML support is a real gem for ADO.NET. Interoperability support is very strong, since all data in ADO.NET is transferred in XML so that any platform can understand the data. This allows developers to separate data processing and the user interface onto separate servers, greatly improving performance and maintainability for systems where scalability is important.

In addition to the XML structure, ADO.NET also supports disconnected datasets along with the typical client-server model, without retaining locks or connections that consume limited system resources. Disconnected datasets also allow for user growth without demanding many additional resources for the server. In addition to disconnected datasets, ADO.NET also includes support for automatic connection pooling.

Even though there is a learning curve, once you have grasped the concepts behind ADO.NET, your overall development time will decrease, and you will produce more bug-free code. Therefore, productivity gains can also be considered when describing the advantages and benefits of ADO.NET.

ADO.NET Object Model

The ADO.NET object model is divided into a couple of group classifications: content components and managed provider components. The content components are those that actually store the data. These components include the `DataSet`, `DataView`, `DataTable`, `DataRelation`, `DataColumn`, and `DataRow` classes. The managed provider components are those that communicate with the data sources to facilitate the retrieval and updating of data. These components include the various connection, command, and data reader classes. In fact, managed provider components themselves are divided into two group classifications. The first group contains provider components that interface with regular data sources (`System.Data.OleDb`). The second group contains a provider that is finely tuned and optimized for use with SQL Server 2000 or higher (`System.Data.SqlClient`).

DataView

The `DataView` class is quite similar to a view you would use in the database. A `DataView` can be customized to display a subset of data from a `DataTable` class. This feature allows you to have two controls bound to the same `DataTable` object but showing a different subset of data. You can also apply filtering and sorting rules against the data rows without altering the actual data itself. For example, you can configure a `DataView` to only show rows that have been deleted from a `DataTable`.

DataSet

The `DataSet` class is very similar to the old `Recordset` class that existed in ADO, except it can hold multiple tables of data. The `DataSet` class also has the ability to define internal constraints and relationships, as well as enforcing them. `DataSet` serves as a storage container for data traveling to and from the database.

In addition to database usage, you can also use a `DataSet` to load and manipulate XML data. Microsoft recognizes that the industry has largely embraced the use of XML for cross-platform communication, and so it has built a number of classes to work with XML data (including the `DataSet` class).

You can access the XML functionality of the `DataSet` class with the `ReadXml()`, `WriteXml()`, and `GetXml()` methods.

DataProvider

There are two group classifications for managed provider components: one to communicate with regular data sources and one that is optimized for communication with SQL Server 2000 and higher. All of these providers comply with the standards defined in the `System.Data.Common` namespace.

The first component is the connection object. Just like ADO, this object manages the connection string and connection state. This object still has the usual `Open()` and `Close()` methods. There is now a `BeginTransaction()` method that is used to control a database transaction. The regular group has the `OleDbConnection`, while the optimized SQL Server provider is `SqlConnection`.

The next component is the command object. This object serves as the transfer pipe for the data. You can execute queries that do not return any rows (using the `ExecuteNonQuery()` method), execute a query that returns a single value like an ID (using the `ExecuteScalar()` method), or execute a query that returns a data reader (using the `ExecuteReader()` method). The regular group has the `OleDbCommand`, while the optimized SQL Server provider is `SqlCommand`.

Another component is the data reader object. This object associates itself with a data stream from the command object and provides a mechanism to perform forward-only reading. This method is very efficient, but intensive queries should be avoided since this uses a server-side cursor, tying up a connection resource until it finishes. The regular group has the `OleDbDataReader`, while the optimized SQL Server provider is `SqlDataReader`.

The last component is the data adapter. This object consolidates many of the other components into this easy-to-use class. A data adapter basically uses your connection to retrieve results, and then passes the data to a `DataSet`, which can then be updated or displayed. If rows are changed, the `DataSet` can be passed back into the data adapter to be persisted into the database. You can set the SQL statements using the `InsertCommand`, `UpdateCommand`, `SelectCommand`, and `DeleteCommand` properties. The regular group has the `OleDbDataAdapter`, while the optimized SQL Server provider is `SqlDataAdapter`.

Working with a DataReader

The following example shows how to select rows from an Access database file and display a message box for all the rows in `SomeTextColumn`.

```
using System;
using System.Data.OleDb;
using System.Data.Common;
using System.Windows.Forms;

string connectionString
    = @"Provider=Microsoft.Jet.OLEDB.4.0;Data Source=C:\YourDB.mdb";
OleDbConnection connection = new OleDbConnection(connectionString);
OleDbCommand command = new OleDbCommand("SELECT * FROM YourTable", connection);
connection.Open();

OleDbDataReader reader = null;

try
{
    command.ExecuteReader();
    while (reader.Read())
    {
        MessageBox.Show((string)reader["SomeTextColumn"]);
    }
}
catch (OleDbException exception)
{
    // ... Handle database exceptions here
}
finally
{
    if (reader != null)
        reader.Close();

    if (connection != null)
        connection.Close();
}
```

Working with a DataAdapter

The following example shows how to select rows from an Access database file, fill a DataSet with the rows, and display a message box for the first row in SomeTextColumn.

```
using System;
using System.Data;
using System.Data.OleDb;
using System.Data.Common;
using System.Windows.Forms;

string connectionString
        = @"Provider=Microsoft.Jet.OLEDB.4.0;Data Source=C:\YourDB.mdb";
OleDbConnection connection = new OleDbConnection(connectionString);
OleDbDataAdapter adapter = new OleDbDataAdapter("SELECT * FROM YourTable",
                                                connection);
DataSet dataSet = new DataSet();
adapter.Fill(dataSet, "YourTable");
MessageBox.Show((string)dataSet.Tables["YourTable"].Rows[0]["SomeTextColumn"]);
```

This example only shows the select, but after any sort of editing, you can call the
following method to persist your changes back to the database.

```
adapter.Update(dataSet);
```

Working with XML

Before showing how to load an XML document, we should first define a simple
XML document that we can load (Books.xml).

```
<?xml version='1.0'?>
<!- This file represents a fragment of a book store inventory database -->
<bookstore>
    <book genre="autobiography" publicationdate="1981" ISBN="1-861003-11-0">
        <title>The Autobiography of Benjamin Franklin</title>
        <author>
            <first-name>Benjamin</first-name>
            <last-name>Franklin</last-name>
        </author>
        <price>8.99</price>
    </book>
    <book genre="novel" publicationdate="1967" ISBN="0-201-63361-2">
        <title>The Confidence Man</title>
        <author>
            <first-name>Herman</first-name>
            <last-name>Melville</last-name>
        </author>
        <price>11.99</price>
```

```
        </book>
        <book genre="philosophy" publicationdate="1991" ISBN="1-861001-57-6">
            <title>The Gorgias</title>
            <author>
                <name>Plato</name>
            </author>
            <price>9.99</price>
        </book>
</bookstore>
```

The following example shows how to load an XML file into a DataSet and then retrieve and update node values.

```
using System;
using System.Data;
using System.Windows.Forms;

DataSet dataSet = new DataSet();
dataSet.ReadXml(@"C:\Books.xml");

MessageBox.Show("Row Count: " + dataSet.Tables["book"].Rows.Count.ToString());
MessageBox.Show("First Author => Last Name: " +
                            (string)dataSet.Tables["author"].Rows[0]["last-name"]);

// Update the last name of the first author
dataSet.Tables["author"].Rows[0]["last-name"] = "Wihlidal";

// Persist the changes back out to the xml file
dataSet.WriteXml(@"C:\Books.xml");
```

Potion Database Editor

The Companion Web site contains an example for this chapter that demonstrates how to use a data reader to build a simple editor. The editor is for a fictitious role-playing game, and it handles the database management of potions. You can add new potions, modify the stats of existing potions, or delete potions from the database. This editor could have been built using any number of the objects discussed throughout this chapter but was done with a data reader because of personal preference. The editor uses a simple Access database file so that you do not have to configure SQL Server to run this example.

Figure 24.1 shows the interface for the potion editor on the Companion Web site.

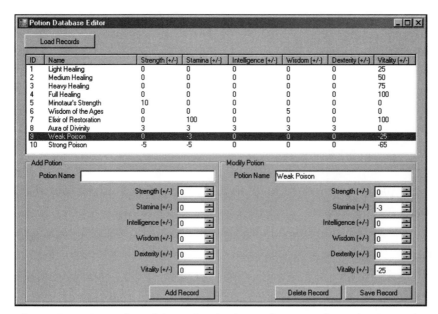

Figure 24.1 Screenshot of the potion database editor example on the Companion Web site.

Conclusion

Many applications store data in some fashion or another, but typically, any application that processes significantly large amounts of data is using some sort of database like SQL Server. The need arises when there are complex queries to perform, or there are a number of associated entities and constraints to enforce. Database servers are optimized for this type of storage and retrieval, so developing a home-grown system will only work in certain situations. Databases also allow you to enforce security settings determining which accounts can do certain tasks, and this can aid in ensuring data integrity and thwarting data tampering.

There are some new features that have just been introduced with .NET 2.0 that are not addressed by this chapter (like the new TableAdapter). Since this chapter only serves as a quick overview of basic ADO.NET functionality, I recommend that you investigate the latest version of ADO.NET in greater detail if you are planning on doing any significant work with it.

PART III

TECHNIQUES FOR GRAPHICAL TOOLS

The programmer, like the poet, works only slightly removed from pure thought-stuff. He builds castles in the air, from air, creating by exertion of the imagination. Few media of creation are so flexible, so easy to polish and rework, so readily capable of realizing grand conceptual structures. Yet the program construct, unlike the poet's words, is real in the sense that it moves and works, producing visible outputs separate from the construct itself. It prints results, draws pictures, produces sounds, moves arms. The magic of myth and legend has come true in our time. One types the correct incantation on a keyboard, and a display screen comes to life, showing things that never were nor could be.... The computer resembles the magic of legend in this respect, too. If one character, one pause, of the incantation is not strictly in proper form, the magic doesn't work. Human beings are not accustomed to being perfect, and few areas of human activity demand it. Adjusting to the requirement for perfection is, I think, the most difficult part of learning to program.

Frederick P. Brooks, *The Mythical Man-Month: Essays on Software Engineering, Anniversary Edition* (2nd Edition)

As time progresses, the technology powering games improves at an exponential rate, and gamers begin to expect more out of a game as each year goes by. Almost all cutting-edge games these days use 3D hardware to render virtual environments that immerse the player in a sort of simulated reality. Earlier 3D games such as *Castle Wolfenstein*, with its 2D ray caster and vertical scan-line rasterization, were rudimentary enough that simple tools could produce suitable game content. Over the years, the capabilities of computers and 3D hardware have grown considerably, and more complex tools are required in order to produce content suitable for today's games.

A large number of content tools for game development visualize data using a 3D API, such as Direct3D. These tools require additional consideration and planning in regards to performance and functionality. The chapters in Part III focus on topics such as swap chain management, texture browsing control creation, converting from screen space to world space, and asynchronous input polling to improve responsiveness and performance.

A graphical tool can be anything that visualizes data using some sort of drawing or rendering API, but the majority of these tools are world editors that create environments for games, or are tools that perform some sort of 3D geometry processing to create static assets like radiosity lightmaps or ambient occlusion maps, and visually display the in-process results to the user. These tools must be designed carefully and pragmatically if they are to be of any value to the intended users. Graphical tools are typically processor- and resource-intensive, so more time must be spent developing these tools than any other.

The chapters in this part will cover some common techniques and approaches to problems that exist in the majority of graphical tools.

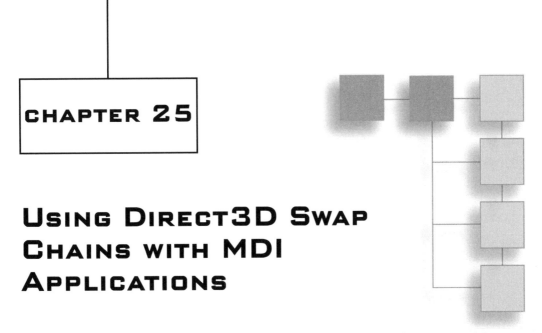

CHAPTER 25

USING DIRECT3D SWAP CHAINS WITH MDI APPLICATIONS

Mostly, when you see programmers, they aren't doing anything. One of the attractive things about programmers is that you cannot tell whether or not they are working simply by looking at them. Very often they're sitting there seemingly drinking coffee and gossiping, or just staring into space. What the programmer is trying to do is get a handle on all the individual and unrelated ideas that are scampering around in his head.

Charles M. Strauss

Almost every game displays itself in a single window, which is a single active device within Direct3D. Many tools, on the other hand, display multiple windows to the users so they may view multiple aspects of the game when designing content. The core purpose of Direct3D is to serve as a high-performance 3D API for real-time games, and because of this, it was designed to be most efficient rendering to a single device. Using a device for every display window in an editor or tool would be extremely inefficient and negatively affect performance.

The efficient way of rendering to multiple windows (or contexts) with a single Direct3D device is through the use of swap chains. Unfortunately, there are a scarce number of examples showing how to use them, and the SDK documentation is extremely vague. The purpose of this chapter is to fill the gap and provide you with extensive information about using swap chains within an MDI (or SDI) application.

What Is a Swap Chain?

An application utilizing Direct3D to render real-time 3D graphics organizes an animated sequence into a series of frames that are stored in a collection of buffers, and renders them in the correct sequence. These buffers are grouped into swap chains that flip to the screen one after the other. A swap chain can render an upcoming frame in the background and present the frame to the screen when ready. This mechanism solves a common problem known as "tearing" and offers smoother animation.

Every Direct3D device that is created automatically instantiates a single implicit swap chain. When a surface flip is requested through the execution of `Device.Present`, the pointers for the front and back buffer(s) are swapped, and a new frame is presented to the viewer. If there is more than one back buffer in a swap chain, the pointers are swapped in a circular order.

Additional swap chains can be created within a given device, though a device can only contain a single full-screen swap chain. Each swap chain renders into a collection of buffers and can be presented to a different window from the main device. The back buffer for a swap chain can be accessed with `SwapChain.GetBackBuffer`.

NOTE

Before continuing, it is important to note that, by the term *window*, I am referring to any control. This association goes back to the unmanaged Win32 API.

A great benefit of using swap chains with a single device is the notion that resources, such as meshes and textures, are shared across all swap chains using a single location in memory.

Creating a swap chain is very easy to do, and the only prerequisite is that a valid Direct3D is already available. The first thing to do is to create a `PresentParameters` object and specify some rendering properties about the swap chain. Most of the properties are familiar from regular device settings, but the important ones to note are `DeviceWindow`, `BackBufferWidth`, and `BackBufferHeight`. All three refer to the handle, width, and height of the window (control) that the swap chain will be bound to for rendering. The variable of this control is called `renderTarget` and is of type `System.Windows.Forms.Control`.

The following code shows how to build present parameters for a swap chain.

```
PresentParameters presentParams = new PresentParameters();
presentParams.AutoDepthStencilFormat = DepthFormat.D16;
```

```
presentParams.Windowed = true;
presentParams.SwapEffect = SwapEffect.Discard;
presentParams.EnableAutoDepthStencil = true;
presentParams.DeviceWindow = renderTarget;
presentParams.BackBufferWidth = renderTarget.Width;
presentParams.BackBufferHeight = renderTarget.Height;
```

With the present parameters built, we can move on to building a swap chain object. The following code shows how to do this, where the first parameter is a reference to the Direct3D device, and the second parameter is a reference to the PresentParameters structure that we just built.

```
SwapChain swapChain = new SwapChain(device, presentParams);
```

The next important piece of code to show is the rendering logic that is executed each time a frame is rendered. This code is similar to a normal Direct3D application, except the back buffer must be set as a render target, and the swap chain presents the frame to the screen, not the device itself.

```
public void RenderSwapChain(SwapChain swapChain, Control renderTarget)
{
    using (Surface backBuffer = swapChain.GetBackBuffer(0,
                                                BackBufferType.Mono))
    {
        swapChain.Device.SetRenderTarget(0, backBuffer);

        // Perform rendering here without calling Device.Present()

        swapChain.Present(renderTarget);
    }
}
```

NOTE

Rendering is performed as normal, except Present() is called on the swap chain rather than the device.

Now that the basics have been covered about how to create and render a Direct3D swap chain, it is time to expand on this topic and cover applicability towards MDI and SDI applications.

Thoughts for SDI and MDI Applicability

There are two common windowing modes for a Windows application: SDI and MDI. An SDI application (Single Document Interface) is typically used when you want to work with one data set at a time in a single window. A commonly known SDI application is Notepad.

An MDI application (Multiple Document Interface) has a primary window (parent) that contains a set of child windows within its client region. A child window is constrained to the boundaries of the parent window, and typically shares the menu bar, tool bar, and other common parts of the parent interface. MDI applications are commonly used in situations where the user wants to work on multiple data sets at the same time.

Swap chains are applicable to either windowing mode, but are more commonly used within MDI applications. An SDI application can use swap chains, but they should only be used when rendering to multiple controls when the problem cannot be solved with the use of viewports. Typically, the swap chains for an SDI application are created after the form is first opened and a Direct3D device is bound to it.

An MDI application has a few more issues to be taken into consideration when using swap chains within the child windows. Swap chains are only valid while the device is still active; the swap chains become invalid as soon as the device is lost or disposed. The device should be bound to the parent window since child windows cannot exist without it, and the swap chains should be created within each individual child window.

Multiple child windows will result in a system that must keep track of the swap chains at a much more intimate level and handle their creation, assignment, and release.

Before diving into the solution and implementation, it is important to discuss several "gotchas" and limitations that must be considered.

Common Pitfalls

An MDI application typically supports the resizing of child windows, so it is important to take this issue into consideration when using swap chains. Direct3D has a built-in mechanism to handle child window resizing, but the results may not be desirable. A stretch blit is used by default to present the frame buffer if the client area dimensions are not the same size as the frame buffer of the swap chain. This mechanism can lead to artifacts and aliasing unless the swap chain is re-created and the render target size is recalculated.

Another issue to take into consideration, which is more of a design concern, is the fact that a device automatically creates an implicit swap chain when it is created. Swap chains can be queried from a device by an indexer, where the implicit swap chain starts at 0 and the other swap chains increment by 1 thereafter. A common approach is to assign the swap chain indexer to the child window associated with it and release the swap chain when the window closes. The problem lies in assigning the implicit swap chain to a child window and trying to release it when the window closes. One solution to this problem is covered in the next section, "The Proposed Solution."

As mentioned earlier, swap chains have the benefit of sharing data from a single device, requiring a single location in memory. While this feature can offer significant memory and performance gains, it can also lead to some headaches. Swap chains do not have their own collection of device settings, so each swap chain must be responsible for the management of settings, such as textures, view state, and render states. It is important that you remain careful and attentive when using swap chains so that you do not end up with settings that transfer over from one swap chain to another by forgetting to set new values.

There are increased render state changes that happen through the use of swap chains, so batching and minimization of changes are important so that performance is not impacted. Swap chains are still much more efficient than using multiple devices, so the performance issues go with the territory of rendering to multiple regions.

Multiple windows are hard to maintain and track, especially when swap chains are associated to them. Luckily, .NET makes MDI application development a breeze, so there is no real concern for this solution.

The Proposed Solution

In this chapter, I present a manager that handles the construction, usage, and destruction of swap chains within either an MDI or SDI application. The manager correctly handles the resizing of child windows to prevent artifacts and aliasing, and it transparently wraps a lot of the swap chain calls into a reusable and extensible framework.

Each child window within the MDI application will be responsible for handling its own rendering, but the swap chain manager must have a way to inform the child window that it should render a frame. The following interface is extremely simplistic but will provide a common mechanism that the manager can call, depending on which child it wants to render. The IRenderWindow interface will be implemented by all child windows to make the Render() method publicly accessible.

```
public interface IRenderWindow
{
    void Render();
}
```

The next section of code describes an associative container class that contains references to a swap chain, present parameters, back buffer, and render target control. This class also contains a unique identifier and makes the association of a swap chain to a child window extremely easy.

```
internal class SwapChainInstance
{
    private int _id;
    private SwapChain _swapChain;
    private PresentParameters _presentParameters;
    private Surface _backBuffer;
    private Control _renderTarget;

    public int Id
    {
        get { return _id; }
        set { _id = value; }
    }

    public SwapChain SwapChain
    {
        get { return _swapChain; }
        set { _swapChain = value; }
    }

    public PresentParameters PresentParameters
    {
        get { return _presentParameters; }
        set { _presentParameters = value; }
    }

    public Surface BackBuffer
    {
        get { return _backBuffer; }
        set { _backBuffer = value; }
```

```
        }

    public Control RenderTarget
    {
        get { return _renderTarget; }
        set { _renderTarget = value; }
    }

    public SwapChainInstance(int id,
                            SwapChain swapChain,
                            PresentParameters presentParameters)
    {
        this._id = id;
        this._swapChain = swapChain;
        this._presentParameters = presentParameters;
    }
}
```

As discussed earlier, there is an issue regarding the implicit swap chain of the device. Perhaps the best way to avoid any problems is to simply ignore the implicit swap chain. This approach is used for the solution, although an alternative approach had been tried with minor success prior to settling on this one.

The next class encompasses the bulk of the swap chain framework. The manager class is responsible for the construction, usage, and destruction of swap chains, and is also accountable for handling the association of a swap chain with a child window.

```
public sealed class SwapChainManager
{
    private List<SwapChainInstance> _swapChainList = new List<SwapChainInstance>();
    private SwapChainInstance _activeSwapChain;
    private int _idCounter;
    private Device _device;
    private bool _ready;
    private Mesh _teapotMesh;
    private Mesh _sphereMesh;

    public Device Device
    {
        get { return _device; }
    }

    public bool Ready
    {
```

```
        get { return _ready; }
    }

    public Mesh TeapotMesh
    {
        get { return _teapotMesh; }
    }

    public Mesh SphereMesh
    {
        get { return _sphereMesh; }
    }
```

The following method is a critical part of the manager. It is responsible for building present parameters and creating a swap chain object that becomes referenced by the manager with a unique identifier.

```
    public int CreateSwapChain(Control renderTarget)
    {
        _idCounter++;

        PresentParameters presentParams = new PresentParameters();

        presentParams.AutoDepthStencilFormat = DepthFormat.D16;
        presentParams.Windowed = true;
        presentParams.SwapEffect = SwapEffect.Discard;
        presentParams.EnableAutoDepthStencil = true;
        presentParams.DeviceWindow = renderTarget;
        presentParams.BackBufferWidth = renderTarget.Width;
        presentParams.BackBufferHeight = renderTarget.Height;

        if (renderTarget != null && _device != null)
        {
            SwapChain swapChain = new SwapChain(_device, presentParams);

            SwapChainInstance instance = new SwapChainInstance(_idCounter,
                                                               swapChain,
                                                               presentParams);

            instance.RenderTarget = renderTarget;

            _swapChainList.Add(instance);
        }
```

```
        return _idCounter;
    }
```

This method is fairly simple. It accepts a unique swap chain identifier, finds the associated object, and releases the swap chain object from the manager.

```
public void DestroySwapChain(int id)
{
    SwapChainInstance instance = FindSwapChainInstance(id);

    if (instance != null)
    {
        DestroySwapChain(instance.SwapChain);
        instance.SwapChain = null;
        _swapChainList.Remove(instance);
    }
}
```

This method works very similarly to DestroySwapChain(), except instead of destroying the swap chain, it simply resets it. A specific use for this method is after a child window has been resized and the swap chain(s) must be reset to reflect the new render target region(s).

```
public void ResetSwapChain(int id)
{
    SwapChainInstance instance = FindSwapChainInstance(id);
    ResetSwapChain(instance);
}
```

This method accepts a unique identifier, locates the referenced swap chain object in the manager, and returns a reference to it.

```
private SwapChainInstance FindSwapChainInstance(int id)
{
    foreach (SwapChainInstance instance in _swapChainList)
    {
        if (instance.Id.Equals(id))
            return instance;
    }

    return null;
}
```

This method is used to re-create a swap chain after a device reset has occurred. First, the old swap chain is destroyed, and then a new swap chain with the new render target size is created.

```
private void ResetSwapChain(SwapChainInstance instance)
{
    if (instance != null)
    {
        DestroySwapChain(instance.SwapChain);

        instance.PresentParameters.BackBufferWidth =
                                    instance.RenderTarget.Width;
        instance.PresentParameters.BackBufferHeight =
                                    instance.RenderTarget.Height;
        instance.SwapChain = new SwapChain(_device,
                                    instance.PresentParameters);
    }
}
```

This method is simply used to release the memory associated with a Direct3D swap chain.

```
private void DestroySwapChain(SwapChain swapChain)
{
    if (swapChain != null)
        swapChain.Dispose();
}
```

This method is very important because it begins the rendering process for a specific swap chain that is referenced by a unique identifier. Notice the ready flag that breaks out of rendering if its value is set to false. This flag is used to prevent errors from occurring if the device is invalid.

```
public void BeginSwapChainRender(int id)
{
    if (!_ready)
        return;

    SwapChainInstance instance = FindSwapChainInstance(id);

    if (instance != null && instance.SwapChain != null)
    {
        _activeSwapChain = instance;
```

```
        instance.BackBuffer = instance.SwapChain.GetBackBuffer(0,
                                                  BackBufferType.Mono);

        if (instance.BackBuffer != null)
        {
            instance.SwapChain.Device.SetRenderTarget(0,
                                              instance.BackBuffer);
        }
    }
}
```

This method completes the rendering process for a specific swap chain that is referenced by a unique identifier.

```
public void EndSwapChainRender(int id)
{
    if (!_ready)
        return;

    SwapChainInstance instance = null;

    if (_activeSwapChain != null)
    {
        if (_activeSwapChain.Id == id)
            instance = _activeSwapChain;
        else
            _activeSwapChain = instance = FindSwapChainInstance(id);
    }

    if (instance != null)
    {
        if (instance.BackBuffer != null && instance.SwapChain != null)
        {
            using (instance.BackBuffer)
            {
                instance.SwapChain.Present(instance.RenderTarget);
            }
            instance.BackBuffer = null;
        }
    }

    _activeSwapChain = null;
}
```

The swap chains are obviously in need of a valid device to render with, and that is the responsibility of this method. A parent window is specified (either the MDI parent form or the SDI form), and the device is created and bound to this window.

```
public void CreateDevice(Form containingWindow)
{
    if (_device != null)
    {
        _device.Dispose();
        _device = null;
    }

    PresentParameters presentParams = new PresentParameters();

    presentParams.AutoDepthStencilFormat = DepthFormat.D16;
    presentParams.Windowed = true;
    presentParams.SwapEffect = SwapEffect.Discard;
    presentParams.PresentationInterval = PresentInterval.Immediate;
    presentParams.EnableAutoDepthStencil = true;

    _device = new Device(0,
                        DeviceType.Hardware,
                        containingWindow,
                        CreateFlags.SoftwareVertexProcessing,
                        presentParams);

    _device.DeviceLost += new EventHandler(DeviceLost);
    _device.DeviceReset += new EventHandler(DeviceReset);

    DeviceReset(null, null);

    _ready = true;
}
```

The following method handles the device lost event. The only job of this method is to flip the ready flag to false so that errors do not occur when the application attempts to render with an invalid device.

```
private void DeviceLost(object sender, EventArgs e)
{
    _ready = false;
}
```

The last method in our manager handles the device reset event. The purpose of this method is to re-create the swap chains with the recalculated render target size, and then re-create the resources that are shared across all swap chains. The ready flag is also flipped to true so that the application can begin rendering the scenes once again.

```
private void DeviceReset(object sender, EventArgs e)
{
    foreach (SwapChainInstance instance in _swapChainList)
        ResetSwapChain(instance);

    _teapotMesh = Mesh.Teapot(_device);
    _sphereMesh = Mesh.Sphere(_device, 1.0f, 30, 30);

    _device.Lights[0].Type = LightType.Directional;
    _device.Lights[0].Diffuse = System.Drawing.Color.White;
    _device.Lights[0].Enabled = true;

    _device.RenderState.Lighting = true;
    _device.RenderState.Ambient = Color.White;
    _device.RenderState.CullMode = Cull.CounterClockwise;
    _device.RenderState.ShadeMode = ShadeMode.Gouraud;

    Material material = new Material();
    material.Ambient = Color.ForestGreen;
    material.Diffuse = Color.Olive;

    _device.Material = material;

    _ready = true;
}
}
```

The implementation of the swap chain manager is complete, so the discussion will now focus on using the manager. The following code insertions are methods and properties extracted directly from the example on the Companion Web site that should offer insight into using the solution if the interfaces alone are not enough. The code snippets are from the single context window that uses the entire window as a display context.

The first property is a unique identifier that references a SwapChainInstance object within the swap chain manager. It is initialized in the DeviceReset() method that is described later in this chapter.

```
private int _swapChain;
```

The next property is a reference to the swap chain manager instance that will typically be created in the parent form if the application uses an MDI windowing mode. In an SDI application, the manager can be instantiated with a device bound to the SDI window.

This example has the manager reference passed in through the child form constructor from the parent form.

```
private SwapChainManager _manager;
```

The next method is executed when the rendering device is lost or reset and the swap chain(s) must be re-created. You will notice that the methods requiring a control are passed a this keyword that references the entire Form. It is perfectly acceptable to pass a reference to a Control residing on the form if you want to target the rendering within a specific Control like a panel. The CreateSwapChain() method creates a swap chain for the entire window and returns a unique identifier back to the user. This unique identifier can be later used to return the swap chain object from the manager.

```
private void DeviceReset()
{
    _swapChain = _manager.CreateSwapChain(this);
}
```

Typically, a device is lost before it is reset, and the purpose of this method is to destroy an existing swap chain before the reset method is executed and a new swap chain is created.

```
private void DeviceLost()
{
    _manager.DestroySwapChain(_swapChain);
}
```

The following event is fired when the window is first loaded, resulting in the creation of a swap chain.

```
private void ContextWindow_Load(object sender, System.EventArgs e)
{
    DeviceReset();
}
```

One of the common pitfalls mentioned in this chapter are the aliasing and artifacts that result from a client region size not matching the size of the swap chain frame buffer. This normally occurs after the swap chain has been created and the associated window resizes. To account for this, there is a ResetSwapChain() method in the manager that will be executed when the window is resized using the event below.

```
private void ContextWindow_Resize(object sender, System.EventArgs e)
{
    _manager.ResetSwapChain(_swapChain);
}
```

Finally, we hit the interesting snippet, the Render() method. It is here that we first make sure the manager exists and is ready to render; if not, we skip the current frame. After that, it is important to set the render and view states for the swap chain in case they were altered by another swap chain in existence on the same device. The example does not employ many render state settings, but it is important to recalculate the projection, world, and view matrices so that the scene renders correctly.

Rendering is then initiated with a call to BeginSwapChainRender(), passing in the unique identifier for the swap chain created when the child window was first loaded. Rendering then proceeds as normal, except at the very end there is a call to EndSwapChainRender() instead of calling Present() on the device.

```
public void Render()
{
    if (_manager == null)
        return;

    if (!_manager.Ready)
        return;

    CalculateProjection();

    _manager.Device.Transform.World = Matrix.Identity;
    Vector3 position = new Vector3(0.0f, 0.0f, -5.0f);
    Vector3 target = new Vector3(0.0f, 0.0f, 0.0f);
    Vector3 upVector = new Vector3(0.0f, 1.0f, 0.0f);
    _manager.Device.Transform.View = Matrix.LookAtLH(position,
                                                     target,
                                                     upVector);
```

```
    _manager.BeginSwapChainRender(_swapChain);
    _manager.Device.Clear(ClearFlags.Target | ClearFlags.ZBuffer,
                        unchecked((int)-8454144),
                        1.0F,
                        0);
    _manager.Device.BeginScene();

    _manager.SphereMesh.DrawSubset(0);

    _manager.Device.EndScene();
    _manager.EndSwapChainRender(_swapChain);
}
```

The following method was included in this topic for completeness, though it does
not directly deal with the swap chain manager. This method recalculates the projection matrix after the render target client region is resized.

```
private void CalculateProjection()
{
    if (this.Height == 0)
        return;

    float aspect = (float)this.Width / this.Height;

    _manager.Device.Transform.Projection = Matrix.PerspectiveFovLH((float)Math.PI / 4,
                                                        aspect,
                                                        1.0f,
                                                        60.0f);
}
```

The example provided on the Companion Web site is an MDI application that
uses the swap chain manager described in this topic to render into multiple child
windows and multiple controls within a child window. You can see two different
types of child windows using the swap chain manager in Figure 25.1, and one of
the child windows is maximized in Figure 25.2.

Both the sphere and teapot meshes are loaded into the single Direct3D device and
are shared across all child windows in the example.

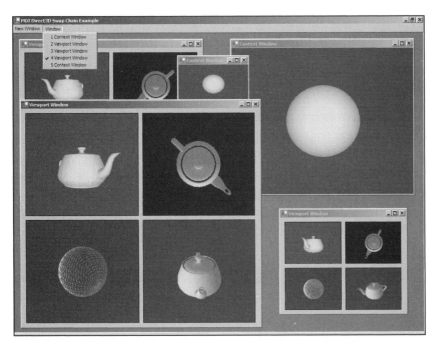

Figure 25.1 Variety of child windows using the swap chain manager.

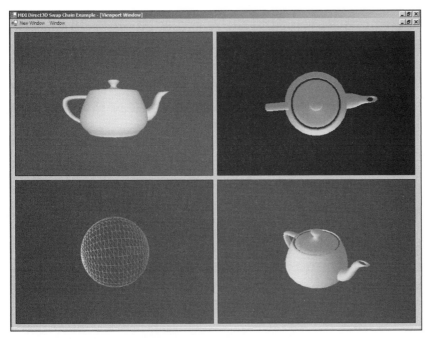

Figure 25.2 Maximized child window using the swap chain manager.

Conclusion

This chapter covered what a swap chain is, how to create them, applicability with MDI applications, and how to effectively create and manage swap chains within an MDI application.

Overall, the solution presented in this chapter is very flexible and extensible, although there are a couple of areas that could be refactored to improve performance or promote more reusability. For example, the device and swap chain creation could be routed through a virtual function that allows the user to specify settings and parameters on a per override basis. On another note, earlier it was mentioned that swap chains increase the number of render state changes, so it would be advantageous to implement a batching mechanism to reduce the total number of changes per frame.

The Companion Web site contains the full source code for the manager presented in this chapter, including a demo application that uses it within an MDI application in a variety of ways.

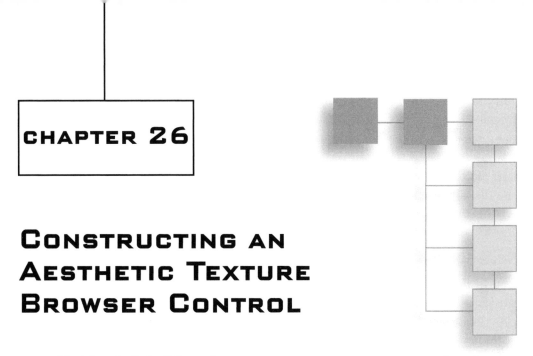

CHAPTER 26

Constructing an Aesthetic Texture Browser Control

If builders built buildings the way programmers wrote programs, then the first woodpecker that came along would destroy civilization.

Weinberg's Second Law

The number of art assets used in the majority of games today can be anywhere from thousands to hundreds of thousands. These assets can be used in numerous places throughout a variety of in-game environments, and typically, the level designers are in charge of determining which assets go where. Some game studios build their own level editors that can manipulate world geometry and handle the placement and scripting of entities. These editors typically offer the ability to select an arbitrary mesh or primitive and assign a texture asset to the geometry. When you have thousands of textures available, designers are more productive if the editor is able to display a thumbnail preview of the different textures available for an environment instead of a textual listing. It is much more appealing to scroll through a collection of texture thumbnails than to scroll through a listing of file-names that might not even describe the contents in an adequate fashion. Texture browsing has its place in a variety of tools, but the most common place to offer it is within a world editor.

This chapter is geared toward building a control that offers texture or image browsing from both local image files and Managed Direct3D Texture resources.

The System.Drawing namespace supports a variety of image formats, but some texture formats, such as DDS, are not supported unless a custom loader is written or the data is loaded through Managed Direct3D. The control will display textures that have been resized to fit within a thumbnail control, with support for both single and multiple selection of texture thumbnails. Each thumbnail will have a label for the filename and a label for the dimensions of the original image. All thumbnails will sit within a parent container control.

Swappable Loader Interface

One of the goals outlined for this component is the ability to switch the loader that processes the image files. While Managed Direct3D and Windows GDI+ are the only loaders supported by this chapter, it would be advantageous to design the component so that any loader implementing the appropriate interface could be plugged into the component. This component makes use of an interface and abstract class to define the common interface of all image loaders so that they can be swapped in and out.

The interface provides two Load methods, which are used to create a Bitmap object from an image file on the hard drive or from a memory stream. Some loaders may also require a handle to a resource, such as a window handle for the Direct3D loader, so this interface provides the ContextHandle property to support this requirement.

The following code defines the base loader interface and abstract class.

```
public interface IAbstractLoader
{
    System.IntPtr ContextHandle
    {
        get;
        set;
    }

    Bitmap Load(string fileName);
    Bitmap Load(MemoryStream stream);
}
```

With the loader interface defined, it is time to define the abstract loader class that implements the interface. This class stores the context handle of a control that certain loaders may need to operate correctly. The GDI+ loader does not use this, but

Direct3D uses this handle to create a device with which the textures can be loaded. The following code defines the abstract loader class.

```
public abstract class AbstractLoader : IAbstractLoader
{
    private System.IntPtr _contextHandle;

    public System.IntPtr ContextHandle
    {
        get { return _contextHandle; }
        set { _contextHandle = value; }
    }

    public virtual Bitmap Load(string fileName)
    {
        return null;
    }

    public virtual Bitmap Load(MemoryStream stream)
    {
        return null;
    }

    protected AbstractLoader(System.IntPtr contextHandle)
    {
        _contextHandle = contextHandle;
    }
}
```

NOTE

You will need to reference System.IO for the MemoryStream object, as well as System.Drawing for the Bitmap object.

Windows GDI+ Loader

This is by far the easiest loader to implement, since it only takes a single line of code to load an image file. Windows GDI+ is available to all .NET applications without the reliance on any external dependencies, so it is an excellent choice when standard image formats like JPEG, BMP and GIF will do the job.

The following code implements the Windows GDI+ image loader.

```
public class NativeLoader : AbstractLoader
{
    public override Bitmap Load(string fileName)
    {
        try
        {
            return new Bitmap(Image.FromFile(fileName));
        }
        catch
        {
            return null;
        }
    }

    public override Bitmap Load(MemoryStream stream)
    {
        try
        {
            stream.Position = 0;
            return new Bitmap(Image.FromStream(stream));
        }
        catch
        {
            return null;
        }
    }

    public NativeLoader(System.IntPtr contextHandle) : base(contextHandle) {}
}
```

NOTE

You will need to reference System.IO for the MemoryStream object, as well as System.Drawing for the Bitmap object.

Managed Direct3D Loader

It is very easy to use Windows GDI+ to load images, unless, of course, the image format is not supported. Image formats that are not supported by Windows GDI+ require a different loader to process any unsupported image formats, so we are presented with two possibilities.

The first option is to write a custom loader that can read in the binary data and extract the image information. After the image information (for instance, the number of channels and the pixel data) has been extracted, the information would be used to build an Image object. This method can be somewhat problematic, especially if the image format comes in different variations, such as different compression options and 3D-specific values such as the Microsoft DirectDraw Surface (DDS) format for example. The custom loader can become quite large in size, and debugging could prove to be difficult.

The alternate solution, and the one covered in this chapter, is to wrap the built-in texture-loading capabilities of Microsoft Direct3D into a loader. There are a number of advantages to building this wrapper over building a custom loader from scratch. The biggest advantage is the time and money saved by not having to reinvent the wheel. Additionally, unless you have a custom image format that neither GDI+ nor Direct3D support, one that requires a custom loader, the formats supported by the TextureLoader utility of Managed Direct3D will almost always suffice for your project.

Now, before you jump into the code, it is important to address the main issue behind wrapping Managed Direct3D into a loader. The TextureLoader loads image files into Texture objects, not Image or Bitmap objects, meaning that a valid device must first be created before any loading can occur. This may sound like a daunting or cumbersome process, but it really isn't all that bad. The main requirement for a device is a window handle, and because Windows defines a window as any control element, we can create a device using the window handle of our texture browsing control!

The loader will create a Managed Direct3D and bind it to the texture browser control, at which point the image files are loaded into texture resources. The image data is then extracted from these resources and saved into Bitmap objects. The device is released after the images are generated; at no point does any actual rendering occur.

The following code implements the Managed Direct3D device and image loader.

```
public class Direct3DLoader : AbstractLoader, IDisposable
{
    private Device _device;

    public override Bitmap Load(string fileName)
    {
        try
```

```csharp
        {
            Bitmap result = null;

            if (_device == null)
            {
                PresentParameters presentParams = new PresentParameters();
                presentParams.Windowed = true;
                presentParams.SwapEffect = SwapEffect.Discard;
                _device = new Device(0,
                                     DeviceType.Reference,
                                     ContextHandle,
                                     CreateFlags.SoftwareVertexProcessing,
                                     presentParams);
            }

            using (Texture texture = TextureLoader.FromFile(_device, fileName))
            {
                using (GraphicsStream stream
                        = TextureLoader.SaveToStream(ImageFileFormat.Bmp, texture))
                {
                    result = new Bitmap(stream);
                }
            }

            return result;
        }
        catch
        {
            return null;
        }
    }

    public override Bitmap Load(MemoryStream stream)
    {
        try
        {
            Bitmap result = null;

            if (_device == null)
            {
```

```
                    PresentParameters presentParams = new PresentParameters();
                    presentParams.Windowed = true;
                    presentParams.SwapEffect = SwapEffect.Discard;
                    _device = new Device(0,
                                        DeviceType.Reference,
                                        ContextHandle,
                                        CreateFlags.SoftwareVertexProcessing,
                                        presentParams);
                }

                stream.Position = 0;

                using (Texture texture = TextureLoader.FromStream(_device, stream))
                {
                    using (GraphicsStream processedStream
                            = TextureLoader.SaveToStream(ImageFileFormat.Bmp, texture))
                    {
                        result = new Bitmap(processedStream);
                    }
                }

                return result;
            }
            catch
            {
                return null;
            }
        }

        public Direct3DLoader(System.IntPtr contextHandle) : base(contextHandle) {}

        public void Dispose()
        {
            if (_device != null)
            {
                _device.Dispose();
                _device = null;
            }
        }
    }
```

Note

You will need to reference `System.IO` for the `MemoryStream` object, as well as `System.Drawing` for the `Bitmap` object. Additionally, you will need to reference both `Microsoft.DirectX` and `Microsoft.DirectX.Direct3D` for the Managed Direct3D support.

Storing Texture Information

The texture browser will support three ways of loading an image as a texture: from an image file stored on the local hard drive, from raw binary data in memory, and from a preloaded bitmap. In order to provide a unified and straightforward way of accessing textures that are loaded in the browser, we need to create a container class that wraps the three load methods into a common interface. This interface will be known as a *texture handle*; it will store the appropriate data depending on the source of the image, and it will keep track of simple state information to support caching.

Texture handles will need to keep track of the image data and where the data originated from, so the `enum` defined below will be used to accomplish this.

```
public enum TextureHandleType
{
    FileSystem,
    Bitmap,
    RawData
}
```

The texture handle class has several different constructors, each with a different signature and parameter list. The texture handle type is set when one of the constructors is fired, and depending on the constructor, the appropriate type value is set.

If one of the constructors accepting a `FileInfo` object is used, then it is assumed that the image is being loaded from the hard drive, so the handle type will be set to `TextureHandleType.FileSystem`.

If a constructor is used that accepts a `Bitmap` object, it is assumed that the object contains the image data, and the handle type should be set to `TextureHandleType.Bitmap`.

Lastly, if a constructor is used that accepts a `MemoryStream` object, it is assumed that the memory stream contains the raw binary data of the image, and that the handle type should be set to `TextureHandleType.MemoryStream`.

Texture handles need a humanly readable way to distinguish themselves from one another. Since the image data does not have to come from the file system and can come directly from raw memory, the filename cannot be used as an identifier. It is for this reason that the Name property was introduced into the texture handle class.

The two boolean properties Generate and Loaded will be covered later in this chapter. They are flags describing whether or not the textures need to be regenerated, and whether or not the image itself was able to be loaded.

You should also notice that the TextureHandle class implements the IDisposable interface. This is because of the MemoryStream object, which the Dispose method will close if required.

The following code implements the texture handle class in its entirety.

```
public class TextureHandle : IDisposable
{
    private string _name;
    private FileInfo _file;
    private Bitmap _image;
    private MemoryStream _data;
    private bool _generate = true;
    private TextureHandleType _type;
    private bool _loaded;

    public string Name
    {
        get { return _name; }
        set { _name = value; }
    }

    public FileInfo File
    {
        get { return _file; }
        set { _file = value; }
    }

    public Bitmap Image
    {
        get { return _image; }
        set { _image = value; }
    }
```

```csharp
public MemoryStream Data
{
    get { return _data; }
    set { _data = value; }
}

public bool Generate
{
    get { return _generate; }
    set { _generate = value; }
}

public TextureHandleType Type
{
    get { return _type; }
    set { _type = value; }
}

public bool Loaded
{
    get { return _loaded; }
    set { _loaded = value; }
}

public TextureHandle(FileInfo file) : this(file, file.Name) { }

public TextureHandle(FileInfo file, string name)
{
    _file = file;
    _name = name;
    _type = TextureHandleType.FileSystem;
}

public TextureHandle(string filePath, string name)
{
    _file = new FileInfo(filePath);
    _name = name;
    _type = TextureHandleType.FileSystem;
}

public TextureHandle(string name, Bitmap image)
{
```

```
        _name = name;
        _image = image;
        _type = TextureHandleType.Bitmap;
    }

    public TextureHandle(string name, MemoryStream stream)
    {
        _name = name;
        _data = new MemoryStream(stream.ToArray());
        _type = TextureHandleType.RawData;
    }

    public TextureHandle(string name, byte[] data)
    {
        _name = name;
        _data = new MemoryStream(data);
        _type = TextureHandleType.RawData;
    }
    public void Dispose()
    {
        if (_data != null)
        {
            _data.Close();
            _data = null;
        }
    }
}
}
```

Note

You will need to reference System.IO for the MemoryStream and FileInfo objects, as well as System.Drawing for the Bitmap object.

Building the Thumbnail Control

With the loaders built, it is time to build the user interface controls. We will start with the thumbnail control, which will show the image to the user, along with a summarized amount of information. This control will operate as an independent and modular unit of code, and it will be used by the texture browser.

The processing of the image data is performed by the loaders, but the original texture size will generally be too big for the thumbnail display. The thumbnail control takes the image data of the associated texture handle, resizes it to the appropriate size, and then uses a resized copy of the original image for the display.

The thumbnail control also handles the visual appearance for selection. The constructor accepts a reference to the texture browser instance so that visual properties can be used and applied to the thumbnail control.

Aside from visual properties, the reference to the texture browser is used by the thumbnail control to relay event information back to the browser control.

The following code defines the thumbnail control and its related properties and functionality.

```
public partial class TextureThumbnail : UserControl
{
    private TextureBrowser _container;
    private TextureHandle _texture;
    private bool _selected;

    public TextureHandle Texture
    {
        get { return _texture; }
    }

    public bool Selected
    {
        get { return _selected; }
        set
        {
            if (_container == null)
                return;

            if (value)
            {
                this.BackColor = Color.Blue;

                FileNameLabel.BackColor = _container.BackgroundColorSelected;
                FileNameLabel.ForeColor = _container.ForegroundColorSelected;

                DimensionsLabel.BackColor = _container.BackgroundColorSelected;
                DimensionsLabel.ForeColor = _container.ForegroundColorSelected;
            }
            else
            {
```

```
                this.BackColor = SystemColors.ActiveCaption;

                FileNameLabel.BackColor = _container.BackgroundColor;
                FileNameLabel.ForeColor = _container.ForegroundColor;

                DimensionsLabel.BackColor = _container.BackgroundColor;
                DimensionsLabel.ForeColor = _container.ForegroundColor;
            }

            _selected = value;
        }
    }

    public TextureThumbnail(TextureBrowser container, TextureHandle texture)
    {
        InitializeComponent();

        _container = container;
        _texture = texture;

        if (_container != null)
        {
            this.FileNameLabel.BackColor = _container.BackgroundColor;
            this.FileNameLabel.ForeColor = _container.ForegroundColor;

            this.DimensionsLabel.BackColor = _container.BackgroundColor;
            this.DimensionsLabel.ForeColor = _container.ForegroundColor;
        }

        GenerateThumbnail();
        DisplayInformation();
    }

    private void GenerateThumbnail()
    {
        if (_texture.Image == null)
            return;

        int maxDimension = Math.Min(MaterialPreview.Width,
                                    MaterialPreview.Height);

        int resizedWidth = _texture.Image.Width;
```

```
        int resizedHeight = _texture.Image.Height;

        if (_texture.Image.Width > maxDimension ||
           _texture.Image.Height > maxDimension)
        {
            if (_texture.Image.Width > _texture.Image.Height)
            {
                resizedWidth = maxDimension;
                resizedHeight = (int)(_texture.Image.Height *
                                    maxDimension / _texture.Image.Width);
            }
            else
            {
                resizedWidth = (int)(_texture.Image.Width *
                                    maxDimension / _texture.Image.Height);
                resizedHeight = maxDimension;
            }
        }

        MaterialPreview.Image = new Bitmap(_texture.Image,
                                    resizedWidth,
                                    resizedHeight);
    }

    private void DisplayInformation()
    {
        if (_texture.Image != null)
        {
            this.FileNameLabel.Text = _texture.Name;
            this.DimensionsLabel.Text = String.Format(CultureInfo.CurrentCulture,
                                            "{0} x {1}",
                                            _texture.Image.Size.Width,
                                            _texture.Image.Size.Height);
        }
    }

    private void ToggleSelection()
    {
        if (_container != null)
            _container.PerformSelect(this);
    }
```

```
    private void MaterialPreview_MouseClick(object sender, MouseEventArgs e)
    {
        if (e.Button == MouseButtons.Left)
        {
            ToggleSelection();
        }
        else if (e.Button == MouseButtons.Right)
        {
            if (_container != null)
                _container.PerformRightClicked(this);
        }
    }

    private void MaterialPreview_MouseDoubleClick(object sender, MouseEventArgs e)
    {
        if (_container != null)
            _container.PerformActivated(this);
    }
}
```

Figure 26.1 shows the texture thumbnail control shown in the designer. There are two labels for the filename and dimensions, as well as a picture box in the middle to display the resized image.

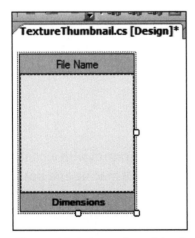

Figure 26.1 Screenshot of the thumbnail control in design mode.

Handling Custom User Events

The various notifications raised by the thumbnail and texture browser controls are going to need a way to reach the application consuming them, so we need to provide events that the consuming application can tie into.

Basically, all of the events provided by the controls will send the same information, so we can define a single class to hold the event arguments that will be sent to the various event delegates. The different events will be covered in the next section when the viewer control is discussed.

The event arguments class only tracks a single texture handle instance, which is a reference to the texture handle associated to the event being executed.

The following code defines the event arguments class for the controls.

```
public class TextureBrowserEventArgs : EventArgs
{
    private TextureHandle _texture;

    public TextureHandle Texture
    {
        get { return _texture; }
        set { _texture = value; }
    }

    public TextureBrowserEventArgs(TextureHandle texture)
    {
        _texture = texture;
    }
}
```

Building the Viewer Control

The viewer control is fairly straightforward. It is basically a user control with a panel that contains the thumbnail controls. This control determines the spacing and positioning of the thumbnails, handles notification events, and exposes appearance and functional settings. It also manages the loading, displaying, and caching of thumbnails using the appropriate loader. The following source code describes the texture browser control in its entirety. The source code listing is somewhat lengthy, one reason why I will not comment much on each piece individually, but the full source is needed to fully enable you to understand the control without referring to the Companion Web site. The source code on the Web site is fully commented if there is a specific piece that you wish to fully investigate.

```csharp
public partial class TextureBrowser : UserControl
{
    public enum LoaderType
    {
        Native,
        Direct3D
    }

    public enum SelectionMode
    {
        Single,
        Multiple
    }

    public event EventHandler<TextureBrowserEventArgs> TextureSelected;
    public event EventHandler<TextureBrowserEventArgs> TextureDeselected;
    public event EventHandler<TextureBrowserEventArgs> TextureActivated;
    public event EventHandler<TextureBrowserEventArgs> TextureRightClicked;

    private LoaderType _loader = LoaderType.Native;

    private SelectionMode _selection = SelectionMode.Single;

    private int _margin = 5;
    private bool _cacheImages;

    private Color _canvasColor = SystemColors.ControlDark;
    private Color _backgroundColor = SystemColors.Control;
    private Color _foregroundColor = SystemColors.ControlText;
    private Color _backgroundColorSelected = SystemColors.Highlight;
    private Color _foregroundColorSelected = SystemColors.HighlightText;

    private AbstractLoader _imageLoader;

    private Size _oldSize;
    private bool _rebuildCache = true;
    private bool _applyAppearance = true;

    private List<TextureHandle> _textures = new List<TextureHandle>();
    private List<TextureThumbnail> _thumbnails = new List<TextureThumbnail>();

    [CategoryAttribute("Texture Browser Settings"),
```

```
    DescriptionAttribute("Loader system to use when processing images")]
    public LoaderType Loader
    {
        get { return _loader; }
        set
        {
            if (_loader != value)
            {
                _rebuildCache = true;
                _loader = value;

                switch (_loader)
                {
                    case LoaderType.Native:
                    {
                        _imageLoader = new NativeLoader(this.Handle);
                        break;
                    }

                    case LoaderType.Direct3D:
                    {
                        _imageLoader = new Direct3DLoader(this.Handle);
                        break;
                    }
                }
            }
            else if (_imageLoader == null)
                _imageLoader = new NativeLoader(this.Handle);
            DisplayThumbnails();
        }
    }

    [CategoryAttribute("Texture Browser Settings"),
     DescriptionAttribute("Selection mode of the control")]
    public SelectionMode Selection
    {
        get { return _selection; }
        set { _selection = value; }
    }
```

```csharp
[CategoryAttribute("Texture Browser Settings"),
 DescriptionAttribute("Whether or not to cache loaded images")]
public bool CacheImages
{
    get { return _cacheImages; }
    set { _cacheImages = value; }
}

[CategoryAttribute("Texture Browser Settings"),
 DescriptionAttribute("Background color of the texture browser panel")]
public Color CanvasColor
{
    get { return _canvasColor; }
    set
    {
        _canvasColor = value;
        ThumbnailPanel.BackColor = _canvasColor;
    }
}

[CategoryAttribute("Texture Browser Settings"),
 DescriptionAttribute("Background color of the thumbnail control")]
public Color BackgroundColor
{
    get { return _backgroundColor; }
    set
    {
        _backgroundColor = value;
        _applyAppearance = true;
        DisplayThumbnails();
    }
}

[CategoryAttribute("Texture Browser Settings"),
 DescriptionAttribute("Foreground color of the thumbnail control")]
public Color ForegroundColor
{
    get { return _foregroundColor; }
    set
    {
        _foregroundColor = value;
        _applyAppearance = true;
```

```
                DisplayThumbnails();
        }
    }


    [CategoryAttribute("Texture Browser Settings"),
    DescriptionAttribute("Background color of selected thumbnails")]
    public Color BackgroundColorSelected
    {
        get { return _backgroundColorSelected; }
        set
        {
            _backgroundColorSelected = value;
            _applyAppearance = true;
            DisplayThumbnails();
        }
    }


    [CategoryAttribute("Texture Browser Settings"),
    DescriptionAttribute("Foreground color of selected thumbnails")]
    public Color ForegroundColorSelected
    {
        get { return _foregroundColorSelected; }
        set
        {
            _foregroundColorSelected = value;
            _applyAppearance = true;
            DisplayThumbnails();
        }
    }


    public TextureBrowser()
    {
        InitializeComponent();
        this.Loader = LoaderType.Native;
    }

    public void AddTexture(TextureHandle texture)
    {
        if (texture != null)
        {
            _textures.Add(texture);
            _rebuildCache = true;
```

```csharp
            DisplayThumbnails();
        }
    }

    public void AddTextures(TextureHandle[] textures)
    {
        foreach (TextureHandle texture in textures)
        {
            AddTexture(texture);
        }
    }

    public void AddTextures(List<TextureHandle> textures)
    {
        foreach (TextureHandle texture in textures)
        {
            AddTexture(texture);
        }
    }

    public void RemoveTexture(TextureHandle texture)
    {
        if (texture != null)
        {
            _textures.Remove(texture);
            _rebuildCache = true;
            DisplayThumbnails();
        }
    }

    public void RemoveTextures(TextureHandle[] textures)
    {
        foreach (TextureHandle texture in textures)
        {
            RemoveTexture(texture);
        }
    }

    public void RemoveTextures(List<TextureHandle> textures)
    {
        foreach (TextureHandle texture in textures)
        {
```

```
            RemoveTexture(texture);
        }
    }

    public void GenerateTexture(TextureHandle texture)
    {
        try
        {
            texture.Loaded = false;

            switch (texture.Type)
            {
                case TextureHandleType.FileSystem:
                {
                    texture.Image = _imageLoader.Load(texture.File.FullName);
                    break;
                }

                case TextureHandleType.RawData:
                {
                    texture.Image = _imageLoader.Load(texture.Data);
                    break;
                }

                case TextureHandleType.Bitmap:
                {
                    // Do nothing, data already there
                    break;
                }
            }

            if (texture.Image != null)
            {
                texture.Loaded = true;

                if (_cacheImages)
                {
                    texture.Generate = false;
                }
            }
        }
        catch (System.OutOfMemoryException)
```

```csharp
        {
            throw;
        }
    }

    public void GenerateTextures(TextureHandle[] textures)
    {
        foreach (TextureHandle texture in textures)
        {
            GenerateTexture(texture);
        }
    }

    public void GenerateTextures(List<TextureHandle> textures)
    {
        foreach (TextureHandle texture in textures)
        {
            GenerateTexture(texture);
        }
    }

    public TextureHandle FindTexture(string name)
    {
        TextureHandle result = null;

        foreach (TextureHandle texture in _textures)
        {
            if (texture.Name.Equals(name))
            {
                result = texture;
                break;
            }
        }

        return result;
    }

    public TextureHandle FindTexture(FileInfo file)
    {
        return FindTexture(file, false);
    }
```

```csharp
public TextureHandle FindTexture(FileInfo file, bool fullPath)
{
    TextureHandle result = null;

    foreach (TextureHandle texture in _textures)
    {
        if (fullPath)
        {
            if (texture.File.FullName.Equals(file.FullName))
            {
                result = texture;
                break;
            }
        }
        else
        {
            if (texture.File.Name.Equals(file.Name))
            {
                result = texture;
                break;
            }
        }
    }

    return result;
}

public void SelectAll()
{
    foreach (TextureThumbnail thumbnail in _thumbnails)
    {
        thumbnail.Selected = true;

        if (TextureSelected != null)
            TextureSelected(this,
                            new TextureBrowserEventArgs(thumbnail.Texture));
    }
}

public void DeselectAll()
{
    DeselectAll(null);
}
```

```csharp
private void DeselectAll(TextureThumbnail skip)
{
    foreach (TextureThumbnail thumbnail in _thumbnails)
    {
        if (skip != null && thumbnail.Equals(skip))
            continue;

        thumbnail.Selected = false;

        if (TextureDeselected != null)
            TextureDeselected(this,
                          new TextureBrowserEventArgs(thumbnail.Texture));
    }
}

private void DisplayThumbnails()
{
    _thumbnails.Clear();

    if (_rebuildCache)
    {
        while (ThumbnailPanel.Controls.Count > 0)
        {
            TextureThumbnail th = (TextureThumbnail)ThumbnailPanel.Controls[0];
            th.Dispose();
            ThumbnailPanel.Controls.Remove(th);
        }

        foreach (TextureHandle texture in _textures)
        {
            if (texture.Generate)
            {
                GenerateTexture(texture);
            }

            if (texture.Loaded)
            {
                TextureThumbnail thumbnail = new TextureThumbnail(this,
                                                            texture);
                _thumbnails.Add(thumbnail);
            }
        }
```

```
            _rebuildCache = false;
        }
        else
        {
            foreach (TextureThumbnail thumbnail in ThumbnailPanel.Controls)
            {
                _thumbnails.Add(thumbnail);
            }

            ThumbnailPanel.Controls.Clear();
        }

        int numberHorizontal = -1;

        foreach (TextureThumbnail thumbnail in _thumbnails)
        {
            if (numberHorizontal < 0)
            {
                // determine how many thumbnails can be displayed on one row
                numberHorizontal = (int)(ThumbnailPanel.Width / (thumbnail.Width != 0
                                                    ? thumbnail.Width : 1));

                if (numberHorizontal <= 0)
                    numberHorizontal = 1;
            }

            thumbnail.Left = _margin + (thumbnail.Width + _margin)
                                        * (ThumbnailPanel.Controls.Count %
                                                numberHorizontal);

            thumbnail.Top = _margin + (thumbnail.Height + _margin)
                                        * (ThumbnailPanel.Controls.Count /
                                                numberHorizontal);

            ThumbnailPanel.Controls.Add(thumbnail);
        }

        if (_applyAppearance)
        {
            foreach (TextureThumbnail thumbnail in ThumbnailPanel.Controls)
            {
                if (thumbnail.Selected)
```

```
            {
                thumbnail.BackColor = BackgroundColorSelected;
                thumbnail.ForeColor = ForegroundColorSelected;
            }
            else
            {
                thumbnail.BackColor = BackgroundColor;
                thumbnail.ForeColor = ForegroundColor;
            }
        }

        _applyAppearance = false;
    }
}

internal void PerformSelect(TextureThumbnail thumbnail)
{
    switch (_selection)
    {
        case SelectionMode.Single:
            {
                DeselectAll();
                thumbnail.Selected = true;
                if (TextureSelected != null)
                    TextureSelected(this,
                            new TextureBrowserEventArgs(thumbnail.Texture));
                break;
            }

        case SelectionMode.Multiple:
            {
                if (Control.ModifierKeys == Keys.Control)
                {
                    thumbnail.Selected = !thumbnail.Selected;

                    if (thumbnail.Selected)
                    {
                        if (TextureSelected != null)
                            TextureSelected(this,
                            new TextureBrowserEventArgs(thumbnail.Texture));
                    }
```

```
                                else
                                {
                                    if (TextureDeselected != null)
                                        TextureDeselected(this,
                                            new TextureBrowserEventArgs(thumbnail.Texture));
                                }

                                break;
                            }
                            else
                            {
                                DeselectAll();

                                thumbnail.Selected = true;

                                if (TextureSelected != null)
                                    TextureSelected(this,
                                        new TextureBrowserEventArgs(thumbnail.Texture));
                            }
                            break;
                    }
                }
            }

    internal void PerformActivated(TextureThumbnail thumbnail)
    {
        if (TextureActivated != null)
            TextureActivated(this, new TextureBrowserEventArgs(thumbnail.Texture));
    }

    internal void PerformRightClicked(TextureThumbnail thumbnail)
    {
        if (TextureRightClicked != null)
            TextureRightClicked(this,
                            new TextureBrowserEventArgs(thumbnail.Texture));
    }

    private void ThumbnailPanel_MouseClick(object sender, MouseEventArgs e)
    {
        DeselectAll();
    }
```

```
private void TextureBrowser_Resize(object sender, System.EventArgs e)
{
    if (_oldSize != ThumbnailPanel.Size)
    {
        _oldSize = ThumbnailPanel.Size;
        this.DisplayThumbnails();
    }
}
}
```

Figure 26.2 shows the texture browser control in design mode. The control is now complete, which means that we can start consuming it in our applications. The next section shows how to use it.

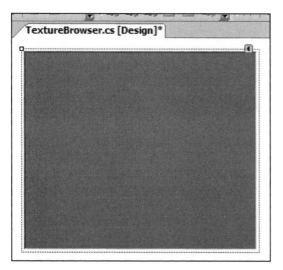

Figure 26.2 Screenshot of the texture browser control in design mode

Using the Control

Using the new control is very easy. The first thing you want to do is add a reference to the control assembly. The next step is to add the texture browser control into your toolbox. You can do this by right-clicking on the toolbox and selecting the Choose Items... option. The Choose Toolbox Items dialog will appear, showing all the assemblies loaded in the Global Assembly Cache (GAC). The control library is not registered in the GAC, so you will need to click the Browse button and navigate to the assembly of the library. An entry called TextureBrowser will be selected in the list. You should now be able to click OK and see the control appear in your toolbox.

You can now drag the texture browser control from the toolbox onto your form. Resize the control to your liking and then go to its properties. Aside from the normal properties that are available for all Windows Forms controls, there is a new section called Texture Browser Settings that are control-specific settings. These settings are shown in Figure 26.3.

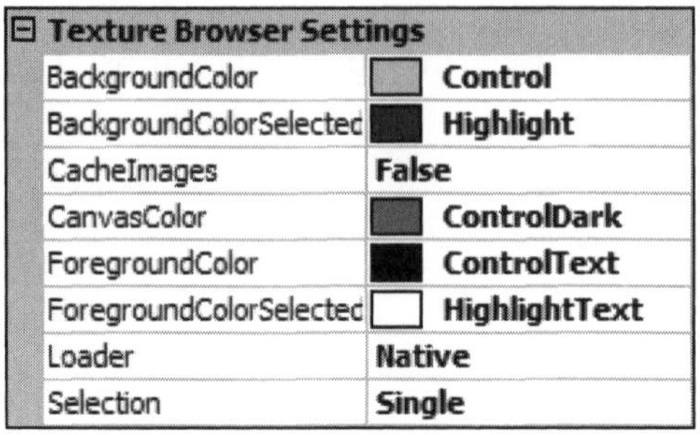

⊟ **Texture Browser Settings**		
BackgroundColor	▢	**Control**
BackgroundColorSelected	◼	**Highlight**
CacheImages	**False**	
CanvasColor	◼	**ControlDark**
ForegroundColor	◼	**ControlText**
ForegroundColorSelected	▢	**HighlightText**
Loader	**Native**	
Selection	**Single**	

Figure 26.3 Properties for the texture browser control.

Change these settings to your liking, and then you can move onto the code for adding textures to the control.

Loading Textures from a Directory

Early in the chapter, I mentioned that the loaders support three different sources for image data. The most common source will be from files located in the file system, and the following code shows how to iterate through a directory and load the image files into the texture browser control. Be sure to reference the System.IO namespace.

```
DirectoryInfo directoryInfo = new DirectoryInfo(path);
if (directoryInfo.Exists)
{
    FileInfo[] files = directoryInfo.GetFiles();

    foreach (FileInfo file in files)
        TextureBrowserInstance.AddTexture(new TextureHandle(file));
}
```

Loading Textures from a MemoryStream

The second source type for loading textures is from raw binary data stored in a MemoryStream object. This type is useful when images are extracted from storage archives, pulled off of a network connection, or programmatically generated. The following code shows how to load an image into the texture browser control from memory. Be sure to reference the System.Drawing and System.IO namespaces.

```
Image image = Image.FromFile(@".\MemoryImage.bmp");
MemoryStream stream = new MemoryStream();
image.Save(stream, ImageFormat.Png);
TextureBrowserInstance.AddTexture(new TextureHandle("My Image", stream));
```

Loading Textures from a Bitmap

The last source type provides the ability to use an existing bitmap image when creating a texture handle. This method does not require any additional loading, since the image data has already been loaded into the bitmap object. This approach is useful when retrieving embedded resource content from an assembly resource stream, or images that are programmatically generated. The following code shows how to load a texture from an existing bitmap.

```
Image image = Image.FromFile(@".\MemoryImage.bmp");
TextureBrowserInstance.AddTexture(new TextureHandle("My Image", image));
```

Texture Browser Demo

The Companion Web site has the complete source code for the library presented in this chapter, along with a simple demo that utilizes it. The demo just loads images located in a folder with the application, but supports the ability to switch image loaders at runtime.

Multiple selection is enabled, and you just have to hold down the Ctrl key while selecting multiple thumbnails. A context menu is bound to the right-click event of the thumbnails to present a dialog that shows simple information about the image. Lastly, the Activated event, (double-click), for the thumbnails shows a simple message box where other functionality could be implemented in a real-world application. An example of real-world functionality might be the ability to double-click a thumbnail and have a selected model mesh reference the texture as its color map.

Figure 26.4 shows a screenshot of the texture browser demo application.

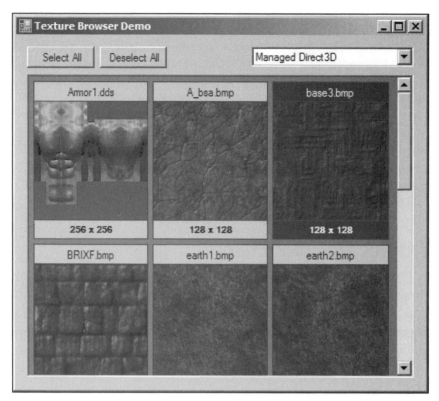

Figure 26.4 Screenshot of the demo application using the texture browser.

Conclusion

This chapter covered the construction of a reusable control that can display images in a visually appealing way, and can also manage the handling and notification of events associated with the control.

There are some places where refactoring could improve the overall design of the component, but the most notable place is the Managed Direct3D loader. The point of having pluggable interfaces is to decouple the reliance on external dependencies when a particular component is not in use. Consider the situation where it is preferred that an application consuming this control does not use the Managed Direct3D loader, but instead uses the native GDI+ version. Sure, the loader can be set to native, but the component is still referencing the managed DirectX assemblies. If the consuming application is launched on a system without these assemblies, then a File Not Found exception would be thrown during execution, even though the Managed Direct3D loader is never used.

This problem could be solved by compiling the abstract loader interface into a separate assembly, along with both loader types compiled into their own assemblies. The texture browser component and both loaders would reference the abstract loader interface, and the texture browser component would dynamically reference the appropriate loader at runtime using reflection.

With such a problem, you are probably wondering why the component was not designed to accommodate this decoupling in the first place. Reflection and plug-in–based architectures would be the ideal "best practice" way to design the component, but this chapter is meant to cover how to build the component itself, hence why the component was designed the way it is. Removing this dependency on Direct3D can be done two ways, both very easily. You can exclude the Direct3D loader code from the texture browser component and recompile it; do not forget to remove the assembly references as well. Or you can refactor the component to support a plugin–based architecture, which is covered in Chapter 38, "Designing an Extensible Plugin-Based Architecture."

Overall, this chapter presents a solid and reusable component that can be employed in a number of tools.

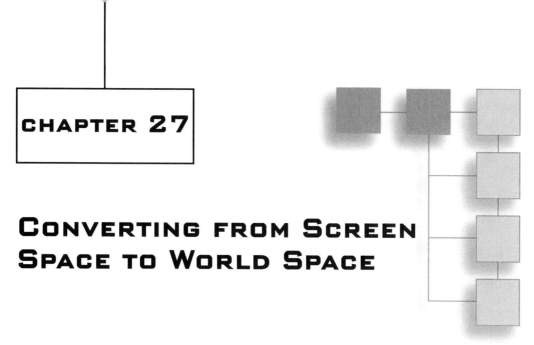

CHAPTER 27

CONVERTING FROM SCREEN SPACE TO WORLD SPACE

A mathematician is a device for turning coffee into theorems.

Paul Erdos

When working with standard applications, users are accustomed to clicking on a control or widget and having some degree of interaction with the control. Take a push button, for example; users click on a push button and a visual cue is used that presents the button in a depressed state, and the button launches an on-click event that performs some action. Users are also accustomed to this same level of interaction with 3D applications.

Many 3D applications have dialogs that can modify and manage data without the need to interact with the scene, but visual interaction is much easier and faster to perform than clicking through dialog after dialog. For example, 3D applications typically allow the user to reposition objects within a scene by using the mouse and by typing in coordinates in a dialog box. It does not take a lot of thought to figure out which method is faster and more productive. If using the mouse is easier and more productive, why bother with field-driven dialog boxes at all? Using the mouse is quick, but typing coordinates into a dialog is much more precise than using the mouse and trying to coerce an object into a specific location.

In order to handle mouse-clicking, the application must be able to read mouse click events, extract the coordinate (X, Y), and perform an intersection test against a particular control to see if it was activated. Thankfully, this process is automatically handled by Win32 user interface controls, but we are not so lucky in the 3D world.

This chapter will cover the math and implementation behind converting coordinates in screen space to world space and performing intersection tests, otherwise known as *picking*.

Transforming Screen Coordinates

Performing intersecting tests against Win32 controls is very simple, since the mouse coordinates and the control bounds are both in screen space (X, Y). Intersection tests from screen space coordinates to world space bounds (X, Y, Z) require a bit of math since we do not know the relationship between the 3D object and its projection. It is also important to state that we are using a left-handed coordinate system, which is the default for Direct3D. OpenGL uses a right-handed coordinate system, so the math and code will have to be adapted to get it working. Take a look at the source code for the gluUnproject function of OpenGL if you are unsure of how to do this.

Figure 27.1 shows the relationship between the origin of projection (screen space) and the projection window (world space).

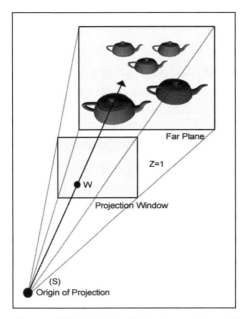

Figure 27.1 Relationship between the origin of project and the projection window.

Figure 27.1 shows that the teapot was projected to the area surrounding **W** on the projection window, corresponding to screen point **S**. With that said, we can compute a picking ray that will project from the origin and pass through **W**. Intersection tests can then be performed against all objects in the scene to determine which objects were picked by the user. It is possible that the intersection tests performed on the scene objects will return no hits. This simply means that the user did not click on any objects.

Note

The point **W** on the projection window corresponds to the clicked screen point **S**.

We must first transform the clicked screen point **S** to point **W** on the projection window. This is done by working backwards from the equations that transform projection window points to screen points. The viewport transformation matrix used in the equations is shown here:

$$\begin{bmatrix} \dfrac{viewportWidth}{2} & 0 & 0 & 0 \\[2ex] 0 & -\dfrac{viewportHeight}{2} & 0 & 0 \\[2ex] 0 & 0 & MaxZ - MinZ & 0 \\[2ex] X + \dfrac{viewportWidth}{2} & Y + \dfrac{viewportHeight}{2} & MinZ & 1 \end{bmatrix}$$

Working backwards, transforming a world space point **W** (X, Y, Z) by the viewport transformation matrix, yields the screen space point **S** (X, Y). Following are the two equations to solve for **S**. The 2D image displayed by your graphics card after rasterization does not contain any depth information (Z).

$$S_x = W_x \left(\frac{viewportWidth}{2} \right) + X + \frac{viewportWidth}{2}$$

$$S_y = -W_y \left(\frac{viewportHeight}{2} \right) + Y + \frac{viewportHeight}{2}$$

These two equations are great when converting from world space to screen space, but they will serve no purpose unless we can get them into a more useful state. Solving for variable **W**, we get the following new equations.

$$W_X = \frac{2S_X - 2X - viewportWidth}{viewportWidth}$$

$$W_Y = \frac{2S_Y + 2Y + viewportHeight}{viewportHeight}$$

The X and Y members of the viewport are almost always 0, so we can go one step further and come up with the following equations. The projection window also coincides with the plane where $Z = 1$, so we can now set the Z component of the 3D coordinate we are trying to calculate.

$$W_X = \frac{2 \cdot S_X}{viewportWidth} - 1$$

$$W_Y = \frac{2 \cdot S_Y}{viewportHeight} + 1$$

$$W_Z = 1$$

There is one last factor that must be considered to correctly solve for **W**. Different fields of view can be used to present a scene, and the projection matrix scales the points on the projection window to simulate these fields of view. To reclaim the original values before scaling occurs, we must transform the points by the inverse of the scaling operations. The variable *projection* will be used to signify the projection matrix, and the subscripts represent the matrix entries. Entries 00 and 11 of a transformation matrix scale the X and Y values, so we can produce the following equations.

$$W_X = \left(\frac{2X}{viewportWidth} - 1 \right) \left(\frac{1}{projection_{00}} \right)$$

$$W_Y = \left(\frac{-2Y}{viewportHeight} + 1 \right) \left(\frac{1}{projection_{11}} \right)$$

$$W_Z = 1$$

Note

The Managed Direct3D Matrix object uses a slightly different numbering convention for row and column entries. The properties M11 and M22 represent the 00 and 11, respectively.

With the final transformation equations, we can move on to computing the picking ray that will test for objects picked by the user.

Computing the Picking Ray

A ray can be represented by the parametric equation $P(t) = P + t * D$, where P is a point in the ray and D is a vector that provides the direction of the ray. In our situation, the origin of the ray is also the origin of the view space, so $P = (0, 0, 0)$. If P is a point on the project window to shoot the picking ray through, then we can solve for D with the following equation.

$$D = P - P_0 = (P_X, P_Y, 1) - (0,0,0) = P$$

The following code is used to compute the picking ray for intersection testing.

```
private PickingRay ComputePickingRay(Entity entity, int x, int y)
{
    float viewportWidth = device.Viewport.Width;
    float viewportHeight = device.Viewport.Height;

    float projection00 = device.Transform.Projection.M11;
    float projection11 = device.Transform.Projection.M22;

    float pX = ((( 2.0F * x) / viewportWidth)  - 1.0F) / projection00;
    float pY = (((-2.0F * y) / viewportHeight) + 1.0F) / projection11;

    Matrix invWorldView = Matrix.Identity;

    invWorldView.Translate(entity.Position);
    invWorldView.Multiply(device.Transform.View);
    invWorldView.Invert();

    Vector3 rayDirection = new Vector3(pX, pY, 1.0f);

    return new PickingRay(rayDirection, invWorldView);
}
```

After computing the picking ray, we must also transform it into world space to correctly represent the objects in the scene. Transforming the picking ray to world space is done in the constructor of the following struct. The transformation matrix supplied to the constructor is the inverse world-view matrix that was created when the picking ray was computed. The following code is used to transform the picking ray into world space so that the ray and the objects are in the same coordinate system.

```
internal struct PickingRay
{
    internal Vector3 Origin;
    internal Vector3 Direction;

    public PickingRay(Vector3 direction, Matrix transform)
    {
        Origin = new Vector3(0.0F, 0.0F, 0.0F);
        Direction = direction;

        Origin.TransformCoordinate(transform);
        Direction.TransformNormal(transform);
        Direction.Normalize();
    }
}
```

Note
_____

Vector3.TransformCoordinate() is used to transform points because it sets the fourth component to W = 1, whereas Vector3.TransformNormal() is used to transform vectors because it sets the fourth component to W = 0.

_____

Bounding Sphere Intersection Tests

At this point, we are converting screen space coordinates to world space and computing a ray that will be used for picking. Intersection tests will be performed against objects in the scene using the computed ray to determine which objects the user has selected.

In order to perform intersection tests, we need a 3D shape to test against. Bounding spheres are common because their approximated nature makes them fast to compute and use. Each object is represented by a bounding sphere that describes the approximated volume of the object.

A sphere is represented by its center c and its radius r. Points can be tested for whether they belong to a sphere if their distance from the center is equal to the radius, shown by the following equation.

$$|c\vec{p}| = |p - c| = r$$

Intersecting a ray with a sphere can be found with the following equation, where p is substituted with $o + t\vec{d}$ to represent the ray.

$$r = |o + t\vec{d} - c| = |c\vec{o} + t\vec{d}|$$

We can square both sides of the equation to obtain the following equation.

$$r^2 = |c\vec{o}|^2 + 2(c\vec{o} \cdot \vec{d})*t + |\vec{d}|^2 * t^2$$

This equation can then be written as a quadratic equation.

$$At^2 + Bt + C = 0$$

$$A = |\vec{d}|^2$$

$$B = 2(c\vec{o} \cdot \vec{d})$$

$$C = |c\vec{o}|^2 - r^2$$

We can calculate the discriminant and use it to determine at first glance whether any solutions exist. Ignoring t, we can calculate the discriminant with $\Delta = B^2 - 4AC$.

When the discriminant is less than zero, there are no solutions, so an intersection did not occur.

When the discriminant is equal to zero, there is only one solution, which is generally a tangency. The solution for this case is given by the following equation:

$$-B/(2A)$$

When the discriminant is greater than zero, there are two solutions. Two solutions for this case are given by the following equation:

$$-B/(2A)$$

Rays only extend in one direction (positive), so any solutions where $t < 0$ have to be ignored. We just need to know if any solution was found, so we can skip the second case altogether and jump right into the third case. If any solution is > 0, we can safely say that an intersection was found.

The following code shows the intersection code for ray-sphere.

```
private bool IntersectRaySphere(Entity entity, int x, int y)
{
    PickingRay ray = ComputePickingRay(entity, x, y);

    Vector3 vec = ray.Origin - entity.BoundingSphere.Center;
```

```
    float b = 2.0F * Vector3.Dot(ray.Direction, vec);

    float center = Vector3.Dot(vec, vec) - (entity.BoundingSphere.Radius *
                                            entity.BoundingSphere.Radius);

    float discriminant = (b * b) - (4.0F * center);

    if (discriminant < 0.0F)
        return false;

    discriminant = (float)Math.Sqrt((double)discriminant);

    float s0 = (-b + discriminant) / 2.0F;
    float s1 = (-b - discriminant) / 2.0F;

    if (s0 >= 0.0F || s1 >= 0.0F)
        return true;

    return false;
}
```

NOTE

The picking ray extends infinitely, so there is a possibility that multiple objects can be intersected. The object closest to the camera is the one the user selected because it will always occlude the other selected objects.

Improving Intersection Accuracy

Testing for object intersection with bounding sphere volumes works, and the tests are straightforward and fast to compute. A disadvantage to using bounding sphere volumes is a fair level of inaccuracy. Bounding sphere volumes are ideal for any spherical object, although most of the time intersections are performed against an arbitrary mesh, which means that selections can occur by clicking near the object.

A solution to this problem is to perform triangle intersections against all the polygons within the arbitrary mesh. This process takes longer to compute, but the results are much more accurate than bounding sphere volumes. For the purposes of this example, we will use the built-in Mesh.Intersect() method of Managed Direct3D to perform intersection at the polygon level. The picking ray is computed in the same way as in the previous example, but the picking ray origin and direction are passed into the intersection method.

The following code shows an intersect variation with improved accuracy.

```
private bool IntersectRayMesh(Entity entity, int x, int y)
{
    PickingRay ray = ComputePickingRay(entity, x, y);
    return entity.Mesh.Intersect(ray.Origin, ray.Direction);
}
```

Using Built-In D3DX Functionality

Reinventing the wheel is generally frowned upon, but a developer can always argue that he would rather reinvent the wheel in some cases if it means he will walk away understanding the mechanics of the solution at a lower level. This chapter has discussed the math and implementation behind converting a screen space coordinate into world space, as well as computing a picking ray that can be used to perform intersection tests against objects. I then went on to showing an improvement to the intersection tests using built-in functionality of the Direct3D Mesh class. There is actually enough built-in functionality with Managed Direct3D to implement a full picking solution with only a few lines of code.

The Vector3 class has a method called Unproject that can be used to project a vector from screen space into world space. We can make two vectors that represent the near and far clipping planes (Z = 0 and 1, respectively), unproject both of them, and then subtract the near vector from the far vector to produce a picking ray suitable for Mesh.Intersect().

The following code shows this.

```
private bool IntersectUnprojectMesh(Entity entity, int x, int y)
{
    Vector3 near;
    Vector3 far;

    near = new Vector3(x, y, 0);
    far = new Vector3(x, y, 1);

    Matrix world = Matrix.Identity;
    world.Translate(entity.Position);

    near.Unproject(device.Viewport,
                   device.Transform.Projection,
                   device.Transform.View,
                   world);
```

```
    far.Unproject(device.Viewport,
                  device.Transform.Projection,
                  device.Transform.View,
                  world);

    far.Subtract(near);

    return entity.Mesh.Intersect(near, far);
}
```

Conclusion

This chapter covered the math and implementation details behind converting screen space coordinates into world space, and performing intersection tests to determine objects that have been picked in a scene.

Remember the following steps:

- Given the screen point **S**, find its corresponding point (**W**) on the projection window.
- Compute the picking ray shooting from the origin through point **W**.
- Transform the picking ray into the same space as each object.
- Perform intersection tests to determine the objects picked by the user.

The Companion Web site has the full source code for the example that is fragmented throughout this chapter. The example displays several teapots; the user can click on a teapot and it will turn a different color when selected. Figure 27.2 shows the example provided with this chapter.

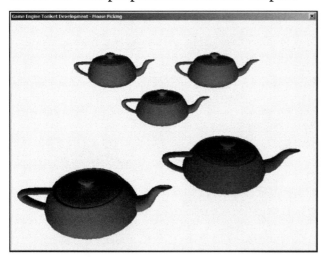

Figure 27.2
Screenshot of the provided example for mouse picking.

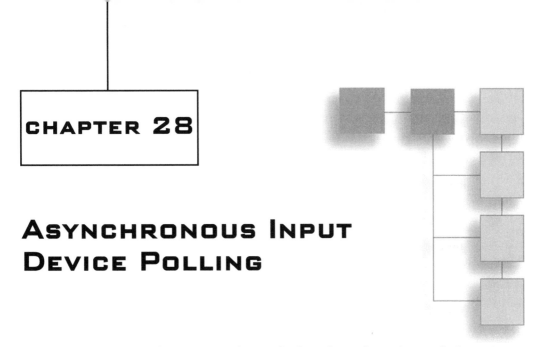

CHAPTER 28

ASYNCHRONOUS INPUT DEVICE POLLING

Why do we never have time to do it right, but always have time to do it over?

Anonymous

The Principle of Feedback (Chapter 7, "Fundamentals of User Interface Design") is perhaps the most important concept of application design. This principle entails visual cues that easily describe the state of the application, but this principle also covers responsiveness of the user interface and cues related to waiting periods.

The standard Microsoft Windows message pump typically works well for most applications, but applications that update their state each time the mouse is moved can suffer from performance penalties. This is usually felt by applications that employ the use of 3D real-time graphics technologies like Direct3D.

The Microsoft DirectX library has a technology called DirectInput that communicates directly with device hardware drivers, completely avoiding the Microsoft Windows message pump. DirectInput offers considerable performance boosts over the message pump, and also supports asynchronous polling and data buffering.

This chapter focuses on using DirectInput to asynchronously read the mouse and keyboard devices. The mouse positions are expressed as deltas (difference) between the current and last positions. This chapter also shows how to read the mouse buttons. This is a useful technique for using the mouse to control a 3D camera. You will also learn how to check whether a key is depressed on the keyboard.

Asynchronous Mouse Polling

The first step is to include and reference the appropriate namespaces. You should add a reference to `Microsoft.DirectX` and `Microsoft.DirectX.DirectInput` and use the following namespaces.

```
using System;
using System.Threading;
using Microsoft.DirectX;
using Microsoft.DirectX.DirectInput;
```

The following class encapsulates all the nitty gritty details of using `DirectInput` for mouse polling. After instantiation, the `Initialize` method is executed to create the mouse input device and to spawn the asynchronous polling thread.

```
public class AsynchronousMouse : IDisposable
{
```

The Device object is used to manage Microsoft DirectInput devices and associated properties, specify behavior, manage force-feedback effects, interact with the device's control panel, and perform device initialization.

```
    private Device _device = null;

    private Thread _threadData = null;
    private AutoResetEvent _eventTrigger = null;

    private byte[] _buttons;
    private int _x;
    private int _y;
    private int _z;

    private System.Windows.Forms.Form _context;

    public delegate void MovementDelegate(int x,
                                          int y,
                                          int z,
                                          bool left,
                                          bool middle,
                                          bool right);

    private delegate void PollTriggerDelegate();

    public event MovementDelegate MouseMovement;
```

```
public byte[] Button
{
    get { return _buttons; }
}

public int X
{
    get { return _x; }
}

public int Y
{
    get { return _y; }
}

public int Z
{
    get { return _z; }
}
```

The initialization method instantiates the device, sets the cooperative level, and sets the notification event that is used to control the polling thread.

The following code shows the initialization method.

```
public bool Initialize(System.Windows.Forms.Form context)
{
    _context = context;
```

The next two lines create a new thread that asynchronously polls the mouse device for state changes and dispatches them back to the user.

```
    _threadData = new Thread(new ThreadStart(this.AsynchronousPolling));
    _threadData.Start();
```

The _eventTrigger is used by DirectInput to notify threads when the mouse state changes. We use this event to control the asynchronous polling thread.

```
    _eventTrigger = new AutoResetEvent(false);

    try
    {
```

SystemGuid contains constant identifiers for system devices for use with DirectInput. SystemGuid.Mouse is associated with a mouse that has up to four buttons, or another device that is behaving like a mouse.

```
        _device = new Device(SystemGuid.Mouse);
        _device.SetDataFormat(DeviceDataFormat.Mouse);
    }
    catch (InputException)
    {
        return false;
    }
```

You must also specify the cooperative level for DirectInput devices. The different flags are described in Table 28.1.

Table 28.1 DirectInput Device Cooperative Level Flags

Flag	Description
Exclusive	This flag means that we want priority for control of the device.
NonExclusive	This flag means that we do not need priority for control of the device.
Foreground	This flag means that we only want data from the device if the window passed into the SetCooperativeLevel method has focus.
Background	This flag means that we always want data from the device.
NoWindowsKey	This flag is used to ignore the Windows logo key, and is generally used in full screen mode to prevent interruptions.

We always want data and we do not want to stall other applications using the input devices, so we use the NonExclusive | Background level.

```
        _device.SetCooperativeLevel(_context,
                                    CooperativeLevelFlags.NonExclusive |
                                    CooperativeLevelFlags.Background);
        _device.SetEventNotification(_eventTrigger);

        Acquire();
        return true;
    }
```

The polling thread runs in a loop, and each cycle is executed when the mouse is moved. A cycle polls the mouse device to update the cached state information, and then the callback method is fired. The callback method is registered by the consumer of the component, and can be used to update the user interface or calculate a 3D camera, for example.

```
private void AsynchronousPolling()
{
    while (_context.Created)
    {
```

The `AutoResetEvent.WaitOne()` method is used to pause thread execution until it receives a notification event (in this case the mouse state changing).

```
        _eventTrigger.WaitOne(-1, false);

        try
        {
            if (_device == null)
            {
                continue;
            }
```

The next line retrieves the current mouse state.

```
            _device.Poll();
        }
        catch (InputException)
        {
            continue;
        }
```

The next two lines are used to asynchronously execute the trigger method that routes mouse state information back to the client through a registered callback.

```
        if (_context.Created && !_context.Disposing)
            _context.BeginInvoke(new PollTriggerDelegate(PollTrigger));
    }
}
```

The following code shows the trigger logic that gets the current mouse information and sends it to the user event.

```
private void PollTrigger()
{
    if (MouseMovement != null)
    {
        MouseState stateData = _device.CurrentMouseState;

        _buttons = stateData.GetMouseButtons();
```

```
            bool left = (_buttons[0] != 0);
            bool right = (_buttons[1] != 0);
            bool middle = (_buttons[2] != 0);

            _x = stateData.X;
            _y = stateData.Y;
            _z = stateData.Z;

            MouseMovement(stateData.X,
                           stateData.Y,
                           stateData.Z,
                           left,
                           middle,
                           right);
        }
    }
```

The following method is used to gain access to the mouse device. This is a required step before data can be read from the device.

```
    public void Acquire()
    {
        if (_device != null)
        {
            try
            {
                _device.Acquire();
            }
            catch
            {
            }
        }
    }
```

The following methods are used to properly dispose of the device and trigger objects using the IDisposable pattern.

```
    public void Dispose()
    {
        Dispose(true);
        GC.SuppressFinalize(this);
    }


    protected virtual void Dispose(bool disposing)
```

```
    {
        if (disposing)
        {
            if (_eventTrigger != null)
                _eventTrigger.Set();

            if (_device != null)
            {
                _device.Unacquire();
                _device.Dispose();
                _device = null;
            }

            _eventTrigger = null;
        }
    }
}
```

Asynchronous Keyboard Polling

Just as with the mouse class, you need to include and reference the appropriate namespaces. You should add a reference to `Microsoft.DirectX` and `Microsoft.DirectX.DirectInput` and use the following namespaces.

```
using System;
using System.Threading;
using Microsoft.DirectX;
using Microsoft.DirectX.DirectInput;
```

The following class encapsulates all the nitty gritty details of using DirectInput for mouse polling. The code is almost identical to the `AsynchronousMouse` class, so only the new sections will be discussed.

```
public class AsynchronousKeyboard : IDisposable
{
    private Device _device = null;
    private Thread _threadData = null;
    private AutoResetEvent _eventTrigger = null;

    private System.Windows.Forms.Form _context;

    private bool _acquired = false;

    private delegate void PollTriggerDelegate();
```

```
public delegate void ActionDelegate();
public event ActionDelegate KeyboardAction;

private KeyboardState _keyboardState;

public bool Initialize(System.Windows.Forms.Form context)
{
    _context = context;

    _threadData = new Thread(new ThreadStart(this.AsynchronousPolling));
    _threadData.Start();

    _eventTrigger = new AutoResetEvent(false);

    try
    {
        _device = new Device(SystemGuid.Keyboard);
        _device.SetDataFormat(DeviceDataFormat.Keyboard);
    }
    catch (InputException)
    {
        return false;
    }

    _device.SetCooperativeLevel(_context,
                               CooperativeLevelFlags.NonExclusive |
                               CooperativeLevelFlags.Background);
    _device.SetEventNotification(_eventTrigger);

    Acquire();

    return true;
}
```

The following method is used to query the keyboard state to determine whether a particular key is depressed. The keyboard state is cached each time the state changes within the asynchronous polling thread.

```
public bool KeyDown(Key key)
{
    if (_keyboardState != null && _keyboardState[key])
    {
```

```
            return true;
        }

        return false;
    }

    private void AsynchronousPolling()
    {
        while (_context.Created)
        {
            _eventTrigger.WaitOne(-1, false);

            try
            {
                if (_device == null)
                {
                    continue;
                }

                Acquire();

                if (_acquired)
                {
```

Retrieve and cache the current keyboard state so that the KeyDown method can use it.

```
                    _keyboardState = _device.GetCurrentKeyboardState();
                }
            }
            catch (InputException)
            {
                continue;
            }

            if (_context.Created && !_context.Disposing)
                _context.BeginInvoke(new PollTriggerDelegate(PollTrigger));
        }
    }

    private void PollTrigger()
    {
        if (KeyboardAction != null)
            KeyboardAction();
    }
```

```csharp
public void Acquire()
{
    if (_device != null)
    {
        try
        {
            if (!_acquired)
            {
                _device.Acquire();
                _acquired = true;
            }
        }
        catch
        {
            _acquired = false;
        }
    }
}

public void Dispose()
{
    Dispose(true);
    GC.SuppressFinalize(this);
}

protected virtual void Dispose(bool disposing)
{
    if (disposing)
    {
        if (_eventTrigger != null)
            _eventTrigger.Set();

        if (_device != null)
        {
            _device.Unacquire();
            _device.Dispose();
            _device = null;
        }

        _eventTrigger = null;
    }
}
```

Sample Usage

Using the two classes in this chapter is very easy. The following code is from the example for this chapter on the Companion Web site. A callback is used to report keyboard state changes, although AsynchronousKeyboard.KeyDown() can be called at any time outside of the callback. The Buttons, X, Y, Z properties of the AsynchronousMouse class can also be called outside of the callback too.

```
public partial class MainForm : Form
{
    private AsynchronousMouse _mouse;
    private AsynchronousKeyboard _keyboard;

    public MainForm()
    {
        InitializeComponent();

        _mouse = new AsynchronousMouse();
        _mouse.MouseMovement +=
                new AsynchronousMouse.MovementDelegate(MouseMovementCallback);

        _keyboard = new AsynchronousKeyboard();
        _keyboard.KeyboardAction +=
                new AsynchronousKeyboard.ActionDelegate(KeyboardActionCallback);
    }

    void KeyboardActionCallback()
    {
        if (_keyboard.KeyDown(Microsoft.DirectX.DirectInput.Key.UpArrow))
        {
            UpArrowState.Text = "Down";
        }
        else
        {
            UpArrowState.Text = "Up";
        }

        if (_keyboard.KeyDown(Microsoft.DirectX.DirectInput.Key.DownArrow))
        {
            DownArrowState.Text = "Down";
        }
        else
        {
```

```
                DownArrowState.Text = "Up";
        }

        if (_keyboard.KeyDown(Microsoft.DirectX.DirectInput.Key.RightArrow))
        {
            RightArrowState.Text = "Down";
        }
        else
        {
            RightArrowState.Text = "Up";
        }

        if (_keyboard.KeyDown(Microsoft.DirectX.DirectInput.Key.LeftArrow))
        {
            LeftArrowState.Text = "Down";
        }
        else
        {
            LeftArrowState.Text = "Up";
        }

        if (_keyboard.KeyDown(Microsoft.DirectX.DirectInput.Key.A))
        {
            AState.Text = "Down";
        }
        else
        {
            AState.Text = "Up";
        }

        if (_keyboard.KeyDown(Microsoft.DirectX.DirectInput.Key.D))
        {
            DState.Text = "Down";
        }
        else
        {
            DState.Text = "Up";
        }
    }

    void MouseMovementCallback(int x,
                               int y,
                               int z,
```

```
                          bool left,
                          bool middle,
                          bool right)
{
    if (left)
    {
        LeftButtonState.BackColor = Color.LimeGreen;
    }
    else
    {
        LeftButtonState.BackColor = Color.Maroon;
    }

    if (middle)
    {
        MiddleButtonState.BackColor = Color.LimeGreen;
    }
    else
    {
        MiddleButtonState.BackColor = Color.Maroon;
    }

    if (right)
    {
        RightButtonState.BackColor = Color.LimeGreen;
    }
    else
    {
        RightButtonState.BackColor = Color.Maroon;
    }

    ListViewItem listItem = new ListViewItem();

    listItem.Text = x.ToString();
    listItem.SubItems.Add(y.ToString());
    listItem.SubItems.Add(z.ToString());

    CoordinateList.Items.Add(listItem);

    Coordinates.Text = String.Format("Coordinates ({0}, {1}, {2})",
                                     x,
                                     y,
                                     z);
```

```
    }

    private void MainForm_Load(object sender, EventArgs e)
    {
        if (!_mouse.Initialize(this))
        {
            MessageBox.Show("Error initializing asynchronous mouse. Exiting.");
            Application.Exit();
        }

        if (!_keyboard.Initialize(this))
        {
            MessageBox.Show("Error initializing async device. Exiting.");
            Application.Exit();
        }
    }

    private void MainForm_Activated(object sender, EventArgs e)
    {
        if (_mouse != null)
        {
            _mouse.Acquire();
        }

        if (_keyboard != null)
        {
            _keyboard.Acquire();
        }
    }
}
```

Conclusion

This chapter briefly discussed DirectInput and some advantages of using DirectInput over the standard Microsoft Windows message pump. A solution was later presented that shows how to read input device data asynchronously from the mouse or keyboard. This technique is very useful for graphic-intensive programs where smooth input is required.

## PART IV

Techniques for Network Tools

The Internet? We are not interested in it.

Bill Gates, 1993

For the most part, tools only need to manage data that exists on the host machine of the tool, but there is an increasing demand for tools of a distributed nature for certain processes. Some tools need to access a remote database containing schemas for game entities, while some tools require the ability to download files off a remote file share when appropriate. Some more advanced topics include distributed computing architectures in order to disperse processor-intensive tasks over multiple processing nodes. Another common use for network tools is to pass information between applications that exist on the same machine. Creating a loopback endpoint has been used by a number of tools to pass information between a managed and an unmanaged application process without worrying about data formatting. However, this approach will not be covered in this book since superior techniques are shown in Part V, "Techniques for Legacy Interoperability," when discussing interoperability with legacy applications.

The chapter in this part does not cover the low-level details of the OSI model or any common network protocols like UDP or TCP\IP because of the abstracted nature of the stream model in .NET. It does, however, cover building a distributed grid computing architecture with .NET remoting, and how to download files asynchronously across HTTP.

There is a growing need for network-oriented tools when dealing with distributed architectures, though the majority of tools do not usually require this functionality. Although fairly specific, the chapters covered in this part will come in handy when the need arises.

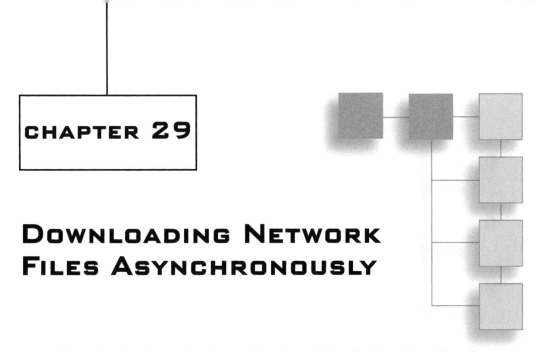

CHAPTER 29

DOWNLOADING NETWORK FILES ASYNCHRONOUSLY

Debugging is twice as hard as writing the code in the first place. Therefore, if you write the code as cleverly as possible, you are, by definition, not smart enough to debug it.

Brian Kernigan

A common task of network applications is the downloading of files off a network or Internet server. Traditionally, the developer would have to implement a TCP\IP socket layer that implemented a subset of the HTTP protocol to retrieve these files. As with many other common tasks, Microsoft has provided this functionality in the .NET framework with the HttpWebRequest and HttpWebResponse classes. These classes provide both synchronous and asynchronous approaches to interacting with universal resource identifiers (URI). The synchronous approach is very straightforward, and requires little instruction on usage. The asynchronous approach, however, can be tricky to implement and use.

In this chapter I will discuss the asynchronous functionality of the HttpWebRequest and HttpWebResponse classes, and present a reusable solution to download files asynchronously off a network or Internet server.

HttpWebRequest and HttpWebResponse

The .NET framework provides the abstract class `WebRequest`, which is the request and response model for accessing data from the Internet. This model is protocol-agnostic, specialized by classes inheriting from the abstract class. There are a variety of specialized descendents of `WebRequest`, like `FileWebRequest` for handling file:// paths, but this chapter will focus on the HTTP protocol using `HttpWebRequest`.

The HTTP protocol is the primary transport mechanism for communicating with Internet resources. A developer may use this mechanism to download application updates and configuration information that constantly changes or even to post messages to a dynamic environment like an ASP.NET application. The `HttpWebRequest` class implements the `WebRequest` class, providing a specialized request class to communicate over the HTTP protocol. This class enables an application to interact directly with servers using HTTP.

Server resources are identified by uniform resource identifiers (URI), and the .NET framework provides the `Uri` class, which defines the properties and methods for handling uniform resource identifiers, such as comparing, combing, and parsing. Requests are sent from an application to a URI, such as a zipped fie or web page. The requests are sent using `HttpWebRequest` to the remote server, using the HTTP protocol as the transport mechanism to access the resource.

Note

If an error occurs with a request, a `WebException` is thrown that contains details about why the request failed. The Status property is of type `WebRequestStatus`, and if the value is `WebRequestStatus.ProtocolError`, the response returned from the server is contained in the `WebException.Response` property.

The remainder of the chapter will cover the construction of an asynchronous wrapper around `HttpWebRequest` and `HttpWebResponse`.

The Request Object

The first component of our asynchronous wrapper is the request object, which serves as the public interface between the application and the rest of the wrapper. This wrapper executes the core system and fires a download complete event when the file has finished downloading. There is also a progress update event that you can subscribe to in order to display download progress to the users.

```
public class AsyncFileDownloadRequest
{
```

```
public event AsyncDownloadCompleteHandler DownloadComplete;
public event AsyncDownloadProgressHandler ProgressUpdate;

private Uri address = null;

public Uri Address
{
    get { return address; }
    set { address = value; }
}

public void Initiate()
{
    Thread thread = new Thread(new ThreadStart(InitiateThread));
    thread.Start();
}

private void InitiateThread()
{
    if (DownloadComplete != null && address != null)
    {
        AsyncFileDownloadSystem system = new AsyncFileDownloadSystem();
        byte[] data = system.DownloadFile(address, ProgressUpdate);
        DownloadComplete(data);
    }
}
}
```

Maintaining Data State

The asynchronous mechanism provided by the HttpWebRequest object relies on a chain of successively executed methods that process data in chunks. In order to associate the data with the asynchronous mechanism, we need to build a simple state object that will be used to store information and data related to state. The asynchronous mechanism allows us to pass an arbitrary object between methods, so the following class will be used as a container to pass within the asynchronous model.

```
internal class AsyncFileDownloadState
{
    public AsyncDownloadProgressHandler ProgressUpdate;
```

```csharp
    private const int bufferSize = 1024;

    private WebRequest request = null;
    private Stream responseStream;
    private bool fixedSizeBuffer = true;
    private byte[] processBuffer;
    private byte[] staticBuffer;
    private List<byte> dynamicBuffer;
    private int dataLength = -1;
    private int bytesRead = 0;

    public WebRequest Request
    {
        get { return request; }
        set { request = value; }
    }

    public Stream ResponseStream
    {
        get { return responseStream; }
        set { responseStream = value; }
    }

    public bool FixedSizeBuffer
    {
        get { return fixedSizeBuffer; }
        set { fixedSizeBuffer = value; }
    }

    public byte[] ProcessBuffer
    {
        get { return processBuffer; }
        set { processBuffer = value; }
    }

    public byte[] StaticBuffer
    {
        get { return staticBuffer; }
        set { staticBuffer = value; }
    }

    public List<byte> DynamicBuffer
```

```
    {
        get { return dynamicBuffer; }
        set { dynamicBuffer = value; }
    }

    public int DataLength
    {
        get { return dataLength; }
        set { dataLength = value; }
    }

    public int BytesRead
    {
        get { return bytesRead; }
        set { bytesRead = value; }
    }

    public AsyncFileDownloadState()
    {
        processBuffer = new byte[bufferSize];
    }
}
```

The Core System

The solution presented in this chapter encapsulates a lot of the implementation details of HttpWebRequest and asynchronous communication into a wrapper class. There are a number of ways to implement an asynchronous model; some are extremely simple, while some are complex and robust. The solution for this chapter sits somewhere between those extremes.

The following code describes the core system that handles asynchronous web requests and responses.

```
public delegate void AsyncDownloadCompleteHandler(byte[] data);
public delegate void AsyncDownloadProgressHandler(int bytesRead,

int dataLength);

internal class AsyncFileDownloadSystem
{
```

The following is a constant that describes the temporary buffer size of incoming data when the content length is unknown.

```
private const int bufferSize = 1024;
```

The following object is used to signal that the download is complete. ManualResetEvent allows threads to communicate with each other; it is typically used when one thread must be completed before others can proceed.

```
public ManualResetEvent completeEvent = new ManualResetEvent(false);
```

The following method downloads the data of a file pointed to by the address string. The specified callback is used to report progress status.

```
public byte[] DownloadFile(string address,
                           AsyncDownloadProgressHandler callback)
{
    Uri addressUri = new Uri(address);
    return DownloadFile(addressUri, callback);
}
```

The following method downloads the data of a file pointed to by the Uri. The specified callback is used to report progress status.

```
public byte[] DownloadFile(Uri address, AsyncDownloadProgressHandler callback)
{
```

Set the complete event state to un-signaled.

```
completeEvent.Reset();
```

Create a new HttpWebRequest object by passing in the address to the resource. Passing in a file:// address will result in a FileWebRequest object being created, working transparently with the existing code because of the protocol-agnostic model used.

```
WebRequest request = WebRequest.Create(address);
```

Instantiate a new asynchronous state object and reference the request for later use.

```
AsyncFileDownloadState state = new AsyncFileDownloadState();
state.Request = request;
```

Set the progress update callback on the state object.

```
state.ProgressUpdate += callback;
```

Launch an asynchronous request to access a web resource.

```
IAsyncResult result =
    request.BeginGetResponse(new AsyncCallback(ResponseCallback),
                                            state) as IAsyncResult;
```

Wait for the complete event to be set so that the data is not returned until the call-back finishes.

```
completeEvent.WaitOne();

if (state.FixedSizeBuffer)
{
    return state.StaticBuffer;
}
else
{
    return state.DynamicBuffer.ToArray();
}
}
```

The following callback is used when an asynchronous response occurs.

```
private void ResponseCallback(IAsyncResult asyncResult)
{
```

Pull the asynchronous state object out of the result object, and then retrieve the request.

```
AsyncFileDownloadState state =
                    (AsyncFileDownloadState)asyncResult.AsyncState;

WebRequest request = state.Request;
```

Complete the asynchronous response and get the response object.

```
WebResponse response = request.EndGetResponse(asyncResult);
```

As an optimization, we check to see whether the data length of the requested resource is known, so that an appropriate storage buffer can be used. With a known length, a static buffer can be used, whereas a dynamic buffer is used when the length is unknown, resulting in decreased performance.

```
if (response.ContentLength != -1)
{
    state.DataLength = Convert.ToInt32(response.Content Length);
    state.StaticBuffer = new byte[state.DataLength];
```

```
        }
        else
        {
            state.FixedSizeBuffer = false;
            state.DynamicBuffer = new List<byte>(bufferSize);
        }
```

Retrieve the response object for the request so that data can now be read from the stream.

```
    Stream responseStream = response.GetResponseStream();
    state.ResponseStream = responseStream;
```

Begin reading stream data asynchronously.

```
    IAsyncResult readResult
            = responseStream.BeginRead(state.ProcessBuffer,
                                        0,
                                        bufferSize,
                                        new AsyncCallback(ReadCallback),
                                        state);
}
```

The following callback is used when an asynchronous data read occurs.

```
private void ReadCallback(IAsyncResult asyncResult)
{
```

Pull the asynchronous state object out of the result object.

```
    AsyncFileDownloadState state =
        (AsyncFileDownloadState)asyncResult.AsyncState;
```

Retrieve the ResponseStream from the state object that was set in the ResponseCallback.

```
    Stream responseStream = state.ResponseStream;
```

Check if there is any more data to read.

```
    int bytesRead = responseStream.EndRead(asyncResult);
    if (bytesRead > 0)
    {
```

Copy the temporary data buffer into the appropriate data buffer that holds the final data.

```
        if (state.FixedSizeBuffer)
        {
```

```
            Array.Copy(state.ProcessBuffer,
                       0,
                       state.StaticBuffer,
                       state.BytesRead,
                       bytesRead);
        }
        else
        {
            byte[] data = new byte[bytesRead];
            Array.Copy(state.ProcessBuffer, 0, data, 0, bytesRead);
            state.DynamicBuffer.AddRange(data);
        }
        state.BytesRead += bytesRead;
```

Notify any callbacks attached to the progress update event.

```
        if (state.ProgressUpdate != null)
            state.ProgressUpdate(state.BytesRead, state.DataLength);
```

Call another data read cycle until there are no more bytes to read.

```
        IAsyncResult readResult
                   = responseStream.BeginRead(state.ProcessBuffer,
                                              0,
                                              bufferSize,
                                              new AsyncCallback(ReadCallback),
                                              state);
    }
    else
    {
```

All the data has been downloaded, so we can now close the response stream and signal the complete event.

```
        responseStream.Close();
        completeEvent.Set();
    }
  }
}
```

Sample Usage

Using the asynchronous download system is very easy. Simply specify the resource address, and bind the two callbacks to handle progress updates and the download complete event. After which, call the Initiate() method to begin downloading.

The following code shows this.

```
AsyncFileDownloadRequest request = new AsyncFileDownloadRequest();

// Specify the address of the file to download
request.Address = new Uri("http://yourdomain/thefile");

// Assign a delegate to handle download complete events
request.DownloadComplete
                += new AsyncDownloadCompleteHandler(DownloadCompleteCallback);

// Assign a delegate to handle progress update events
request.ProgressUpdate
                += new AsyncDownloadProgressHandler(DownloadProgressCallback);

// Request the file
request.Initiate();
```

Conclusion

This chapter discussed the HttpWebRequest and HttpWebResponse classes, and then presented a reusable solution using these classes to asynchronously download files off a network or Internet server.

The Companion Web site has the full source code to the download system, including a simple demo that shows how to use the system. Figure 29.1 shows the main interface of the provided example.

As mentioned earlier, there are a number of ways that files can be downloaded asynchronously from a network location, but the solution presented in this chapter fully utilizes the built-in functionality of the .NET Class Framework.

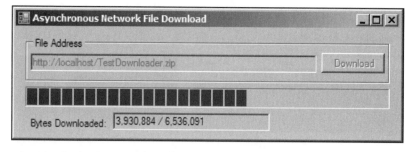

Figure 29.1 Screenshot of the demo application on the Companion Web site.

PART V

TECHNIQUES FOR LEGACY INTEROPERABILITY

Programming is like sex: one mistake and you have to support it for the rest of your life.

Michael Sinz

The .NET platform is relatively new technology, so the majority of game development studios still have legacy code that they have invested large amounts of time and money into developing. Conversions and ports do not happen overnight, and some situations require that a wrapper or interface be built around legacy technology instead of updating it. Considerable resources have been spent on researching and attempting ways to interoperate between managed and unmanaged applications. The long-term goal of a tools team should be to have a purely managed code base, but it will take some time and commitment to reach such an objective. For a short-term plan, a solid course of action will be to slowly migrate key components over to managed code, exposing wrappers that allow the existing legacy applications to still consume them without errors. As each component is migrated and as dependencies on legacy components are reduced, you will be able to start getting rid of unmanaged wrappers. Obviously, any new components will targeted at the managed runtime. Over time, you will end up with a purely managed solution that exists solely on the managed runtime.

In order to accomplish even the short-term goal, an understanding must be fostered regarding how to go about writing wrappers and exposing unmanaged interfaces from managed components. In addition to exposing unmanaged interfaces, some conversion strategies may include migrating the application harness to the managed runtime, and slowly move the unmanaged components across. In this situation, you will need to know how to consume an unmanaged component from within a managed application or component.

The chapters in Part V focus on such topics as exchanging data between applications, and exposing wrapper interfaces between various components. These techniques can be used to support a solid migration plan for legacy components to managed code.

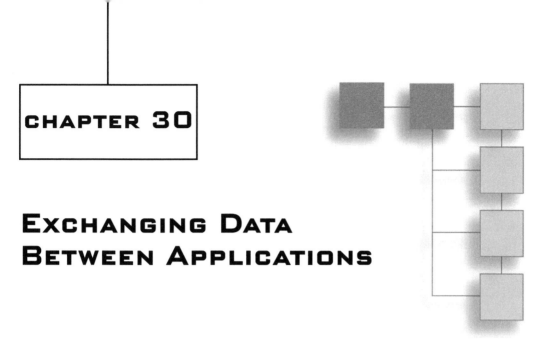

CHAPTER 30

EXCHANGING DATA
BETWEEN APPLICATIONS

*Less than 10% of the code has to do with the ostensible purpose of the system;
the rest deals with input-output, data validation, data structure maintenance,
and other housekeeping.*

Mary Shaw

Inter-Process Communication, also known as IPC, addresses the techniques and mechanisms that allow processes to communicate and share data with each other. The processes can exist on the same machine or on a network. Now, why do processes require special mechanisms to facilitate communication with each other? If you ever took a class on operating system fundamentals, you should remember that each running instance of a program, a process if you would, is allotted a unique memory space by the operating system kernel. No memory spaces will ever overlap, which allows for the safe operation of processes but prohibits processes from sharing data with each other. This is the reason that a communication medium is required to handle the exchange of data between applications.

Why do processes need to communicate? Well, the reason is not very apparent simply because you do not notice the ongoing exchange of data between processes. If Inter-Process Communication were not possible and you, as a user, had to manage the communication of shared data, the critical need for IPC mechanisms would be perceptible.

As discussed in Chapter 18, "Ensuring a Single Instance of an Application," imagine that you have Adobe Photoshop open and you double-click on another image file on your desktop and, instead of the image opening up within the current instance of Photoshop, the application remains silent. Once an already running process of a particular application is located, the common approach to inform the current instance of the new file is, you guessed it, Inter-Process Communication.

Now that we have discussed the importance of a process communication medium, what can be used? Since the operating system kernel is in charge of memory and process management, the kernel can be utilized to handle the communication for us.

What Microsoft.NET Provides

The .NET framework provides a number of mechanisms for inter-process communication, each with its own advantages and disadvantages. A brief overview of each built-in IPC mechanism will be described, but only a few of them will be implemented.

Web Services

A Web Service is often defined as being a software system identified by a Universal Resource Indicator (URI), whose public interfaces are defined and described using the XML format. Its definition can then be discovered by other software systems by communicating with Universal Description Discovery and Integration (UDDI) registries. Other software systems can then interact with a Web Service-enabled application through the manner described by its definition, using XML-based messages conveyed over common Internet protocols like TCP\IP.

This method of communication is excellent for applications that exist on remote machines, and because the transport protocol is XML-based, both applications can be written in entirely different languages yet still communicate effectively with each other. Web Service communication comes at a fairly hefty price though. Deployment requires an HTTP server that understands Web Services such as IIS, packet sizes tend to be fairly large because of plain text XML messages, XML serialization incurs a significant performance cost, and transport speed is quite slow.

Remoting

Web Services are very powerful, but surely there must be another method of working with remote objects with increased performance? Welcome to the world of .NET Remoting.

Remoting accomplishes nearly the same inter-process communication goals of Web Services, but it does not have the same level of overhead, making it both a powerful and high-performance method of working with remote objects between different applications. The applications can be located on the same computer, on different computers located on the same network, or on computers existing in different network domains. Remoting is much easier to use than Java Remote Method Invocation (RMI), but it is not as easy to use as Web Services. In the past, the majority of inter-process communication was made possible using the Distributed Component Object Model (DCOM), which accomplishes many of the goals that Web Services and Remoting do, except DCOM uses a proprietary binary protocol that hinders object models from supporting platform neutrality.

Remoting has two main types of communications methods: TCP and HTTP. Communication via the TCP protocol is accessible through the `TcpServerChannel` object and is best for local networks because of the increased performance over the HTTP protocol. Firewalls generally block Remoting using the TCP protocol, thus making `HttpServerChannel` the common choice for Internet-based communication.

Note

In order to use the Remoting functionality present in the .NET framework, you must reference the `System.Runtime.Remoting.dll` assembly.

A solid design for Remoting architecture entails creating a separate library that contains the shared vocabulary of all serializable objects both client and server will use to communicate. The definition to all serializable objects must be available to every application handling those objects; hence the need for an external library to house them.

Figure 30.1 shows the relationship between the client, server, and shared vocabulary assemblies.

The Companion Web site includes a simple server that accepts a string from a client, converts the text to Pig Latin, and returns the modified string back to the client. The vocabulary library for this example is quite simple, and only contains one class that facilitates the communication between client and server; `PigLatinController` has only one method called `Convert`, which accepts a string containing the text to convert, and returns a string containing the converted text.

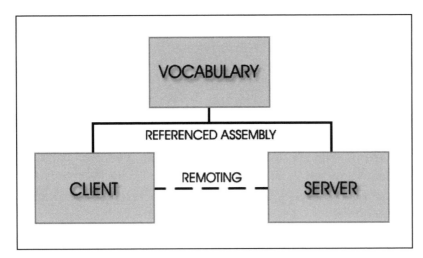

Figure 30.1 Relationship between the client, server, and shared vocabulary assemblies.

You should notice that `PigLatinController` is inheriting from `MarshalByRefObject`, which is necessary to make the object available to clients requesting it. Remoting does not return a copy of the object; instead a proxy object is used to invoke methods in the remote object.

Every public method you define in the remote object will be available to clients, with the same rules that would apply if the object were accessed locally in a system.

```
using System;

namespace PigLatinRemoting
{
    public class PigLatinController : MarshalByRefObject
    {
        public string ConvertToPigLatin(string input)
        {
            ...
        }
    }
}
```

As you can see in the preceding code, there is one public method the server will make available to all clients requesting the proxy of this object.

Once the vocabulary is defined, a server must be created that registers the vocabulary over a channel which clients will use to request the proxy. This is accomplished by first instantiating either TcpServerChannel or HttpServerChannel, depending on the protocol you wish to use. The constructor accepts the port number that this channel resides on over the protocol used.

Note

The server application must reference the shared vocabulary assembly so that the remote object definition is available to the server.

```
TcpServerChannel serverChannel = new TcpServerChannel(9978);
```

This code creates a Remoting channel on port 9978 using the Tcp protocol. The following code shows the same thing using the Http protocol.

```
HttpServerChannel serverChannel = new HttpServerChannel(9978);
```

After the channel is initialized, it must be registered with the static ChannelServices object, used in the registration of Remoting channels, resolution, and URL discovery.

```
ChannelServices.RegisterChannel(serverChannel);
```

After the channel is registered, it is time to register the vocabulary so that clients can begin requesting the proxy objects. This is done using the static RemotingConfiguration object, used for configuring the Remoting infrastructure.

Remote object lifetime management is an important factor to consider when designing your system. There are two lifetime types available to remote objects: SingleCall and Singleton. SingleCall means that every incoming message will be serviced with a new instance of the registered type. Singleton means that every incoming message will be serviced with a shared instance of the registered type.

Since our object does not even have variables to store data, it would be most efficient to use a singleton instance of the remote object. We call RegisterWellKnown ServiceType to register our class as a well known type on the service end.

```
RemotingConfiguration.RegisterWellKnownServiceType(typeof(PigLatinController),
                                    "PigLatinController",
                                    WellKnownObjectMode.Singleton);
```

That's it! The server has been created and is now making our remote object vocabulary accessible to any clients that request it. The last step is to create the client application that will use the remote object.

Creating the client is even easier than creating the server; the remote object can be accessed using just one line of code!

```
PigLatinController controller = Activator.GetObject(typeof(PigLatinController),
                                        "tcp://localhost:9978/PigLatinController")
                                                          as PigLatinController;
```

Note

In order to use the Remoting functionality present in the .NET framework, you must reference the `System.Runtime.Remoting.dll` assembly.

Now we can use our public method `ConvertToPigLatin()` and see Remoting in action.

```
string result = controller.ConvertToPigLatin("Remoting Rocks");
```

When this line is executed, the result is *Emotingray Ocksray*.

Remoting is an excellent choice for managed inter-process communication over a network between multiple machines, but it is overkill for many projects. This section briefly skimmed the surface of .NET Remoting, so it is recommended that you read up on additional information if you plan on using Remoting extensively in your applications.

Clipboard

The Clipboard mechanism is a collection of functions and messages that allow for the transfer of data between multiple applications or within a single application. Since all applications have access to the Clipboard, it can also serve as an IPC mechanism. Its usage is a special case though, and is generally used as a storage system for a user to manually move data in memory between multiple applications. Using the Clipboard mechanism is covered in a separate chapter of this book.

TCP\IP Loopback Communication

Another common method of inter-process communication is though the use of TCP\IP communication to pass data between processes. This approach can be used to communicate between different machines, or the loopback address (127.0.0.1) can be used to communicate with endpoints on the same machine. While this approach has its uses, it may not be the best way if you are doing a large number of chatty calls, or if you do not want to manage designated port numbers for your applications. This approach is natively supported in Microsoft.NET, so it may be useful to you if performance isn't critical and you just want an easy way to pass data between processes on the same machine or across a network.

What Microsoft.NET Should Provide

There are a couple mechanisms that Microsoft.NET should provide that are only accessible through unmanaged Interop.

Named Pipes

A common IPC mechanism that exists on the majority of modern operating systems is referred to as a pipe. Windows has named pipes, which are one-way or duplex for communication between a pipe server and one-to-many pipe clients. All instances of a named pipe share the same name, though each instance has a reserved and separate set of buffers and handles. Any process can function as both a server and a client, which allows for peer-to-peer communication. Named pipes can also provide communication between processes on the same machine or between processes across a network.

Named pipes can be accessed by any process, making them ideal candidates for simple communication between related or unrelated processes. Named pipes are also much more efficient than Remoting when using chatty calls, as named pipes avoid binary serialization. Named pipes are not natively supported by Microsoft.NET, so developers must resort to legacy Interop in order to use them.

WM_COPYDATA

A simple communication method that Win32 applications can use to send data between processes is the WM_COPYDATA message in the Windows API. WM_COPYDATA runs at a low level, so it is capable of sending data between process address spaces. This message is very useful for sending data between applications, but it requires cooperation between the sending and receiving applications. Both applications must know the format of the data being sent, and must respond to it appropriately. The sender must ensure that it does not modify any data referenced by pointers sent to receiving applications, and any pointers used must be accessible from any application. This means that you cannot send a pointer that references memory in the local address space of the sender application.

Building a Wrapper Around WM_COPYDATA

WM_COPYDATA is not natively supported by Microsoft.NET, so it is only accessible through Platform Invocation Services. The remainder of this chapter will focus on sending and receiving data between managed and unmanaged applications.

The Companion Web site contains a robust wrapper and manager around WM_COPYDATA. There is a version for managed applications and also a version for unmanaged applications.

Communicating from Unmanaged Applications

In order to focus purely on the implementation details behind WM_COPYDATA, we will first look at usage from an unmanaged application so we can avoid Platform Invocation Services.

The WM_COPYDATA message is sent to an application by calling the SendMessage() method; the PostMessage() method should not be used. The first parameter is the window handle of the target you are sending the data to; this handle will be referencing a window that is in use by another application. The second parameter is the event ID that is being sent. In this case we are using the WM_COPYDATA identifier. The third parameter (WPARAM) is the handle of the window that is sending the data. Finally, the last parameter (LPARAM) is a pointer to a COPYDATASTRUCT structure that contains the data that will be sent to the other application.

COPYDATASTRUCT has three members: dwData allows you to send 32 bits of data, and the remaining two members are used to pass a pointer to the other application. The cbData member describes the data length (in bytes) that is pointed to by the member lpData. You do not have to pass a pointer; lpData can be null if you just wish to pass values in dwData.

```
COPYDATASTRUCT copyData;
copyData.dwData = 0;
copyData.cbData = dataPointerSize;
copyData.lpData = dataPointer;
```

The following code shows how to construct the SendMessage() call. That's all there is to sending data with WM_COPYDATA!

```
SendMessage(targetHWND,
            WM_COPYDATA,
            (WPARAM)senderHWND,
            (LPARAM)(LPVOID)&copyData);
BOOL success = (GetLastError() == 0 ? 1 : 0);
```

In order to receive WM_COPYDATA messages, you must add a message handler in the Windows message processing loop. When a WM_COPYDATA message is received, you have a pointer to a COPYDATASTRUCT instance where you can extract the data sent to you.

Caution

The receiving application should consider the data read-only, as the data is only valid during processing. The receiving application should also not attempt to free the memory sent to it. If the receiving application needs to manipulate the data, it should store a local copy.

The following code shows a culled version of a message handler, only showing the WM_COPYDATA handler.

```
LRESULT CALLBACK WinProc(HWND handle,
                         UINT message,
                         WPARAM wParam,
                         LPARAM lParam)
{
    switch (message)
    {
        case WM_COPYDATA:
        {
            PCOPYDATASTRUCT copyData = (PCOPYDATASTRUCT)lParam;
            // Start using the elements in copyData
            return 0;
        }
    }

    return DefWindowProc(handle, message, wParam, lParam);
}
```

Communicating from Managed Applications

Using WM_COPYDATA from a managed application is pretty much identical to using it from an unmanaged application, except that we need to declare some of the types and identifiers we will need.

The following code shows the P/Invoke signature for the COPYDATASTRUCT type.

```
[StructLayout(LayoutKind.Sequential)]
private struct COPYDATASTRUCT
{
    public IntPtr _dataType;
    public int _dataSize;
    public IntPtr _dataPointer;
}
```

As mentioned earlier, we pass the WM_COPYDATA identifier into the SendMessage() method. In order to do so, we need to define the WM_COPYDATA identifier because Microsoft.NET does not natively recognize its value.

```
private const int WM_COPYDATA = 0x4A;
```

The following two lines of code show the P/Invoke signature for the SendMessage() method that is located in user32.dll.

```
[DllImport("user32.dll", CharSet=CharSet.Auto)]
private extern static int SendMessage(IntPtr handle, int msg, int param, ref
COPYDATASTRUCT copyData);
```

In order to send a data pointer to another process, we need to allocate a global block of memory that is not managed by the garbage collector. We can do this by calling Marshal.AllocCoTaskMem(). It will return a pointer to an allocated block of memory that can now have contents copied into it. A subsequent call to Marshal.Copy() can copy a byte array to that location in memory.

```
byte[] dataToSend = new byte[123];
IntPtr dataPointer = Marshal.AllocCoTaskMem(dataToSend.Length);
Marshal.Copy(dataToSend, 0, dataPointer, dataToSend.Length);
```

Just like using WM_COPYDATA in an unmanaged application, we need to instantiate a COPYDATASTRUCT instance and specify the data that we will be sending to the receiving application.

```
COPYDATASTRUCT copyData = new COPYDATASTRUCT();
copyData._dataType = IntPtr.Zero;
copyData._dataSize = dataToSend.Length;
copyData._dataPointer = dataPointer;
```

The next few lines of code show the call to SendMessage(). You can get an unmanaged handle (HWND) to any managed Form in .NET by accessing the Handle property. You need to find out the handle of the target form, which again is not natively supported by .NET, although you can use a function like FindWindow() to help you out. You will have to tap into P/Invoke for this one too. The example and library on the Companion Web site show how to do this.

```
IntPtr target = TargetForm.Handle;
IntPtr sender = YourForm.Handle;
int result = SendMessage(target, WM_COPYDATA, sender.ToInt32(), ref copyData);
// Successful if result is 0
```

After you have successfully sent the data, it is important that you free the memory from Windows, because this memory is not managed by the .NET garbage collector. Remember that receiving applications are not supposed to manipulate or free the memory referenced by this pointer, so it is your responsibility to do so.

```
Marshal.FreeCoTaskMem(dataPointer);
```

Perhaps the trickiest part about using WM_COPYDATA with a managed application is that you cannot just tap into the message handler of a form. You need to create a wrapper class that inherits from NativeWindow, and assign to NativeWindow the handle of the form you are using. The following code shows the implementation of the NativeWindow wrapper class. You will also notice that the pointer we received gets Marshaled back into a COPYDATASTRUCT instance.

```
public sealed class CopyDataWindow : NativeWindow, IDisposable
{
    protected override void WndProc(ref System.Windows.Forms.Message message)
    {
        switch (message.Msg)
        {
            case WM_COPYDATA:
            {
                COPYDATASTRUCT copyData = Marshal.PtrToStructure(message.LParam,
                                                    typeof(COPYDATASTRUCT))
                                            as COPYDATASTRUCT;

                if (copyData._dataSize > 0)
                {
                    byte[] data = new byte[copyData._dataSize];
                    Marshal.Copy(copyData._dataPointer,
                                 data,
                                 0,
                                 copyData._dataSize);
                    message.Result = (IntPtr)1;
                }
            }

            break;
        }

        base.WndProc(ref message);
    }
}
```

You can instantiate this class after your form exists and call `AssignHandle()` on the `NativeWindow` instance, passing in the `Handle` property of your form instance.

Conclusion

This chapter started off by discussing what inter-process communication is and why it is important, and then described some IPC mechanisms that are native to Microsoft.NET, and then some IPC mechanisms that are only available through Platform Invocation Services. Remoting was briefly covered, but nowhere near close to the level of detail that is available from books that are dedicated to the subject. I recommend that you pick up the book *Advanced .NET Remoting* by Ingo Rammer (ISBN: 1590590252) if you want to investigate this awesome technology in greater detail.

A large number of IPC mechanisms were at least briefly covered in this chapter, though some were left out since the chapter is generally directed towards `WM_COPYDATA`. Some excluded IPC mechanisms are shared memory spaces and overlapped I/O.

Be sure to check out the Companion Web site for a robust library that wraps and manages communication between managed and unmanaged applications, including an example that shows library usage. There are two flavors of the library: one for managed applications and one for unmanaged applications. This library allows you to group messages into channels, so that you can perform filtering or classification of messages and associated data.

CHAPTER 31

INTERACTING WITH THE CLIPBOARD

I object to doing things that computers can do.

Olin Shivers

Microsoft has always spearheaded the movement to constantly increase productivity using the Windows operating system. One productivity feature that has allowed people to work smarter and faster is the Windows Clipboard. The Clipboard is a temporary storage area that Windows uses to hold information that is being transferred between documents or applications. Most Windows applications support cutting or copying data to the Clipboard and pasting data from the Clipboard.

The Windows Clipboard can store many types of data, including text, formatted text, images, audio, and binary files. Even though any Clipboard data can be shared by all Windows applications, it is important to note that supported data formats vary between applications. Most applications know how to handle text, but not all applications know how to handle other data formats.

The Clipboard can only hold one data item at a time. When the Clipboard receives new data, the previous data is overwritten with the new contents. Contents can be pasted numerous times, because the contents remain in the Clipboard until cleared, overwritten by newer contents, or when Windows is shut down.

This chapter describes how to use the standard Windows Clipboard API from within your .NET applications.

The Clipboard Class and IDataObject

Accessing the Clipboard and storing data is made possible by the Clipboard class in the `System.Windows.Forms` namespace, specifically the `SetDataObject()` and `GetDataObject()` methods.

`SetDataObject()` is used to store arbitrary data on the Clipboard, and it defines whether or not the data remains persisted after the application exits. Similarly, `GetDataObject()` is used to retrieve arbitrary data that is stored on the Clipboard. `GetDataObject()` can also be used to determine whether data exists on the Clipboard, and what format the data is. Both methods use the `IDataObject` interface, which is a format-independent mechanism that is used for data transfer and notification of changes in data. The `IDataObject` interface is used in this situation because arbitrary data can be stored on the Clipboard, and we need an initial way to determine what format the data is before we can work with it.

The `SetDataObject()` method has two overloaded definitions. The first one (shown in the following line of code) is used to store an object on the Clipboard, releasing the data when the application exits.

```
public static void SetDataObject(object data);
```

The following method has a copy parameter that specifies whether the data should be persisted on the Clipboard after the application exits.

```
public static void SetDataObject(object data, bool copy);
```

The `GetData()` method can be used to get the associated data and convert it to the appropriate type.

Storing Built-In Types

Storing built-in types is very simple, especially since .NET automatically handles conversion between similar data formats (ANSI and Unicode text, for example).

The following code shows how to store a built-in type (`DataFormats.Text` for this example).

```
string text = "This is a test!";

IDataObject dataObject = new DataObject();
dataObject.SetData(DataFormats.Text, true, text);
Clipboard.SetDataObject(dataObject, true);
```

The following code shows how to retrieve the text from the Clipboard.

```
IDataObject dataObject = Clipboard.GetDataObject();

string text = null;

if (dataObject.GetDataPresent(DataFormats.Text))
{
    text = (string)dataObject.GetData(DataFormats.Text);
}
```

There are many built-in types available, as shown in Table 31.1.

Table 31.1 Available Data Formats

Data Format	Description
Bitmap	Specifies a Windows bitmap format.
CommaSeparatedValue	Specifies a comma-separated value (CSV) format that is a common interchange format for spreadsheet applications.
Dib	Specifies the Windows device-independent bitmap format.
Dif	Specifies the Windows data interchange format.
EnhancedMetafile	Specifies the Windows enhanced metafile format.
FileDrop	Specifies the Windows file drop format.
Html	Specifies text consisting of HTML data.
Locale	Specifies the Windows culture format.
MetafilePict	Specifies the Windows metafile format.
OemText	Specifies the standard Windows original equipment manufacturer (OEM) text format.
Palette	Specifies the Windows palette format.
PenData	Specifies the Windows pen data format, used to store pen strokes for handwriting software.
Riff	Specifies the Resource Interchange File Format (RIFF) audio format.
Rtf	Specifies text consisting of rich text format data.
Serializable	Specifies a format that encapsulates any type of Windows Forms object.
StringFormat	Specifies the Windows Forms string class format, used by Windows Forms to store string objects.
SymbolicLink	Specifies the Windows symbolic link format.
Text	Specifies the standard ANSI text format.
Tiff	Specifies the Tagged Image File format.
UnicodeText	Specifies the standard Windows Unicode text format.
WaveAudio	Specifies the wave audio format.

Storing Custom Data Formats

Situations arise when your application needs to store custom data on the Clipboard, either for use within the same application or so that other related applications can use the data. The .NET framework allows you to store any serializable data type on the Clipboard. To start, we will define a simple custom data object that will be stored on the Clipboard. This object is described with the following code.

```
[Serializable]
public class CustomData
{
    private static DataFormats.Format dataFormat;

    public static DataFormats.Format DataFormat
    {
        get { return dataFormat; }
    }

    static CustomData()
    {
        dataFormat = DataFormats.GetFormat(typeof(CustomData).FullName);
    }

    private string testString;
    private int testInteger;

    public CustomData()
    {
        testString = string.Empty;
        testInteger = 0;
    }

    public CustomData(string testString, int testInteger)
    {
        this.testString = testString;
        this.testInteger = testInteger;
    }

    public string TestString
    {
        get { return testString; }
        set { testString = value; }
    }
```

```
    public int TestInteger
    {
        get { return testInteger; }
        set { testInteger = value; }
    }

    public override string ToString()
    {
        return string.Format("TestString:{0}, TestInteger{1}",
                                        testString,
                                        testInteger);

    }
}
```

Custom data requires a unique format descriptor, which is created with the following line of code.

```
dataFormat = DataFormats.GetFormat(typeof(CustomData).FullName);
```

The simple data object has a static constructor that sets the static dataFormat property so that the format can easily be plugged into the storage operation of the Clipboard.

The following code shows how to copy the CustomData object to the Clipboard.

```
CustomData data = new CustomData();
data.TestString = "This is a test";
data.TestInteger = 12345;

IDataObject dataObject = new DataObject();
dataObject.SetData(format, true, data);
Clipboard.SetDataObject(dataObject, true);
```

Similarly, the following code shows how to retrieve the CustomData object from the Clipboard.

```
IDataObject dataObject = Clipboard.GetDataObject();

CustomData data = null;

if (dataObject.GetDataPresent(CustomData.DataFormat.Name))
{
    data = (CustomData)dataObject.GetData(CustomData.DataFormat.Name);
}
```

Querying Available Data Formats

You already know that only a single chunk of data can be stored on the Clipboard at any one time, but it is also important to point out that some data types can be easily converted to a variety of different formats. .NET supports both implicit and explicit conversions between multiple data formats, but you generally need to be aware of the formats that a certain type format can convert to; attempting to convert data to an unsupported format will cause exceptions.

IDataObject has a useful method called GetFormats() that can be used to query the formats that the stored data can be converted to, provided that auto conversion was true when the data was stored on the Clipboard.

There are two overloaded definitions for GetFormats() shown in the following. The first definition retrieves all the formats that the stored data can be converted to.

```
public string[] IDataObject.GetFormats();
```

The next definition allows you to specify whether or not to include all convertible formats, or only list native types.

```
public string[] IDataObject.GetFormats(bool autoConvert);
```

Note

Call GetFormats() to get the supported formats before calling GetData().

Complete Solution

The code snippets in this chapter have been consolidated into a helper class that makes it easier to work with the Clipboard. .NET 2.0 has introduced several wrapper methods around SetDataObject() and GetDataObject() that are specific to certain data types. The intent of this chapter is to show how the low-level API for the Clipboard works, because all the wrapper methods do is encapsulate the SetDataObject() approach.

The complete source code for the helper class is shown below.

```
internal static class ClipboardHelper
{
    internal static string[] GetCurrentFormats()
    {
        IDataObject dataObject = Clipboard.GetDataObject();
        string[] formats = dataObject.GetFormats(true);
```

```
        return formats;
}

internal static void CopyText(string text)
{
        CopyArbitraryData(DataFormats.Text, (object)text);
}

internal static void CopyImage(Image image)
{
        CopyArbitraryData(DataFormats.Bitmap, (object)image);
}

internal static void CopyCustomData(CustomData data)
{
        CopyArbitraryData(CustomData.DataFormat.Name, (object)data);
}

internal static string PasteText()
{
        object rawData = PasteArbitraryData(DataFormats.Text, true);

        string text = null;

        if (rawData != null && rawData is string)
        {
            text = (string)rawData;
        }

        return text;
}

internal static Image PasteImage()
{
        object rawData = PasteArbitraryData(DataFormats.Bitmap, true);

        Image image = null;

        if (rawData != null && rawData is Image)
        {
            image = (Image)rawData;
        }
```

```
        return image;
    }

    internal static CustomData PasteCustomData()
    {
        object rawData = PasteArbitraryData(CustomData.DataFormat.Name,
                                            false);

        CustomData data = null;

        if (rawData != null && rawData is CustomData)
        {
            data = (CustomData)rawData;
        }

        return data;
    }

    private static void CopyArbitraryData(string format, object data)
    {
        IDataObject dataObject = new DataObject();
        dataObject.SetData(format, true, data);
        Clipboard.SetDataObject(dataObject, true);
    }

    private static object PasteArbitraryData(string format, bool autoConvert)
    {
        object data = null;

        IDataObject dataObject = Clipboard.GetDataObject();

        if (dataObject.GetDataPresent(format))
        {
            if (autoConvert)
            {
                data = dataObject.GetData(format, true);
            }
            else
            {
                data = dataObject.GetData(format);
            }
        }
```

```
        return data;
    }
}
```

Conclusion

This chapter described what the Windows Clipboard is used for and how to store and retrieve arbitrary data on it. The Clipboard is a standard Windows feature that users expect to work in all applications, so it is advisable that you implement Clipboard functionality where appropriate in order to promote comfortable user interfaces.

Additionally, Clipboard functionality in terms of availability in the user interface is only meaningful in certain contexts. The Cut and Copy commands should only be enabled when data is selected. The Paste command should only be enabled when appropriate data is on the Clipboard. Be sure to design user interfaces that are easy for users to intuit and understand.

The Companion Web site includes the complete source code shown in this chapter, including a simple WinForms application that uses the Clipboard helper class. This demo application is shown in Figure 31.1.

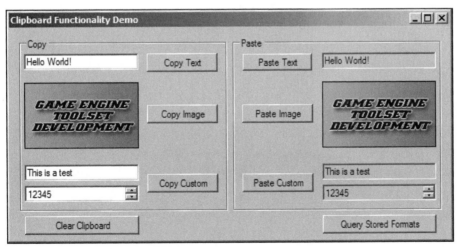

Figure 31.1 Screenshot of the demo application on the Companion Web site.

The Clipboard is fairly simple to understand, though it is important to properly implement its functionality because users are so accustomed to its existence.

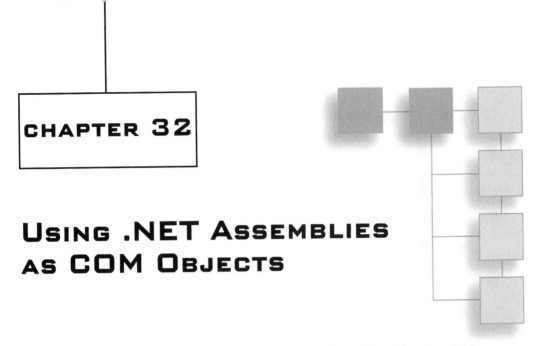

CHAPTER 32

USING .NET ASSEMBLIES AS COM OBJECTS

The lowest form of thinking is the bare recognition of the object. The highest, the comprehensive intuition of the man who sees all things as part of a system.

Plato

Microsoft engineers have devoted a significant amount of work to the Component Object Model (COM) since its inception in 1998. Many software projects invested a lot of time and resources into adopting COM because it made sense at the time. With the introduction of the .NET platform, software projects are starting to build reusable components as strongly named .NET assemblies rather than dealing with COM. Some companies have the available resources to migrate entire projects over to .NET, while most companies only have the resources to migrate individual subsystems to the .NET platform one component at a time.

Thankfully for projects on a tight budget or schedule, the .NET framework provides tools and strategies to promote easy integration with legacy components, and the ability to allow legacy components to interact with .NET components. This chapter covers the interoperability support that allows .NET components to be registered for COM, thus allowing legacy applications to communicate with managed code without being managed themselves.

COM Callable Wrappers (CCW)

The Component Object Model is a binary format that represents reusable objects with a model that can be used from any programming language that can interface with COM. When a COM client asks for an instance of an object, the server will instantiate that object and return a reference to the client. COM acts as a binary contract between the caller and callee, defined in a document called a Type library (.tlb). This library document describes the services that are exposed to clients from an object.

Figure 32.1 describes the communication between a client and a COM component.

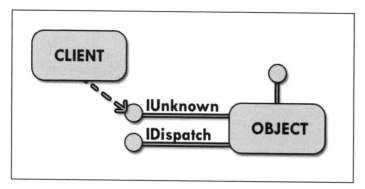

Figure 32.1 Communication between a client and a COM component.

Note

Figure 32.1 is meant to provide a high-level overview of communication. Methods specific to the COM mechanism, such as AddRef, QueryInterface, and Release, are not shown because we do not need to directly invoke them in this chapter.

COM components communicate with clients through a set of common interfaces, while .NET communicates with components directly through assembly metadata in the objects. This object-based communication is not understandable by COM applications, so a mechanism known as a COM Callable Wrapper (CCW) can be used to wrap .NET components so that they are accessible by COM and legacy applications. Creating a CCW is covered later in this chapter.

Figure 32.2 shows communication between a client and a .NET object through a COM Callable Wrapper.

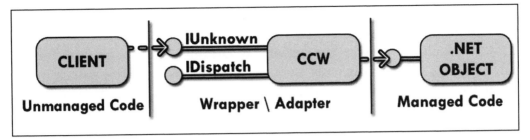

Figure 32.2 Communication between a client and a .NET object through a COM Callable Wrapper.

An additional layer of overhead is introduced to your application when using COM Interop, but this penalty is typically quite small and often unnoticeable. The biggest performance bottleneck comes from marshaling between wrappers and environments. So if you suspect that your performance problems are coming from COM Interop, verify this by creating a COM worker class to wrap your chatty calls into a single function that can be invoked by your managed application; doing so will decrease the amount of marshaling between the two layers.

Applying Interop Attributes

Exposing .NET components as COM objects is nearly autonomous, though there are some attributes that must be decorated on exposed classes so that COM can understand them correctly.

COM relies on identifying public components through the Windows registry, so perhaps the most important attribute is decoration of unique identifiers on all exposed classes and interfaces. This is done with the Guid attribute, as shown in the following example.

```
[Guid("04F08063-8226-4b5d-941C-C2F5E3027126")]
public interface IMyComponent
{
    // …
}
```

You can easily create unique identifiers for your types with the Tools->Create GUID->Registry Format menu item in the Visual Studio IDE. Globally unique identifiers (GUID) are the equivalent of CLSIDs. Also good to know, you can set a humanly readable form of the unique identifier using the ProgId attribute, although the accompanying example does not use it.

The next attribute to cover is InterfaceType, which is used to explicitly set how a managed interface is exposed to COM. Managed interfaces are exposed as dual to COM by default, which offers the flexibility of late binding or the performance of early binding. You can explicitly state that a managed interface can only be exposed as IDispatch, only supporting late binding. The following example shows this attribute.

```
[Guid("50B39BFD-FC05-4f28-AF75-084E0394A55E"),
InterfaceType(ComInterfaceType.InterfaceIsIDispatch)]
public interface IMyComponentEvents
{
    // ...
}
```

Similar to the InterfaceType attribute, the ClassInterface attribute is used to specify how classes are wrapped for COM. By default, a boilerplate interface is generated for classes exposed to COM, but this can be turned off using this attribute if a custom interface is desired. While the ability to automatically generate interfaces may seem easy, their use is strongly discouraged. The positioning of methods can change to the point where clients think they are calling one method, but are in fact calling a completely different method. Explicitly defining a custom interface for your components is the safe way around this problem. The following example shows how to use this attribute so that no interfaces are generated automatically.

```
[Guid("9DB1F428-B027-408d-BEDF-6A8398F0AAF8"),
ClassInterface(ClassInterfaceType.None)]
public class MyComponent : IMyComponent
{
    // ...
}
```

You can explicitly set the COM dispatch identifier (DISPID) for a member, property, or field with the DispId attribute. The constructor for this attribute takes an integer that specifies the identifier to associate with the type. The following example shows this attribute in action.

```
 [Guid("AB8C32F0-9DA1-4afb-8B91-E8B035412DBD")]
public interface IMyComponent
{
    [DispId(1)]
    void CustomMethod1();
```

```
    [DispId(2)]
    int CustomMethod2();

    [DispId(3)]
    string CustomMethod3(string param);
}
```

Okay, I lied. The most important attribute is ComVisible, which identifies a class or interface within an assembly as a COM object when registered. Adding a ComVisible(true) attribute to a class or interface exposes the type to COM. The following code shows the source code for the.NET-based COM component for the accompanying example. The first code snippet describes the interface that clients can communicate to the object with.

```
 [Guid("AB8C32F0-9DA1-4afb-8B91-E8B035412DBD"),
ComVisible(true)]
public interface IMyComponent
{
    [DispId(1)]
    void CustomMethod1();

    [DispId(2)]
    int CustomMethod2();

    [DispId(3)]
    string CustomMethod3(string param);
}
```

The next code snippet describes the event source interface that would serve more of a purpose if the accompanying example used COM events. We cannot use regular .NET event delegates with a regular COM client, so we will not cover COM events aside from showing how to register the event source interface.

```
[Guid("50B39BFD-FC05-4f28-AF75-084E0394A55E"),
InterfaceType(ComInterfaceType.InterfaceIsIDispatch),
ComVisible(true)]
public interface IMyComponentEvents
{
    // This is where events would be defined.
    // This example does not use them
}
```

Finally, the following class implements the functionality of our COM component that implements the `IMyComponent` interface. The `ComSourceInterfaces` attribute is used to specify all the event source interfaces for our component.

```
using System.Windows.Forms;

[Guid("9DB1F428-B027-408d-BEDF-6A8398F0AAF8"),
ClassInterface(ClassInterfaceType.None),
ComSourceInterfaces(typeof(IMyComponentEvents)),
ComVisible(true)]
public class MyComponent : IMyComponent
{
    public void CustomMethod1()
    {
        // Do something useful
        MessageBox.Show("This was called from CustomMethod1()!");
    }

    public int CustomMethod2()
    {
        return 1234;
    }

    public string CustomMethod3(string param)
    {
        return String.Format("You entered the string: '{0}'!", param);
    }
}
```

The type library generator for .NET components does a fine job of wrapping almost every type, though there are some rules to follow in order to ensure interoperability. These rules are:

- Avoid using parameterized constructors and static methods.
- Define interfaces for event sources in managed code.
- Utilize HRESULT for user-defined exceptions.
- Understand that differences in inheritance may occur.
- Supply unique identifiers for appropriate types.

Following these rules will ensure that type library generation goes smoothly and is utilized seamlessly.

Registering with COM

After your .NET component is compiled, you have to generate a type library file (.tlb) so that COM clients can consume and invoke the new functionality. There are a couple of ways to do this.

The first approach is to use the type library exporter utility (tlbexp.exe) to convert the exposed classes and interfaces into a COM type library. This approach creates a type library, but does not register the COM component in the registry. This step must be performed elsewhere.

Another approach is to use the TypeLibConverter class in the System.Runtime. InteropServices namespaces to programmatically generate a type library. This class produces the same output as the type library exporter utility.

A third approach is to use the .NET services installation tool (regsvcs.exe), which can generate, register, and install type libraries into existing COM+ 1.0 applications, in addition to loading and registering assemblies.

One of the easiest ways is to use the assembly registration tool (regasm.exe) which generates a type library using the /tlb switch, but it also places the appropriate entries into the Win32 registry to make COM clients aware of the component. The following line shows how to generate a type library for a .NET component and install it into the Win32 registry.

```
regasm.exe MyComponent.dll /tlb:MyComponent.tlb
```

You can automatically perform this step during the build process in the Visual Studio IDE by enabling Register for COM Interop in the Build project page, as shown in Figure 32.3.

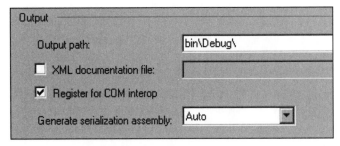

Figure 32.3 The Register for COM Interop property in the Visual Studio IDE Build page.

We can use the Microsoft Oleview utility to inspect the generated type library to see what is there. Figure 32.4 shows Oleview inspecting the type library for MyComponent.

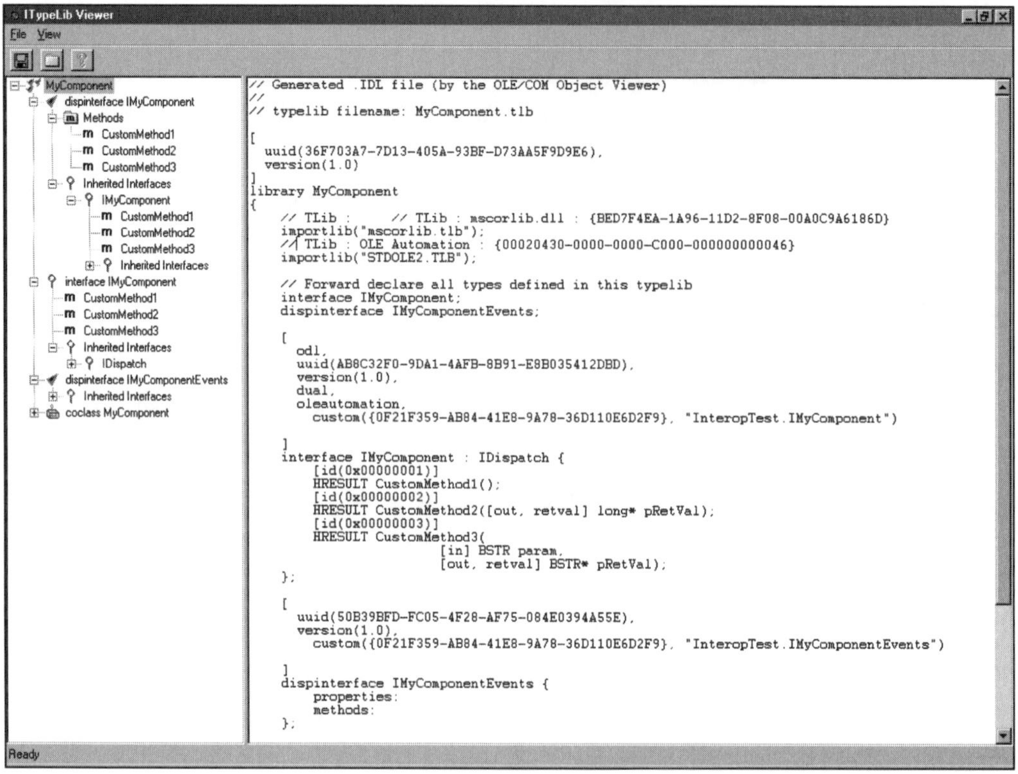

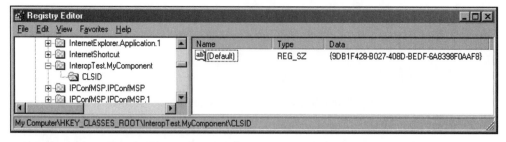

Figure 32.4 Oleview utility inspecting the type library for MyComponent.

Note

Microsoft's Oleview utility is available for download from their web site (http://www.microsoft.com).

Inspecting the registry, you will notice entries related to the registered component, as shown in Figure 32.5.

Figure 32.5 Registry entry for the InteropTest.MyComponent registration.

Accessing from Unmanaged Code

The hardest part is over; you can now work with your exposed component and start invoking its methods. As covered in the last section, you are now left with a type library file (.tlb) that you can import into a C++ application (or any other platform or language supporting COM) to recognize your exposed component. The unmanaged ClientTest example located on the Companion Web site shows how to consume the exposed component. The following code describes the source code to the ClientTest executable (standard Win32 project, unmanaged C++). Notice how the type library file (.tlb) is referenced with the import directive. The linker will actually generate a second file from this one called a type library header, which contains some specific C++ wrapper functionality. Both files can be used to get a better understanding of what is going on behind the scenes of COM Interop.

```cpp
#include <windows.h>
#include <atlbase.h>
#include <atlcom.h>
#include <comutil.h>

#import "MyComponent.tlb" no_namespace

int WINAPI WinMain(HINSTANCE, HINSTANCE, LPSTR, int)
{
    ::CoInitialize(NULL);

    CComPtr<IMyComponent> myComponent;

    // Acquire the unique identifier of the COM server (.NET Component)
    CLSID myComponentClassID = __uuidof(MyComponent);

    // Acquired a reference to the COM server (.NET Component)
    if (SUCCEEDED(myComponent.CoCreateInstance(myComponentClassID,
                                        0, CLSCTX_ALL)))
    {
        char output[64];

        if (SUCCEEDED(myComponent->CustomMethod1()))
        {
            ::MessageBox(0,
                    "Successfully invoked CustomMethod1()!",
                    "Test CustomMethod1()",
                    0);
        }
```

```
            long result = myComponent->CustomMethod2();
            sprintf(output, "Result: %d", result);
            ::MessageBox(0, output, "Test CustomMethod2()", 0);

            //Note: System.String is Marshaled into a _bstr_t with COM Interop
            _bstr_t inputMessage = _T("This is a test");

            _bstr_t message = myComponent->CustomMethod3(inputMessage);

            sprintf(output, "Message: %s", (char *)message);
            ::MessageBox(0, output, "Test CustomMethod3()", 0);
    }
    else
    {
        ::MessageBox(0, "Error loading MyComponent COM object!", "Error", 0);
    }

    ::CoUninitialize();
}
```

As you can see, consuming exposed .NET components is easy once they have been properly configured and registered for COM Interop. The biggest gotcha when consuming exposed components is finding out what complex types in .NET are marshaled, as in the type library (System.String to _bstr_t, for example). This is easy enough to spot by looking at the generated type library file.

Deployment Considerations

Managed .NET assemblies can be deployed as private or shared. Private deployment makes an assembly only available to clients that exist in the same directory as the private assembly, while shared assemblies are installed into the Global Assembly Cache (GAC), making them available to any local client. Ultimately, the choice about whether to deploy your .NET assemblies as private or shared is up to you.

If you choose to use private assemblies, you should also use the /codebase switch with the regasm.exe utility. You must ensure that you deploy all private assemblies alongside the client applications that utilize them.

COM exposed assemblies must be strongly named, so you can use the sn.exe tool to create a strong name key that that you can sign your assembly with. Afterwards, you can install your shared assembly into the GAC by using the gacutil.exe tool.

The following line shows how to install the MyComponent.dll assembly into the Global Assembly Cache.

```
gacutil.exe /i MyComponent.dll
```

An important deployment issue to consider is the system requirements for COM Interop. Because COM Interop merely provides a wrapper around a .NET component, you now have a dependency on the minimum system requirements to host the .NET framework. The .NET framework must be installed or the exposed components will not be able to function.

Lastly, there is also a way to support registration-free activation through the use of component and client manifest files that are linked or deployed with the appropriate executables after compiling. Although registration-free activation is not covered in this chapter, it may be worthwhile for you to look into if you want to avoid registering your exposed components in the Win32 registry.

Conclusion

This chapter started off by introducing COM Callable Wrappers and how they can be used to wrap a .NET component so that COM clients can utilize its functionality. Afterwards, the appropriate attributes to expose a .NET component were discussed, and then used in the context of the example on the Companion Web site. Component registration was then addressed, including a number of ways to perform the registration and type library generation. Finally, some deployment considerations were discussed that may not be the most obvious when working with COM Interop.

COM Interop and COM Callable Wrappers offer easy migration from traditional COM to the .NET platform by allowing individual components to be migrated one at a time, rather than trying to migrate an entire application or system in one go. Having such a powerful migration strategy can prove to be extremely advantageous in terms of budget and time constraints, and also makes debugging much easier by decreasing the volume of new code to test at a single time.

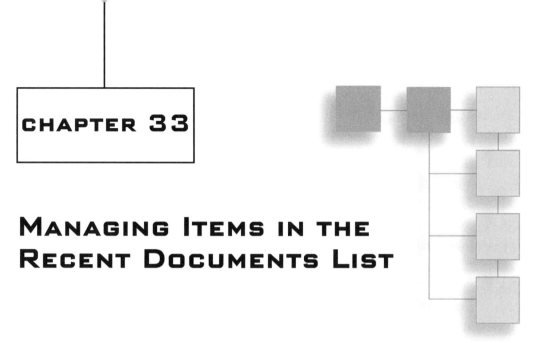

CHAPTER 33

MANAGING ITEMS IN THE RECENT DOCUMENTS LIST

Technology… the knack of so arranging the world that we don't have to experience it.

Max Frisch

An important feature of almost any software application is the ability to persist and remember settings between different instances of the application. Putting user interface customization aside, remembering commonly or previously accessed files and providing the ability to reopen those files with a shortcut can be quite a useful feature. Having recent document shortcuts without the need to navigate through the traditional file system dialog can save a significant amount of time, increasing productivity in the end.

The Documents folder (My Recent Documents folder on Windows XP and 2003) on the Start menu contains a listing of recently accessed files and documents. One of the most important design considerations for software is the concept of interface transparency. An application should behave the same as other applications on the operating system. This is so the user can easily navigate the application by using knowledge learned from other applications. Users have come to expect that recently opened or saved files from your application appear in the recent documents list, so this topic will show how to programmatically interact with this feature of Windows.

Implementation

The code to implement this feature is very simple. The solution involves a few P\Invoke calls, so the first logical step is to include the appropriate namespace.

```
using System.Runtime.InteropServices;
```

The API signatures we will invoke are described in the following code. The first signature is sent the pointer type, along with a pointer to the actual data. The second signature is nearly identical to the first, except a string is passed into it instead of a pointer.

```
[DllImport("shell32.dll")]
internal static extern void SHAddToRecentDocs(UInt32 pointerType, IntPtr pointer);


[DllImport("shell32.dll")]
internal static extern void SHAddToRecentDocs(UInt32 pointerType,
                    [MarshalAs(UnmanagedType.LPWStr)] string pointer);
```

There are three flavors of the SHAddToRecentDocs method that can be used, specified by the PointerType enumeration. These pointer types are defined in the following code, and are described in Table 33.1.

```
internal enum PointerType
{
    SHARD_PIDL = 0x00000001,
    SHARD_PATHA = 0x00000002,
    SHARD_PATHW = 0x00000003,
}
```

TABLE 33.1 SHAddToRecentDocs Pointer Types

Pointer Type	Description
SHARD_PIDL	Pointer to a PIDL (ITEMIDLIST structure) identifying the file to add to the recent documents menu
SHARD_PATHA	Pointer to a null terminated string with the path and filename of the object
SHARD_PATHW	Pointer to a null terminated string with the path and filename of the object; Unicode formatting

Using the method is very easy. You can either pass in the PIDL of the file if you have it, or simply specify the system path to the file as a string. Doing so will create a shortcut to the file and place it in the Recent Documents folder. The following code shows how to do this.

```
SHAddToRecentDocs(Convert.ToUInt32(PointerType.SHARD_PATHW),
                                path);
```

Clearing the Recent Documents folder is even easier! Passing a null PIDL pointer into the method will clear all the entries. The following code shows how to do this.

```
SHAddToRecentDocs(Convert.ToUInt32(PointerType.SHARD_PIDL)
                                IntPtr.Zero);
```

Note

The SHAddToRecentDocs method does not check if the files passed to it are valid, so it is the responsibility of your application to pass qualified file paths.

Example Usage

Using the code is extremely straightforward. The following example clears all current entries in the Recent Documents menu, and then adds four new entries to it.

```
SHAddToRecentDocs(Convert.ToUInt32(PointerType.SHARD_PIDL),
                                IntPtr.Zero);

SHAddToRecentDocs(Convert.ToUInt32(PointerType.SHARD_PATHW),
                                @"C:\MyFolder\File1.txt");

SHAddToRecentDocs(Convert.ToUInt32(PointerType.SHARD_PATHW),
                                @"C:\MyOtherFolder\File2.doc");

SHAddToRecentDocs(Convert.ToUInt32(PointerType.SHARD_PATHW),
                                @"C:\Images\File3.gif");

SHAddToRecentDocs(Convert.ToUInt32(PointerType.SHARD_PATHW),
                                @"C:\MyFolder\File4.zip");
```

Conclusion

Managing items in the recent documents folder is extremely trivial, but do not underestimate the significance of implementing features like this. Users expect all applications to function the same way; if they don't, you end up breaking interface transparency, and users will hate your program because of it.

## PART VI

Techniques to Improve Performance

…with proper design, the features come cheaply. This approach is arduous, but continues to succeed.

Dennis Ritchie

Regardless of what a tool does, it has to feel responsive to the user and report appropriate status information and visual cues to the user when a long-running task is being performed. Performance is a measurement of how well an application handles responsiveness, scalability, memory footprint, or throughput. While some optimizations can be done later on in development, the majority of performance improvements originate from an architecture that is well designed and constructed. It is important to build responsiveness and scalability into your processor- and resource-intensive tools early on in order to achieve optimal performance.

The chapters in Part VI cover ways to investigate and improve performance in a managed environment, where performance can be any process or task that can be measured quantitatively with a stopwatch. Performance testing and optimization has been around since pretty much the beginning of software development, but .NET is a relatively new platform, so there is a learning curve that developers must follow in order to learn the techniques and approaches to improve performance and write efficient code. The chapters in this part will attempt to alleviate most of the burden on developers new and old to the .NET platform who are building performance-critical tools.

CHAPTER 34

PLAYING NICE WITH THE GARBAGE COLLECTOR

In software, the chain isn't as strong as its weakest link; it's as weak as all the weak links multiplied together.

Steve C McConnell

A common concern about using managed code and the .NET platform is the idea that control over the allocation and deallocation of memory is handled by an automated process, otherwise known as the *garbage collector* (GC) intrinsic to the Common Language Runtime. Automated memory management has been around for quite some time, most notably in the Java world, but there have been some innovative deviations from the norm to produce a more efficient and better performing garbage collector. One reason that C++ developers generally feel uneasy making the transition from unmanaged to managed code is because they love the control and power offered by such a low-level language and do not wish to give it up. On the other hand, those same developers are torn because even experienced C++ developers have to utilize patterns like smart pointers to produce reliable software.

The inner workings of the GC are by no means simplistic, resulting in developers making mistakes that considerably degrade performance. Although the .NET runtime handles a lot of the nitty gritty aspects of automated memory management, there are some best practices that should be followed to maximize performance in this area. This topic covers some of the proper ways to work with managed data and the .NET garbage collector.

Overview of the Garbage Collector

The CLR garbage collector is a generational mark-and-compact collector (also known as an ephemeral garbage collector), offering excellent performance and efficiency by taking some fundamental notions into consideration. The primary notion is that short-lived objects tend to be smaller and are accessed more often. The GC divides the memory allocation graph into sub-allocation graphs titled *generations*, each with a specific purpose. The three generations are shown in Table 34.1.

Table 34.1 CLR Garbage Collector Generations

Generation	Description
Generation 0 (Gen0)	This generation contains newly allocated objects that are frequently used. This generation is typically the smallest in size, taking roughly 10 milliseconds to collect.
Generation 1 (Gen1)	This generation is for larger and older objects that are used infrequently. When Gen1 is collected, Gen0 is collected as well.
Generation 2 (Gen2)	This generation is for larger and older objects that are used infrequently, except it is also a full collection that can be optimized for intelligent CPU caching by the underlying system if supported.

The managed heap originally starts in an empty state. Objects that are allocated initially go into the generation 0 portion. When a collection occurs, the GC determines which objects are garbage (no more references pointing to them) and which objects are surviving and need to be *compacted*. When an object is compacted, it moves into an older generation.

Currently there are three generations, but you can query the maximum number of generations if needed. You do so by getting the value from the GC.MaxGeneration property, which will always return 2. This may change in future versions of the GC. Any objects in generation 2 that get compacted will remain in generation 2. More information on interacting with the garbage collector is covered later in this chapter.

The main advantage of a generational garbage collector is that collections of a portion of the heap take less time than collecting the entire heap. The garbage collector can choose to examine only objects in generation 0, and because it mostly contains objects with a short life span, there is a good chance that a lot of memory will be reclaimed without the need to examine other generations.

Another performance benefit of the managed garbage collector comes from locality of reference. With the traditional unmanaged heap, memory was allocated wherever free space was found. Sometimes related data could be separated by megabytes. However, the managed heap allocates consecutive objects in a contiguous manner. There is an assumption that short-lived objects tend to have strong relationships with each other and are typically accessed around the same time. Many situations will allow all the related objects to reside in the CPU cache, which provides extremely fast access without having cache misses that require RAM access.

Collecting the Garbage

Garbage collection is automatically called by the CLR runtime, alleviating the burden of you having to explicitly do it yourself. It is important to know when and how collections occur in order to optimize effectively. Understanding how the GC works internally can offer some great insight into ways that your applications should be built to maximize memory management performance.

Developers transitioning from an unmanaged to a managed environment are often concerned with the performance of automatic memory management, more specifically, how the GC compares to the explicit management of memory like in C++.

When a memory allocation occurs, the CLR garbage collector determines whether or not a collection should occur. The GC looks at different factors, such as the current size of each generation, the size of each collection, and the size of the data that must be allocated. The GC then uses a heuristic evaluation to decide if a collection should occur. CLR garbage collection is as fast as or faster than C++ until a collection occurs. Essentially, a collection occurs when generation 0 does not have enough free space to accommodate a new object.

Collection usually occurs because:

- The application explicitly calls the collection routine of the GC.
- Generation 0 reaches max storage size.
- An AppDomain is unloaded by the CLR.
- The CLR itself is unloaded.

Each application has a set of *roots*, which identify storage locations for objects on the managed heap and objects that are set to null. These roots are made accessible by the garbage collector to determine whether a particular object is strongly referenced or if it should be collected (garbage).

The algorithm used by the CLR garbage collector is fairly straightforward, but has been optimized extensively. When a collection occurs, the GC starts with the assumption that all objects in the heap are garbage. It begins building a hierarchical graph of the roots and walks the tree to determine which objects cannot be accessed by the application. Objects that are unreachable from the application are considered garbage and can be removed during the next collection. The GC then walks the roots in a linear fashion, looking for contiguous blocks of memory that can be freed. The garbage is removed and all the remaining objects are shifted down in memory to remove gaps in the heap.

Allocation Profile

The level of exertion required by the garbage collector to handle the memory of a managed application is known as an allocation profile, which is a function of the object allocation count, the lifetime of each object, and the size of the allocations. As the level of exertion increases, so does the number of processor cycles the garbage collector takes, resulting in less time for the processor to run the application code. There are a couple techniques to optimize the allocation profile for your application, alleviating a good percentage of overhead as a result of garbage collection.

The most apparent way to relieve pressure is by allocating fewer objects. While the object-oriented paradigm introduced many great design and development concepts, it also resulted in a vast increase in the number of objects used to solve a problem.

An allocation profile is known to be either friendly or unfriendly with the garbage collector. An unfriendly profile will have many short life span objects allocated in the Large Object Heap, or many objects surviving in generation 2 for a long time before being collected. Objects in older generations that reference objects in younger generations increase the level of exertion by the garbage collector to manage collection. A friendly profile will allocate most of the objects when the application loads for the first time, and other objects will have a short life span and exist mainly in generation 0. Additionally, any objects with a long life span will contain few or no references to objects with a short life span.

It is important that you determine and constantly tune your allocation profile so that you can eliminate many performance issues as a result of automatic garbage collection.

CLR Profiler and GC Monitoring

Proper measurement metrics are a necessity when performance tuning an application, so you will need quantifiable methods to determine your allocation profile. Two such methods are described in this section: performance counters and the CLR Profiler.

Performance Counters

The Microsoft runtime team created a variety of performance counters to evaluate a few core .NET components, including the garbage collector, which can be used to study the garbage collector in a multitude of ways.

The first thing to do is launch the Performance Counter utility, which you can do by typing perfmon.exe into the Run dialog from the Start Menu or directly at the command prompt. Once the utility launches, you need to add the appropriate performance counter(s) by pressing Ctrl+I, or by clicking on the plus sign button like the one shown in Figure 34.1.

Figure 34.1
The button to add counters to the performance monitor utility.

The performance counters applicable to the garbage collector reside in the .NET CLR Memory performance object. Perhaps the most important counter metric in this performance object is the total processor time that is spent on garbage collection, known as the % Time in GC performance counter. Launch the managed application that you wish to profile and select it from the instance list for the % Time in GC counter. You should be presented with a dialog similar to the one shown in Figure 34.2.

After selecting the performance counters that you wish to analyze, you will immediately begin seeing the graph display data for the metrics you have selected. You can now test functionality in your application and witness the level of exertion by the GC in managing your memory. Figure 34.3 shows the performance monitor utility displaying the % Time in GC performance counter for the World Builder application.

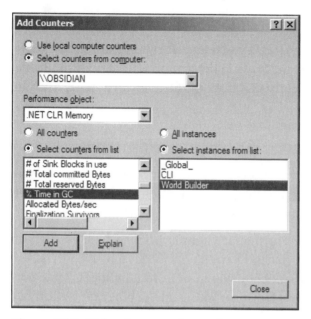

Figure 34.2 Dialog shown to select performance counters to utilize.

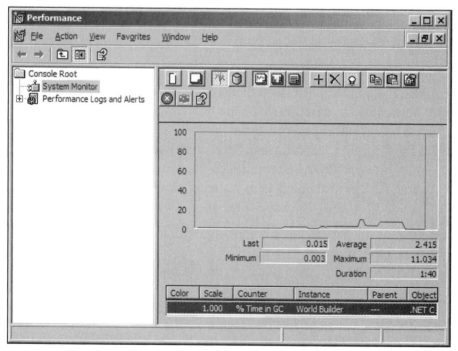

Figure 34.3 Example of the % Time in GC performance counter.

If the total processor time spent on garbage collection falls on average above 30%, you should consider tuning your allocation profile. Some applications can warrant high activity, whereas others cannot; having an average above 30% does not necessarily mean that your application is inefficient with memory. The course of action to take is a judgment call, depending on the type of application and whether or not there are performance issues.

An application with a good allocation profile will have most of its objects in generation 0. You can tune this aspect of your profile by comparing the # Gen 0 Collections and # Gen 2 Collections. Figure 34.4 shows the performance monitor utility with a variety of additional counters installed.

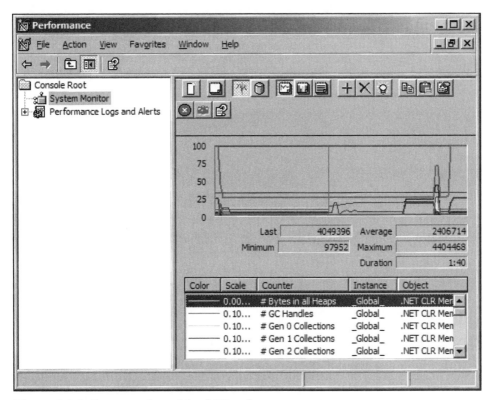

Figure 34.4 Showcase of a variety of GC performance counters.

The performance counters available in the .NET CLR Memory performance object are described in Table 34.2.

Table 34.2 Performance Counters in .NET CLR Memory

Performance Counter	Description
# Bytes in all Heaps	Total bytes in all three generations, including the large object heap. This value indicates the total amount of memory used by the garbage collector to store allocated objects.
# GC Handles	Total number of active handles used by the garbage collector.
# Gen 0 Collections	Number of collections of objects in generation 0.
# Gen 1 Collections	Number of collections of objects in generation 1.
# Gen 2 Collections	Number of collections of objects in generation 2.
# Induced GC	Number of times garbage collection was run from an explicit call, rather than during an allocation.
# Pinned Objects	This performance counter has not yet been implemented.
# of Sink Blocks in use	Sink blocks are used by synchronization primitives, and their data is allocated on demand belonging to an object. This metric determines the number of sink blocks currently in use.
# Total Committed Bytes	Total committed byte count from all managed heaps.
# Total Reserved Bytes	Total reserved byte count of the virtual memory reserved by the garbage collector for the application.
% Time in GC	Total time a sample spent performing garbage collection, divided by the total time since the last sample.
Allocated Bytes/Sec	Rate of bytes allocated per second by the garbage collector. This value is updated during a collection, and the time between garbage collections will be 0 because this metric evaluates to a rate.
Finalization Survivors	Number of garbage-collected classes that have survived because of a strong reference to them created by their finalizer.
Gen 0 Heap Size	Total size (in bytes) of the generation 0 managed heap.
Gen 0 Promoted Bytes/Sec	Total size (in bytes per second) of memory that has been promoted from generation 0 to generation 1 after surviving a garbage collection.
Gen 1 Heap Size	Total size (in bytes) of the generation 1 managed heap.
Gen 1 Promoted Bytes/Sec	Total size (in bytes per second) of memory that has been promoted from generation 1 to generation 2 after surviving a garbage collection.
Gen 2 Heap Size	Total size (in bytes) of the generation 1 managed heap.
Large Object Heap Size	Total size (in bytes) of the large object heap.

Table 34.2 Performance Counters in .NET CLR Memory *(continued)*

Performance Counter	Description
Promoted Memory from Gen 0	Total bytes of memory that are promoted from generation 0 to generation 1 after a garbage collection.
Promoted Memory from Gen 1	Total bytes of memory that are promoted from generation 1 to generation 2 after a garbage collection.
Promoted Finalization Memory from Gen 0	Total bytes of memory that are promoted from generation 0 to generation 1 because they are waiting to be finalized. This counter is non-cumulative, so the value observed at the end of the last garbage collection is displayed.
Promoted Finalization Memory from Gen 1	Total bytes of memory that are promoted from generation 1 to generation 2 because they are waiting to be finalized. This counter is non-cumulative, so the value observed at the end of the last garbage collection is displayed. If the last collection was generation 0 only, then the counter is reset to 0.

There are many performance counters available to track the .NET garbage collection, reducing the amount of work required to analyze your allocation profile in a quantitative manner.

Profiling API and the CLR Profiler

The CLR contains an extremely powerful API that allows third parties to create custom applications that can profile managed applications. In addition to the API, the Microsoft CLR runtime team developed an unsupported tool that can analyze managed memory using the Profiling API. This tool is called the CLR Profiler, and has a variety of uses.

Note

Download the tool by navigating to the following URL or accessing the Companion Web site: http://msdn.microsoft.com/netframework/downloads/tools/default.aspx

Launching the application will present a dialog like the one shown in Figure 34.5. From here you can target an application to test, and specify what you want to profile.

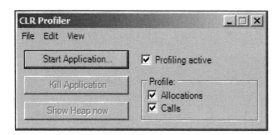

Figure 34.5
Main dialog of CLR Profiler.

Start by targeting an application to profile by using the main menu and selecting File>Profile Application... as shown in Figure 34.6. After targeting and application, you can click the Start Application... button to begin profiling.

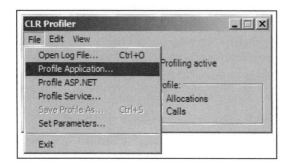

Figure 34.6
Menu to specify an application for profiling.

You now begin using the functionality that you want to profile in your application. The profile reports are accessible when the application is running or after it has been closed down, so you can either profile as you use the application or view the reports after the application has closed.

There is a wide variety of reports that you can view, such as the Histogram by Size for Allocated Objects shown in Figure 34.7. This report is useful in determining how much data was allocated, and separated by object type.

Another way to analyze your allocation profile is by viewing the memory management time line that depicts usage patterns for object types in your application as well as generation statistics for the garbage collector. This report is shown in Figure 34.8.

Another useful report is the allocation graph, which allows you to walk through the allocation tree for any objects in the application. This report is shown in Figure 34.9.

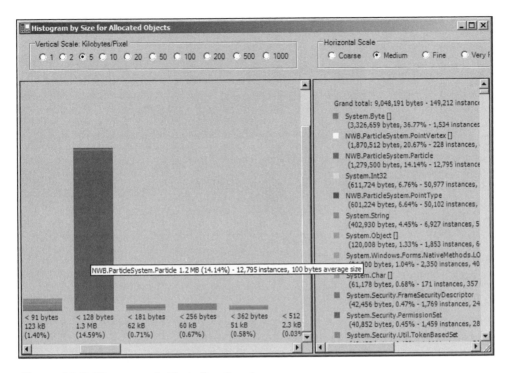

Figure 34.7 Histogram of object allocation sizes.

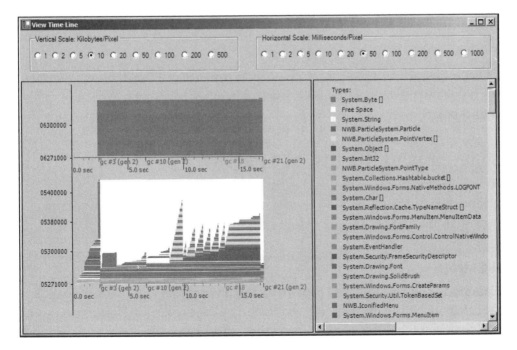

Figure 34.8 Time line of memory management by object type.

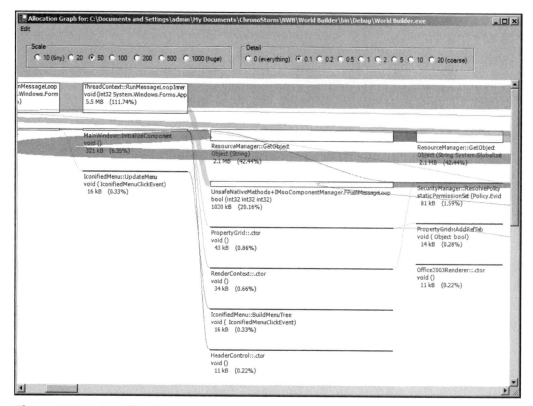

Figure 34.9 CLR Profiler allocation graph.

The CLR Profiler is accompanied by a high-performance overhead, making certain analysis tests difficult to do, but it is very useful in other areas, such as memory efficiency and usage.

Finalization and the Dispose Pattern

Even though automatic memory management handles releasing the memory of an allocation when the resource is no longer needed, some resources have some special steps that must be performed before releasing the memory.

Finalization

The Common Language Runtime provides a mechanism that automatically handles resource cleanup before memory is freed by the garbage collector. This mechanism is called *finalization*, and it is used to release native resources such as operating system handles or database connections.

The CLR does not use reference counting, so finalization was created to accommodate the issue behind releasing resources when references reach zero. Finalization is used in situations where an object's lifetime is unknown and the object requires cleanup.

The finalization mechanism increases the level of exertion required by the garbage collector, so it should be used appropriately. Objects requiring finalization are entered in a finalizable queue (f-reachable) that is searched by the garbage collector during a collection. The garbage collector manages a separate finalizer thread that processes objects that require finalization. Objects being finalized are moved into the next generation because the garbage collector may require their state. The memory for finalized objects will be released during the following collection.

There are two ways to implement finalization, each accomplishing the same thing but using different syntax. The first approach is overriding the Finalize method available to any object. This approach is illustrated by the following code:

```
public class YourClass
{
    public YourClass ()
    {
    }

    protected override void Finalize()
    {
        // Perform cleanup here
    }
}
```

The other method to implement finalization is using the same syntax that C++ uses for class destructors. It is important to know that even though the syntax is identical, the C# version does not fire when the object goes out of scope. Instead, it fires when the finalization thread gets around to releasing the object. This approach is illustrated by the following code:

```
public class YourClass
{
    public YourClass ()
    {
    }

    ~YourClass()
    {
```

```
            // Perform cleanup here
        }
}
```

Objects requiring finalization should be wrapped into the smallest object possible. If your class accesses both managed and unmanaged memory, you should make a child finalizer class that releases the unmanaged resources and encapsulates them in the parent object. Keep in mind that in order for this to work, there cannot be any strong references to the parent object.

Caution

Never implement a finalizer that blocks the finalization thread. Remember that there is only one thread for it, and blocking this thread will prevent resources from being freed.

Finalization is a great feature to have, but it is also very important that you are aware of the expensive performance implications. Another negative attribute of finalization is that you do not really have control over when the finalizer will execute or when the garbage collector will perform cleanup. A solution to these problems is to implement the dispose pattern which supports both the implicit and explicit freeing of resources.

The Dispose Pattern

For situations where the lifetime of an object is explicitly known, the dispose pattern is used to release unmanaged resources. Functionality for disposable objects is implemented through the IDisposable interface by providing an implementation for the Dispose method. In fact, you never know how your object will be used, so implementing a finalizer and IDisposable is the proper way of handling the release of unmanaged resources.

Both the finalizer and the Dispose method will call the same code, and it is advisable to route them both to the same function so that the code is maintainable and in one place only. When the Dispose method is called, it is important to inform the garbage collector that finalization is not needed. This is done by calling the GC.SuppressFinalization method.

The following code shows the proper way to implement IDisposable with support for finalization and multi-threading:

```
public class YourClass : IDisposable
{
```

```
public void Dispose()
{
    Dispose(true);
    GC.SuppressFinalize(this);
}

protected virtual void Dispose(bool disposing)
{
    // Prevent issues with multi-threading
    lock (this)
    {
        if (disposing)
        {
            // Perform cleanup on managed objects
        }

        // Perform cleanup on unmanaged objects
    }
}

~YourClass()
{
    Dispose(false);
}
}
```

Note

The disposing boolean parameter passed into the Dispose method will be true if explicitly called by the user, and false if called by the garbage collector during finalization.

The following code shows the proper way to implement IDisposable with support for finalization in a derived class. It is important to note that this code does not have a Finalize method or a non-parameterized Dispose method because these methods are inherited from the base class.

```
public class YourDerivedClass : YourClass
{
    protected override void Dispose(bool disposing)
    {
        // Prevent issues with multi-threading
        lock (this)
        {
```

```
                    if  (disposing)
                    {
                        // Perform cleanup on managed objects
                    }

                    // Perform cleanup on unmanaged objects

                    base.Dispose(disposing);
                }
            }
        }
```

Certain cases, like a database connection or network socket, are better suited to a Close method instead of Dispose. The best way to handle this situation is to have a Dispose, finalizer, and a Close method that all point to the same function. In most cases, the Dispose method will be privately declared.

The general rule of thumb is to implement IDisposable and provide a Dispose method if the class has a finalizer. Also, in situations where you know you are done with an object, you should call the Dispose method explicitly instead of waiting for the finalizer to fire.

The C# language provides a great mechanism that automatically disposes objects that implement the IDisposable interface. The using keyword allows you to specify a block of code that will call the Dispose method when program execution leaves the construct.

The following code shows how to use the construct:

```
using (DisposableType disposableObject)
{
    // Use disposableObject for something
}
// At this point the disposableObject.Dispose() method has been called.
```

Another great feature about the using keyword is that you can be guaranteed the Dispose method will fire, even if an exception is thrown from within the construct.

Note

Implement the dispose design pattern on resources that need to be explicitly freed, and always implement IDisposable if the class provides a finalizer.

Lastly, throw an ObjectDisposedException from methods where the unmanaged resources are needed but have already been disposed. The only place you should not do this is in the dispose method itself because it should be callable any number of times without throwing an exception.

Weak Referencing

As discussed earlier, an object cannot be collected if there is a root pointing to it (strong reference). However, this is not the only way of referencing an instantiated object. The GC also supports the notion of weak references. A weak reference to an object allows the garbage collector to perform collection if needed, but also allows the application to use the object. The first thing that probably popped into your head was having a `NullReferenceException` thrown when the application attempts to access an object after being collected; using weak references is an issue of timing.

Note

It is important to note that an application must obtain a strong reference to access a weakly referenced object. If this strong reference has been obtained before the garbage collector runs, the object cannot be collected.

The WeakReference object offers two constructors:

```
WeakReference(object target);
WeakReference(object target, bool trackResurrection);
```

The `target` parameter specifies which object a weak reference should be obtained for, and the `trackResurrection` parameter specifies whether or not the `WeakReference` should track the target after its `Finalize` method has been called; the `trackResurrection` parameter defaults to false with the first constructor.

A `WeakReference` that does not track resurrection is known as a short weak reference, while one that tracks resurrection is known as a long weak reference. It is advisable to refrain from using long weak references unless necessary; the state of resurrected objects can be very unpredictable.

Note

A long weak reference and a short weak reference will behave identically if the object does not offer a `Finalize` method.

Weak references are useful in situations where a certain data structure requires a lot of memory, and performance begins to degrade or you run out of memory because the garbage collector has no objects to collect. The most common data structure that benefits from the use of weak references is a tree structure that has a lot of references and depth.

The user might not be requiring the use of a particular area of the tree, so weak referencing the tree nodes will allow for the garbage collector to collect unused portions of the data structure if necessary. If a tree node gets collected, you simply reload that node and its children when you need them again.

As the user navigates away from a particular region of the tree, you can create some weak references and release the strong references for the objects in that region. If memory becomes low enough that the garbage collector requires collection, it will start to reclaim the weakly referenced tree objects. When the user navigates back to that same region, the application will try to recreate a strong reference for that tree. If successful, no memory operations are needed, and if the tree has already been collected, the application will simply reload that region again.

A prime example of using weak references is a directory browser that loads files and directories into a hierarchical tree. Keeping a weakly referenced tree in memory is much more efficient than loading all the data from the hard drive. If a file or directory node is collected, you can simply reload its contents from that location on the hard drive.

Once the WeakReference has been instantiated to point at the target object, you should set the strong reference from the root to null. The garbage collector will not be able to collect the object if any strong references to it remain.

The proper way to release the weak reference and reobtain a strong reference to the object is by assigning a root to the Target property of the WeakReference object. If the property returns null, the object was collected by the GC. Another way to determine whether the object has been collected is to check the IsAlive property of the WeakReference object.

The following code shows how to create a weak reference in C#:

```
MyClass instance = new MyClass ();

WeakReference weakReference = new WeakReference(instance);
instance = null; // Object is no longer rooted

if (weakReference.IsAlive)
{
    instance = weakReference.Target;
    // Object is rooted and can be used again (strong reference)
}
else
{
```

```
    // Recreate the object
    instance = new MyClass();
}
```

Explicit Control

The automated memory management of the .NET platform is very efficient and optimized, but certain situations may require direct control over the garbage collector to improve performance. Every application has a fairly unique allocation profile in terms of memory requirements and the intervals or patterns in which memory is managed, presenting some opportunities for performance tuning using explicit control over the garbage collector.

The System.GC type provides functionality for your application to interface with the garbage collector directly. There are a variety of things that can be done with this class, such as the ability to induce a collection, wait for the finalization thread to complete a pass, and query the garbage collector for some useful statistics, like the maximum number of generations.

Garbage collection is a fairly multi-threaded process, so performance optimizations typically come in the form of timing. For example, if you run a process that allocates a substantial number of objects, it is fair to say that you should explicitly invoke the garbage collector before returning control back to the user. If the user is already waiting for a long-running process to complete, where is the harm in running a collection when the process completes, so that the application does not hit a random pause when the GC finally fires up to release memory that was used? Your application knows more about how it works than the garbage collector does, so some strategically placed calls can offer some performance boosts. It is important to keep in mind that collections also degrade performance, so use them sparingly and wisely.

One of the most important operations you can do is invoke a collection. There are two flavors of the GC.Collect method: one version that takes in an integer specifying which generation to collect, and another version that invokes a collection across all generations and is the equivalent of calling GC.Collect(GC.MaxGeneration).

```
GC.Collect(Int32 Generation)
GC.Collect()
```

Note

Normally, you should avoid calling the collection methods explicitly, but as discussed earlier, there is a definite need for direct control in certain situations.

Another useful operation is the GC.WaitForPendingFinalizers method that suspends the calling thread until the finalization thread has emptied the f-reachable queue and all finalizers have been executed. It is uncommon that you should need to call this method directly unless you know what you are doing.

Aside from statistics like GC.MaxGeneration that returns the maximum number of generations, you can query any object or WeakReference to determine the generation that it is currently stored in.

```
Int32 GetGeneration(Object obj)
Int32 GetGeneration(WeakReference weakRef)
```

The value returned will be inclusively within the range of 0 and GC.MaxGeneration.

Conclusion

This chapter covered many aspects of the garbage collector intrinsic to the .NET platform, along with ways to optimize your allocation profile and program flow to increase performance and responsiveness. First, you were introduced to a high-level overview of the garbage collector and the purposes that it serves. Then the discussion became low-level and centered on everything that goes on behind the scenes. A number of rules and best practices were mentioned, along with some warnings about possible trouble spots.

Techniques for profiling the allocation profile of your application were also covered, as well as techniques to properly release unmanaged resources that require explicit disposal.

While fairly comprehensive, this chapter did not cover absolutely everything about the .NET garbage collector. The purpose of this chapter was not for you to walk away with an intimate knowledge of how the GC works, but rather with the knowledge to develop your applications to take advantage of automated memory management without suffering much of a performance hit. Some things that were not covered include the AddMemoryPressure and HandleCollector mechanisms that were introduced in .NET 2.0.

Automated memory management is a wonderful benefit to using the .NET platform for tools development due to the increased stability and reliability. The garbage collector will never go away, so learning the specifics of what goes on behind the scenes will make development and optimization much more straightforward.

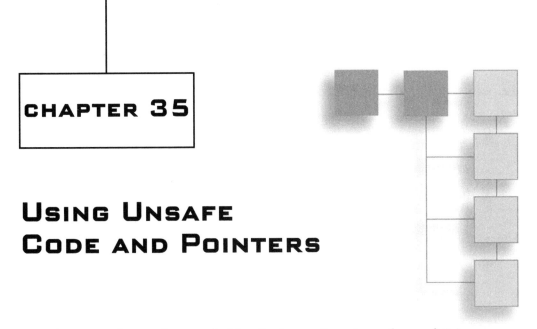

CHAPTER 35

USING UNSAFE CODE AND POINTERS

At some point you have to decide whether you're going to be a politician or an engineer. You cannot be both. To be a politician is to champion perception over reality. To be an engineer is to make perception subservient to reality. They are opposites. You can't do both simultaneously.

H. W. Kenton

One of the best features of .NET is the automatic memory management provided by the Common Language Runtime, reference types, and the Garbage Collector. C# hides most of its memory management, which makes life a lot easier for developers. In almost all situations, this censorship from the nitty gritty details of memory management is a good thing, though the need does arise when low-level access to memory is needed.

Memory in C++ is accessed and managed through the use of pointers. C# supports the concept of pointers, but only when absolutely necessary. The use of pointers in C# is discouraged, though there are a few rare situations that require them.

These situations are:

- When dealing with existing structures on disk, or when you need direct access to memory.

- When using Platform Invoke or Advanced COM that involve structures with pointers in them.

- When there is a strong need for performance-critical code, such as applications that require enhanced performance to make things as "real time" as possible.

Pointers in C# should not be used except for the three situations listed above. Only use pointers when absolutely necessary.

Caution

Never use pointers as an attempt to write C code in C#.

Before continuing on, it is important to list the advantages and disadvantages of using C# pointers.

The advantages are:

- Enhanced performance and increased flexibility. You can use a pointer to access and manipulate data in the most efficient way.

- There have obviously been a large number of Windows and third-party libraries that were developed prior to the .NET platform. Some functions may require that pointers be passed as parameters. Though this can be accomplished with DLLImport and System.IntPtr, it can often be cleaner to do it with pointers if you are already using them. Pointers offer extensive compatibility with legacy components.

- Some situations require that you track memory addresses, in which case a pointer is the only way to accomplish this.

The disadvantages are:

- Using pointers in C# increases the complexity of the language syntax. While C\C++ developers are accustomed to it, C# developers may struggle a bit with the rarely used concepts.

- Pointers are much harder to use, and even harder to use safely, than using reference types. It is quite easy to overwrite other variables, cause stack overflows, and access areas of memory that do not contain valid data, and in some cases, you can even overwrite process data for the .NET runtime. Doing so will result in a fatal application crash, defeating the purpose of using managed code for robust fault tolerance in the first place.

Now that I have successfully scared you away from using pointers in C#, it is time to continue on into the implementation and usage details.

Rudiments of Pointer Notation

The concept of pointers is well known and loved by C++ developers, but developers accustomed to other languages may find the idea and syntax difficult to grasp at times. Because of this, it is important to briefly discuss pointer notation, though only scratching the surface of a complex topic. If you are new to using pointers, it is recommended that you do further reading before attempting to use them in your code.

What is a pointer? **A pointer is a variable that holds the memory address of another type.** In C#, pointers are implicitly declared using the *dereferencer* symbol (*). After declaring the pointer variable, prefixing the variable with a dereferencer symbol will allow you to refer to the type located at the memory location held by the pointer; this is commonly known as *dereferencing a pointer*.

For example, the following code creates an integer with a pointer to it (intPtr) and uses integer assignment to set its value to 27.

```
int* intPtr = 27;
```

Later on, should you wish to change the integer value, you can use the following code to set the value to 15.

```
*intPtr = 15;
```

Caution

It is very important that you prefix the variable with the dereferencer symbol when trying to work with the data.

Consider the following code:

```
intPtr = 56;
```

The intent was to set the integer value to 56, but in actuality the pointer will now point to the start of the four bytes at memory location 56 (which could be anything).

Another symbol that is essential when working with pointers is the address operator (&) (in the context of pointer notation). Prefixing a variable with this operator will return the memory address of the variable.

The following code declares an integer and creates a pointer that points to the location of the integer in memory.

```
int myNumber = 42;
int* myNumberPtr;
myNumberPtr = &myNumber;
```

At this time, we have a pointer (myNumberPtr) that points at the memory location of an integer (myNumber) in memory.

The following code can now be used to set the value of myNumber to 13 through the pointer myNumberPtr.

```
*myNumberPtr = 13;
```

Note

> *myNumberPtr can be read as "the integer located at the memory value address held by myNumberPtr."

Finally, pointers can also be declared for structs.

Consider the following struct definition and code:

```
struct CartesianCoord
{
    public int x;
    public int y;
    public int z;
}

CartesianCoord coord = new CartesianCoord();
CartesianCoord* coordPtr = &coord;
```

You can now use the pointer coordPtr to access public fields of coord.

This can be done with the following code:

```
(*coordPtr).y;
```

Or the following equivalent code, which uses the indirection operator:

```
coordPtr->y;
```

Caution

> C++ developers are used to declaring statements like the following to save typing:
> ```
> int* int1, int2;
> ```
> Those developers would assume that int1 is a pointer to an integer, and int2 is just an integer. C# handles this statement differently, as the pointer declaration is on the type, not the variable. In this example, both int1 and int2 are pointers to integers.

Using an Unsafe Context

C# code executes in either a safe or unsafe context. Safe is the default, but any use of pointers requires that an unsafe context be used. The unsafe keyword is used to denote an unsafe context. Unsafe code is still managed by the Common Language Runtime, just like safe code, the only difference being that programmers can use pointers to manipulate memory directly. Unsafe code runs outside of the automatic memory management capabilities provided by the garbage collector, though the Common Language Runtime is always aware of the code. The unsafe keyword is an enhancement to make unsafe code a little bit safer. Code executing in an unsafe context is not verified to be safe, so the code must be fully trusted in order to execute the unsafe code. Unsafe code cannot be executed in an untrusted environment like the Internet.

The unsafe keyword can be applied on methods, properties, constructors (exception static), and extenders. Running code in an unsafe context is much more efficient than using references because the garbage collector and an extra layer are bypassed to decrease overhead. Unsafe code also increases performance by getting rid of array bounds checking (though you are now responsible for it).

Aside from placing code within an unsafe construct, you must also configure the compiler to allow unsafe code to be used. This can be done through the property pages for the project or by using the /unsafe switch flag with csc.exe.

The following code shows how to properly use the unsafe keyword in a couple of ways.

```csharp
public void unsafe MyMethod(int* arg)
{
    // Use arg parameter here
}

public void MyMethod(int arg)
{
    unsafe
    {
        fixed (int* argPtr = arg)
        {
            // Use argPtr parameter here
        }
    }
}
```

Pinning Memory with the Fixed Statement

The automatic memory management provided by the Garbage Collector runs in a background thread, so you can never tell when memory will be assigned to a new data location. This can create a serious problem when dealing with pointers, because the pointers will not update their addresses when the memory changes, resulting in pointers that point at incorrect or invalid memory blocks.

C# supports the fixed statement, which is used to signal that a particular variable should not be touched by the garbage collector. This is known as memory pinning, which means that the specified memory is pinned to a particular location, and that you are guaranteed that the location will remain constant until the code exits the fixed statement. The fixed statement has similar syntax to the using statement.

The following code shows the fixed statement being used.

```
byte[] data = new byte[10000];
unsafe
{
    fixed (byte* dataPtr = data)
    {
        // Code using dataPtr here
    }
}
```

Some situations require that you have two fixed variables that use each other. This is perfectly acceptable by nesting fixed statements. The following code shows this being done.

```
byte[] data1 = new byte[10000];
byte[] data2 = new byte[5000];
unsafe
{
    fixed (byte* data1Ptr = data1)
    {
        fixed (byte* data2Ptr = data2)
        {
            // Code using data1Ptr and data2Ptr here
        }
    }
}
```

Note

The compiler will not even permit a variable address with pointers unless the memory for the variable is pinned within a `fixed` statement.

Disabling Arithmetic Overflow Checking

Another keyword that is relevant to unsafe pointer usage is the unchecked keyword. Specifying unchecked allows you to suppress overflow-checking for integral-type arithmetic operations and conversions. If an expression produces a value that is outside the range of the destination data type, then the result is truncated. For example, trying to evaluate the following code will set myNumber equal to -1014837864.

```
unchecked
{
    int myNumber = (int)3181555928472; // Evaluates to -1014837864
}
```

The unchecked keyword causes the compiler to ignore the fact that the value is too large for the integer data type. Had the unchecked keyword not been specified, then the compiler would have thrown compile time errors because the sizes are known and the values are constant. Otherwise, an OverflowException would have been thrown at runtime.

You can also use the unchecked keyword as an operator, as in the following example.

```
public int AddNumbers(int left, int right)
{
    return unchecked(left + right);
}
```

Running code, especially numeric-intensive calculations, within an unchecked block can boost the overall speed and performance of the executing code. You have to be careful to watch your data type sizes though.

Allocating High Performance Memory

You can use the keyword stackalloc to allocate a block of memory on the stack. This only works with value types, and the memory is not subject to garbage collection, so it does not have to be pinned. The lifetime of the memory block is limited to the scope of the executing method; stackalloc is only valid in local variable initializers.

Note

Stackalloc is very similar to the _alloca method in the C runtime library. Stackalloc depends on the use of pointers, so you can only use it within an unsafe context.

The memory is only allocated by stackalloc, so initialization is up to you. One common usage for stackalloc in terms of performance is when dealing with arrays. The .NET platform provides excellent mechanisms for dealing with arrays, but the data are still objects instantiated from System.Array and stored on the heap, so all the related overhead is incurred when dealing with them.

You can allocate enough memory to store 10 integers with the following code.

```
int* intArray = stackalloc int[10];
```

There are a couple of ways to access the array members.

You can use *(intArray + i), where i is the index of the array element to access.

```
*(intArray + 0) = 123;
*(intArray + 1) = 456;
*(intArray + 2) = 789;
```

You can also use intArray[i] to access the array elements.

```
intArray[0] = 123;
intArray[1] = 456;
intArray[2] = 789;
```

Normally, when you access a member outside of the array bounds, an out of bounds exception will be thrown. When using stackalloc, however, you are accessing an address located somewhere on the stack. Writing to an incorrect address could corrupt a variable, or even return an address from a method currently being executed.

For example:

```
int* intArray = stackalloc int[5];
intArray[7] = 123; // This means that (intArray + 7 * sizeof(int)) had
                   // a value of 123 assigned to it.
```

Caution

The moral of the story is, be very careful!

Getting Size of Data Types

Just as in C\C++, you can use the sizeof operator to determine the number of bytes occupied of the given data type. You must do so within an unsafe context.

The following code can be executed to print out a list of data type sizes for handy reference. As of .NET 2.0, it is optional to use the sizeof operator within an unsafe context.

```
unsafe
{
    Console.WriteLine("sbyte: {0}", sizeof(sbyte));
    Console.WriteLine("byte: {0}", sizeof(byte));
    Console.WriteLine("short: {0}", sizeof(short));
    Console.WriteLine("ushort: {0}", sizeof(ushort));
    Console.WriteLine("int: {0}", sizeof(int));
    Console.WriteLine("uint: {0}", sizeof(uint));
    Console.WriteLine("long: {0}", sizeof(long));
    Console.WriteLine("ulong: {0}", sizeof(ulong));
    Console.WriteLine("char: {0}", sizeof(char));
    Console.WriteLine("float: {0}", sizeof(float));
    Console.WriteLine("double: {0}", sizeof(double));
    Console.WriteLine("decimal: {0}", sizeof(decimal));
    Console.WriteLine("bool: {0}", sizeof(bool));
}
```

Executing the above code will print out the following:

```
sbyte: 1
byte: 1
short: 2
ushort: 2
int: 4
uint: 4
long: 8
ulong: 8
char: 2
float: 4
double: 8
decimal: 16
bool: 1
```

You may be wondering why char prints a size of 2. This is because System.Char (char) is a Unicode type (two bytes), and sizeof returns the size of the data types allocated by the CLR. There is another method to get the size of data types after marshaling has occurred. `System.Runtime.InteropServices.Marshal.SizeOf()` returns the size of a data type when converted to an unmanaged representation. Using `Marshal.SizeOf(char)` will return one byte since at this point the char has been converted to a one-byte ANSI character.

You can also get the size of a struct that contains value types. The following code shows this.

```
public struct SimpleStruct
{
    public char firstChar;
    public char secondChar;
    public int myInteger;
}
```

Evaluating `sizeof(SimpleStruct)` will return 10 bytes with padding, and `Marshal.SizeOf(SimpleStruct)` will return 6 bytes.

Example: Array Iteration and Value Assignment

The following example shows how to loop through an array and assign values to each array element. This example also profiles the elapsed time between using checked and unchecked arithmetic.

```
private static void ArrayValueAssignment()
{
    byte[] data = new byte[100000000];

    int unsafeTime = 0;
    int uncheckedTime = 0;

    unsafeTime = Environment.TickCount;

    unsafe
    {
        fixed (byte* dataPtr = data)
        {
            byte* dataByte = dataPtr;

            for (int index = 0; index < data.Length; index++)
            {
                *dataByte++ = (byte)index;
                // Can also do:  *(dataByte + index) = (byte)index;
            }
```

```
        }
    }

    unsafeTime = Environment.TickCount - unsafeTime;

    uncheckedTime = Environment.TickCount;

    unsafe
    {
        unchecked
        {
            fixed (byte* dataPtr = data)
            {
                byte* dataByte = dataPtr;

                for (int index = 0; index < data.Length; index++)
                {
                    *dataByte++ = (byte)index;
                    // Can also do:  *(dataByte + index) = (byte)index;
                }
            }
        }
    }

    uncheckedTime = Environment.TickCount - uncheckedTime;

    Console.WriteLine("Unsafe Elapsed Time: " +
                            unsafeTime.ToString() + " ticks");

    Console.WriteLine("Unchecked Elapsed Time: " +
                            uncheckedTime.ToString() + " ticks");
}
```

Example: Data Block Copying

The following example copies the data from a source array into a destination array, serving as a replacement for Array.Copy().

```
static void DataBlockCopy()
{
    int dataLength = 100000000;

    byte[] sourceData = new byte[dataLength];
```

```
        byte[] destinationData = new byte[dataLength];

        for (int index = 0; index < dataLength; index++)
        {
            sourceData[index] = (byte)index;
        }

        UnsafeCopy(sourceData, 0, destinationData, 0, dataLength);

        Console.WriteLine("The first 15 elements are:");

        for (int index = 0; index < 15; index++)
        {
            Console.Write(destinationData[index] + " ");
        }

        Console.WriteLine("\n");
    }

    static unsafe void UnsafeCopy(byte[] source,
                                  int sourceIndex,
                                  byte[] destination,
                                  int destinationIndex,
                                  int count)
    {
        Debug.Assert(source != null);
        Debug.Assert(sourceIndex >= 0);

        Debug.Assert(destination != null);
        Debug.Assert(destinationIndex >= 0);

        Debug.Assert(!(source.Length - sourceIndex < count));
        Debug.Assert(!(destination.Length - destinationIndex < count));

        unchecked
        {
            int countDiv = count / 4;
            int countMod = count % 4;

            fixed (byte* sourcePtr = source, destinationPtr = destination)
            {
                byte* sourceByte = sourcePtr;
                byte* destinationByte = destinationPtr;
```

```
        for (int blockIndex = 0; blockIndex < countDiv; blockIndex++)
        {
            *((int*)destinationByte) = *((int*)sourceByte);

            destinationByte++;
            sourceByte++;
        }

        for (int blockIndex = 0; blockIndex < countMod; blockIndex++)
        {
            *destinationByte = *sourceByte;

            destinationByte++;
            sourceByte++;
        }
    }
  }
}
```

Example: Win32 API Access

The following example shows how to interact with Win32 API calls through
PInvoke and unsafe pointers. There are alternatives to this approach, but this example shows how to do it with unsafe code. This example retrieves the name of the
local machine.

```
[System.Runtime.InteropServices.DllImport("Kernel32")]
static extern unsafe bool GetComputerName(byte* lpBuffer, long* nSize);

private static void Win32APIAccess()
{
    byte[] buffer = new byte[512];
    long size = buffer.Length;

    unsafe
    {
        long* sizePtr = &size;

        fixed (byte* bufferPtr = buffer)
        {
            GetComputerName(bufferPtr, sizePtr);
        }
    }
```

```
    byte[] nameBytes = new byte[size];

    Array.Copy(buffer, 0, nameBytes, 0, size);

    Console.WriteLine("Computer Name: " + Encoding.ASCII.GetString(nameBytes));
}
```

Conclusion

Figure 35.1 shows all three examples after execution. Notice the speed difference between the unsafe context and the unsafe + unchecked context.

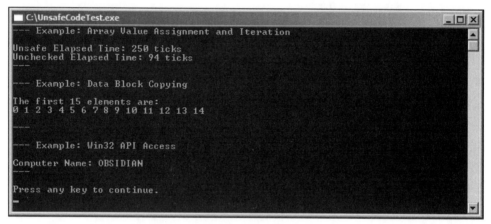

Figure 35.1 Screenshot of all three examples after execution.

This chapter covered the usage of pointers and unsafe code within the C# language. There are only a few situations where it should be used, but pointers can solve a lot of problems when used appropriately.

It is important to keep in mind that unsafe code contexts require elevated security permissions to execute, so do not use unsafe code within applications that need to run under a least privilege account.

Lastly, only use pointers for performance gains if the gain itself is substantial. A great deal of the .NET framework has been optimized to its fullest potential, and while you may think your unsafe code implementation is faster than the built-in functionality, you cannot be certain unless you profile. Even then, if the difference between your code and the built-in functionality is pretty close, you are better off using the built-in functionality instead.

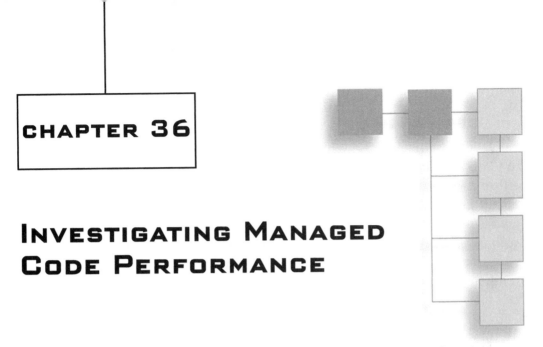

CHAPTER 36

INVESTIGATING MANAGED CODE PERFORMANCE

You cannot teach beginners top-down programming, because they don't know which end is up.

C. A. R. Hoare

An important of element of software development, especially when dealing with important tools and tools that perform complex calculations, is performance and optimization. Performance testing and optimization techniques for pretty much every language have been around for quite some time, and developers making the switch, or developers who are hesitant to make the switch, are worried about code performance and not having the understanding to write optimized code. The truth for developers worried about managed code optimizations is that much of the advice remains the same as it did prior to the introduction of .NET and the managed runtime.

In this chapter, I will briefly cover two approaches for investigating performance and then lead into a substantial number of considerations for writing efficient code for the .NET platform.

Investigating Performance

There are two discrete approaches for investigating performance: white box investigation and black box investigation. Both approaches have different strengths and weaknesses, and sometimes it is beneficial to use both approaches to conduct a robust and thorough performance investigation.

407

Using the white box approach involves studying the implementation details behind a particular component or function, and deriving a list of characteristics to factor into performance testing based on the complexity and perceived cost of completing a particular task. White box testing is great when trying to understand the technology in greater detail, and it allows you to easily identify and address performance pitfalls related to implementation. White box testing makes it very difficult to produce quantitative performance metrics. Relative performance can be measured using an order of magnitude, but only on a piece of functionality in isolation from other components in the system or various software and hardware configurations. Code that may appear slow or overly complex may run quite fast on different hardware with a caching strategy or with an optimizing compiler. Code that may appear efficient has the potential to run extremely slowly or inefficiently on different hardware or software configurations.

Using the block box approach involves disregarding the implementation details and instead basing test results on overall execution time. Black box testing is great in the sense that you can end up with a set of strong and unambiguous metrics to measure performance, including a fairly precise resolve understanding of the capacity of a particular test case. The downside to black box testing results from the nearly infinite number of software and hardware combinations, also known as a combinatorial explosion. The sheer volume of combinations makes it nearly impossible to determine a set of distinct systems that tests can be performed against.

Choosing the best approach depends on the type of investigation being conducted, and how large the system is. White box testing will not suffice for large systems where there is a massive amount of code, or for systems that rely on third-party components that do not have source code available. Black box testing is really to determine which operations or tasks are problematic, making it difficult to determine exactly where the problem originates, unless the slowdown results from architecture and the communication between distributed and isolated components. Quite often, it makes sense to perform a little bit of white box testing in complex areas and then perform a thorough investigation of performance using the black box approach.

Avoid Manual Optimization

Many developers, especially the ones who have been in the industry for a while, are used to optimizing code so tightly that they are concerned with how the compiler is going to execute each segment of critical code, and so they use alternate syntax in an attempt to compile more efficient code. There is no point in trying to perform low-level optimizations manually. Current compilers on the market are quite intelligent when it comes to low-level optimizations, even smarter than you. Just make sure that you enable compiler optimizations when building a final release so that the compiler can work its magic. Be sure to test your application in release mode because preprocessor symbols and conditionally compiled function calls can perform unexpectedly when executed in a different compilation mode. Certain bugs may be masked in debug mode and only appear in an optimized compilation.

The optimizations that you should be concerned with are high-level, such as memory allocation, network traffic, and using inappropriate data structures and algorithms. Make sure that you profile your code before attempting to optimize. It is a waste of time to incorrectly guess where code is suffering from poor performance and attempt to optimize in an area that does not need it.

Use code analysis tools such as FxCop to help identify performance bottlenecks. Some bottlenecks are very hard to identify without a robust tool to help you. Lastly, pass your assemblies through a commercial obfuscator. The main purpose of an obfuscator is to make it difficult to decompile your application by mangling your private and internal type and variable names, but some obfuscators can increase performance by a slight amount through shorter names and optimized memory layouts.

String Comparison

Pretty much every application performs comparisons between strings, with the variant being the number of comparisons performed. String equality can be defined as two strings with the identical sequence of characters, also known as *binary equality*. This type of string comparison works for most situations, but binary equality does not suffice when multiple locales are used, or case sensitivity matters. The term *logical equality* is used to describe two strings that are equivalent despite binary differences.

The System.String data type of the .NET framework provides numerous ways to store and manipulate string data, including methods of performing binary and logical equality comparisons. Three methods exist that provide the ability to check for binary equality: two instance methods and one static method. The first instance method is strongly typed to accept a string parameter, and the other instance method overrides the Equals method inherited from System.Object. The overridden method is not recommended unless you are comparing more than just strings, because this method suffers a performance penalty by needing to perform type checking. The static method uses a performance tuned approach that is employed throughout the .NET framework. First, a check is performed to see if any of the strings are null. Then a reference equality check is performed to see if the two strings refer to the same object. If no result has been returned yet, the virtual instance method is called.

Note

The C# equality operator ==, represented by the MSIL op_Equality, simply makes a call to the static Equals method of System.String, so you do not have to worry about performance with this one.

Logical equality is provided through the use of the overloaded Compare method, which has parameters for locale formatting and case insensitive comparisons. Unlike the Equals method, which returns a boolean value, the Compare method returns an integer that describes the lexical difference between the two strings, with a value of zero stating that the two strings are lexicographically identical.

Being able to perform locale-aware and case insensitive comparisons comes at a significant performance cost. The cost is dependent on the locale used and the complexity of the rules related to the locale. Because of the fairly significant performance hit when using the Compare method, it is important to minimize calls to it whenever possible. One approach is to identify comparisons where case and locale rules can be ignored, using String.Equals() instead of String.Compare(). This approach works well for situations where the data originates from back-end or embedded systems, to name a couple examples. Situations where case and locale rules cannot be ignored, but binary equality is common, are best served by calling String.Equals() before String.Compare(). Doing so can result in a considerable performance gain if most of the comparisons exhibit binary equality. The following code shows this.

```
string string1 = "This is from one place";
string string2 = "This is from elsewhere";
if (string1 == string2 || String.Compare(string1, string2) == 0)
{
    // Handle identical strings
}
```

In terms of case insensitive comparisons, String.Compare() is able to perform these comparisons without allocating new strings, whereas a call to String.Equals() with calls to String.ToUpper() will result in two new strings being allocated.

It is a common mistake to think that checking whether the length of a string is zero is faster than comparing the string to the empty string constant. There is a sliver more performance when checking the length because only the string metadata must be examined, but this increase is marginal and it is doubtful that you will see any measurable performance bonus. It is important to note that you should use the canonical `String.Empty` instance as a constant when comparing against an empty string rather than `""` since an allocation will be avoided in this case.

String Formatting

Having the ability to insert, remove, and replace data inside strings is a common task in almost every application. This functionality is provided through a couple of mechanisms of the .NET platform and class framework. The first mechanism, also the easiest to use, is the `ToString()` method that is available on data types that inherit from `System.Object`. The default behavior of this method is to return the full name of the type, though it can be overridden to support extended functionality. The typical implementation will return a partial representation of the class with the help of the member variables inside the class. Pretty much all the string formatting features of the .NET framework boil down to using `ToString()` at some point. Therefore, it is important that you make sure that this method performs efficiently and quickly.

Another formatting mechanism is `String.Format`, which functions like `sprintf` in the C realm. This function is used to format a string against a pattern where certain tokens are substituted with values in the supplied arguments array. This function is perhaps the slowest of the bunch, because it lacks the efficiency of type overloading provided by a class like `StringBuilder`, causing a number of boxing and unboxing operations to occur. Classes can also inherit from `IFormattable` to extend the formatting capabilities of `ToString()`.

One of the biggest slowdowns when dealing with strings is that they are immutable, which means that any time a string is modified, a new string object is created. Immutable strings are great when they are shared frequently and are modified infrequently. Reading is cheap in terms of performance because locking or reference counting is unnecessary, and you can avoid abstraction and sharing schemes. The class framework provides the `StringBuilder` class, which is used to perform high-performance string operations against a mutable Unicode character array. After modifications on the string within a `StringBuilder` are complete, you can call `ToString()` to retrieve the contents of the internal string.

N o t e

Calling ToString() on a StringBuilder object will simply reference the internal character array, but a copy operation occurs as soon as the result is assigned to a string object and further operations are performed on the StringBuilder. The recommended approach is to only call ToString() after all modifications on the StringBuilder are complete. Otherwise, it is advisable to use the ToString() overload that allows only a substring of the internal character array to be returned.

StringBuilder manages an internal character buffer that is allocated during instantiation. The initial capacity defaults to an array of 16 characters, but you can specify a different value for the initial capacity as a parameter in the constructor. When an operation requires that the internal size of the StringBuilder be increased, a new array that is double the size of the old one is created, and the old data is copied into the new array. The reallocation is quite expensive, and it should be avoided as much as possible. It is highly recommended that you explicitly set the initial capacity if you have enough information to estimate the value that works best for your situation.

There are some downsides to working with a StringBuilder object over a String object. The first downside is that StringBuilder only implements a fraction of the functions offered by String. StringBuilder also incurs a significant overhead cost when first initialized, so there are times where using StringBuilder for only a handful of manipulations can actually decrease your performance. The rule of thumb is to only consider using StringBuilder when the number of manipulations reaches double digits. StringBuilder is great to use when appending strings within a loop. There is no real definitive answer on when to use StringBuilder, because the performance is dependent on system parameters and design. It may not be such a bad idea to profile critical code when using StringBuilder or another formatting mechanism to determine which approach is faster.

Concatenating strings is a form of string formatting, but there are additional performance increases that can be investigated. String.Concat() is, by far, the fastest and most efficient way to join a couple of strings together. Use this method over anything else if you can combine all your strings in one call to String.Concat(). Otherwise, you can resort to a more flexible mechanism like StringBuilder if you need to join many strings together. Never use normal String instances and the concatenation operator to join strings together; this is the most inefficient way you could possibly use to accomplish the task.

String Reversal

The unification of text storage and manipulation into a single String data type was an excellent decision, although the .NET Framework is missing a way to efficiently reverse the contents of a string. String reversal is an uncommon activity but not extremely rare. There are a number of ways to accomplish string reversal, such as appending each string character to a StringBuilder in reverse order, generating a character array and calling Array.Reverse, or calling the StrReverse method in the Microsoft.VisualBasic.Strings library. All three methods will perform the task, but they are not the most efficient way to accomplish it.

The fastest way to perform string reversal is by using a character array with each character from the input string appended to the array in reverse order, afterwards constructing a new string from the reversed character array.

The following code shows how to do this.

```
string ReverseString(string input)
{
    chars[] chars = new char[input.Length];

    int index1 = input.Length -1;
    int index2 = 0;

    while (index1 >= 0)
    {
        chars[index1--] = input[index2++];
    }

    return new string(chars);
}
```

Compiling Regular Expressions

In a nutshell, regular expressions are a very powerful text manipulation tool that compresses verbose and suboptimal text manipulation and matching patterns into a couple of lines composing an efficient regular expression. The .NET framework provides a number of robust classes for working with regular expressions, like the Regex type that exists in the System.Text.RegularExpressions namespace. Regex provides a mechanism to execute a regular expression against a text string. When a regular expression is set on the Regex object, it is converted to a partially compiled representation, which is cached for execution during the application lifetime.

In order to further increase performance when executing a regular expression, there is support for pre-compiling a regular expression to MSIL, which will then be JIT'ed (Just-in-Time compiled) to native code before execution. Pre-compiled regular expressions are placed in dynamically generated assemblies that can be loaded at runtime within an application domain. Assemblies cannot be unloaded, so there is a potential problem with this approach where you will not be able to unload regular expressions from memory until the application domain itself is released. To solve this problem, you can persist the dynamically generated assemblies to the hard drive and load them at runtime into a second application domain. This functionality is available through the Regex.CompileToAssembly() method.

The following code shows how to compile a regular expression to a dynamically generated assembly.

```
using System;
using System.Reflection;
using System.Text.RegularExpressions;

string name = "AlphaNumericTest";
string nameSpace = "CompiledExpression";
string assembly = "RegularExpressionTest";
string expression = "[^a-zA-Z0-9]";

RegexOptions options = RegexOptions.None;
RegexCompilationInfo info = new RegexCompilationInfo(expression,
                                                     options,
                                                     name,
                                                     nameSpace,
                                                     true);
AssemblyName assemblyName = new AssemblyName();
assemblyName.Name = assembly;
Regex.CompileToAssembly(new RegexCompilationInfo[]{info}, assemblyName);
```

The following code shows how to use the regular expression that has been compiled into the RegularExpressionTest assembly.

```
using System;
using System.Text.RegularExpressions;
string searchString = "Your Search String Here";
CompiledExpression.AlphaNumericTest expression
                              = new CompiledExpression.AlphaNumericTest();
foreach (Match match in expression.Matches(searchString))
{
```

```
    // Do something with match.Value
}
```

Note

The performance improvement from using precompiled expressions is dependent on the regular expression used.

Use the Most Specific Type

In the majority of object-oriented programming languages that support inheritance, it is generally possible to use any data type in the inheritance tree to declare a variable. For example, you could instantiate a SpeedBoat object and reference it with a variable of type Boat. Unless there is a specific reason, the general rule is to use the most specific type possible, because doing otherwise can cause performance problems. An example could be declaring a variable of type Object and storing an integer with it. In this particular example, Object is a reference type, and integer is a value type. Treat an integer as an object and you end up with boxing operations.

Luckily, VB.NET is more prone to errors of this nature than C#, because in C# you have to explicitly cast a reference type storing a value type to that correct type before using it in arithmetic operations, for example. This explicit casting will give C# enough information to generate relatively efficient code, although using the most specific type in the first place would still be the most efficient.

Avoid Boxing and Unboxing

There are two data types in the .NET platform—value and reference—and new developers can introduce significant performance penalties without fully understanding the implications behind boxing and unboxing operations.

Value types are lightweight objects that are allocated on the stack, unless the value type is allocated as an array element, or if the value type is a field of a reference type. All primitives and structures are value types that are derived from System.ValueType. Value types are stack-based, which means that allocating and accessing them is much more efficient than using reference types.

Reference types are heavyweight objects that are allocated on the heap, unless the stackalloc keyword is used. Reference layers impart a level of indirection, meaning that they require a reference to access their storage location. These types cannot be accessed directly, so a variable always holds a reference to the actual object or it is null. Reference types are allocated on the heap, so the runtime must check to see that each allocation is successful.

A boxing operation occurs when a value type needs to behave like a reference type. The Common Language Runtime allocates enough memory to hold a copy of the value type, including the necessary information to create a valid reference type. There is a significant amount of performance overhead because of the heap allocation and storage of the value type state. This conversion can occur explicitly through a cast operation, or implicitly by an assignment operation or a method call.

An unboxing operation occurs when a boxed value type is to be explicitly converted back to a value type on the stack. The Common Language Runtime returns a pointer to the referenced data, and then the data is typically copied to a location on the stack through an assignment operation. The boxed value type will still remain on the heap until the garbage collector is able to reclaim it.

It is important to be aware of areas of your code where large numbers of boxing and unboxing operations occur. Also be aware that the .NET framework has many methods and properties that can cause implicit conversions to occur when used with value types. If a method takes an object as a parameter, then value type instances will be boxed.

Use Value Types Sensibly

Using value types in performance-critical code can lead to some performance gain, but only if used correctly. Performance can be significantly decreased if value types are overused or are used inefficiently. Value types are much faster to instantiate and uninstantiate, and they also take up less space in memory. The size difference between a value type and a reference type on a 32-bit machine is three words. This is because reference types store the reference to the object data, a sync block index, and a method table index. Three words may seem insignificant, but consider situations where you have a large number of objects. You do need to also consider the performance implications when value types need to behave as objects, resulting in a boxing and unboxing operation.

Working with structures can also offer the potential for performance improvements. Classes are specified as auto layout so that the CLR can arrange fields in the optimal manner for speed and memory size, taking byte alignment into account. Structures are specified as sequential layout by default, which makes things easy when passing structures to P/Invoke and unmanaged code, because the layout of the structure easily maps to the structure in unmanaged code. Performance in this situation is ideal because hardly any marshaling is required. However, using structures with sequential layout without interacting with unmanaged code is very inefficient. If you are using structures for performance reasons, without the intent to communicate with legacy code, you can explicitly declare a struct as auto layout with the following code.

```
[StructLayout(LayoutKind.Auto)]
public struct MyStructure
{
    // ...
}
```

The Myth About Foreach Loops

A common misconception with code optimization is that using a for loop instead of a foreach loop will offer better performance. In actuality, this advice used to be correct back when compilers were not intelligent enough to determine the logical equality between a for and a foreach loop in like situations. This thought is based on the assumption that an enumerator is instantiated inside a foreach loop to iterate through the elements of a collection, which is not a factor anymore because of processor speeds and compiler optimization. Using a foreach loop to iterate through the elements of an array will make no substantial difference in performance, if any at all.

To review, writing a for loop like the following code:

```
for (int index = 0; index < array.Length; index++)
{
    // Do processing on array[index]
}
```

will perform the same as a foreach loop like the following code (assuming an array of bytes for the sake of argument).

```
foreach (byte element in array)
{
    // Do processing on element
}
```

There is one situation where a for loop might be more efficient than a foreach loop, and that is when the size of the collection is a fixed value that you are aware of when writing the code. Consider the following code.

```
for (int index = 0; index < 15; index++)
```

Being able to write a `for` loop with a constant iteration count will give the JIT compiler a lot more flexibility and scope for optimization.

Use Asynchronous Calls

The .NET platform offers mechanisms to provide both asynchronous and synchronous execution. Typically, synchronous execution is used for the bulk of your application, though some situations warrant an asynchronous model in order to increase performance and responsiveness. An example would be downloading a file from a network or the Internet, which is generally a processor-intensive task depending on the size of the file. The file could be downloaded asynchronously while the user interface displays the running process of the operation.

An asynchronous model can be extremely advantageous when used correctly, although it can destroy your performance if used incorrectly.

Note

There is a small overhead penalty incurred when using asynchronous calls. When an asynchronous call is invoked, the security state of the call stack is copied and attached to the thread that is executing the asynchronous call. This penalty is insignificant if the callback executes a fair chunk of code, or if the asynchronous calls are infrequently executed.

Efficient IO Buffer Sizes

The .NET framework provides a number of data buffers that inherit from `BufferedStream`. These buffers have a default buffer size value, but you are able to set the value to any size that you want. Even though you have this freedom, in almost every case you will be getting sub-optimal performance unless you have the buffer size set to a value between 4000 and 8000 bytes. Generally, the only time where a large buffer size is efficient occurs when a very predictable size is being managed, such as files that are usually around the same size.

Minimize the Working Set

Managed code takes care of many low-level responsibilities and handles them transparently, but managed code does not always handle things in the most efficient way possible. External assemblies are loaded into the main application domain when they are used for the first time, which increases memory usage and decreases performance by a slight amount. Therefore, it is important to minimize the number of assemblies that you use in order to keep the working set small.

The more types in an assembly, the more memory it will take up and the more time it will take to be JIT'ed. Consider moving types that are rarely used into separate assemblies that can be loaded into a second AppDomain on demand. The same goes for large resources; keep them in external assemblies instead of embedding them into the main assembly. Lastly, if you are only using a couple methods out of a fairly large assembly, you might consider implementing your own copy of those methods to avoid having to load the assembly.

N o t e

You can use the VaDump tool, downloadable from Microsoft.com, to track your working set. You can also use Performance Counters (perfmon.exe) to give you detailed feedback about a number of useful statistics like the number of classes that you load.

The .NET platform provides transparent support for automatic memory management, but there are some tasks that you should explicitly do in order to design for optimum performance. The first task is to ensure that Dispose() is called on the appropriate objects as soon as possible. Also, ensure that you do not reference objects once you are done using them. References to unused objects will prevent the garbage collector from collecting and removing the objects from the application memory.

Perform Chunky Calls

There are generally two types of calls when working with data across managed and unmanaged interfaces: "chatty" and "chunky." Chatty calls are those that occur quite often and do very little work, while chunky calls are those that occur less frequently, but generally do more work when they occur.

I should mention that chunky calls are not always the best solution. A chatty call that passes simple data may be less computationally expensive than a chunky call. The incurred performance costs are cheaper because the data marshaling is not as complex. P/Invoke, Interop, and Remoting calls all carry significant overhead, so you want to minimize the number of calls using them. The best approach is to prototype both call types early in the development phase so that you can make the best decision for the solution.

When a call is sent between managed and unmanaged code, there are some events that transpire in order to facilitate this communication. First, data marshaling must be performed to get the source data into the appropriate target format for the receiver. Next, the calling convention signatures must be fixed to pass data between the sender and receiver. The next step is to protect callee-saved registers and switch the threading mode so that the garbage collector does not block unmanaged threads. Lastly, a frame to handle exceptions is created to supervise calls into managed code. The events equate to roughly 30 x86 instructions when using P/Invoke (roughly 10 when marshaling is not required), and roughly 60 x86 instructions when using COM Interop. Therefore, it is important to use P/Invoke over COM Interop whenever possible to speed up the calls between managed and unmanaged code.

The biggest slowdown occurs during data translation, such as converting text from ASCII to Unicode. Classes with explicit layout are extremely cheap, and primitive types require almost no marshaling at all. Blittable types are those that can be transferred directly across managed and unmanaged code with no marshaling at all. These types are byte, sbyte, double, float, long, ulong, int, uint, short, and ushort. You can also freely pass value types and single-dimensional arrays that contain blittable types.

Minimize Exception Throwing

One of the best features of the .NET platform is the exception handling model that is available to all applications. This model offers the ability to develop robust applications that can handle and respond to exceptions and errors gracefully in almost all situations. However, this model must be used carefully, or some significant performance costs can be introduced into your application. Throwing exceptions is expensive in terms of performance, so throw as few as possible. You can check how many exceptions your application throws at runtime through the use of Performance Counters (perfmon.exe). Also, be aware that the .NET runtime can throw its own exceptions. It is advisable to use Performance Counters to check this, and use the debugger to locate the source of the exceptions.

One myth that circulates around developers working with managed code is that try/catch blocks introduce performance overhead. The truth is that you only incur a performance cost when an actual exception is thrown. You can use as many try/catch blocks as you want. Do not use exceptions to control program flow.

Thoughts About NGen

The methods of a managed application are Just-in-Time compiled (JIT'ed) the first time they are used during runtime. This dynamic compilation can lead to a significant startup penalty if the application invokes a lot of methods during startup.

Also, there are many shared libraries in the .NET class framework that incur significant overhead on top of your own code. There is a tool provided with the .NET framework (ngen.exe) that can generate native images of assemblies and store them in the Global Assembly Cache, essentially precompiling your code for faster startup times and overall runtime execution in certain situations.

While NGen sounds like the silver bullet for increasing runtime performance, there are only certain situations when performance can be improved through its use. Native images cannot be used when crossing application domains, so there is no real benefit from using NGen for ASP.NET applications. However, generating native images for Windows Forms can result in a performance increase.

Note

NGen must be run on the assemblies after they have been deployed to the target machine. Doing so allows the application to be optimized for the machine it is installed on.

There are some situations where your application may perform better with JIT compilation instead of native images. Some optimizations cannot be done with native images, so make sure that you profile the startup and operating times of your application while using native images and JIT compilation. You should also profile combinations of native images and regular assemblies.

Conclusion

This chapter examined performance considerations when developing applications for the .NET platform. First, two approaches for investigating performance were discussed: white box and black box. The rest of the chapter focused on performance considerations for commonly used and abused areas of everyday .NET development. A misconception regarding performance optimization is that a considerable amount of time should be spent on optimizing code down to the compiler level. In reality, especially with .NET, the majority of performance loss results from application architecture and design. These problems occur at a high level, and can be identified using black box performance testing.

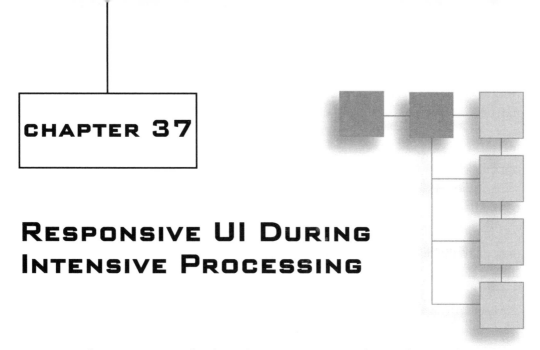

CHAPTER 37

RESPONSIVE UI DURING INTENSIVE PROCESSING

Complexity is a sign of technical immaturity. Simplicity of use is the real sign of a well designed product whether it is an ATM or a Patriot missile.

Daniel T. Ling

It is fairly common to use applications that fail to repaint their windows, displaying an empty or partially empty frame on the screen. Or you may use applications that execute a long-running task, ignoring you until the task completes. In some instances, you may even wish to abort the task rather than wait for completion, which is not supported by these applications. A responsive user interface is very important, so it is crucial that you design your application so the user knows the current state of the application: whether a message sent to the application has been received, and that the application has not stalled when processing a complex task or operation. Users want to feel in control of the application, so be sure that the user can always control the flow of the application.

To fully understand the importance of a responsive user interface, a few common problems will be addressed that users typically come across. The first problem is a window that takes a long time to repaint during a time-consuming operation. During this operation, the application does not give any CPU cycles to the user interface, which results in the user waiting for the window to update or for keyboard and mouse events to be processed. These wait times make the user interface seem sluggish, or even cause the application to be unusable.

Another problem occurs when the application performs a long-running task but does not provide any control to the user during this period. Many times these tasks are developed to execute in entirety and then return, maybe updating the progress and displaying it to the user, but the user will still not be able to interact with the application until the task completes. This can lead to a few problems, such as the user being unable to cancel the task if the need arises, and keeping the user from taking advantage of other application features that logically should be available during the long process.

While performing a long task, you should make sure the application informs the user of the progress by periodically updating the window with a progress bar or similar control. Let the user know that the application is executing normally and that the task is progressing. Additionally, you should also support interaction by the user or the ability to access logical features while the task is processing.

For years, one of the most difficult and time-consuming tasks in Windows programming has been the development and debugging of multi-threaded solutions. Developers using .NET typically write asynchronous code using an asynchronous pattern that returns an IAsyncResult using Begin and End methods. Otherwise, developers use delegates or an explicit threading technique such as thread pools. Some developers even resort to writing custom threading systems for various reasons, despite the pain and suffering that occurs during the development of such solutions. Generally, it is better to have an intrinsic approach, based on infrastructure, than to build a custom approach from the ground up. Additional patterns have been introduced in version 2.0 of the .NET framework. One of these new patterns is AsyncOperationManager and AsyncOperationFactory, coupled with a set of custom events and delegates. While this approach is fairly straightforward to use, advanced tasks will not benefit from this new mechanism.

An excellent component introduced in .NET 2.0 is the BackgroundWorker class, which is a convenient way to start and monitor asynchronous operations, with the ability to cancel the operation and report progress to the user. This chapter shows how to use BackgroundWorker safely and how to correctly marshal control between the worker thread and the Windows Forms thread in a thread-safe fashion. The demo presented in this solution calculates Fibonacci numbers, and will be used to introduce you to the implementation details of BackgroundWorker.

Implementing the Worker Logic

The first step is to create a new BackgroundWorker object, specify the appropriate settings, and rig the instance up with event handlers. Table 37.1 shows the important members of the BackgroundWorker class.

Table 37.1 Important Members of BackgroundWorker

Member	Description
CancelAsync	Invoking this method will cancel the progressing task.
CancellationPending	Invoking CancelAsync will set this property to true, signifying that the user has requested cancellation of the task.
DoWork	This event is fired when RunWorkerAsync is invoked.
ProgressChanged	This event is fired when ReportProgress is invoked.
ReportProgress	Invoking this method will fire the ProgressChanged event, updating the progress of the operation.
RunWorkerAsync	Executes the task asynchronously on a worker thread.
RunWorkerCompleted	This event is fired when the task is completed or cancelled, or when an unhandled exception is thrown within the DoWork event.
WorkerReportsProgress	Boolean property that specifies whether or not to report progress.
WorkerSupportsCancellation	Boolean property that specifies whether or not the task can be cancelled.

You can create BackgroundWorker programmatically or by dragging it onto your form from the Components tab of the Visual Studio toolbox. The example in this chapter shows programmatic instantiation and configuration. The following code shows how to instantiate the BackgroundWorker.

```
backgroundWorker = new BackgroundWorker();
backgroundWorker.WorkerReportsProgress = true;
backgroundWorker.WorkerSupportsCancellation = true;

backgroundWorker.DoWork += new DoWorkEventHandler(backgroundWorker_DoWork);

backgroundWorker.ProgressChanged += new ProgressChangedEventHandler
(backgroundWorker_ProgressChanged);

backgroundWorker.RunWorkerCompleted += new RunWorkerCompletedEventHandler
(backgroundWorker_RunWorkerCompleted);
```

The DoWork event provides an instance of DoWorkEventArgs as a parameter, which handles the input, output, and cancellation properties of the worker thread. Table 37.2 shows the properties of DoWorkEventArgs.

Table 37.2 Properties of DoWorkEventArgs

Property	Description
e.Argument	Defined as an object, so any arbitrary data type can be used as an input argument for the DoWork event. This parameter is passed into the RunWorkerAsync method.
e.Cancel	This property allows you to cancel the progressing task. Setting this property to true will cancel the task and move the context to the RunWorkerCompleted event with a cancelled status. This property is used in conjunction with the CancellationPending property to determine whether or not the user has issued a cancellation request.
e.Result	Defined as an object, so any arbitrary data type can be used as an output result to the RunWorkerCompleted event. This property is a way to communicate the result or status back to the user interface.

The following code shows the implementation behind the DoWork event for the Fibonacci calculator. Notice the exception that is thrown when the compute number has an invalid value. This is because any values higher than 91 will result in an overflow with the long data type.

```
private void backgroundWorker_DoWork(object sender, DoWorkEventArgs e)
{
    if (((int)e.Argument < 0) || ((int)e.Argument > 91))
    {
        throw new ArgumentException("Compute number must be >= 0 and <= 91");
    }

    e.Result = ComputeFibonacci((int)e.Argument, (BackgroundWorker)sender, e);
}
```

The following code shows the actual processing logic behind the Fibonacci calculations. This logic is in its own method because it calculates the numbers using recursion.

```
private long ComputeFibonacci(int computeNumber,
                             BackgroundWorker worker,
                             DoWorkEventArgs e)
{
    long result = 0;
```

```
    if (worker.CancellationPending)
    {
        e.Cancel = true;
    }
    else
    {
        if (computeNumber < 2)
        {
            result = 1;
        }
        else
        {
            result = ComputeFibonacci(computeNumber - 1, worker, e) +
                     ComputeFibonacci(computeNumber - 2, worker, e);
        }

        int percentComplete = (int)((float)computeNumber /
                                        (float)((int)e.Argument) * 100);

        if (percentComplete > percentageReached)
        {
            percentageReached = percentComplete;
            worker.ReportProgress(percentComplete);
        }
    }

    return result;
}
```

Note

The DoWork method can complete in three ways: the process completes successfully, the user requests cancellation, or an unhandled exception occurs.

Reporting Operation Progress

The ProgressChanged is used to report status to the user interface. This event is fired whenever the ReportProgress method is invoked.

Note

Do not make excessive calls to the ReportProgress method, because each call adds additional over-head to your background processing, taking longer to complete; however, it is also important to enable users to witness the current progress of the tasks, making it tricky to find the right balance of use.

The PercentageProgress property of the ProgressChanged event arguments will return the percentage completed value, set by the ReportProgress method. You can also access the user state within the ProgressChanged event handler arguments. The following code shows the implementation details for the progress changed event.

```
private void backgroundWorker_ProgressChanged(object sender,
ProgressChangedEventArgs e)
{
    OperationProgressBar.Value = e.ProgressPercentage;
    ResultLabel.Text = String.Format("Calculating: {0}%",
                                    e.ProgressPercentage.ToString());
}
```

BackgroundWorker events are not marshaled across AppDomain boundaries; therefore you must not use BackgroundWorker to process tasks in more than one AppDomain. You must be careful not to manipulate the user interface in your DoWork event handler. The proper way is to communicate with the user interface through the ProgressChanged and RunWorkerCompleted events.

Supporting User Cancellation

Allowing the user to cancel the progressing task is extremely easy. Just invoke the CancelAsync method on the BackgroundWorker instance and then handle the CancellationPending property in the DoWork event appropriately.

```
private void CancellationButton_Click(object sender, EventArgs e)
{
    backgroundWorker.CancelAsync();
    CancellationButton.Enabled = false;
}
```

Note

It is important to know that if a call to CancelAsync sets CancellationPending to true just after the last invocation of the DoWork event, then the code will not have the opportunity to set the DoWorkEventArgs.Cancel flag to true. This results in the Cancelled flag being set to false in the RunWorkerCompleted event. This problem occurs because of a race condition.

Executing the Worker Thread

BackgroundWorker executes the DoWork event in a separate thread so the user interface remains responsive. Executing the worker thread is very easy; it's done by invoking the RunWorkerAsync method on the BackgroundWorker. This method optionally allows you to pass in an argument that the worker logic can use during processing. The following code shows the implementation details behind the demo that is available on the Companion Web site for this book.

```csharp
private void ComputeButton_Click(object sender, EventArgs e)
{
    ResultLabel.Text = string.Empty;

    ComputeNumberField.Enabled = false;
    ComputeButton.Enabled = false;
    CancellationButton.Enabled = true;

    int computeNumber = (int)ComputeNumberField.Value;
    percentageReached = 0;

    backgroundWorker.RunWorkerAsync(computeNumber);
}
```

No matter how the DoWork event completes, whether successfully or in an erroneous manner, the RunWorkerCompleted event will always fire, providing an instance of RunWorkerCompletedEventArgs that contains the status and result of the operation. This event will allow you to respond appropriately to whatever result is returned by the worker thread. When an error occurs, you can retrieve the exception object from the Error property. This property will be null if no errors occurred during processing. When a cancellation occurs at the request of the user, the Cancellation property will be set to true. Otherwise, you can retrieve the result from the Result property if there is one. The following code shows the completed event handler that is fired when the processing task is finished.

```csharp
private void backgroundWorker_RunWorkerCompleted(object sender,
                                              RunWorkerCompletedEventArgs e)
{
    if (e.Error != null)
    {
        ResultLabel.Text = String.Format("Error: {0}", e.Error.Message);
    }
    else if (e.Cancelled)
    {
```

```
            ResultLabel.Text = "Cancelled";
    }
    else
    {
        ResultLabel.Text = e.Result.ToString();
    }

    ComputeNumberField.Enabled = true;
    ComputeButton.Enabled = true;
    CancellationButton.Enabled = false;
}
```

Conclusion

Creating a user interface that is responsive is not that difficult, provided that you know the techniques required to do so. Your code must divide time between processing a long-running task and interacting with the user; one should not be sacrificed for the other. You cannot think in a linear fashion when building a long-running task; your application cannot wait around for the task to complete. Think about a good place in the processing logic to stop and report status back to the user. Thankfully, you do not have to worry about processing application events while using the BackgroundWorker object, because this is done behind the scenes for you.

Figure 37.1 shows a screenshot of the demo application provided on the Companion Web site.

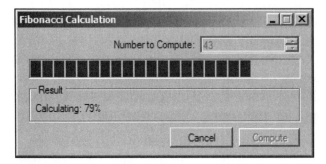

Figure 37.1
Screenshot of the demo application on the Web site.

Asynchronous processing can drastically improve the responsiveness of your application. However, do not assume that an asynchronous model is always the best approach; sometimes a synchronous model is a better choice. Thankfully, .NET 2.0 simplifies the tasks related to using either execution model.

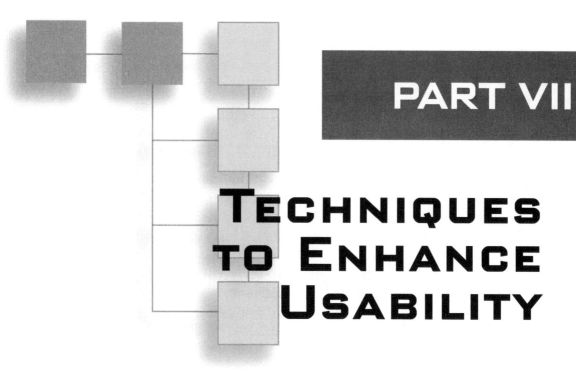

PART VII

TECHNIQUES TO ENHANCE USABILITY

The best programmers write only easy programs.

Michael A. Jackson

Improving the usability of your tools is a sound business strategy when appropriate, and you can differentiate your work from the competition, and enhance your success simply by following good engineering practices. Enhanced usability can reduce development time and costs by ensuring earlier detection of problems. Problems detected later in development or even during transition can cost 10 to 100 times more to resolve than problems detected early on. Much more testing can be done on a tool when it is responsive and users can readily understand how to correctly operate the tool. Making a tool easier for a user to work with will make it easier for you and your team to accomplish your business objectives. One important process to follow in order to develop a successful tool is the regular measurement of user satisfaction; otherwise, you cannot be sure that you are delivering a successful user experience. User satisfaction objectives must take part in driving the development of your tools.

At this point, you are probably wondering what is meant by usability, and how you can enhance it. There are many definitions, but essentially, usability is the efficiency with which a user can perform a required task or business function with a tool. Efficiency can also spin into multiple examples, but the most common efficiency metrics are performance, errors, productivity, and user-subjective preferences and interface characteristics. The chapters in Part VII investigate ways to enhance usability, mainly from a productivity standpoint. Performance is an important aspect of usability engineering, but you can read performance-related chapters in Part VI, "Techniques to Improve Performance."

A positive user experience is critical to the success of a tool, so it is vital that you deliver it.

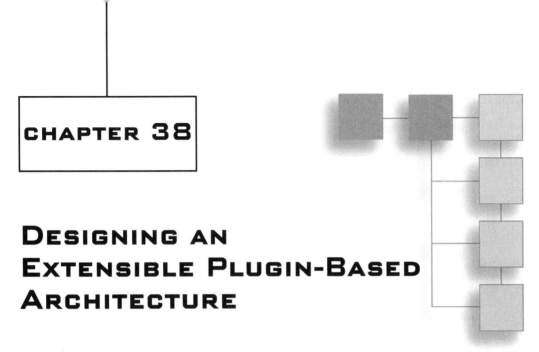

CHAPTER 38

DESIGNING AN EXTENSIBLE PLUGIN-BASED ARCHITECTURE

When I am working on a problem, I never think about beauty. I think only of how to solve the problem. But when I have finished, if the solution is not beautiful, I know it is wrong.

R. Buckminster Fuller

Many applications provide a mechanism to support extensibility through the use of external code modules, also known as plugins, which are linked into the application at runtime. Plugin support is generally used so that the application can be extended with additional functionality without the need to recompile the source code and distribute the executable to users. Some applications have business rules that change frequently, or they have new business rules added on a regular basis. Plugins allow business rules to be added or changed easily without recompilation or redistribution.

The .NET framework and the Common Language Runtime provide a variety of classes and mechanisms for dynamically loading assemblies at runtime and peering into the metadata of these assemblies. This dynamic support makes .NET an ideal platform for plugin-based architectures.

Making your application plugin-aware is also an excellent way to promote a longer lifetime. While not all applications are suitable for this kind of architecture, many are, especially within tools development. This chapter will cover the rudiments and advanced topics surrounding plugin-based architectures and the .NET platform.

Designing a Common Interface

Each plugin is unique in terms of functionality, but there must be some common elements between all plugins in order to load them with a generic framework, and this is best accomplished through the use of interfaces. Interfaces are reference types and contain only abstract members. Interfaces are, in essence, a contract, so any classes implementing an interface are enforced to implement all members on the interface. This means that an application only needs to know about the interface in order to communicate with the class.

Information about classes can also be inspected with reflection, so we can use this common interface's type to dynamically locate plugin classes within an assembly. Classes that do not implement this common interface will not be loaded as plugins.

The common interface should be placed in a separate assembly so that the application and the plugins can reference the interface as a shared assembly. You can even go a step further by placing the shared assembly in the Global Assembly Cache so that the application and plugins do not need local copies to compile or run.

The following code shows the common interface from the example for this chapter. The two methods are used, respectively, to initialize and release plugin resources. The actual implementation details for these two methods are left up to the individual plugins.

```
namespace Plugin.API
{
    public interface IPlugin
    {
        void Initialize();

        void Release();
    }
}
```

Embedding Plugin Metadata Information

A common feature of most plugin-aware applications is a plugin manager or browser that can display a listing of all the plugins referenced by the application. Some of these browsers go even further by showing information about each plugin to describe functionality and author credits.

The same functionality can easily be accomplished by decorating a plugin with an attribute that describes what the plugin does.

Figure 38.1 shows an example of a plugin browser. The Component property describes the short name of the plugin, while the Description property provides a more lengthy description of what the plugin actually does.

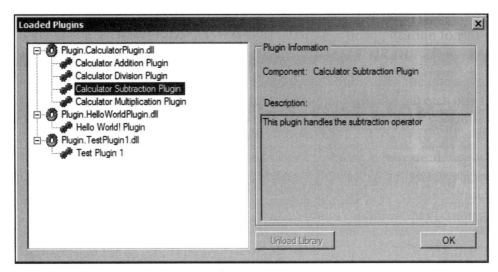

Figure 38.1 Screenshot of the plugin browser example.

The following code is for the Calculator Subtraction Plugin shown in Figure 38.1. Notice the PluginAttribute decoration.

```
namespace Plugin.CalculatorPlugin
{
    using API;
    using ExampleInterfaces;

    [Plugin(Component = "Calculator Subtraction Plugin",
    Description = "This plugin handles the subtraction operator")]
    public class CalculatorSubtraction : MarshalByRefObject,
                                         IPlugin,
                                         ICalculatorPlugin
    {
        public void Initialize()
        {
        }

        public void Release()
        {
```

```
        }

        public double Operation(double left, double right)
        {
            return left - right;
        }
    }
}
```

Note

You may have noticed that the class is decorated with `Plugin` instead of `PluginAttribute`. It is optional to append the Attribute text when decorating a class with an attribute.

The following code shows the `PluginAttribute` decoration. It would be very easy to add to this attribute over time if there is additional information you want to be embedded with each plugin.

```
namespace Plugin.API
{
    [AttributeUsage(AttributeTargets.Class)]
    public class PluginAttribute : Attribute
    {
        private string component = string.Empty;
        private string description = string.Empty;

        public string Component
        {
            get { return component; }
            set { component = value; }
        }

        public string Description
        {
            get { return description; }
            set { description = value; }
        }
    }
}
```

The `PluginAttribute` decoration should be located in the same assembly as the `IPlugin` interface.

Building a Proxy Wrapper

Here is where things get slightly more complicated. Typically, many of the plugin systems created with .NET load external plugin assemblies into the main AppDomain of the application. Although this works and you can use event-driven plugins to your heart's content, these external assemblies can never be unloaded from the main AppDomain until the application quits. With a lot of loaded plugins, especially plugins that are only run for a short period of time, the AppDomain can quickly become swamped with loaded assemblies that degrade performance and consume valuable system memory.

The solution to this problem does require additional work, but the external plug-in assemblies will be unloadable. By creating another AppDomain, you can load external assemblies into it, execute the needed functionality, and then dump the extra AppDomain when the plugin is no longer needed. There is a catch though. There is no restriction that can be enforced to stop types within the extra AppDomain from leaking into the main AppDomain in certain situations.

One particular situation, which frustrated me and required a code refactoring, was to avoid the use of delegates and events between the two AppDomains. Doing so will load the plugin class into the main AppDomain, preventing the extra AppDomain from being unloaded.

You cannot directly instantiate a plugin class using the Activator object directly from the main AppDomain. You must use a MarshalByRefObject that will serve as a proxy between the two AppDomains. It is also important that you do not return any object references or types from the proxy class. Use only types that are available to the main AppDomain (strings to represent type and interface names, for example).

The extra AppDomain is not found in the proxy class, because the proxy class will be instantiated within the extra AppDomain. The following code describes the proxy wrapper; the extra AppDomain code will be covered in the next section.

```
using System;
using System.IO;
using System.Reflection;
using System.Collections.Generic;

namespace Plugin.Manager
{
    using Plugin.API;

    public class PluginProxy : MarshalByRefObject
```

```
    {
        List<Type> pluginTypes = new List<Type>();
        List<PluginInfo> pluginInfo = new List<PluginInfo>();
        List<IPlugin> pluginInstances = new List<IPlugin>();
```

The following method is used to load a plugin assembly into a temporary AppDomain and build a collection of information about each class that implements the IPlugin interface.

```
        public bool LoadAssembly(AppDomain appDomain, byte[] data)
        {
            try
            {
                Assembly assembly = appDomain.Load(data);

                foreach (Type type in assembly.GetTypes())
                {
                    if (!type.IsAbstract)
                    {
                        foreach (Type interfaceType in type.GetInterfaces())
                        {
                            if (interfaceType == typeof(IPlugin) &&
                                type.IsDefined(typeof(PluginAttribute), false))
                            {
                                pluginTypes.Add(type);

                                PluginAttribute pluginAttrib =
                                type.GetCustomAttributes(typeof(PluginAttribute),
                                                    false)[0] as PluginAttribute;
```

As mentioned earlier, it is important that the proxy does not return any of the types within the plugin library. We want users to be able to view the plugin attribute information about each plugin, so the following two lines instantiate a wrapper class designed to hold the attribute information.

```
                                PluginInfo info = new PluginInfo(pluginAttrib.Component,
                                                    pluginAttrib.Description);
                                pluginInfo.Add(info);
                            }
                        }
                    }
                }
```

```
            return true;
        }
        catch (Exception)
        {
            return false;
        }
    }
```

The following method is used to determine whether the plugin assembly contains any plugin classes that implement a particular interface. This is used to determine which assemblies can handle a particular application component.

```
public bool ImplementsInterface(string interfaceName)
{
    foreach (Type type in pluginTypes)
    {
        foreach (Type interfaceType in type.GetInterfaces())
        {
            if (interfaceType.Name.Equals(interfaceName))
                return true;
        }
    }
    return false;
}
```

The following method is used to instantiate all the plugins within an assembly, execute the Initialize() method, and add the instantiated plugins to a list to keep track of them.

```
public void Initialize()
{
    bool exists = false;

    foreach (Type type in pluginTypes)
    {
        foreach (IPlugin plugin in pluginInstances)
        {
            if (plugin.GetType().Equals(type))
            {
                exists = true;
                break;
            }
        }
```

```
            if (!exists)
            {
                IPlugin plugin = Activator.CreateInstance(type) as IPlugin;
                ExecuteInitializeMethod(plugin);
                pluginInstances.Add(plugin);
            }

            exists = false;
        }
    }
```

The following method loops through all the instantiated plugins and calls the Release() method.

```
    public void Release()
    {
        foreach (IPlugin plugin in pluginInstances)
        {
            ExecuteReleaseMethod(plugin);
        }
    }
```

The following method is a wrapper around executing a method of the plugin with no return value. Remember that we cannot access objects directly from outside of the proxy.

```
    public void ExecuteMethodNoReturn(string interfaceName,
                                      string method,
                                      object[] parameters)
    {
        foreach (IPlugin plugin in pluginInstances)
        {
            foreach (Type interfaceType in plugin.GetType().GetInterfaces())
            {
                if (interfaceType.Name.Equals(interfaceName))
                {
                    ExecuteMethodNoReturn(plugin,
                                          method,
                                          parameters);
                }
            }
        }
    }
```

The following method is a wrapper around executing a method of the plugin, except this time with return values.

```
public object[] ExecuteMethodWithReturn(string interfaceName,
                                        string method,
                                        object[] parameters)
{
    List<object> results = new List<object>();

    foreach (IPlugin plugin in pluginInstances)
    {
        foreach (Type interfaceType in plugin.GetType().GetInterfaces())
        {
            if (interfaceType.Name.Equals(interfaceName))
            {
                results.Add(ExecuteMethodWithReturn(plugin,
                                                    method,
                                                    parameters));
            }
        }
    }

    return results.ToArray();
}
```

The following method is used to return metadata information about all the plugins within the assembly.

```
public PluginInfo[] QueryPluginInformation()
{
    return pluginInfo.ToArray();
}


#region Plugin Method Invocation
```

The following method uses reflection to call the Initialize() method directly on the IPlugin instance.

```
private void ExecuteInitializeMethod(IPlugin plugin)
{
    ExecuteMethodNoReturn(plugin, "Initialize", null);
}
```

The following method uses reflection to call the Release() method directly on the IPlugin instance.

```
private void ExecuteReleaseMethod(IPlugin plugin)
{
    ExecuteMethodNoReturn(plugin, "Release", null);
}
```

The following method uses reflection to call a method directly on the IPlugin instance. This call does not return any values.

```
private void ExecuteMethodNoReturn(IPlugin plugin,
                                   string methodName,
                                   object[] parameters)
{
    MethodInfo method = plugin.GetType().GetMethod(methodName);

    if (method != null)
        method.Invoke(plugin, parameters);
}
```

The following method uses reflection to call a method directly on the IPlugin instance. This call returns values.

```
private object ExecuteMethodWithReturn(IPlugin plugin,
                                       string methodName,
                                       object[] parameters)
{
    MethodInfo method = plugin.GetType().GetMethod(methodName);

    if (method != null)
        return method.Invoke(plugin, parameters);

    return null;
}

    #endregion
    }
}
```

Loading Plugins Through the Proxy

With the proxy created, we can now move on to loading plugins and accessing them through the proxy. The following class wraps each plugin assembly and

routes messages to and from the proxy object. This class also handles a temporary
AppDomain used to load the plugin assembly independent from the main AppDomain.

```
using System;
using System.IO;
using System.Security;
using System.Security.Permissions;
using System.Security.Policy;
using System.Collections;

namespace Plugin.Manager
{
    using Plugin.API;

    public sealed class PluginLibrary
    {
        private AppDomain appDomain;

        private PluginProxy proxy;

        private string name = string.Empty;

        public string Name
        {
            get { return name; }
        }
```

The following method is used to load a plugin assembly from the file system into
memory, create a temporary AppDomain with enforced security permissions, and
instantiate the proxy object within the temporary AppDomain. If the plugin file is
source code, then the plugin is compiled and loaded afterwards. The supported source
code languages are C#, VB.NET, and J#. The default settings for the security policy
will deny the ability to compile source code at runtime, but you can either change
the policy file or disable security by commenting out EnforceSecurityPolicy().
Remember to only do this in a fully trusted environment.

```
        public bool Load(DirectoryInfo pluginDirectory, FileInfo plugin)
        {
            try
            {
                if (plugin.Exists)
                {
                    using (FileStream stream = plugin.OpenRead())
```

```csharp
{
    byte[] assemblyData = new byte[stream.Length];

    if (stream.Read(assemblyData,
                             0,
                             (int)stream.Length) < 1)
    {
        return false;
    }

    AppDomainSetup setup = new AppDomainSetup();
    setup.ApplicationName = "Plugins";
    setup.ApplicationBase = AppDomain.CurrentDomain.BaseDirectory;
    setup.ShadowCopyFiles = "true";
    setup.ShadowCopyDirectories = pluginDirectory.FullName;

    appDomain = AppDomain.CreateDomain("PluginDomain" +
    plugin.Name.Replace(".dll", "").Replace(".", ""), null, setup);

    EnforceSecurityPolicy();

    proxy = appDomain.CreateInstanceAndUnwrap("Plugin.Manager",
                    "Plugin.Manager.PluginProxy") as PluginProxy;

    if (plugin.Extension.EndsWith("cs") ||
        plugin.Extension.EndsWith("js")  ||
        plugin.Extension.EndsWith("vb"))
    {
        if (!proxy.CompileAssembly(appDomain, plugin.FullName))
        {
            return false;
        }
    }
    else if (!proxy.LoadAssembly(appDomain, assemblyData))
    {
        return false;
    }

    name = plugin.Name;

    return true;
}
```

```
            }
            else
            {
                return false;
            }
        }
        catch (IOException)
        {
            return false;
        }
    }

    public void Unload()
    {
        if (appDomain == null)
            return;

        Release();

        AppDomain.Unload(appDomain);

        appDomain = null;
    }

    public PluginInfo[] QueryPluginInformation()
    {
        return proxy.QueryPluginInformation();
    }

    public void Initialize()
    {
        proxy.Initialize();
    }

    public void Release()
    {
        proxy.Release();
    }

    public bool ImplementsInterface(string interfaceName)
    {
        return proxy.ImplementsInterface(interfaceName);
    }
```

```
public bool ImplementsInterface(Type interfaceType)
{
    return proxy.ImplementsInterface(interfaceType.Name);
}

public void ExecuteMethodNoReturn(string interfaceName,
                                  string methodName,
                                  object[] parameters)
{
    proxy.ExecuteMethodNoReturn(interfaceName,
                                methodName,
                                parameters);
}

public void ExecuteMethodNoReturn(Type interfaceType,
                                  string methodName,
                                  object[] parameters)
{
    proxy.ExecuteMethodNoReturn(interfaceType.Name,
                                methodName,
                                parameters);
}

public object[] ExecuteMethodWithReturn(string interfaceName,
                                        string methodName,
                                        object[] parameters)
{
    return proxy.ExecuteMethodWithReturn(interfaceName,
                                         methodName,
                                         parameters);
}

public object[] ExecuteMethodWithReturn(Type interfaceType,
                                        string methodName,
                                        object[] parameters)
{
    return proxy.ExecuteMethodWithReturn(interfaceType.Name,
                                         methodName,
                                         parameters);
}
```

The following two methods are covered later on in the "Enforcing a Security Policy" section.

```
private void EnforceSecurityPolicy()
{
    IMembershipCondition condition;
    PolicyStatement statement;

    PolicyLevel policyLevel = PolicyLevel.CreateAppDomainLevel();

    PermissionSet permissionSet = new PermissionSet(PermissionState.None);
    SecurityPermission permission
    = new SecurityPermission(SecurityPermissionFlag.Execution)
    permissionSet.AddPermission(permission);

    condition = new AllMembershipCondition();

    statement = new PolicyStatement(permissionSet,
                                    PolicyStatementAttribute.Nothing);

    // The root code group of the policy level combines all
    // permissions of its children.
    UnionCodeGroup codeGroup = new UnionCodeGroup(condition, statement);

    NamedPermissionSet localIntranet
                            = FindNamedPermissionSet("LocalIntranet");

    condition = new ZoneMembershipCondition(SecurityZone.MyComputer);
    statement = new PolicyStatement(localIntranet,
                                    PolicyStatementAttribute.Nothing);

    // The following code limits all code on this machine
    // to local intranet permissions when running in this
    // application domain.
    UnionCodeGroup virtualIntranet = new UnionCodeGroup(condition,
                                                        statement);
    virtualIntranet.Name = "Virtual Intranet";

    // Add the code groups to the policy level.
    codeGroup.AddChild(virtualIntranet);
    policyLevel.RootCodeGroup = codeGroup;

    appDomain.SetAppDomainPolicy(policyLevel);
}
```

```
        private NamedPermissionSet FindNamedPermissionSet(string name)
        {
            IEnumerator policyEnumerator = SecurityManager.PolicyHierarchy();

            while (policyEnumerator.MoveNext())
            {
                PolicyLevel currentLevel = policyEnumerator.Current
                                                        as PolicyLevel;

                if (currentLevel.Label == "Machine")
                {
                    IList namedPermissions = currentLevel.NamedPermissionSets;

                    IEnumerator namedPerm = namedPermissions.GetEnumerator();

                    while (namedPerm.MoveNext())
                    {
                        if (((NamedPermissionSet)namedPerm.Current).Name == name)
                        {
                            return ((NamedPermissionSet)namedPerm.Current);
                        }
                    }
                }
            }

            return null;
        }
    }
}
```

Each instance of the plugin library class represents a plugin assembly or source file in the plugins directory. Therefore, each plugin has its own temporary AppDomain that can be unloaded at will without affecting the rest of the system.

Reloading Plugins During Runtime

The majority of plugin-enabled applications load and initialize all plugins when the application first launches, but plugins would not be reloaded if they had changed on the file system. The new version of the plugins would not be visible until the application had relaunched. It would be even better if the application could detect file system changes and automatically reload plugins that had changed. This would greatly speed up plugin debugging and development.

The following class keeps track of the loaded plugins, but it also contains the code to watch the file system for changes, reloading the plugins when appropriate.

```
using System;
using System.IO;
using System.Collections.Generic;
using System.Threading;
using System.Windows.Forms;

namespace Plugin.Manager
{
    public class PluginCatalogue
    {
        private FileSystemWatcher fileSystemWatcher = null;
        private string lockObject = "{RELOAD_PLUGINS_LOCK}";
        private DateTime changeTime = new DateTime(0);
        private Thread pluginReloadThread = null;
        private readonly List<PluginLibrary> plugins
                                        = new List<PluginLibrary>();
        private bool beginShutdown = false;
        private bool active = true;
        private bool started = false;
        private bool autoReload = true;
        private string pluginDirectory = string.Empty;

        public event EventHandler ReloadedPlugins;
        public event EventHandler UnloadedPlugins;

        public List<PluginLibrary> Plugins
        {
            get { return plugins; }
        }
```

The following property is used to stop and start automatic plugin reloading at runtime, which is useful if you want to make it a user setting.

```
        public bool AutoReload
        {
            get
            {
                return autoReload;
            }
            set
```

```
        {
            if (autoReload != value)
            {
                autoReload = value;

                if (!autoReload)
                {
                    fileSystemWatcher.EnableRaisingEvents = false;
                    ReleasePluginRuntime();
                    pluginReloadThread = null;
                    fileSystemWatcher = null;
                }
                else
                {
                    CreateFileSystemWatcherAndThread();
                }
            }
        }
    }

    public PluginCatalogue(string pluginDirectory)
    {
        this.pluginDirectory = pluginDirectory;
    }

    public void FireUnloadEvent()
    {
        if (UnloadedPlugins != null)
            UnloadedPlugins(this, EventArgs.Empty);
    }
```

The following method creates the FileSystemWatcher object, points it at the plugin directory, and binds the event handlers to the appropriate method. The reload plugin thread is also created here.

```
    private void CreateFileSystemWatcherAndThread()
    {
        DirectoryInfo directory = new DirectoryInfo(pluginDirectory);

        if (!directory.Exists)
            directory.Create();
```

```
fileSystemWatcher = new FileSystemWatcher(pluginDirectory);
fileSystemWatcher.EnableRaisingEvents = true;
fileSystemWatcher.Changed
    += new FileSystemEventHandler(fileSystemWatcher_Changed);

fileSystemWatcher.Deleted
    += new FileSystemEventHandler(fileSystemWatcher_Changed);

fileSystemWatcher.Created
    += new FileSystemEventHandler(fileSystemWatcher_Changed);

pluginReloadThread
    = new Thread(new ThreadStart(this.ReloadPluginsThread));

pluginReloadThread.Start();
}
```

The following method is used to get a listing of valid plugin files from the plugin directory. Then the plugins themselves are loaded, initialized, and added to the plugin list.

```
private void LoadPluginDirectory()
{
    UnloadPluginDirectory();

    DirectoryInfo pluginDirectoryInfo
                            = new DirectoryInfo(pluginDirectory);

    foreach (FileInfo pluginFile
            in GetPluginFiles(pluginDirectoryInfo))
    {
        PluginLibrary plugin = LoadPlugin(pluginDirectoryInfo,
                                        pluginFile);

        if (plugin != null)
        {
            plugin.Initialize();
            plugins.Add(plugin);
        }
    }
}
```

The following method is used to unload all the plugins and clear the plugin list. This method is generally used when reloading plugins.

```
private void UnloadPluginDirectory()
{
    bool subsequentCall = false;

    foreach (PluginLibrary existingLibrary in plugins)
    {
        subsequentCall = true;
        existingLibrary.Unload();
    }

    plugins.Clear();

    if (subsequentCall)
    {
        if (UnloadedPlugins != null)
            UnloadedPlugins(this, EventArgs.Empty);
    }
}
```

The following method is the starting point for the system at runtime. This method will create the FileSystemWatcher object and the reload plugins thread, after which the plugins are loaded from the plugins directory.

```
public void InitializePluginRuntime()
{
    started = true;

    if (autoReload)
    {
        CreateFileSystemWatcherAndThread();
    }

    ReloadPlugins();
}
```

The following method is used to stop the FileSystemWatcher and the reload plugins thread, unloading all the plugins in the process.

```
public void ReleasePluginRuntime()
{
    try
```

```
    {
        started = false;
        UnloadPluginDirectory();
        beginShutdown = true;

        while (active)
        {
            Thread.Sleep(100);
        }
    }
    catch
    {
        //Quietly ignore unload exceptions
    }
}
```

The following method is the logic for the reload plugins thread. This method continuously loops while active, and the plugins are reloaded when the change time is set by the FileSystemWatcher object.

```
protected void ReloadPluginsThread()
{
    if (!started)
    {
      throw new InvalidOperationException("PluginManager not started.");
    }

    DateTime invalidTime = new DateTime(0);

    while (!beginShutdown)
    {
        if (changeTime != invalidTime && DateTime.Now > changeTime)
        {
            ReloadPlugins();
        }

        Thread.Sleep(5000);
    }

    active = false;
}
```

The following method is invoked from the `ReloadPluginsThread` method, and is used to reload the plugin list from the plugins directory.

```
private void ReloadPlugins()
{
    if (!started)
    {
        throw new InvalidOperationException("PluginManager not started.");
    }

    lock (lockObject)
    {
        LoadPluginDirectory();

        changeTime = new DateTime(0);

        if (ReloadedPlugins != null)
            ReloadedPlugins(this, EventArgs.Empty);
    }
}
```

The following method is the event handler for the `FileSystemWatcher` object. This handler is invoked whenever the plugin directory changes. A new change time is set so that the reload thread will fire 10 seconds from the current time.

```
void fileSystemWatcher_Changed(object sender, FileSystemEventArgs e)
{
    changeTime = DateTime.Now + new TimeSpan(0, 0, 10);
}
```

The following method is used to load a plugin from the specified path. A new `PluginLibrary` instance is created for the plugin and returned if successful.

```
private PluginLibrary LoadPlugin(DirectoryInfo pluginDirectory,
                                 FileInfo pluginFile)
{
    bool success = false;

    PluginLibrary plugin = null;

    try
    {
        plugin = new PluginLibrary();
```

```
            if (plugin.Load(pluginDirectory, pluginFile))
            {
                success = true;
            }
        }
        catch (Exception)
        {
            success = false;
        }

        if (!success)
        {
            MessageBox.Show(String.Format("Could not load plugin [{0}].",
                                            pluginFile.Name));
            plugin = null;
        }

        return plugin;
    }
```

The following method is used to check the loaded plugin list and see if any of the instances support the specified interface. This is used to return a list of compatible plugins for the given interface. This method can be considered a caching optimization so that the entire plugin list does not have to be checked when invoking a method on a plugin interface.

```
    public List<PluginLibrary> DeterminePluginTargets(Type interfaceTarget)
    {
        List<PluginLibrary> targets = new List<PluginLibrary>();

        foreach (PluginLibrary library in plugins)
        {
            if (library.ImplementsInterface(interfaceTarget.Name))
            {
                targets.Add(library);
            }
        }

        return targets;
    }
```

The following method is used to return a list of valid plugin files from the specified directory. This list will be the one that the plugin catalogue uses to load all the plugins.

```
        private FileInfo[] GetPluginFiles(DirectoryInfo pluginDirectory)
        {
            FileInfo[] plugins;

            if (pluginDirectory.Exists)
            {
                List<FileInfo> filteredPlugins = new List<FileInfo>();

                filteredPlugins.AddRange(pluginDirectory.GetFiles("*.dll"));
                filteredPlugins.AddRange(pluginDirectory.GetFiles("*.cs"));
                filteredPlugins.AddRange(pluginDirectory.GetFiles("*.vb"));
                filteredPlugins.AddRange(pluginDirectory.GetFiles("*.js"));

                plugins = filteredPlugins.ToArray();
            }
            else
            {
                pluginDirectory.Create();
                plugins = new FileInfo[0];
            }

            return plugins;
        }
    }
}
```

Runtime Compilation of Plugins

Plugins are an excellent way to extend an application without the need to recompile the application. However, the plugins themselves must be recompiled when modified, and the new version must then be deployed to the installation applications. We can try to improve this by introducing a runtime plugin compiler into the solution. Doing so will allow us to place source code files in the plugins directory and have them loaded into the application at runtime as compiled assemblies. Obviously, you would only want to use this feature in a trusted environment. In fact, the security policy introduced in this chapter will not permit this kind of code to execute without readjusting the default settings.

The following code shows the full source code to the plugin factory that is used to compile plugins at runtime. The only real functionality is in `CompilePluginSource()`, where the appropriate `CodeDom` compiler is created, and many of the most commonly used class framework libraries are referenced so that they are available to the plugins.

```csharp
using System;
using System.IO;
using System.Reflection;
using System.CodeDom;
using System.CodeDom.Compiler;
using System.Collections.Generic;

namespace Plugin.Manager
{
    internal class PluginFactory
    {
        private CompilerErrorCollection compileErrors
                = new CompilerErrorCollection();

        public CompilerErrorCollection CompileErrors
        {
            get { return compileErrors; }
        }

        public Assembly CompilePluginSource(string fileName)
        {
            return CompilePluginSource(new List<string>
                                    (new string[]
                                    { fileName }),
                                    null);
        }

        public Assembly CompilePluginSource(List<string> fileNames)
        {
            return CompilePluginSource(fileNames, null);
        }

        public Assembly CompilePluginSource(string fileName,
                                            List<string> references)
        {
            return CompilePluginSource(new List<string>
                                    (new string[]
                                    { fileName }),
                                    references);
        }

        public Assembly CompilePluginSource(List<string> fileNames,
                                            List<string> references)
```

```
{
    string fileType = null;

    foreach (string fileName in fileNames)
    {
        string extension = Path.GetExtension(fileName);

        if (fileType == null)
        {
            fileType = extension;
        }
        else if (fileType != extension)
        {
            throw new ArgumentException("All source code files must be " +
                                        "written in the same language!");
        }
    }

    CodeDomProvider codeProvider = null;

    switch (fileType)
    {
        case ".cs":
        {
            codeProvider = new Microsoft.CSharp.CSharpCodeProvider();
            break;
        }
        case ".vb":
        {
            codeProvider = new Microsoft.CSharp.CSharpCodeProvider();
            break;
        }
        case ".js":
        {
            codeProvider = new Microsoft.VJSharp.VJSharpCodeProvider();
            break;
        }
        default:
        {
            throw new InvalidOperationException("Invalid source code " +
                                                "file extension!");
        }
    }
```

```
CompilerParameters parameters = new CompilerParameters();

parameters.CompilerOptions = "/target:library /optimize";

parameters.GenerateExecutable = false;

parameters.GenerateInMemory = true;

parameters.IncludeDebugInformation = false;

parameters.ReferencedAssemblies.Add("mscorlib.dll");

parameters.ReferencedAssemblies.Add("System.dll");

parameters.ReferencedAssemblies.Add("Plugin.API.dll");

parameters.ReferencedAssemblies.Add("Plugin.ExampleInterfaces.dll");

parameters.ReferencedAssemblies.Add("System.Configuration.Install.dll");

parameters.ReferencedAssemblies.Add("System.Data.dll");

parameters.ReferencedAssemblies.Add("System.Design.dll");

parameters.ReferencedAssemblies.Add("System.DirectoryServices.dll");

parameters.ReferencedAssemblies.Add("System.Drawing.Design.dll");

parameters.ReferencedAssemblies.Add("System.Drawing.dll");

parameters.ReferencedAssemblies.Add("System.EnterpriseServices.dll");

parameters.ReferencedAssemblies.Add("System.Management.dll");

parameters.ReferencedAssemblies.Add("System.Runtime.Remoting.dll");

parameters.ReferencedAssemblies.Add(
    "System.Runtime.Serialization.Formatters.Soap.dll");

parameters.ReferencedAssemblies.Add("System.Security.dll");

parameters.ReferencedAssemblies.Add("System.ServiceProcess.dll");

parameters.ReferencedAssemblies.Add("System.Web.dll");

parameters.ReferencedAssemblies.Add("System.Web.RegularExpressions.dll");

parameters.ReferencedAssemblies.Add("System.Web.Services.dll");

parameters.ReferencedAssemblies.Add("System.Windows.Forms.Dll");
```

```
            parameters.ReferencedAssemblies.Add("System.XML.dll");

            parameters.ReferencedAssemblies.Add("Accessibility.dll");

            parameters.ReferencedAssemblies.Add("Microsoft.Vsa.dll");

            if (references != null)
            {
                foreach (string reference in references)
                {
                    if (!parameters.ReferencedAssemblies.Contains(reference))
                    {
                        parameters.ReferencedAssemblies.Add(reference);
                    }
                }
            }

            CompilerResults results
                = codeProvider.CompileAssemblyFromFile(parameters,
                                                        fileNames.ToArray());

            compileErrors = results.Errors;

            if (compileErrors.Count > 0)
            {
                throw new Exception("Error(s) occurred while " +
                                                "compiling source file(s).");
            }

            return results.CompiledAssembly;
        }
    }
}
```

Note

One restriction on the code compilation system presented in this chapter is that each source code file must be a fully functional module. Plugins cannot be spread over multiple files in the plugins directory, because each file will be compiled as a standalone plugin.

Enforcing a Security Policy

A common concern when making an application plugin-aware is how code security can be handled. Malicious plugins can do a lot of damage to the application or even the operating system itself. This is even more of a concern when allowing dynamic runtime compilation of plugins. There are two main approaches to solving this problem with the .NET platform: code access security and setting a security policy on the temporary AppDomain that plugins run under. This chapter will not cover code access security, but it will discuss how to enforce a security policy.

Windows has a variety of security zones that restrict what applications and web sites can do under them. The actual restrictions for these security zones can be customized to your needs.

The following two methods show how to set the security policy of the temporary AppDomain so that code within it runs under the Local Intranet security zone.

```
private void EnforceSecurityPolicy()
{
    IMembershipCondition condition;
    PolicyStatement statement;

    PolicyLevel policyLevel = PolicyLevel.CreateAppDomainLevel();

    PermissionSet permissionSet = new PermissionSet(PermissionState.None);
    permissionSet.AddPermission(
                    new SecurityPermission(SecurityPermissionFlag.Execution));

    condition = new AllMembershipCondition();
    statement = new PolicyStatement(permissionSet,
                                    PolicyStatementAttribute.Nothing);

    UnionCodeGroup codeGroup = new UnionCodeGroup(condition, statement);

    NamedPermissionSet localIntranet = FindNamedPermissionSet("LocalIntranet");

    condition = new ZoneMembershipCondition(SecurityZone.MyComputer);
    statement = new PolicyStatement(localIntranet,
                                    PolicyStatementAttribute.Nothing);
```

The following code restricts all code on this machine to the Local Intranet permissions when running within this AppDomain.

```
    UnionCodeGroup virtualIntranet = new UnionCodeGroup(condition, statement);
    virtualIntranet.Name = "Virtual Intranet";
```

Add the code group to the policy level.

```
    codeGroup.AddChild(virtualIntranet);
```

The root code group combines all permissions of its children.

```
policyLevel.RootCodeGroup = codeGroup;
```

Set the new policy level of the temporary `AppDomain`.

```
appDomain.SetAppDomainPolicy(policyLevel);
}
```

The following method is used to locate a named permission set within Windows. In this example, we use it to locate the Local Intranet permission set.

```
private NamedPermissionSet FindNamedPermissionSet(string name)
{
    IEnumerator policyEnumerator = SecurityManager.PolicyHierarchy();

    while (policyEnumerator.MoveNext())
    {
        PolicyLevel currentLevel = (PolicyLevel)policyEnumerator.Current;

        if (currentLevel.Label == "Machine")
        {
            IList namedPermissions = currentLevel.NamedPermissionSets;
            IEnumerator namedPermission = namedPermissions.GetEnumerator();

            while (namedPermission.MoveNext())
            {
                if (((NamedPermissionSet)namedPermission.Current).Name == name)
                {
                    return ((NamedPermissionSet)namedPermission.Current);
                }
            }
        }
    }

    return null;
}
```

Note

The default settings for Local Intranet disable runtime compilation of source code within the temporary `AppDomain` enforcing it. Runtime code compilation can open the door to malicious scripts, so it is recommended that you only support this feature in a trusted environment.

Conclusion

This chapter covered the implementation of an architecture that supports plugins loaded from the file system. Additional features, such as reloading the plugins when the plugin directory is modified, and the ability to dynamically compile source code in the plugin directory at runtime, were covered. There are definitely areas that could be improved, including the security section. Code access security could be used, for example, to deny file system access from the plugins. You could also sign each plugin with a common strong name key, and demand that linked plugins contain that public key. This would prevent malicious attempts to drop an unknown plugin into the plugin directory and execute it.

Another modification could be having a class that represents a proxy to an individual function within a plugin library. This way, you get improved caching instead of just caching the supported libraries and then finding the appropriate function each time you need to invoke it.

The Companion Web site contains the full source code to the plugin system, including a solid example showing the plugin system in action.

Figure 38.2 shows the main screen of the provided example.

There is also an integrated debug tool that will display the list of assemblies loaded in the main AppDomain. This was of great use when testing my system to make sure that plugins were not leaking into the main AppDomain.

Figure 38.3 shows the debug tool in action.

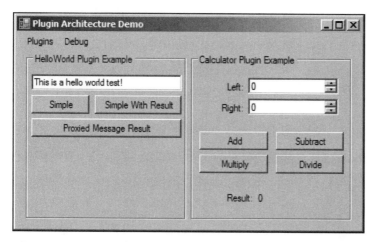

Figure 38.2 Screenshot of the main interface for the provided example.

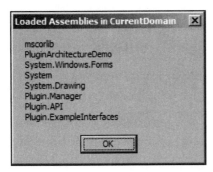

Figure 38.3 Screenshot of the debug tool in action.

I advise you to use a similar technique when building your system so that you can be sure of the same thing.

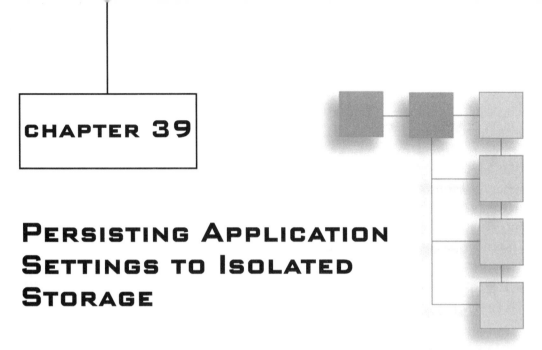

CHAPTER 39

PERSISTING APPLICATION SETTINGS TO ISOLATED STORAGE

It's very good for an idea to be commonplace. The important thing is that a new idea should develop out of what is already there so that it soon becomes an old acquaintance. Old acquaintances aren't by any means always welcome, but at least one can't be mistaken as to who or what they are.

Penelope Fitzgerald

Almost every application requires the ability to store session and state information. This is especially true when dealing with disconnected applications or applications that cache data when possible to reduce load times. Traditionally, settings were persisted to INI files when working with 16-bit Windows, but this approach had fairly substantial limitations. Maximum file size was a factor when using the APIs provided by Microsoft, and the settings were stored in flat file format, so hierarchical relationships could not be represented. Another problem was determining where INI files should be located. Typically, these files were deployed alongside the executables or in the Windows directory because it was the only directory guaranteed to be available on all computers. Additionally, multiple users were not supported by this mechanism. This deployment strategy created a configuration nightmare, and was very hard to support and maintain.

Microsoft tried to introduce a new approach to solve these problems by creating the registry on 32-bit Windows. This solution could represent hierarchical data, so complex data could be nested to make configuration much cleaner. There was also no size limit on the amount of data that could be stored. One of the biggest problems with INI files is deciding where to place the physical files, which is not an issue with the registry because it is globally accessible. The registry solved a number of problems with INI configuration, but other problems were introduced in doing so. With all configuration data for the system stored in a single location, the entire system slows down at an exponential rate as more entries are added. Having large amounts of configuration data in the same place also makes finding a particular entry challenging. Additionally, the registry is only accessible via an API, so backing up configuration info is extremely difficult. Security is also a big concern, because it can be risky to allow application access to the registry to save a few configuration settings, especially if the application is untrusted. Lastly, the entire system depends on the registry, so any accidents using the regedit tool can cripple the operating system.

The .NET framework introduced application configuration files that allow applications to be configurable without the need for recompilation of source code. This approach is widely used by .NET applications, but a major limitation is that this is a read-only mechanism, because `ConfigurationSettings` does not support writing. The `app.config` files can be manipulated as normal XML documents, but this considered a hack and bad practice.

A custom solution could be used to save settings as either binary or text to regular files, but then there are even more deployment and maintenance issues that arise. Issues like data protection, where to save the files, and additional code to support loading and saving these files must also be written.

The ideal solution to the mentioned problems would be a mechanism that can separate files per application or per Windows user so that multiple users on the same machine can have their own settings. The ability to save arbitrary data is important, especially if the proposed solution is intended to be generic and widely reusable. Data should be storable in a variety of formats such as flat text, hierarchical, or binary. Lastly, the mechanism must be secure, so that untrusted callers like downloaded executables cannot access sensitive system information. Microsoft introduced another approach with the .NET framework called *isolated storage* that is the recommended approach when the need for data persistence arises.

Concept of Isolated Storage

Isolated storage is basically a virtual folder that only your application can access. You can create files and directories in your isolated storage and treat it pretty much like normal disk space. Application users never have to actually know where data is physically located on the hard drive. The physical location for isolated storage varies for each operating system, so you just have to tell .NET framework to persist data to isolated storage and it handles all the implementation details. Isolated storage can also be specific to each assembly, or to each Windows user. Perhaps one of the best features about isolated storage is that the application does not require file system permissions. This makes it even easier for an application to run under a least privilege account.

Isolated storage cannot be accessed by a different assembly than the one assigned to do so. Isolated storage locations for assemblies are even isolated from each other within the same process. The same security restriction applies to different Windows users.

Note

It is important to know that isolated storage data is limited to 10 MB per each assembly. Just be sure to efficiently manage the data placed in isolated storage and clean out cached data when it is no longer needed.

Accessing Isolated Storage

The code to access isolated storage for this chapter also makes use of binary serialization, generics, and the hashtable collection. The following code shows the appropriate namespaces that are needed for this functionality.

```
using System;
using System.IO;
using System.IO.IsolatedStorage;
using System.Collections;
using System.Deployment.Application;
using System.Runtime.Serialization.Formatters.Binary;
```

The first step for either the load or the save method is to retrieve the isolated storage file that represents the top-level directory in the storage. This object can be used to manipulate both files and directories. There are a couple different deployment situations that must be taken into consideration when working with isolated storage. The differences are later discussed in detail, but at this point you can be aware that network deployed means that the application has been installed using ClickOnce. The following code retrieves the appropriate isolated storage depending on the deployment situation.

```
private static IsolatedStorageFile OpenIsolatedStorage()
{
```

```
    IsolatedStorageFile storage = null;

    if (ApplicationDeployment.IsNetworkDeployed)
    {
        storage = IsolatedStorageFile.GetUserStoreForApplication();
    }
    else
    {
        storage = IsolatedStorageFile.GetUserStoreForDomain();
    }


    return storage;
}
```

Now that we have retrieved the isolated storage reference, we can begin saving files to it. Any type of data can be saved into isolated storage, but the purpose of this chapter is to show application state persistence.

Our system is going to operate on a single file that will store all the persisted information, so we are going to want a data structure to hold our state information while in memory. This will be accomplished through the use of the hashtable collection. A hashtable will be used to store the state information referenced by unique key. The save will serialize the hashtable into the isolated storage, while the load will deserialize the hashtable from the isolated storage and back into object form. Hashtable cannot be serialized to XML because it inherits from an interface, but BinaryFormatter can be used instead to serialize it to binary. The following code shows the save routine for the isolated storage interface.

```
public static void WriteSetting<KEY, TYPE>(string fileName,
                                           KEY key,
                                           TYPE setting)
{
    try
    {
        IsolatedStorageFile storage = OpenIsolatedStorage();

        BinaryFormatter formatter = new BinaryFormatter();
        Hashtable settings = null;

        using (Stream loadStream = new IsolatedStorageFileStream(fileName,
                                        FileMode.OpenOrCreate, storage))
        {
            try
```

```
            {
                settings = (Hashtable)formatter.Deserialize(loadStream);
            }
            catch (Exception)
            {
                // Quietly handle this error
            }
        }

        if (settings == null)
        {
            settings = new Hashtable();
        }

        settings[key] = setting;

        using (Stream writeStream = new IsolatedStorageFileStream(fileName,
                                                  FileMode.Create, storage))
        {
            formatter.Serialize(writeStream, settings);
        }
    }
    catch (Exception)
    {
        // Quietly handle this error
    }
}
```

The load routine for the isolated storage interface is just as easy as the save. First, we check to make sure the settings file exists in isolated storage, and we open it as a stream if possible. The data from the stream is then sent into BinaryFormatter, and data is deserialized into a hashtable containing the settings. The appropriate value referenced by the supplied key is then returned. The following code shows the load routine for the isolated storage interface.

```
public static TYPE ReadSetting<KEY, TYPE>(string fileName, KEY key)
{
    try
    {
        IsolatedStorageFile storage = OpenIsolatedStorage();

        string[] fileMatches = storage.GetFileNames(fileName);
```

```
            if (fileMatches.Length > 0 && fileMatches[0].Length > 0)
            {
                using (Stream loadStream = new IsolatedStorageFileStream(fileName,
                                                        FileMode.Open, storage))
                {
                    BinaryFormatter formatter = new BinaryFormatter();
                    Hashtable settings = formatter.Deserialize(loadStream)
                                                                as Hashtable;

                    if (settings != null)
                    {
                        return (TYPE)settings[key];
                    }
                }
            }

            return default(TYPE);
        }
        catch (Exception)
        {
            return default(TYPE);
        }
    }
```

Using the code is very straightforward, but you may want to know if an application is launching for the first time or not so you can save default settings into isolated storage. The following code shows how to determine whether an application is launching for the first time.

```
bool firstRun = !ReadSetting<string, bool>("MySettingsFile.dat",
                                        "FirstTimeLaunching");
if (firstRun)
{
    WriteSetting("MySettingsFile.dat", "FirstTimeLaunching", true);
}
```

Levels of Isolation

The whole idea behind isolated storage is that the physical location of stored files is managed by the .NET framework, not the application directly. Ignoring politics, it is important to understand how the framework associates an isolated storage location with a particular application. The association with an isolated storage location all comes down to how applications are identified by the framework.

Every user gets a collection of isolated storages, which are contained in a unique directory on the hard drive. This prevents interference between different users. Remember that the physical location of isolated storage files varies among operating systems, but typically they can usually be found at:

```
\Documents and Settings\<username>\Local Settings\Application Data\IsolatedStorage
```

Each record in isolated storage is referenced by a tag. If the assembly is signed, then this tag is the strong name as described by the Global Assembly Cache (GAC), and its location on the hard drive is not used for association. If the assembly is not signed, then the tag is the URL to where the assembly resides on the hard drive. Two identical copies of an assembly residing in different directories will be allotted separate isolated storages. This does mean that if an unsigned assembly is moved, the association to that assembly is broken and a new isolated storage will be created for it.

At this point, you may be wondering about the dangers of sharing assemblies between multiple applications, and corrupting data that does not belong to you. Another type of identification used by the framework for associations is at the domain (AppDomain) level. This level refers to the location where the code was executed from. A program executed from the local hard drive will have the same domain as the assembly tag. A program downloaded from the web would have a domain that is the URL where the program was downloaded from.

Management and Debugging

Isolated storage enforces a 10 MB data size limit per assembly, but it is still important to clean up data when it is no longer needed. There is a tool provided with the .NET framework that handles administration of isolated storage for each user. This tool is very simple and only offers limited functionality, but it is useful when debugging your storage.

Typing the command storeadm /help will produce the following usage text:

```
Microsoft (R) .NET Framework Store Admin 2.0.50215.44
Copyright (C) Microsoft Corporation. All rights reserved.

Usage     : StoreAdm [options]
options   : [/LIST] [/REMOVE] [/ROAMING | /MACHINE] [/QUIET]
/LIST     : Displays the existing isolated storage for the current user.
/REMOVE   : Removes all existing isolated storage for the current user.
/ROAMING  : Select the roaming store.
/QUIET    : Only error messages will be output.
/MACHINE  : Select the machine store.
```

Execute the demo application without a strong name key. Running the command storeadm /list will produce results similar to the following:

```
Microsoft (R) .NET Framework Store Admin 2.0.50215.44
Copyright (C) Microsoft Corporation. All rights reserved.


Record #1
[Domain]
<System.Security.Policy.Url version="1">
<Url>file:///C:/GETD/IsolatedStorageDemo.exe</Url>
</System.Security.Policy.Url>

[Assembly]
<System.Security.Policy.Url version="1">
<Url>file:///C:/GETD/IsolatedStorageDemo.exe</Url>
</System.Security.Policy.Url>


        Size : 1024
```

Notice that the domain and the assembly Url tags are identical. This means that if you move the assembly, the association to the isolated storage will be broken and a new one will be created.

Now give the assembly a strong name key and run the same command again. You should be shown results similar to the following:

```
Microsoft (R) .NET Framework Store Admin 2.0.50215.44
Copyright (C) Microsoft Corporation. All rights reserved.


Record #1
[Domain]
<StrongName version="1"
Key="00240000048000009400000006020000002400005253413100040000010001007353FE7EBDA40
8B323B72D672E003AF9F09659AF60C233333CDE3C7AC02AC57864B746E0029B3FBC66A31DA8BD75084
27A271E52EA5B7295D97839A038932D4BA50920BE848BDDBB2F536FCB396B9CE422C1AEE47730607D4
D20F22586D4B73AC5A39FA03D1DC796F34E5ABB6041416C13CCE66CDBAAB15D353978332AEB5BB"
Name="IsolatedStorageDemo"
Version="1.0.0.0"/>

[Assembly]
<StrongName version="1"
Key="00240000048000009400000006020000002400005253413100040000010001007353FE7EBDA40
8B323B72D672E003AF9F09659AF60C233333CDE3C7AC02AC57864B746E0029B3FBC66A31DA8BD75084
27A271E52EA5B7295D97839A038932D4BA50920BE848BDDBB2F536FCB396B9CE422C1AEE47730607D4
```

D20F22586D4B73AC5A39FA03D1DC796F34E5ABB6041416C13CCE66CDBAAB15D353978332AEBC5BB"
Name="IsolatedStorageDemo"
Version="1.0.0.0"/>

```
        Size : 1024
```

Notice now that the `Url` tag has disappeared, and the public strong name key is now set. The assembly can now reside at any location on the local hard drive and remain associated to this isolated storage.

You may at times wish to remove isolated storages. Removing all the storages for the current user can be done using the `storeadm /remove` command. This operation requires elevated permissions, generally admin status for the local machine. Finer control has to be done programmatically. `storeadm` is a managed application, so disassembling the executable will give you an idea of how it works, and how to enumerate isolated storages for the current user. It is generally common practice to create a hook in the assembly to remove data in isolated storage when it is no longer needed.

Conclusion

This chapter discussed traditional methods for storing legacy application data, and later covered the concept of isolated storage. Ideal uses for isolated storage include user settings and preferences, queued data waiting for a connection to be established to the Internet, and cached data retrieved from web services and databases.

So, having looked at the details of what isolated storage is and how it works, we looked at some general ideas of when and how to use it form. Do not store user documents or downloaded assemblies, because users will have a difficult time locating these documents on the hard drive for transfers or backups. Downloaded assemblies that are placed in isolated storage will also not be loadable because there is no path name. Finally, any data you place in isolated storage has the potential to be read by users because stored data is not encrypted. Do not store private or sensitive information in isolated storage unless you handle the encryption.

Isolated storage is a great concept, and the .NET framework provides a solid foundation for it. The standard is to use application configuration files (`app.config`) when handling read-only settings, and to use isolated storage when you need bidirectional data persistence.

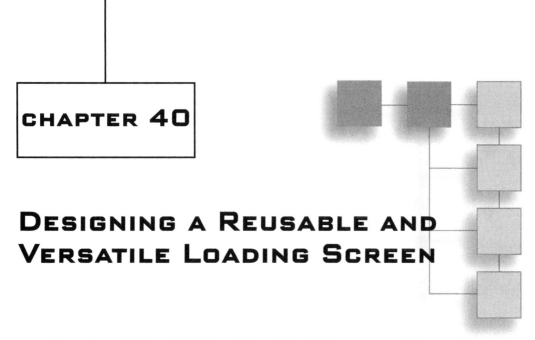

CHAPTER 40

DESIGNING A REUSABLE AND VERSATILE LOADING SCREEN

I'm a strong believer in being minimalistic. Unless you actually are going to solve the general problem, don't try and put in place a framework for solving a specific one, because you don't know what that framework should look like.

Anders Hejlsberg

Many large applications have a considerable waiting period that occurs when the application first launches. One reason can be the loading of numerous dependencies on external components, such as a plugin that must be interrogated and assimilated into the runtime of the application. Another reason can be a substantial amount of preprocessing that occurs before the application is handed to the user. Preprocessing is generally used to generate and cache commonly used data when the application first starts so that this data is not calculated when the user expects responsiveness.

Some applications also use the concept of a *splash screen*, which is basically a loading screen that is only used for aesthetic purposes. These screens typically display a title image and some supporting text, like copyright messages or development credits. Splash screens are usually dismissed when a certain amount of time has elapsed or the user clicks the mouse or presses a key.

As discussed in Chapter 7, "Fundamentals of User Interface Design," the Principle of Feedback describes how the application should notify the user of long-running processes so the user does not suspect that the application has stalled. Almost every application that has a significant waiting period during startup uses a loading screen to display the status of long-running processes. Typically, these loading screens run as modal dialogs that appear centered on top of the underlying application windows and do not allow the user to interact with anything in the application until the processing is finished and the loading screen closes.

This chapter will describe some fundamental aspects of loading screens, and then will focus on implementing a reusable component that will display process status to the user when an application first starts. The component will also support the concept of splash screens.

Splash Dialog

The general idea is to build a reusable form that has a variety of customization options depending on the needs of the project. Splash dialogs can be designed in virtually any way, so this chapter will cover the features found in the example on the Companion Web site. The main feature is the ability to specify a background image that defines the width and height of the form.

There are a couple of properties that must be customized on the default form. The starting position of the form should be set to center screen, the form should be displayed without a title box, and the border style should be set to none. Another good flag to enable is top most, which causes the splash dialog to be shown on top of all other windows. Lastly, specify the splash dialog to not show up in the task bar. Splash dialogs should not create additional window entries in the task bar because they should be considered part of the main window.

The framework presented in this chapter makes use of a class that contains all the settings and handles the launching of the splash screen dialog. The settings class passes itself as a reference to the dialog constructor so that the splash screen can configure the appropriate settings as it launches. The splash dialog is an internal class within the library, so consumers of the library cannot access the dialog directly, and must do so through the settings and launcher class.

The following code describes the settings and launcher class in its entirety. I will not yet explain what each property does, but they will be discussed when needed as you read on in the chapter. You will need to make sure that you reference the `System.Drawing` and `System.Collections.Generic` namespaces as well.

```
public class SplashScreen
{
    private List<ILoadingJob> _loadingJobs = new List<ILoadingJob>();
```

```csharp
private bool _interruptible = true;
private bool _fading = true;
private bool _displayVersion = true;
private bool _displayStatus = false;
private int _splashInterval = 3000;
private Image _splashImage = null;
private string _windowTitle = string.Empty;
private bool _blackBorder = true;
private string _versionText = string.Empty;

public List<ILoadingJob> LoadingJobs
{
    get { return _loadingJobs; }
    set { _loadingJobs = value; }
}

public bool Interruptible
{
    get { return _interruptible; }
    set { _interruptible = value; }
}

public bool Fading
{
    get { return _fading; }
    set { _fading = value; }
}

public bool DisplayVersion
{
    get { return _displayVersion; }
    set { _displayVersion = value; }
}

public bool DisplayStatus
{
    get { return _displayStatus; }
    set { _displayStatus = value; }
}

public int SplashInterval
{
```

```
            get { return _splashInterval; }
            set { _splashInterval = value; }
        }

        public Image SplashImage
        {
            get { return _splashImage; }
            set { _splashImage = value; }
        }

        public string WindowTitle
        {
            get { return _windowTitle; }
            set { _windowTitle = value; }
        }

        public bool BlackBorder
        {
            get { return _blackBorder; }
            set { _blackBorder = value; }
        }

        public string VersionText
        {
            get { return _versionText; }
            set { _versionText = value; }
        }

        public void Launch()
        {
            (new SplashDialog(this)).ShowDialog();
        }
    }
```

It is now time to jump into the meat of our framework, the splash dialog form itself.

The VersionText property enables the user to set the version of the application to display in the top-right corner of the splash dialog, and the dimensions of the text box are dynamically calculated based on the width of the version string specified.

The dialog constructor takes an instance of the settings and launcher class and configures the appropriate settings for the splash screen.

When the dialog first loads, it checks to see if it should function as a splash screen or as a loading screen. Basically, the dialog checks to see if any jobs have been designated for loading; if there are no jobs, it will function as a splash screen. In splash screen mode, the dialog will start the display timer that will run for the specified interval and then close. In loading screen mode, the dialog will remain open until all jobs have been processed.

The key down and mouse click events call the interrupt method that attempts to close the splash screen dialog early. The ability to do this is determined by the Interruptible property in the settings and launcher class.

Note

A loading screen cannot be interrupted in our framework because all jobs must complete before the application can be considered ready for use. Canceling the loading process has the potential to make the application unstable.

The following code implements the functionality of the splash screen and loading dialog form.

```
public partial class SplashDialog : Form
{
    private ILoadingJob _currentJob = null;
    private SplashScreen _splashScreen = null;
    public string VersionText
    {
        set
        {
            VersionLabel.Text = String.Format("Version: {0}", value);
            int offset = this.Width - VersionLabel.Bounds.Right;
            Graphics graphics = VersionLabel.CreateGraphics();

            Size size = (graphics.MeasureString(VersionLabel.Text,
                                            VersionLabel.Font)).ToSize();
            int newX = this.Width - offset - size.Width;

            VersionLabel.Bounds = new Rectangle(newX,
                                            VersionLabel.Bounds.Y,
                                            size.Width,
                                            size.Height + 4);
        }
    }
```

```csharp
public string StatusText
{
    set
    {
        StatusLabel.Text = String.Format("Status: {0}", value);
    }
}

public SplashDialog(SplashScreen splashScreen)
{
    InitializeComponent();

    _splashScreen = splashScreen;

    if (_splashScreen != null)
    {
        if (_splashScreen.SplashImage != null)
        {
            this.Width = _splashScreen.SplashImage.Width;
            this.Height = _splashScreen.SplashImage.Height;

            this.SplashPanel.BackgroundImage = _splashScreen.SplashImage;
        }

        VersionLabel.Visible = _splashScreen.DisplayVersion;
        StatusLabel.Visible = _splashScreen.DisplayStatus;

        DisplayTimer.Interval = _splashScreen.SplashInterval;

        if (_splashScreen.BlackBorder)
        {
            SplashPanel.BorderStyle = BorderStyle.FixedSingle;
        }
        else
        {
            SplashPanel.BorderStyle = BorderStyle.None;
        }

        if (_splashScreen.WindowTitle != null &&
            _splashScreen.WindowTitle.Length > 0)
        {
            this.FormBorderStyle = FormBorderStyle.FixedDialog;
```

```csharp
                this.Text = _splashScreen.WindowTitle;
            }
            else
            {
                this.FormBorderStyle = FormBorderStyle.None;
            }

            this.VersionText = _splashScreen.VersionText;
        }
    }

    private void SplashDialog_Load(object sender, EventArgs e)
    {
        this.Opacity = 1.0;

        if (_splashScreen.LoadingJobs == null ||
            _splashScreen.LoadingJobs.Count <= 0)
            DisplayTimer.Start();
        else
            ProcessJobs();
    }

    private void DisplayTimer_Tick(object sender, System.EventArgs e)
    {
        DisplayTimer.Stop();
        this.Close();
    }

    private void SplashDialog_KeyDown(object sender,
                                System.Windows.Forms.KeyEventArgs e)
    {
        InterruptSplash();
    }

    private void SplashPanel_MouseClick(object sender, MouseEventArgs e)
    {
        InterruptSplash();
    }

    private void InterruptSplash()
    {
        if (_splashScreen.Interruptable)
```

```csharp
        {
            if (_splashScreen.LoadingJobs == null ||
                _splashScreen.LoadingJobs.Count <= 0)
            {
                DisplayTimer.Stop();
                this.Close();
            }
        }
    }

    public void RefreshStatus()
    {
        if (_currentJob != null)
        {
            this.StatusText = _currentJob.StatusText;
            Application.DoEvents();
        }
    }

    public void ProcessJobs()
    {
        Application.DoEvents();

        if (_splashScreen.LoadingJobs != null &&
            _splashScreen.LoadingJobs.Count > 0)
        {
            MethodInvoker refreshInvoker = new MethodInvoker(RefreshStatus);

            foreach (ILoadingJob jobObject in _splashScreen.LoadingJobs)
            {
                _currentJob = jobObject;

                if (_currentJob != null)
                {
                    LoadingResult result = _currentJob.Load(refreshInvoker);

                    switch (result)
                    {
                        case LoadingResult.Success:
                        {
                                // Generally ignore this return value
                                break;
                        }
```

```
                    case LoadingResult.Warning:
                    {
                            // Could log this somewhere or notify the user
                            break;
                    }

                    case LoadingResult.Failure:
                    {
                            // Could cancel all remaining jobs
                            // and perform a rollback
                            break;
                    }
                }
            }
        }

        this.StatusText = "Finished";
        this.Close();
    }
  }
}
```

The splash dialog looks something like Figure 40.1 at this point in time.

As we continue on in this chapter, some more features and functionality will be added to make the component more robust.

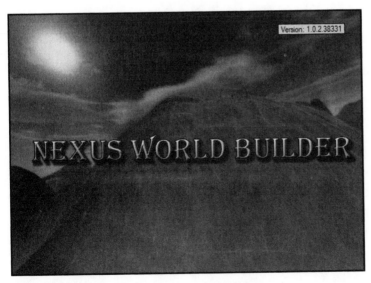

Figure 40.1 Preview of the splash screen dialog.

Go for the Gusto

We now have the dialog component built for our splash screen launcher, but we can take it one step further and enhance the visual effects if we want. A nice touch that is common among many splash screens is the fade-in and fade-out transition effect. You may skip this step if you do not want this extra functionality, or if you feel that doing so would not be an effective use of your time.

Thankfully, .NET WinForms support an Opacity property that lets you modify the transparency factor of a window and all the contained child controls. We can utilize this property in conjunction with a couple of timer objects to create a fading effect that will make our splash dialogs look really slick!

The fading effect will be orchestrated by two timers in addition to the first one used to time the duration of the splash dialog.

```
private void FadeInTimer_Tick(object sender, System.EventArgs e)
{
    if (this.Opacity < 0.9)
        this.Opacity += 0.1;
    else
    {
        FadeInTimer.Stop();

        if (_splashScreen.LoadingJobs == null ||
            _splashScreen.LoadingJobs.Count <= 0)
        {
            DisplayTimer.Start();
        }
        else
        {
            ProcessJobs();
        }
    }
}
```

The fade-in timer will be started in the form load event instead of the display timer. When the form is fully visible and if the dialog is timed, the display timer will fire and begin counting towards closing the dialog. The event code for the display timer presented earlier will require a small modification to support the new fading feature. The change is shown in the following code.

```
private void DisplayTimer_Tick(object sender, System.EventArgs e)
{
    DisplayTimer.Stop();
```

```
    if (_splashScreen.Fading)
        FadeOutTimer.Start();
    else
        this.Close();
}
```

Lastly, another timer is used to fade out the window visibility and then close the window when it becomes hidden. The following code implements the fade out timer event.

```
private void FadeOutTimer_Tick(object sender, System.EventArgs e)
{
    if (this.Opacity > 0.01)
        this.Opacity -= 0.1;
    else
    {
        FadeOutTimer.Stop();
        this.Close();
    }
}
```

The load event for the dialog must also be updated to support the new fading effect. The following code implements the updated dialog load event.

```
private void SplashDialog_Load(object sender, EventArgs e)
{
    if (_splashScreen.Fading)
        FadeInTimer.Start();
    else
    {
        this.Opacity = 1.0;

        if (_splashScreen.LoadingJobs == null ||
            _splashScreen.LoadingJobs.Count <= 0)
            DisplayTimer.Start();
        else
            ProcessJobs();
    }
}
```

The splash interrupt method must also be updated to cancel the active timers and start the fade out timer, if appropriate. The following code implements the updated splash interrupt method.

```
private void InterruptSplash()
{
    if (_splashScreen.Interruptable)
    {
        if (_splashScreen.LoadingJobs == null ||
            _splashScreen.LoadingJobs.Count <= 0)
        {
            if (_splashScreen.Fading)
                FadeInTimer.Stop();

            DisplayTimer.Stop();

            if (_splashScreen.Fading)
                FadeOutTimer.Start();
            else
                this.Close();
        }
    }
}
```

The last modification that must be performed is near the end of the job processing method. The following code shows where the change must be done.

```
public void ProcessJobs()
{
    Application.DoEvents();

if (_splashScreen.LoadingJobs != null &&
        _splashScreen.LoadingJobs.Count > 0)
    {
        ...

        this.StatusText = "Finished";

        if (_splashScreen.Fading)
            FadeOutTimer.Start();
        else
            this.Close();
    }
}
```

Concept of Loading Jobs

At this point, we have an attractive splash dialog that does not provide much in terms of processing functionality. The next thing on the agenda is to create a mechanism where jobs can be designed and plugged into the job manager for execution. If you have not figured it out yet, we need an interface to do this!

The interface `ILoadingJob` is described in the following code and should be fairly simple to understand. The `StatusText` property will be called by the job manager to update progress messages. The load method takes a `MethodInvoker` that is used to relay update requests back to the job manager during loading (more on this later).

The following code implements the `ILoadingJob` interface.

```
public interface ILoadingJob
{
    string StatusText
    {
        get;
    }

    LoadingResult Load(MethodInvoker refreshInvoker);
}
```

The load method also returns a result code that indicates the success or failure of the job. The result codes are described in the following. The values are self-explanatory, and the job manager can handle each code in a certain way, depending on the implementation.

```
public enum LoadingResult
{
    Success,
    Warning,
    Failure
}
```

The success code is fairly trivial; generally, this result will be ignored and processing will continue. The warning code can be used to alert the user if a potential problem or risk is identified and leave it up to her to react to it. The error code can be used to halt further processing and perform a rollback if desired.

Responsive Processing

Launching the splash screen is simple enough, but the complexity of the solution increases when the component must facilitate the processing of jobs. Single-threaded applications typically hang when a long-running process executes, and the application must wait to dispatch its usual messages. It is important that the user interface remain responsive while jobs are being processed.

The MethodInvoker mechanism provides a generic delegate that is used to invoke a method with a void parameter list. This mechanism can be used when you need a simple delegate but do not want to create one yourself. MethodInvoker is used by jobs to notify the application when processing status has changed. The application defines a method that updates the status text label and calls Application.DoEvents() to allow the application to update the user interface with the changes. This method is bound to a MethodInvoker object and is passed to all jobs by the controlling logic. The ProcessJobs() method has the code that creates a MethodInvoker bound to the refresh method and then passes it to all jobs being processed.

With the addition of responsive job processing, the loading job component is now complete and should resemble that shown in Figure 42.2. Notice the addition of the status text label at the bottom of the form. The visibility of this label is controlled by the DisplayStatus property in the settings and launcher class.

Figure 42.2 Preview of the splash screen dialog.

Simple Example

Now that development of the component is complete, we can finally start using it! The example presented in this chapter has a form with two buttons where one launches a splash screen and the other launches a loading dialog. The user interface code will not be discussed because it is redundant and rudimentary, but the full source code can be found on the Companion Web site.

We will start off by building three sample jobs that can be used to test the loading dialog and show how to properly implement the ILoadingJob interface. Finally, the code will be shown that properly configures the component to function as a splash screen or a loading dialog.

The first sample job merely waits for two seconds before completing. This wait time is to simulate actual processing that would occur if the job did something remotely useful. The StatusText property will be used by the job manager to update the processing status, so it is important that this property always return the most up-to-date description of the operation.

```
public class SampleLoadingJob1 : SplashScreenLibrary.ILoadingJob
{
    public SplashScreenLibrary.LoadingResult Load(MethodInvoker refreshInvoker)
    {
        refreshInvoker.Method.Invoke(refreshInvoker.Target, new object[0]);
        System.Threading.Thread.Sleep(2000);
        return SplashScreenLibrary.LoadingResult.Success;
    }

    public string StatusText
    {
        get
        {
            return "Processing Sample Job 1 : Waiting for 2 Seconds";
        }
    }
}
```

You should notice the following line that invokes the method that refreshes the status description.

```
refreshInvoker.Method.Invoke(refreshInvoker.Target, new object[0]);
```

The preceding code should never be altered, but it is important that this line appear either before a job begins processing or before each task within a job begins processing.

The second sample job shows how to execute multiple tasks within a job and correctly handle the StatusText property. The job executes 10 tasks, each one taking 0.6 seconds to complete.

```
public class SampleLoadingJob2 : SplashScreenLibrary.ILoadingJob
{
    private int _currentTask = 1;

    public SplashScreenLibrary.LoadingResult Load(MethodInvoker refreshInvoker)
    {
        for (_currentTask = 1; _currentTask <= 10; _currentTask++)
        {
            refreshInvoker.Method.Invoke(refreshInvoker.Target, new object[0]);
            System.Threading.Thread.Sleep(600);
        }

        return SplashScreenLibrary.LoadingResult.Success;
    }

    public string StatusText
    {
        get
        {
            return String.Format("Processing Sample Job 2 : Task {0} of 10",
                                  _currentTask);
        }
    }
}
```

This sample job works in a very similar way to the second sample job, except that there are a greater number of tasks to complete and a much shorter waiting period between tasks.

```
public class SampleLoadingJob3 : SplashScreenLibrary.ILoadingJob
{
    private int _currentTask = 1;

    public SplashScreenLibrary.LoadingResult Load(MethodInvoker refreshInvoker)
    {
        for (_currentTask = 1; _currentTask <= 100; _currentTask++)
        {
            refreshInvoker.Method.Invoke(refreshInvoker.Target, new object[0]);
            System.Threading.Thread.Sleep(50);
        }
```

```
        return SplashScreenLibrary.LoadingResult.Success;
    }

    public string StatusText
    {
        get
        {
            return String.Format("Processing Sample Job 3 : Task {0} of 100",
                                  _currentTask);
        }
    }
}
```

The component is ready, and we now have some sample jobs at our disposal to work with. The last step is to instantiate the settings and launcher class, configure it appropriately (splash screen or loading dialog), and finally activate it. The following code shows how to configure and launch a splash screen.

```
SplashScreen splash = new SplashScreen();
splash.BackgroundImage = new System.Drawing.Bitmap(@"PathToSplash.bmp");
splash.DisplayStatus = false;
splash.DisplayVersion = true;
splash.VersionText = Application.ProductVersion;
splash.DisplayTime = 3000;
splash.Launch();
```

The code to launch the loading dialog is quite similar to the splash screen, except the display time is not set, and the job objects are bound to the job manager for processing. The following code shows how to configure and launch a loading dialog.

```
SplashScreen splash = new SplashScreen();
splash.BackgroundImage = new System.Drawing.Bitmap(@"PathToSplash.bmp");
splash.DisplayStatus = true;
splash.DisplayVersion = true;
splash.VersionText = Application.ProductVersion;
splash.LoadingJobs.Add(new SampleLoadingJob1());
splash.LoadingJobs.Add(new SampleLoadingJob2());
splash.LoadingJobs.Add(new SampleLoadingJob3());
splash.Launch();
```

The background image can also be loaded from the assembly if it has been compiled as an embedded resource. Simply add the appropriate bitmap image to the project, right-click on it, select Properties, and set the Build Action to Embedded

Resource. If the assembly is called SplashTest, and the image is called Splash.bmp, the following code will return a bitmap from the data embedded in the assembly.

```
using System.Reflection;
Assembly mainAssembly = Assembly.GetExecutingAssembly();
splash.SplashImage    = new Bitmap(mainAssembly.GetManifestResourceStream
("SplashTest.Splash.bmp"));
```

This approach is generally superior to loading the bitmap from the file system because the user cannot easily modify or remove the image, and there is one less file that you have to worry about deploying with your tool.

Conclusion

This chapter provided a reusable and customizable component, suitable for displaying splash screens or loading screens that prohibit users from accessing the application until processing has finished.

One area that could be improved is where a method is passed into each job to handle refreshing of the status text. This approach was used to decouple the interface from a lot of the implementation specifics, but it would be an improvement to refactor the framework where this method invocation is unnecessary.

The full source code to this component can be found on the Companion Web site in the Chapter 40 folder.

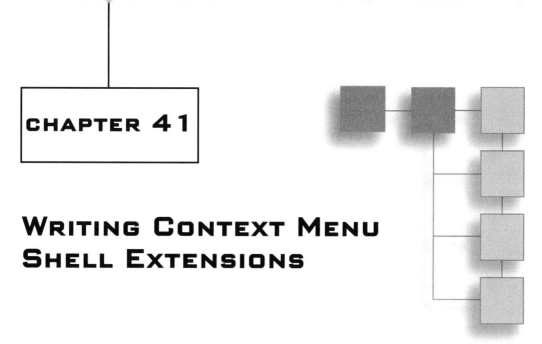

CHAPTER 41

WRITING CONTEXT MENU SHELL EXTENSIONS

Mankind always sets itself only such tasks as it can solve; since, looking at the matter more closely, we will always find that the task itself arises only when the material conditions necessary for its solution already exist or are at least in the process of formation.

Karl Marx

Most developers have myriad tools they have developed over the course of their projects. Command line tools are a common choice because they are effortless to develop, and they are easy to integrate with a scripting process. These tools are moderately easy to operate through the command line, but require a fair amount of typing to specify settings and files to process. These useful tools can be consumed by a Windows Forms application, but an even better approach is to integrate with the Windows shell (Explorer) so that a simple right-click on a particular file could present options specific to the tools.

A shell extension is a COM object that adds additional functionality to the Windows shell. There are many different types of extensions that can be developed, such as a context menu that is presented to the user when she right-clicks on a file with a certain extension. Shell extensions are in-process servers that facilitate the communication with the shell by implementing common interfaces that the shell understands.

Microsoft .NET is a powerful platform to develop on, but unfortunately, it is not yet a native part of Windows. Most applications are still unmanaged, and while interaction between managed and unmanaged application is possible, managed and unmanaged applications remain in their own independent worlds.

Windows Explorer is an unmanaged application that cannot differentiate between a managed application and an unmanaged application. Explorer only understands how to load COM interfaces, so there is no special base class we can inherit from; we have to do things the messy way. Shell extensions can be written in a managed language like C#, but the component must be visible as a COM object and employ a proxy that the shell can understand. Supposedly, Windows Vista (Longhorn) provides a variety of managed mechanisms, but our current operating systems do not work like that.

In this chapter, you will learn how to create a shell extension, and register it with the Windows shell as a standalone assembly, or integrated within an application.

Unmanaged Interfaces

The first step is to import the native structures, interfaces, types, and methods that we require in order to build our shell extension.

Every COM interface is associated with a unique GUID (Globally Unique Identifier), and is a required attribute to specify when importing a COM interface in a .NET application. When importing a COM interface, you must specify the correct GUID for the interface as defined in the Win32 registry. Additionally, you must also specify the interface type to determine how the interface is exposed to COM callers. The different interface types available are described in Table 41.1.

Table 41.1 Enumerated Types for ComInterfaceType

COM Interface Type	Description
InterfaceIsDual	Exposes an interface as a dual interface, supporting both early and late binding.
InterfaceIsIUnknown	Exposes an interface that is derived from IUnknown, supporting only early binding.
InterfaceIsIDispatch	Exposes an interface that is a dispinterface, supporting only late binding.

By default, a COM interface is exposed as dual, but the interfaces needed for shell extensions do not require late binding, so their types are all set to InterfaceIsIUnknown.

The [GuidAttribute] is used to assign a GUID to the interface. This GUID must be the correct one to use for the COM interface you are importing, as defined in the Win32 registry. This is so COM clients can invoke methods of the interface, regardless of how the .NET implementation works.

Note

.NET interfaces and classes do not require an explicit GUID to be set as they are automatically generated.

The [PreserveSig] attribute is used to specify that there is a direct translation between the managed signature and the unmanaged entry point. More specifically, most COM interfaces return method success as an HRESULT, and use a memory buffer pointer to pass this value back to callers. The default behavior of the CLR is to automatically transform the managed signature, but the [PreserveSig] attribute is used to ensure that this transformation does happen.

The IShellExtInit interface is called by the shell, and is used to initialize property sheets, drag-and-drop handlers, and context menu extensions. The parameters for this method vary depending on the type of extension, but we will focus on content menu extensions. The pidlFolder is null when dealing with file objects, or it specifies the folder for which the context menu is being requested. The objectPointer identifies the selected files, and the keyProgID identifies the file class of the object with focus.

```
[ComImport(), InterfaceType(ComInterfaceType.InterfaceIsIUnknown),
GuidAttribute ("000214e8-0000-0000-c000-000000000046")]
public interface IShellExtInit
{
    [PreserveSig()]
    int Initialize(IntPtr pidlFolder, IntPtr objectPointer, uint keyProgID);
}
```

Note

IShellExtInit is only used by property sheet, context menu, and drag-and-drop handler extensions. Be sure to use the correct interface when building other types of shell extensions.

The IContentMenu interface is used by the shell when creating or merging a context menu associated with a shell object. This interface can be used to dynamically add items to a shell object's context menu.

```
[ComImport(), InterfaceType(ComInterfaceType.InterfaceIsIUnknown),
                        GuidAttribute("000214e4-0000-0000-c000-000000000046")]
public interface IContextMenu
{
    [PreserveSig()]
    int QueryContextMenu(uint menu,
                         uint menuId,
                         int firstCommand,
                         int lastCommand,
                         uint flags);

    [PreserveSig()]
    void InvokeCommand(IntPtr pointer);

    [PreserveSig()]
    void GetCommandString(int command,
                          uint flags,
                          int reserved,
                          StringBuilder commandString,
                          int max);
}
```

The IDataObject interface provides a mechanism through which data can be transferred; it is also used to handle notifications related to the data, such as changes. The data transfer mechanism specifies the format of the data, along with the medium through which the data is transferred.

Note

The term *data object* refers to any object that implements the IDataObject interface.

The IShellExtInit.Initialize() method is given a pointer to an IDataObject that contains our file objects; we must define the IDataObject interface so that we can cast the pointer to a data object. The only method we need in this interface is GetData(), which is supplied with the data format, along with a storage medium container, and we are given the data itself.

```
[ComImport(), InterfaceType(ComInterfaceType.InterfaceIsIUnknown),
                        GuidAttribute("0000010e-0000-0000-C000-000000000046")]
public interface IDataObject
{
    [PreserveSig()]
    int GetData(ref ClipFormat a, ref StorageMedium b);
```

```
[PreserveSig()]
void GetDataHere(int a, ref StorageMedium b);

[PreserveSig()]
int QueryGetData(int a);

[PreserveSig()]
int GetCanonicalFormatEtc(int a, ref int b);

[PreserveSig()]
int SetData(int a, int b, int c);

[PreserveSig()]
int EnumFormatEtc(uint a, ref Object b);

[PreserveSig()]
int DAdvise(int a, uint b, Object c, ref uint d);

[PreserveSig()]
int DUnadvise(uint a);

[PreserveSig()]
int EnumDAdvise(ref Object a);
}
```

There are a number of unmanaged Win32 types that must also be defined so that the unmanaged methods can use them. There are also several unmanaged types within the structures that will be covered later. It is also important to note the use of the [StructLayout] attribute. By default, the CLR automatically chooses a layout for structure members when compiled. This can lead to format problems when interacting with COM callers. By specifying LayoutKind.Sequential, the structure layout is defined in the order in which members appear.

The InvokeCommandInfo structure defined below is known as CMINVOKECOMMANDINFO in the unmanaged world. It contains information needed by IContextMenu.InvokeCommand() to execute a context menu command.

```
[StructLayout(LayoutKind.Sequential, CharSet = CharSet.Unicode)]
public struct InvokeCommandInfo
{
    public uint Size;
    public uint Mask;
    public uint Window;
```

```
    public int Verb;
    [MarshalAs(UnmanagedType.LPStr)]
    public string Parameters;
    [MarshalAs(UnmanagedType.LPStr)]
    public string Directory;
    public int Show;
    public uint HotKey;
    public uint Icon;
}
```

The `MenuItemInfo` structure defined below is known as `MENUITEMINFO` in the unmanaged world. It contains information about a menu item. This structure is used when adding new menu items to the context menu for a file object.

```
[StructLayout(LayoutKind.Sequential)]
public struct MenuItemInfo
{
    internal uint Size;
    internal uint Mask;
    internal uint Type;
    internal uint State;
    internal int ID;
    internal int SubMenu;
    internal int BitmapChecked;
    internal int BitmapUnchecked;
    internal int ItemData;
    internal string TypeData;
    internal uint Max;
    internal int BitmapItem;
}
```

The `ClipFormat` structure defined below is known as `FORMATETC` in the unmanaged world. It is a generalized clipboard format that describes the format of arbitrary data. This structure is used when calling the `IDataObject.GetData()` method.

```
[StructLayout(LayoutKind.Sequential)]
public struct ClipFormat
{
    internal Native.ClipFormatFlags Format;
    internal uint DevicePointer;
    internal Native.DvAspectFlags Aspect;
    internal int Index;
    internal Native.TypeMediumFlags Medium;
}
```

The `StorageMedium` structure defined below is known as `STGMEDIUM` in the unmanaged world. It is a generalized global memory handle used in data transfer operations like `IDataObject.GetData()`.

```
[StructLayout(LayoutKind.Sequential)]
public struct StorageMedium
{
    public uint Medium;
    public uint Global;
    public uint ReleasePointer;
}
```

There are some enumerated values that must also be defined in order for the unmanaged interfaces and methods to operate. These types are defined in an internal class called `Native` so that they are not accessible outside of the assembly.

```
internal sealed class Native
{
```

The following flags enumeration is used to determine when a context menu should be shown. There are many more flags that can be used as a filter, but this chapter only focuses on one flag, so the rest have been truncated out. The `Explore` flag (`CMF_EXPLORE`) will be set when the context menu is being generated by the shell from an Explorer mode window.

```
    internal enum QueryContextMenuFlags : uint
    {
        Explore = 0x00000004
    }
```

When one of the items added by a context menu extension is highlighted, the `IContextMenu.GetCommandString()` method is called to request a help text string or a verb string assigned to the command (canonical). Both ANSI and Unicode strings can be requested. This functionality is generally used for localization and will not be covered in this chapter. Feel free to consult MSDN for more information.

```
    internal enum GetCommandStringFlags : uint
    {
        Verb = 0x00000000,        // Canonical verb
        HelpText = 0x00000001    // Help text (for status bar)
    }
```

The following flags enumeration is used when specifying the data format for `IDataObject`. There are many more format types available, but this chapter only focuses on one type, so the rest have been truncated out. The `DropHandle` type (`CF_HDROP`) is used when transferring the location of a group of existing files.

```
internal enum ClipFormatFlags : uint
{
    DropHandle = 15
}
```

The following flags enumeration is used when creating menu items. There are many more flags available, but this chapter only focuses on the following flags, so the rest have been truncated out. All menu items have the `Type` flag set, and all menu items except separators have `State` and `ID`, which are standard Win32 menu flags. `SubMenu` is fairly self-explanatory; the parent menu has it set because it contains submenu items. The rest of the menu items do not set this flag.

```
internal enum MaskFlags : uint
{
    State = 0x00000001,
    ID = 0x00000002,
    SubMenu = 0x00000004,
    Type = 0x00000010
}
```

The following flags enumeration is used when accessing data contained in a storage medium (`TYEMED`). We only define the `Global` type because that is the only one we use in this chapter. `Global` represents a global memory handle.

```
internal enum TypeMediumFlags : uint
{
    Global = 1
}
```

The following flags enumeration is used when building the data format for `IDataObject.GetData()`. There are more types available, but this chapter only focuses on one type, so the rest have been truncated out. The `Content` type (`DVASPECT_CONTENT`) represents an object that can be displayed as an embedded object inside a container. This type is for compound document objects.

```
internal enum DvAspectFlags : uint
{
    Content = 1
}
```

The following flags enumeration is used when specifying the Type or State property of a menu item. Enabled is a state property, which is fairly self-evident. The String type is used to say that the menu item is displayed as text, and the Separator type is used to create a separator line menu item.

```
internal enum MenuFlags : uint
{
    Separator = 0x00000800,
    Enabled = 0x00000000,
    String = 0x00000000
}
```

The following method creates a new menu and returns a handle to it if successful.

```
[DllImport("user32")]
internal static extern uint CreatePopupMenu();
```

The following method adds a menu item to an existing menu created with CreatePopupMenu().

```
[DllImport("user32")]
internal static extern int InsertMenuItem(uint menu,
                                          uint position,
                                          uint flags,
                                          ref MenuItemInfo menuItemInfo);
```

The following method is used to extract information from a group of files, referenced by a drop handle from IDataObject.GetData(). The file parameter is a zero-based index into the array of files, and the buffer will be set to the full path to the file. The max parameter is set to the maximum string length; set it to zero for no maximum.

```
[DllImport("shell32")]
internal static extern uint DragQueryFile(uint dropHandle,
                                          uint file,
                                          StringBuilder buffer,
                                          int max);
}
```

You can also use this method to retrieve the number of files referenced by a drop handle. Set the file parameter to 0xffffffff, the buffer to null, and max to zero. The result will be the number of files in the query.

Reusable Framework

With all of the unmanaged types defined, we can finally jump into the framework class itself. Reusability is an important consideration when building any component. There is a lot of functionality that is common to any context menu extension, so naturally this code will reside in an extendable class. Extensions will inherit from this base class and configure the necessary options and logic. We will call this class ShellExtensionBase, it will implement IShellExtInit and IContextMenu, and it will be abstract so that it cannot be instantiated directly.

```
public abstract class ShellExtensionBase : IShellExtInit, IContextMenu
{
    ...
}
```

The first configurable option is the menu title. This property is the text used for the context menu entry that contains all the submenu command items.

```
protected abstract string MenuTitle
{
    get;
}
```

The next configurable option is the list of file extensions that will be associated with the extension. This can be one to many entries. For example, having .txt would associate the extension with any text file. If you want to associate the extension with any file, simply use * (an asterisk) as the extension.

```
protected abstract string[] Extensions
{
    get;
}
```

Extensions using this framework need a way of registering commands with the underlying system, and that is the purpose of the following method. The file path array is passed into the method so that filtering can be done based on the files selected. This provides a mechanism where dynamic menus can be created.

```
protected abstract void CommandRegistration(string[] files);
```

Commands are registered using literal strings. The command strings are used as the display text for the submenu item, as well as the command identifier itself. The following method is called when a submenu item is selected on a group of files.

```
protected abstract void HandleCommand(string command, string[] files);
```

When an error occurs, it is the job of the following method to handle the error gracefully.

```
protected abstract void HandleError(Exception exception);
```

Even though it's not necessarily used in our framework, we still need to implement the IContextMenu.GetCommandString() method to a certain extent.

```
void IContextMenu.GetCommandString(int command,
                                   uint flags,
                                   int reserved,
                                   StringBuilder commandString,
                                   int max)
{
    switch (flags)
    {
        case (uint)Native.GetCommandStringFlags.Verb:
        {
            commandString = new StringBuilder("...");
            break;
        }

        case (uint)Native.GetCommandStringFlags.HelpText:
        {
            commandString = new StringBuilder("...");
            break;
        }
    }
}
```

When our context menu extension initializes, we need to get a handle to the data in the storage medium through the IDataObject interface. The following code shows how to do this.

```
int IShellExtInit.Initialize(IntPtr folderPidl, IntPtr pointer, uint keyProgID)
{
    try
    {
        if (pointer != IntPtr.Zero)
        {
            IDataObject dataObject = Marshal.GetObjectForIUnknown(pointer)
                                                          as IDataObject;

            ClipFormat format = new ClipFormat();
```

```
                    format.Format = Native.ClipFormatFlags.DropHandle;
                    format.DevicePointer = 0;
                    format.Aspect = Native.DvAspectFlags.Content;
                    format.Index = -1;
                    format.Medium = Native.TypeMediumFlags.Global;

                    StorageMedium medium = new StorageMedium();

                    dataObject.GetData(ref format, ref medium);

                    _dropHandle = medium.Global;
                }
            }
            catch (Exception exception)
            {
                    HandleError(exception);
            }

            return 0;
        }
```

The `IContextMenu.QueryContextMenu()` method is called whenever the context menu is supposed to be displayed. This is where the menu is created and populated. First, the popup menu is created. Then each file in the query is filtered against the extensions array. Then the commands specific to the extension are registered, and the submenu items are created and added to the parent menu item; finally, the parent menu item is inserted into the Explorer context menu.

```
int IContextMenu.QueryContextMenu(uint menu,
                                  uint menuId,
                                  int firstCommand,
                                  int lastCommand,
                                  uint flags)
{
    int id = 1;

    try
    {
        if ((flags & 0xf) == 0 ||
            (flags & (uint)Native.QueryContextMenuFlags.Explore) != 0)
        {
            _popupMenu = Native.CreatePopupMenu();
```

```
uint fileCount = Native.DragQueryFile(_dropHandle, 0xffffffff, null, 0);

List<string> filteredFiles = new List<string>();

if (fileCount >= 1)
{
    for (uint index = 0; index < fileCount; index++)
    {
        StringBuilder buffer = new StringBuilder(1024);

        Native.DragQueryFile(_dropHandle,
                             index,
                             buffer,
                             buffer.Capacity + 1);

        string fileExtension = Path.GetExtension(buffer.ToString());

        foreach (string filterExtension in Extensions)
        {
            if (fileExtension == filterExtension)
            {
                filteredFiles.Add(buffer.ToString());
                break;
            }
        }
    }

    _fileNames = filteredFiles.ToArray();

    _commandIdentifier = (firstCommand + id) - 1;

    CommandRegistration(_fileNames);

    id = (_commandIdentifier++);
}

MenuItemInfo menuItemInfo = new MenuItemInfo();

menuItemInfo.Size = 48;
menuItemInfo.ID = id++;
menuItemInfo.SubMenu = (int)_popupMenu;
menuItemInfo.TypeData = MenuTitle;
menuItemInfo.Mask = (uint)Native.MaskFlags.Type |
```

```
                                        (uint)Native.MaskFlags.State |
                                        (uint)Native.MaskFlags.SubMenu |
                                        (uint)Native.MaskFlags.ID;
                menuItemInfo.Type = (uint)Native.MenuFlags.String;
                menuItemInfo.State = (uint)Native.MenuFlags.Enabled;

                Native.InsertMenuItem(menu, (uint)menuId, 1, ref menuItemInfo);

                AddMenuSeparator(menu, menuId + 1);
            }
        }
        catch (Exception exception)
        {
            HandleError(exception);
        }

        return id;
    }
```

The base class exposes a method that is used to register commands with the underlying framework and create the submenu items for the context menu. The following code shows this method. Specifying - (a hyphen) as the command text will insert a separator entry, which is useful for cleaning up menus with multiple groups of commands.

```
protected void RegisterCommand(string command)
{
    _commandPosition++;
    _commandIdentifier++;

    if (command == "-")
    {
        AddMenuSeparator(_popupMenu, (uint)(_commandPosition));
    }
    else
    {
        _commands.Add(_commandPosition, command);

        AddMenuItem(_popupMenu,
                    command,
                    _commandIdentifier,
                    (uint)(_commandPosition));
    }
}
```

The following method is used to add a submenu item to the parent menu item at the specified position.

```
void AddMenuItem(uint menu, string text, int id, uint position)
{
    MenuItemInfo menuItemInfo = new MenuItemInfo();

    menuItemInfo.Size = 48;
    menuItemInfo.ID = id;
    menuItemInfo.TypeData = text;
    menuItemInfo.Mask = (uint)Native.MaskFlags.ID |
                        (uint)Native.MaskFlags.Type |
                        (uint)Native.MaskFlags.State;
    menuItemInfo.Type = (uint)Native.MenuFlags.String;
    menuItemInfo.State = (uint)Native.MenuFlags.Enabled;

    Native.InsertMenuItem(menu, position, 1, ref menuItemInfo);
}
```

The following method is very similar to AddMenuItem(), except it inserts a separator into the parent menu item at the specified position.

```
void AddMenuSeparator(uint menu, uint position)
{
    MenuItemInfo separator = new MenuItemInfo();

    separator.Size = 48;
    separator.Mask = (uint)Native.MaskFlags.Type;
    separator.Type = (uint)Native.MenuFlags.Separator;

    Native.InsertMenuItem(menu, position, 1, ref separator);
}
```

As mentioned earlier, IContextMenu.InvokeCommand() is called when a submenu item is activated from the context menu. This is where we get the command information and pass it off to the extension to handle.

```
void IContextMenu.InvokeCommand(IntPtr pointer)
{
    try
    {
        Type type = typeof(InvokeCommandInfo);

        InvokeCommandInfo info = Marshal.PtrToStructure(pointer, type)
                                            as InvokeCommandInfo;
```

```
            HandleCommand(_commands[info.Verb - 1].ToString(), _fileNames);
        }
        catch (Exception exception)
        {
            HandleError(exception);
        }
    }
}
```

Registration of the extension component is covered later in the chapter, but it is important that the following two methods are discussed.

The RegisterExtension() method is used to place an entry in the approved shell extensions (for WINNT), and to associate the extension component with the file extensions array.

```
protected static void RegisterExtension(System.Type type,
                                        string[] extensions,
                                        string handlerName)
{
    try
    {
        string guid = InterogateGuid(type);

        if (guid.Length > 0)
        {
            RegistryKey key;

            key = Registry.LocalMachine.OpenSubKey("Software\\" +
                                                   "Microsoft\\" +
                                                   "Windows\\" +
                                                   "CurrentVersion\\" +
                                                   "Shell Extensions\\" +
                                                   "Approved", true);
            key.SetValue(guid,
                    String.Format("{0} shell extension", handlerName));
            key.Close();

            foreach (string extension in extensions)
            {
                string path = String.Format("{0}\\shellex\\ContextMenuHandlers\\{1}",
                                    extension,
                                    handlerName)
                key = Registry.ClassesRoot.CreateSubKey(path);
                key.SetValue(string.Empty, guid);
```

```
                key.Close();
            }
        }
    }
    catch (Exception)
    {
        throw;
    }
}
```

The UnregisterExtension() method is called to undo the registry changes applied by the RegisterExtension() method.

```
protected static void UnregisterExtension(System.Type type,
                                          string[] extensions,
                                          string handlerName)
{
    try
    {
        string guid = InterogateGuid(type);

        if (guid.Length > 0)
        {
            RegistryKey key;

            key = Registry.LocalMachine.OpenSubKey("Software\\" +
                                                   "Microsoft\\" +
                                                   "Windows\\" +
                                                   "CurrentVersion\\" +
                                                   "Shell Extensions\\" +
                                                   "Approved", true);
            key.DeleteValue(guid);
            key.Close();

            foreach (string extension in extensions)
            {
                string path = String.Format(
                                "{0}\\shellex\\ContextMenuHandlers\\{1}",
                                extension, handlerName)
                Registry.ClassesRoot.DeleteSubKey();
            }
        }
    }
```

```
        catch (Exception)
        {
            throw;
        }
    }
}
```

The importance of explicitly setting a guid for the extension is vital so that the Win32 registry can point to the class. The class must be decorated with a [Guid] attribute so that it can be registered with COM, but the class must also be registered with Windows, as previously discussed. Rather than hardcode the guid in the assembly and in the register and unregister methods, the following method uses reflection to extract the guid value right out of the attribute decoration. This approach is much more maintainable because the guid is only declared in a single location. The type passed to this method is the type of the extension class that is inheriting from ShellExtensionBase; that is where the [Guid] attribute is decorated.

```
private static string InterogateGuid(Type type)
{
    try
    {
        GuidAttribute[] attributes = type.GetCustomAttributes(typeof(GuidAttribute),
                                                              false)
                                                          as GuidAttribute[];

        if (attributes.Length != 0)
        {
            return "{" + attributes[0].Value + "}";
        }

        return string.Empty;
    }
    catch (Exception)
    {
        throw;
    }
}
```

The base class is now complete, so we can move on to usage. There are two ways that the extension can be built using our framework; both methods are discussed in the next two sections.

Sample Usage—Standalone

Using the framework is very easy, and most of the implementation details for the extension have already been covered. The most notable parts to mention are the RegisterServer() and UnregisterServer() methods. You will notice the ComUnregisterFunctionAttribute and ComRegisterFunctionAttribute decorations on both methods. These attributes specify the methods to call when registering or unregistering an assembly from COM; this allows for the execution of custom code during component registration. More on component registration later in this chapter, but just be aware that these methods are entry points from COM, and they simply call the RegisterExtension() and UnregisterExtension() methods in ShellExtensionBase.

```
[Guid("45A92DA6-3559-4d20-88F7-552E10779D5A"), ComVisible(true)]
public class StandAloneExtension : ShellExtensionBase
{
    protected static string[] _extensions = new string[2] { ".nxe", ".nxw" };
    protected static string _handlerName = "SimpleToolStandAlone";

    protected override string MenuTitle
    {
        get { return "SimpleTool - Stand Alone"; }
    }

    protected override string[] Extensions
    {
        get { return _extensions; }
    }

    protected override void CommandRegistration(string[] fileNames)
    {
        RegisterCommand("Do Something");
        RegisterCommand("Do Something Else");
        RegisterCommand("-");
        RegisterCommand("View Stuff");
        RegisterCommand("-");
        RegisterCommand("Simple Command 1");
        RegisterCommand("Simple Command 2");
    }

    protected override void HandleCommand(string command, string[] files)
    {
```

```csharp
        StringBuilder buffer = new StringBuilder();

        buffer.AppendFormat("Handle Command '{0}':{1}{1}",
                            command,
                            Environment.NewLine);

        foreach (string file in files)
        {
            string fileName = Path.GetFileName(file);
            buffer.AppendFormat("{0}{1}", fileName, Environment.NewLine);
        }

        MessageBox.Show(buffer.ToString());
    }

    protected override void HandleError(Exception exception)
    {
        MessageBox.Show(exception.ToString());
    }

    [System.Runtime.InteropServices.ComRegisterFunctionAttribute()]
    internal static void RegisterServer(string description)
    {
        try
        {
            RegisterExtension(typeof(SimpleToolExtension),
                                _extensions,
                                _handlerName);
        }
        catch (Exception e)
        {
            MessageBox.Show(exception.ToString());
        }
    }

    [System.Runtime.InteropServices.ComUnregisterFunctionAttribute()]
    internal static void UnregisterServer(string description)
    {
        try
        {
            UnregisterExtension(typeof(SimpleToolExtension),
                                _extensions,
                                _handlerName);
```

```
        }
        catch (Exception e)
        {
            MessageBox.Show(exception.ToString());
        }
    }
}
```

Standalone shell extensions exist as separate assemblies. This is ideal for extensions that contain the actual tool logic, or for extensions that cannot be integrated into the source code of an existing tool.

Sample Usage—Integrated

If you are able to modify the source code to your tool and if it is managed code, you can integrate the shell extension right into the code base. There are a number of benefits to this approach, but the most important is ease of deployment.

To start, we generally want to keep the logic called by the extension and the logic called by the tool in the same location for maintainability. The following code implements a simple class that processes a collection of files using a specified command.

```
public static class SimpleTool
{
    public static void ProcessFiles(string command,
                                    string[] files,
                                    bool fromExtension)
    {
        if (fromExtension)
        {
            StringBuilder buffer = new StringBuilder();

            buffer.AppendLine(String.Format("Handle Command '{0}':", command));
            buffer.AppendLine("---");

            foreach (string file in files)
            {
                buffer.AppendLine(file);
            }

            System.Windows.Forms.MessageBox.Show(buffer.ToString());
        }
        else
```

```
            {
                Console.WriteLine(String.Format("Handle Command '{0}':", command));
                Console.WriteLine("--");

                foreach (string file in files)
                {
                    Console.WriteLine(file);
                }
            }
        }
    }
}
```

For the most part, the extension code can stay the same. We will, however, modify the method that handles menu commands so that it points to the static logic class for the tool. The `fromExtension` parameter for `SimpleTool.ProcessFiles()` is set to true so that a message box is shown instead of writing the messages to the console. There is no console when executing the standalone extension.

```
protected override void HandleCommand(string command, string[] files)
{
    SimpleTool.ProcessFiles(command, files, true);
}
```

As an example, we will create a simple console application. You can pass it several files as command-line arguments, or you can use a switch to register or unregister the shell extension with the operating system. The `fromExtension` parameter for `SimpleTool.ProcessFiles()` is set to `false` so that the messages are written to the console.

```
class Program
{
    static int Main(string[] args)
    {
        Console.WriteLine("SimpleTool.exe - Simple demo to show " +
                        "how to link a tool to a shell extension.");

        if (args.Length == 1)
        {
            string option
                = args[0].Replace('-', '/').ToLower(CultureInfo.InvariantCulture);

            if (option == "/?" || args[0] == "/help")
            {
```

```
        Usage();
        return 0;
    }
    else if (option == "/u")
    {
        try
        {
            Assembly assembly = Assembly.GetExecutingAssembly();

            RegistrationServices registration
                                        = new RegistrationServices();

            registration.UnregisterAssembly(assembly);
            SimpleToolExtension.UnregisterServer("");

            Console.WriteLine("Extension unregistered successfully");
        }
        catch (Exception)
        {
            Console.WriteLine("Extension is not currently registered");
        }
    }
    else if (option == "/r")
    {
        try
        {
            Assembly assembly = Assembly.GetExecutingAssembly();
            RegistrationServices registration = new RegistrationServices();

            registration.RegisterAssembly(assembly,
                            AssemblyRegistrationFlags.SetCodeBase);
            SimpleToolExtension.RegisterServer("");

            Console.WriteLine("Extension registered successfully");
        }
        catch (Exception exception)
        {
            Console.WriteLine("Extension failed to register: " +
                            exception.ToString());
        }
    }
    else
```

```
                    {
                        Console.WriteLine("Invalid option: " + args[0]);
                        Usage();
                        return 1;
                    }
                }
                else if (args.Length >= 2)
                {
                    List<string> files = new List<string>(args);

                    string command = files[0];

                    files.RemoveAt(0);

                    SimpleTool.ProcessFiles(command, files.ToArray(), false);
                }
                else
                {
                    Usage();
                }

            return 0;
        }

        private static void Usage()
        {
            Console.WriteLine("/r - Register the shell extension " +
                            "for this tool with Explorer");
            Console.WriteLine("/u - Unregister the shell extension " +
                            "for this tool from Explorer");
        }
    }
}
```

The simple tool shell extension is now built, but it must be registered before it is functional. The next section covers how to do this.

Component Registration

Before our extension will work, we need to register it with Windows. This involves a few entries into the registry so the shell is aware of the new functionality, and it requires installation of the component into the Global Assembly Cache (GAC).

First, you must register the extension assembly as a COM component. When using a standalone extension assembly, you can do this with the `regasm.exe` command. Open the Visual Studio command prompt and execute:

```
Regasm.exe NameOfYourExtension.dll
```

This tool creates all the necessary entries to configure the assembly as a COM object. With the assembly correctly configured for COM, we now need to register the object as a shell extension. This is done with Win32 registry entries, and the code for this is in the `RegisterExtension()` method within `ShellExtensionBase`. Remember the `RegisterServer()` method that was decorated with `ComRegisterFunctionAttribute`? `Regasm` will call this static method automatically when executed, which is where we then call `RegisterExtension()` to configure the registry appropriately. Conveniently, there is also a method for unregistration that calls `UnregisterExtension()`.

After the object has been successfully configured as a shell extension, the Win32 registry will have new entries for each of the configured file extensions pointing to the `extension` class. Figure 41.1 shows the extension registered for an .nxw file.

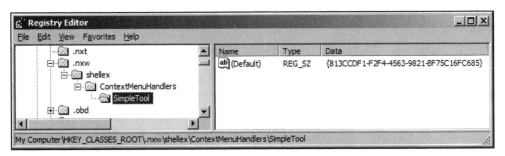

Figure 41.1 Registry key added for shell extension association.

Extensions that have been integrated with an existing managed tool are typically in the form of an executable, which will not be successfully registered with `Regasm`. To get around this, we simply use the `RegistrationServices` class of the COM interop layer, which essentially calls the same functionality that `Regasm` does, except programmatically.

You can register the extension integrated in our test console application by executing:

```
SimpleTool.exe /r
```

The /r runs the registration code, which will call the same static method that Regasm does. Conveniently, you can also use /u to unregister the integrated extension from Explorer as well.

Lastly, you must install the extension assembly (exe or dll) into the Global Assembly Cache, including the ShellExtensionBase library so that windows can find them based on the guid specified in the registry.

You can do this by either executing:

```
Gacutil.exe -i TheAssemblyToInstall
```

or by dragging the file into the assembly folder in your Windows directory.

Note

You must sign your assemblies with a strong name key in order to install them into the Global Assembly Cache. You can generate a strong name key with the sn.exe utility, or through the Signing property page for the project.

After the extension has been successfully registered, the last step is to restart the explorer.exe process so that your extension can be installed. See the next section for a way to do this.

If everything has been done correctly, you should now be able to right-click on any file with a .nxw or .nxe extension (using our example) and be able to see the new context menu. Figure 41.2 shows this context menu with both extension types installed.

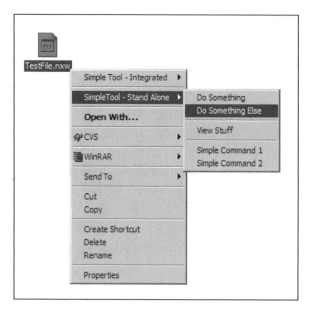

Figure 41.2
Screenshot of the context menu extension in action.

If you select a command from the extension, you will see a message similar to the one shown in Figure 41.3.

Figure 41.3
Command executed through the context menu extension.

Running the integrated executable as a normal console application will result in a message similar to the one shown in Figure 41.4.

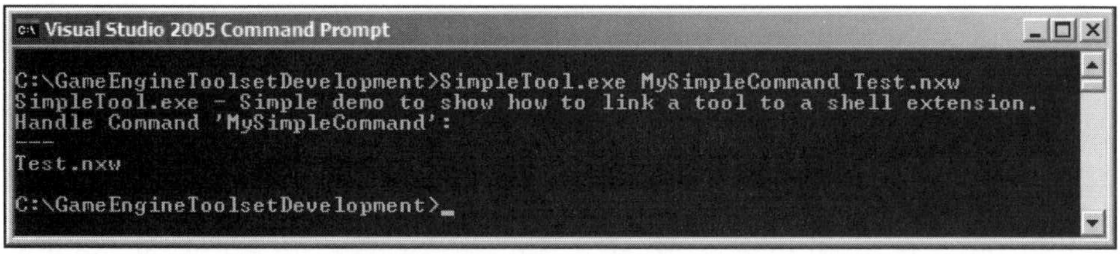

Figure 41.4 Command executed through the integrated console application.

Debugging Techniques

Developing and debugging shell extensions has never been an easy task, especially because the shell holds a copy of the previously loaded DLL. This can lead to problems overwriting the file or a change not being reflected until the shell is restarted because of the local copy in memory.

A useful trick is to build a simple Win32 C++ application using the following code, which will stop and restart the shell, removing the cached copy of the DLL.

```
#include <windows.h>
int WINAPI WinMain(HINSTANCE hInstance, HINSTANCE hPrevInstance,
                   PSTR szCmdLine, int iCmdShow)
{
    HWND hwnd = FindWindow("Progman", NULL);
    PostMessage(hwnd, WM_QUIT, 0, 0);
    ShellExecute(NULL, NULL, "explorer.exe", NULL, NULL, SW_SHOW);
    return 0;
}
```

There are some additional steps that must be taken as well. Here is the usual process for reloading a new extension dll.

1. Remove the existing extension dll and ShellExtension.dll file from the GAC.
2. Recompile your extension dll.
3. Place your extension and the ShellExtension.dll file back into the GAC.
4. Restart the Windows shell using the above technique.

Note

You do not need to register your associations in the registry again unless the guid for your component changes.

Conclusion

In this chapter, I discussed what a shell extension is, and how to create a context menu extension in C#. Although extensions can be tricky to write and debug at times, they can offer a significant boost to productivity and workflow. There are a number of types of shell extensions that can be created, but covering them all would require a book in itself.

It was the intent of this chapter to discuss shell extensions, and then ramp up into the development of a reusable framework that can be used to quickly develop context menu extensions in the shortest amount of time possible.

TECHNIQUES TO INCREASE PRODUCTIVITY

Computer /nm./: a device designed to speed and automate errors.
—From the Jargon File

Perhaps the goal of every single company is to increase productivity, and although the idea may sound simple, actually doing so can be quite a feat to accomplish. There are many levels where productivity could be increased, but the chapters in Part VIII will focus on a couple of techniques that can be employed in your tools to boost productivity for your users. Part VIII focuses on process automation, while Part VII mainly focused on productivity from a user interface perspective.

Essentially, productivity is the overall measure of an output quantity generated by a given input quantity. An increase in productivity comes from an existing process generating a larger output quantity using the regular input quantity. The increase mainly results from a more efficient use of resources due to process improvements or other achievements. The chapters in this part describe a couple of techniques for automating components of your tools in order to produce more output quantity compared to the original approach.

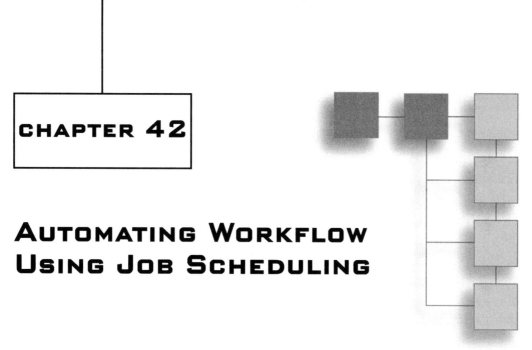

CHAPTER 42

AUTOMATING WORKFLOW
USING JOB SCHEDULING

Just because you don't know a technology, doesn't mean you won't be called upon to work with it.

Mike Bongiovanni

Job scheduling has become an increasingly important role of computers. They are most effective at automatically carrying out the scheduled routines of an organization. Some analysts believe that the level of job scheduling and process automation is altering the way workflow and business is done today. In actuality, the level of automation used within software products or workflow pipelines is a result of the growing needs of the industry. The industry is largely responsible for the increased reliance on enhanced process automation, not the technology itself.

Some common applications for job scheduling include report generation, batch conversion or compression of game assets, nightly system backups of source code and game assets, and moving concept art from the "completed" folder on one artist's machine into the "to be modeled" folder on another artist's machine. The possibilities for this technology and how it relates to workflow enhancement are nearly limitless.

There are a variety of job scheduling systems on the market that all support an exhausting number of features, but essentially there are two fundamental components: job and scheduler.

A job can be defined as a unit of work orchestrated by a computer to perform a task in an automated fashion. Multiple jobs can be composed together to form a larger workflow process, or they can operate independently of each other. Jobs can be run at a specific date and time or on a reoccurring basis specified by a time span interval.

The job scheduler is typically responsible for the continuous monitoring and notification of processes and event-driven jobs, scheduling of operational reports, and the monitoring of performance. Jobs are registered with the scheduler, and it is the duty of the scheduler to provide the mechanism that ensures the orderly and timely processing of the jobs at the time or interval specified.

Most of the leading scheduling systems provide a graphical user interface that offers a single point of control for a distributed environment of processes. This chapter addresses the development of a reusable core framework that offers a flexible mechanism for generic job scheduling.

Benefits

Most companies have a multitude of processes and workflows that define how their business operates. There are some significant benefits that result from the integration of all the disparate processes into a cohesive and automated workflow.

It is a commonly known fact that an automated process will be more reliable and less prone to error than a human operator. The less time required from human effort to perform a particular task will free that human effort for assignment to more thought-intensive problems, resulting in a considerable cost savings.

Another benefit is the increase in productivity. Almost every software company, especially within the gaming industry, is faced with the dilemma that product development must be crunched into a seemingly impossible time span. Batch processing and workflow automation allow for an increase in the amount of work performed in a shorter period of time.

Aside from the financial and increased resource gains, there are a number of operational and quality assurance benefits that result from automation. Human effort is prone to errors, whereas a properly configured computerized job will execute in the same manner every time it is run, reducing the probability of error.

Solution Goals

It may seem silly, but the key goal of the solution is to support the automation of processes. The user should be able to define a job, register the job within the scheduler, and feel confident that the process will be executed at the appropriate time.

Earlier, workflow management was discussed as a common application for job scheduling, but this chapter is meant to focus on the technology behind the scheduling itself, not business process or workflow. Near the end of the chapter, some goals are discussed that would be applicable to a scheduling system that managed workflow.

The solution must also ensure that data is efficiently processed in a generic manner. Each job performs a different role, but the core functionality remains the same. The framework must provide a mechanism to pass arbitrary data through a job efficiently.

Two job scheduling modes are available: exact and time span. The exact mode specifies a specific date and time that a job will be executed. The job will fire once and then be promptly removed from the scheduler. The time span mode specifies an interval at which a job will be executed on a recurring basis.

Implementation

The namespaces used in the implementation are very simple, shown with the following code. Be sure to reference System.Timers so that you have access to the .NET Timer object.

```
using System;
using System.Timers;
```

As outlined in the solution goals, the core framework will support two different scheduling modes. The following enumeration will be used within the job and scheduler components to distinguish between the two modes.

```
public enum ScheduleMode
{
    Exact,
    Span
}
```

The following class implements the event arguments that are passed in the event handler when a job is executed.

```
public class JobTriggeredEventArgs : EventArgs
{
    private ScheduleMode _mode;
    private Object   _userData;
```

```
    public ScheduleMode Mode
    {
        get { return _mode; }
    }

    public Object UserData
    {
        get { return _userData; }
    }

    public JobTriggeredEventArgs(ScheduleMode mode, Object userData)
    {
        _mode = mode;
        _userData = userData;
    }
}
```

The following class implements the functionality behind a job and the timing mechanism that controls it.

```
public abstract class JobBase
{
    private ScheduleMode    _mode;
    private Timer           _jobTimer;
    private Object          _userData;
    private Scheduler       _schedule;

    protected JobBase(Scheduler schedule, ScheduleMode mode)
    {
        _schedule = schedule;
        _mode = mode;
    }

    public Timer JobTimer
    {
        get { return _jobTimer; }
        set { _jobTimer = value; }
    }

    public ScheduleMode Mode
    {
        get { return _mode; }
    }
```

```csharp
    public object UserData
    {
        get { return _userData; }
        set { _userData = value; }
    }

    internal void ElapsedInterval(object sender, ElapsedEventArgs e)
    {
        if (Triggered != null)
            Triggered(sender, new JobTriggeredEventArgs(_mode, _userData));

        _schedule.Trigger(_mode, _userData);

        if (_mode.Equals(ScheduleMode.Exact))
        {
            _schedule.Remove(_userData);
        }
    }

    public event EventHandler<JobTriggeredEventArgs> Triggered;
}
```

The following class describes a job that occurs at a specific date and time.

```csharp
public class JobExact : JobBase
{
    public JobExact(Scheduler schedule,
                    DateTime startTime,
                    DateTime finishTime)
        : base(schedule, ScheduleMode.Exact)
    {
        TimeSpan period = finishTime - startTime;

        base.JobTimer = new Timer(period.TotalMilliseconds);
        base.JobTimer.Elapsed += new ElapsedEventHandler(ElapsedInterval);
        base.JobTimer.AutoReset = false;
    }
}
```

The following class describes a job that occurs at a recurring interval.

```csharp
public class JobSpan : JobBase
{
```

```
    public JobSpan(Scheduler schedule, TimeSpan interval)
        : base(schedule, ScheduleMode.Span)
    {

        base.JobTimer = new Timer(interval.TotalMilliseconds);
        base.JobTimer.Elapsed += new ElapsedEventHandler(ElapsedInterval);
        base.JobTimer.AutoReset = true;
    }
}
```

The final step in implementing a job scheduler is to develop the scheduling component itself. At this point, we have two different flavors of jobs that can be registered: jobs that execute at a particular date and time and jobs that can execute at a given interval on a recurring basis. Basically, each JobBase object has an internal timer that is configured for the job, and it is the responsibility of the scheduler to manage the timers and track all registered jobs. While relatively simple, the scheduler is an important part of an automation system. The following code describes the implementation of the scheduler in its entirety.

```
using System;
using System.Collections.Generic;

public class Scheduler : IDisposable
{
    private SortedList<Object, JobBase> _jobList;

    public SortedList<Object, JobBase> JobList
    {
        get { return _jobList; }
    }

    public Scheduler()
    {
        _jobList = new SortedList<Object, JobBase>();
    }

    public void Add(object key, JobBase job)
    {
        try
        {
            _jobList.Add(key, job);
            job.UserData = key;
            job.JobTimer.Start();
```

```csharp
        }
        catch (Exception exception)
        {
            System.Diagnostics.Debug.WriteLine(exception.Message);
            throw;
        }
    }

    public void Remove(object key)
    {
        _jobList[key].JobTimer.Dispose();
        _jobList.Remove(key);
    }

    public JobBase this[object key]
    {
        get { return _jobList[key]; }
        set { _jobList[key] = value; }
    }

    public void Trigger(ScheduleMode mode, Object userData)
    {
        if (Triggered != null)
        {
            Triggered(this, new JobTriggeredEventArgs(mode, userData));
        }
    }

    public void IDisposable.Dispose()
    {
        foreach (JobBase job in _jobList.Values)
        {
            job.JobTimer.Dispose();
        }
    }

    public event EventHandler<JobTriggeredEventArgs> Triggered;
}
```

Conclusion

In this chapter, I discussed the need for job scheduling, some common uses for it, and how to implement a framework that provides enough of a mechanism to create jobs and register them within a scheduler for execution. At the beginning of this chapter, it was stated that all scheduling systems have jobs and a scheduler, no matter what other enhancements or "cool features" are included. Some systems support a transaction layer that can recover from a job failure and, in some cases, can even restart the job!

You may also be wondering what type of harness is needed to control the job system, and typically a Windows service would do the job nicely. Building a Windows service is beyond the scope of this chapter, but it would be ideal to place the code for your job manager within such a service.

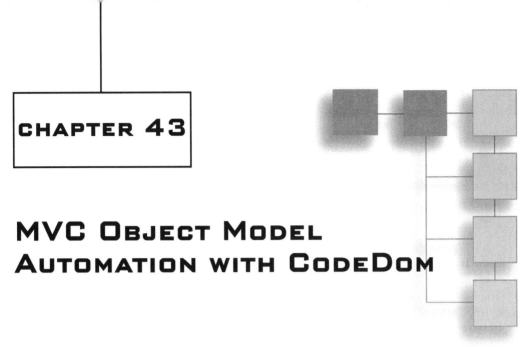

CHAPTER 43

MVC OBJECT MODEL AUTOMATION WITH CODEDOM

"Every minute spent on infrastructure programming is a wasted minute."

Juval Lowy, .NET Software Legend, April 2003

Users of an application or tool vary in their levels of knowledge and technical competence. Some users can alter configuration files to optimize the application for their environment, or access public APIs to extend the software, while others barely get by with the self-help guides and manuals. Catering to this diversity of simple users and power users can be quite challenging, and doing so in a clean and maintainable way is even harder. How can you provide enough advanced functionality to power users, without cluttering up the interface and confusing simple users? Welcome to the wonderful concept of extensibility.

There are a number of ways to develop an extensible application, such as plugin support, but one concept that is repeatedly ignored or abused is having a rich object model that is decoupled from the presentation layer, with support for script interaction and automation. Almost every Microsoft application, especially those included in the Office suite, is built on top of a rich object model that has support for automation. This level of extensibility allows any developer to create and manipulate content or to automate functionality and actions within the application. Scripts can be written to extend these applications to suit the needs of the power users.

Sadly, the majority of applications available do not offer the level of extensibility that the Microsoft products provide, and this is generally because of budget and time constraints. The ideal solution to this problem would be a solid and proven design from the ground up that would pave the way for flexible extensibility support. Typically, rich object models that support extensibility are developed with respect to the Model-View-Controller design pattern, but this chapter will present a slight deviation from this common approach, using .NET delegates to provide a truly decoupled architecture. This chapter will also show how to embed a command window, such as the one found in Visual Studio .NET, to write and execute script macros at runtime within the application.

Advantages of an Automatable Object Model

Many benefits are derived from developing an object model that supports automation, but I will list only a handful of them since that should be enough to convince you. One of the biggest benefits is that a rich object model decouples the user interface from the business logic. Quite often, the user interface is entangled with business logic and becomes hard to maintain. The user interface code can be so dependent on the business logic that a single change to the business logic can break the entire application, and vice versa for changes to the user interface code. This occurrence is generally a result of developers focusing first on the user interface when they are assigned a task. Building the user interface, even a rough prototype, before the business logic is a bad idea because the design of your business logic will reflect the constraints and design ideas behind the way your user interface is designed. Business logic should be user interface-agnostic.

A rich object model causes developers to focus on the design behind small units of work instead of the entire application, or "the big picture." Focusing on a small unit of work usually results in cleaner and more reliable code. For example, imagine a part of the application that shows the user a file listing in a tree view. Normally, a developer would design the system with the tree view control in mind. A developer thinking about the object model, however, would ignore the fact that there is a user interface. He would focus strictly on file and directory entities, processing functionality such as determining a hierarchical list of files and folders from a parent folder, and how these entities fit into the rest of the model. The new functionality in the object model can then be consumed by whatever component is using it, in this case the user interface of the application. The developer could now display this relationship of entities in multiple tree view controls, or other controls altogether, without altering the model. If the user interface had been considered, he might have been stuck with file loading code mixed in with the code of the tree view control, forcing him to copy and paste code or refactor.

On the other side of the fence, developers working on the user interface only have to know that any files added to a collection in the object model are to be displayed in the appropriate controls. They do not care where these files come from, just so long as they are notified accordingly when files are made available for display.

Another nice feature of a decoupled object model is the ability to distribute responsibility for the implementation of certain aspects to different developers without their having to worry about how the other components work. Again, as long as the appropriate notifications are fired, the villagers are content. If you have a developer who shows the file listing in a tree view, she will not care about another developer who shows the same listing in an HTML page that is generated with XSL transforms. Both developers only care that the object model contains model objects that will fire the appropriate notifications when certain situations arise.

Lastly, having an object model that supports automation is a godsend to functional and defect testing. It is very easy to write scripts to test user interface and business logic behaviors when the underlying architecture supports this automation natively.

Comparison with Model-View-Controller Pattern

To start, it is important to cover the Model-View-Controller (MVC) pattern before doing a comparison because this chapter discusses a slightly enhanced version of MVC. The MVC pattern, or paradigm, encompasses breaking a section or all of an application into three parts: the model, the view, and the controller.

The *model* manages information and handles the notification of observers when the related information changes. The model only contains information and functionality that match a common purpose. If you need to model multiple groups of unrelated information and functionality, you create multiple models. This is important so that your business logic remains modular and decoupled. The model serves as an abstraction of a real world system or process. As an example, a model could be a relationship between file and directory entries, and could contain functionality to load them from the file system or network. There is no user interface code for displaying the entities within the model; the user interface code is handled by the views.

The *view* handles transforming the models to be displayed in an appropriate display context. A view is usually attached to a single display surface and renders to that surface using transformed information from the models attached to it. The view automatically renders the information again when the information in the model changes. It is quite common to have multiple views attached to the same model but rendering information to many unique display surfaces. A view can be composite, containing sub-views that can each themselves contain sub-views. As an example, a view could be a tree view that will display hard drive files in a hierarchical fashion.

The *controller* is the interface point between the user and the application. The controller reads input sent by the user and instructs the model and view to act according to the type of input received. As an example, when the user clicks a button, the controller is responsible for determining how the application will respond.

The model, view, and controller form a triumvirate, so they must reference each other as shown in Figure 43.1.

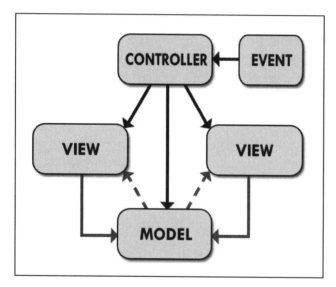

Figure 43.1
Common approach to the Model-View-Controller pattern.

To explain, an event occurs that propagates to the controller. The controller then changes the model, the view, or both accordingly. If the model changes, events can be sent to the views; an example could be a request for a redisplay of information. If need be, the views can go fetch data from the model to display. This pattern requires that each view must understand the relationship and schema of the model.

It is for this reason that I present a slightly different spin on this paradigm, using the native event mechanisms of the .NET platform in an attempt to further decouple this excellent pattern from being directly tied between views and model. The pattern used in this chapter is basically the Model-View-Controller paradigm, except .NET delegates, and events are used to pass data between model and views. Such a variation can resemble Figure 43.2.

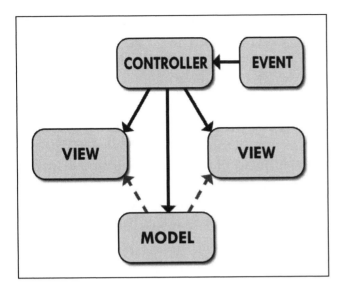

Figure 43.2
Modified version of the
Model-View-Controller pattern.

The variation will still require that the controller know the type of views and model used, but we should be able to build a system where a view does not need to know the type of model being observed. You may be wondering why a view does not know about the controller sending commands to it. This is so there are as few dependencies as possible, making it easy to swap controllers in and out of the system without breaking any references.

A Simple Object Model Architecture

Microsoft Word is an excellent case study when studying object models, but covering the entire design would be a complete book in itself. Instead, I will give you a very small overview of a small subset of the object model so that hopefully you will understand the way the object model in Word is designed. After that I will discuss the small object model that the example in this chapter employs, along with some of the more important code snippets.

The root of the Microsoft Word object model starts with the `Application` class, which is basically a singleton that provides access to all the toolbars, documents, windows, menus, status bars, alerts, dialogs, and so forth. The entire application can be accessed by this singleton, which can do things like manipulate content in documents, change menu labels, update a status bar, click user interface elements such as buttons, add command bars, and so forth. As an example, you can display an open file dialog by calling `Application.Documents.Open()`. If you need to change a value such as the title of the document, you do not have to worry about executing the code that Word invokes to change a document title. You can instead find the `Document` instance in the `Application.Documents` collection and modify the `Name` property. The user interface will automatically reflect the new change, thanks to the power of an object model that supports automation.

Prior to learning the Model-View-Controller paradigm, I used to think that large applications like Word or Visual Studio just had a massive amount of code that performed a whole slew of tasks when an event, such as a file being deleted, occurred. The complexity and unmaintainability of such a solution gave me shivers. When I discovered this wonderful pattern, I began to relax and understand that these applications are actually not that complicated. But experience and learning from past mistakes is the way to constantly improve and write better code.

The object model for the example in this chapter is far from a real world system. Instead, it exists solely to show how all the pieces fit together into an architecture that has decoupled views from the model, and automation script support using the `CodeDom` compiler. Showing a full-featured object model in this chapter would make it even more difficult to understand the underlying principles behind what this chapter really covers.

The actual implementation details behind the example on the Companion Web site are covered near the end of this chapter.

Plugin-Based Architectures

I will not talk much about plugin architectures, since this topic is addressed in Chapter 38, "Designing an Extensible Plugin-Based Architecture." I will, however, discuss how a robust object model can make your life much easier when building a system that supports plugin extensibility.

When it comes to extensibility, having a rich object model that supports automation is ideal for plugin-based architectures. Theoretically, if your object model is robust enough that you can perform all tasks programmatically, any plugins that are exposed to this object model can extend all aspects of the application.

Supporting extensibility with a rich object model and plugins reduces the amount of code that exists in the core assemblies, resulting in a number of advantages. The first advantage is that your working set is greatly reduced, only loading plugins when needed (provided you are unloading the assemblies from a second application domain when they are no longer in use). A reduced working set results in less memory being required to run your application, and overall loading and execution times are reduced.

In addition to a reduced working set, the core application will be lightweight and contain very little business logic. Such a design would make patching and repairing the application really easy because you would just have to patch or repair a subset of the logic that exists within an external plugin assembly.

As an example, say, for instance, that you have a model viewer application, which renders 3D models that are structured in your proprietary format. You could have plugins that add import options for different third-party formats to the file menu. These import plugins could extend the application to be able to handle different formats and convert the end result into the proprietary format. If you deploy the application on a machine where importing is unnecessary, you could simply remove the external assemblies from the plugins directory.

Controlling an Object Model with Scripts

Perhaps the most powerful extensibility feature of an application is the ability to write scripts to automate processes and use case flows. Automation can lead to a number of benefits, including a substantial increase in productivity for tedious and repetitive tasks. Imagine that you have hundreds of source code files, to which you must prepend a new copyright comment block. You could do this manually, but it could take you an hour or more, depending on the project. To save a significant amount of time, you could write a script in Visual Studio .NET that iterates through the documents in the solution tree and modifies the text within them automatically.

Another excellent application for integrated script support is in the realm of testing: functional, performance, and defects. A script could be written to verify that a particular process or flow works, or a script that determines the elapsed running time for an intensive calculation, or a script that unit tests the user interface and business logic looking for errors.

As an example, let's look at the Visual Studio .NET 2005 IDE. One mechanism for script support is the Command Window, which lets you write a line of code and instantly execute it. This feature is shown in Figure 43.3.

The Command Window is great for simple evaluations and expressions, but the functionality of this feature pales in comparison to the power of the macro support in Visual Studio .NET. As mentioned earlier, almost all Microsoft products use the same object model, which is probably the most robust object model available for any application on the market. There are a variety of ways to access this object model, such as extensions and plugins, but one approach is to script macros within the IDE. These macros can be saved and reused across projects. Figure 43.4 shows the macro editor in Visual Studio .NET 2005.

Figure 43.3
Visual Studio .NET 2005
Command Window.

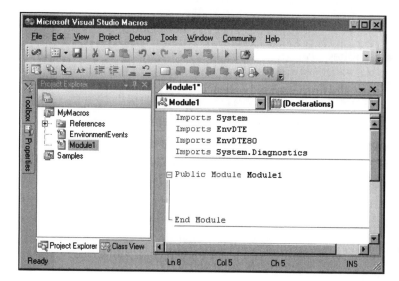

Figure 43.4
Visual Studio .NET 2005
Macro Editor.

The interface is very similar to the regular code editor that you are used to, just with fewer options. After a macro has been written to perform a particular task, you can map the macro to a key-binding or a toolbar button, or you can access it directly from the macro explorer pane, as shown in Figure 43.5.

Figure 43.5
Visual Studio .NET 2005 Macro Explorer.

The Microsoft object model takes automation even further and allows you to record scripts based on actions you perform in the application, which can later be played back to repeat. This level of extensibility is very powerful, but it's tricky to get right. You must build your architecture from the ground up with this level of extensibility in mind, or you will fail. If you manage to pull it off though, your power users will kiss the ground you walk on for making their productive lives that much more enjoyable.

Implementing a C# Command Window

Before moving on to the implementation details behind the object model and the Model-View-Controller pattern, let's focus on code generation with CodeDom. We will use this powerful .NET feature to compile C# code at runtime with which we can automate our application (through the object model).

We can start by referencing the namespaces that we will be using.

```
using System;
using System.Text; // For StringBuilder
using System.Reflection; // For the Assembly type
using System.CodeDom.Compiler; // For CSharpCodeProvider support
using System.Collections.Specialized; // For StringCollection
using Microsoft.CSharp; // For CSharpCodeProvider support
```

Basically, what we are building is a class that can take a string of C# source code and compile it to an in-memory assembly. This assembly will contain a method that can be invoked to run whatever script we have written.

```
namespace SampleApp.Scripting
{
    using ObjectModel;

    public class ScriptEngine
    {
```

Regardless of the script logic, there will always be identical stub code that must be compiled in order to generate correct source code that will support runtime automation. Rather than having the user write the same stub code every time, we will provide a simple method that takes in a string containing C# code and wraps it within a default layer of stub code. The following code shows the method to generate the stub wrapper code. Take note of the namespace, class, and method names.

```
        private string StubWrapper(string innerCode)
        {
```

```
        }
```

The next method is the meat of our scripting engine; it is in charge of building complete source code, including the stub code, setting up the CodeDom compiler instance, and building the in-memory assembly for execution. A notable area is the list of references where you specify the dependencies to include. Keep this reference list as small as possible for security. The user should only have access to the functionality you provide.

Caution

Do not add every class library in the .NET framework for the heck of it. Many problems will arise from this, including a number of security vulnerabilities, even with code access security configured. The rule of thumb is to list only the references you need after carefully considering what your users need access to.

The next important area is where compilation errors are handed. Do not worry about the code lines that reference ObjectHost; we will cover that shortly. You can, however, notice the information that is available for each error. We can use this information to display compilation errors to the user when we build the user interface for our command window.

Finally, the most important area is near the end, where reflection is used to find the Run() method within our in-memory assembly after compilation. This method is then executed to run the script logic sent to this class.

The following method describes the compilation logic for the script engine.

```
        public bool Execute(string innerCode)
        {
```

```
        }
    }
}
```

The harness code that uses the scripting engine is not overly complex, but is large enough that it would be a waste of space and reading time to place it all in this chapter. Rather, I will just show you a couple of screenshots of the command window, error listing, and script output window.

Figure 43.6 shows our new command window. Clicking Run passes the code within the textbox into the scripting engine and executes it. If no errors are encountered, the tab control switches to the Output page, otherwise the tab control switches to the Errors and Warnings page.

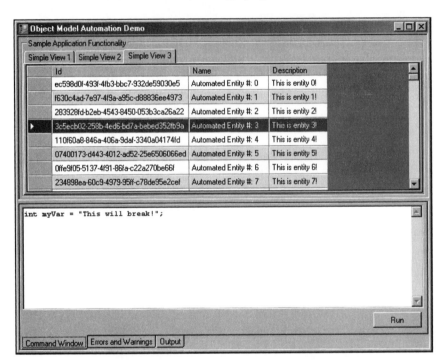

Figure 43.6 Integrated C# command window for automation.

As you can see from the code in Figure 43.6, we are trying to initialize an integer value to a string. Obviously, this will generate a compilation error and inform us that we are too tired to write any worthwhile code. When attempting to run this code, you will end up with an error like the one shown in Figure 43.7.

If a script executes successfully, you will be redirected to the Output page of the tab control, which displays any script output that was printed during execution. Figure 43.8 shows some output that is printed when executing the example provided with this chapter.

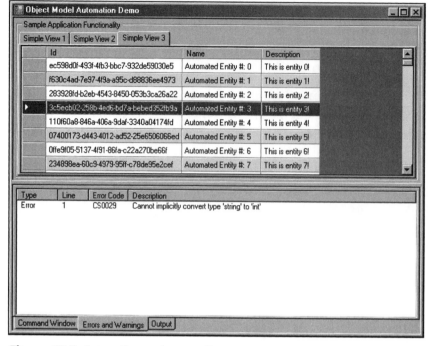

Figure 43.7 Automation engine compiler errors.

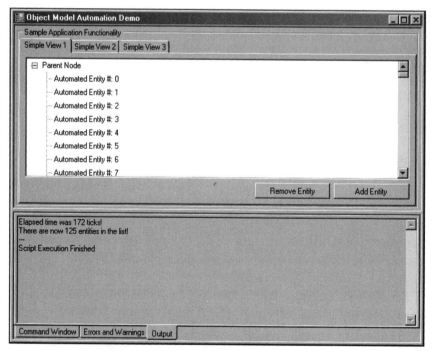

Figure 43.8 Output results shown after execution.

By referencing the object model assembly in the CodeDom instance, we can now execute any code in the command window that can be expressed in the compiled code for the application that uses the object model.

Simple Automation and MVC Example

The previous section gave a quick inside look at the example for this chapter, and now we are going to dive right into the heart of everything. We are going to make an application that serves no real world applicability, but it demonstrates all of the concepts discussed in this chapter. To start, we are going to need some sort of data object to exist in our model, so let's declare the following entity class.

```
namespace SampleApp.Entities
{
    public class SimpleEntity
    {
```

Note

The full source code for this class is available on the Companion Web site.

```
    }
}
```

Note

The full source code for the example will not be presented, so it may be difficult to see how the assemblies are composed and where each class belongs. It is safe to assume that whatever namespace a class is declared in is also the name of the assembly in which it resides.

Before covering the event system for our object model, we will need a custom EventArgs class that can store a SimpleEntity object. This class will be used to transport entity data between views and the controller inside the events.

The following code defines the EventArgs class for SimpleEntity events.

```
namespace SampleApp.Entities
{
    public class SimpleEntityEventArgs : EventArgs
    {
```

Note

The full source code for this class is available on the Companion Web site.

```
        }
    }
```

Note

The entity object and `EventArgs` class exist in a separate assembly from the rest of the application, so that the assembly containing the views does not have to reference the object model assembly.

The example has three sample views, each of which displays the `SimpleEntity` data in a different way. The beauty of the Model-View-Controller paradigm is that the object model does not care about the views, so the user interface code is decoupled from the business logic. We can also add or remove views without breaking the object model.

Earlier in this chapter, I gave a very brief overview of how the root level of the Microsoft Word object model is designed. The accompanying example has a similar approach to the Application object, except it is called `ObjectHost` so that I do not have to override the type name used by the `System.Windows.Forms.Application` class.

```
namespace SampleApp.ObjectModel
{
    using Entities;

    public class ObjectHost
    {
```

Note

The full source code for this class is available on the Companion Web site.

```
    }
}
```

You probably noticed the `EnhancedBindingList` class. This class is an inherited version of the `BindingList` collection that exists in `System.ComponentModel`. This class is a generic collection template just like `List<T>`, except it supports event notifications for when the data in the list changes. These events are used to notify the views of changes to the data. Unfortunately, the delete event for `BindingList` does not store a reference to the object being deleted; it only references the index where the object used to be stored.

I did not want to have an associated list of references to return the deleted object, so I added an override for the `RemoveItem` method so I could store a reference to the object being deleted. The following code describes the `EnhancedBindingList` collection.

```
namespace SampleApp.ObjectModel
{
    public class EnhancedBindingList<T> : BindingList<T>
    {
```

Note

The full source code for this class is available on the Companion Web site.

```
    }
}
```

Our object model is now built (I did not lie when I said it was too simple to be real-world applicable!) so we can start linking events. The first events we will link are related to the script engine. Specifically, we want to handle the event for errors that occur, the event for displaying script output, and the event for code execution that uses our scripting engine. Additionally, we will tie into the event the handles application exceptions.

The following code shows how these events are linked and implemented in the example on the Companion Web site.

```
namespace SampleApp
{
    using ObjectModel;
    using Scripting;
    using Entities;

    public partial class MainForm : Form
    {
```

Note

The full source code for this class is available on the Companion Web site.

```
    }
}
```

We now want to link up some views to display the information contained in the object model. The first view we will implement is a TreeView that just lists SimpleEntity nodes under a parent node. The following code shows the event handling for this type of view.

```
namespace SampleApp
{
```

```
using ObjectModel;
using Entities;

public partial class SimpleView1 : UserControl
{
```

Note

The full source code for this class is available on the Companion Web site.

```
}
}
```

This first view resembles the one shown in Figure 43.9 when shown in the running application.

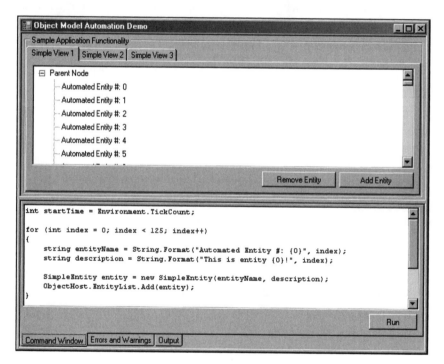

Figure 43.9 Screenshot of tree style display of the object model data.

The second view we will implement is a ListView in detail mode that displays more information about the entity data than was shown in the first view. The following code shows the event handling for this type of view.

```
namespace SampleApp
{
    using ObjectModel;
    using Entities;

    public partial class SimpleView2 : UserControl
    {
```

Note

The full source code for this class is available on the Companion Web site.

```
    }
}
```

This second view resembles Figure 43.10 when shown in the running application.

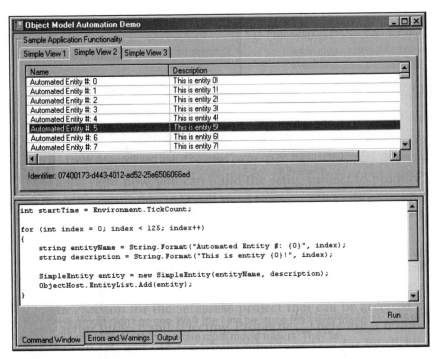

Figure 43.10 Screenshot of list style display of the object model data.

Finally, the third view we will implement is to show the power of .NET databinding. This view is a DataGrid control that is bound to the EnhancedBindingList class that holds our SimpleEntity objects. We do not need to implement any logic behind adding and removing objects because this is all handled beautifully by the built-in features of databound controls.

```
namespace SampleApp
{
    using ObjectModel;
    using Entities;

    public partial class SimpleView3 : UserControl
    {
```

Note

The full source code for this class is available on the Companion Web site.

```
    }
}
```

This third view resembles the one shown in Figure 43.11 when shown in the running application.

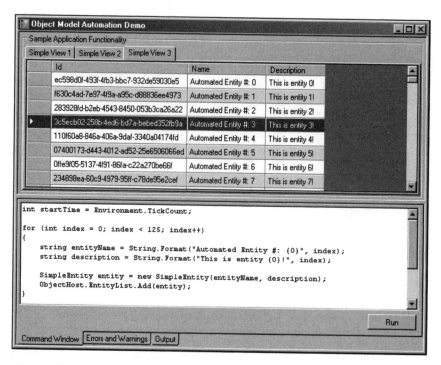

Figure 43.11 Screenshot of a DataGrid bound to the object model data.

The DataGrid view is great because we do not have to put in much code to get it up and running. The downside is a little bit of a performance hit compared to the other views because of an insane number of reflection calls when the row count gets fairly high. It's all about the right tool for the job!

Conclusion

A number of problems arise when an application contains a variety of presentation layer code, business logic, and data access code. These applications are often difficult to maintain and extend because of all the dependencies between different components. Usually any change, even the smallest one, breaks compilation and calls for a bit of refactoring to get the application back together. Tightly coupled architectures make it difficult to reuse components, often resulting in copy-paste solutions or other ungodly hacks. The Model-View-Controller design pattern is widely used for desktop application development, and I guarantee that you will see a significant improvement in the overall maintainability and extensibility of your application if you consider this wonderful paradigm. It will make your application and components much more reusable, provide you with a decoupling of your business logic and presentation layer, and cleanly support extensibility mechanisms such as plugins and integrated scripting.

Integrated scripting is not necessary for many applications, especially small throwaway tools, but for large applications where you anticipate a fair amount of content to be created, you should definitely consider implementing some form of automation support to reduce the time spent on performing tedious and repetitive tasks. Doing so can save a significant amount of time, money, and patience.

## PART IX

TECHNIQUES FOR DEPLOYMENT AND SUPPORT

"Dating a girl is just like writing software. Everything's going to work just fine in the testing lab (dating), but as soon as you have a contract with a customer (marriage), then your program (life) is going to be facing new situations you never expected. You'll be forced to patch the code (admit you're wrong) and then the code (wife) will just end up all bloated and unmaintainable in the end."

scott1853

As technology advances, the complexities surrounding deployment and support increase, causing some concern with the Total Cost of Ownership (TCO). The endless permutations of hardware, software, and security constraints cause migraines for deployment managers everywhere. If you cannot get your software into the hands of your users, and easily, then what good is your software? Some tools are meant for internal use, where you often know the hardware and software profile of your target machines, but external tools that are available to the general public are a different story. External tools require additional machine profile testing, and they require an efficient way to access any software updates that are available.

There is never a single "correct solution" in regards to deployment, as the appropriateness of a solution is dependent on project-specific factors. There are, however, common techniques and approaches that can be applied to your tools when the time comes, in order to lessen the burden of deployment management.

The chapters in Part IX focus on these techniques and approaches, and show you some situations where a particular technology is an ideal match for the end solution. A couple of traditional deployment techniques are covered, as well as technology that is new to Microsoft .NET 2.0.

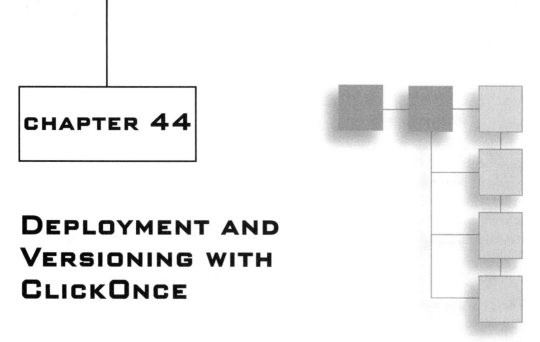

CHAPTER 44

DEPLOYMENT AND VERSIONING WITH CLICKONCE

Version 1 of any software is full of bugs. Version 2 fixes all the bugs and is great. Version 3 adds all the things users ask for, but hides all the great stuff in Version 2.

Fred Blechman

Configuration management has always been an integral component of the software development life cycle because its main purpose is to efficiently handle the evolving nature of software design. The deployment and support of a product often causes many headaches and problems, especially with regards to updating the user base with the latest software version. It is for this reason that there is such a following around thin-client architectures and web-based solutions. A change is generally only needed in a single location on the server to affect all connected users. Imagine a company with a thousand machines that use a particular software application. If it is deployed as a desktop application, you must rely on the user to perform updates because of the large user base.

There are virtually limitless varieties of machine configurations within the user base of a software product, and the components and code of desktop applications must run on all of them. So many different configurations of software can also lead to the infamous "DLL Hell" that has haunted configuration management for many years. There is also a large assortment of security profiles within any organization of reasonable size, so it is important that software run under a diverse range of security permissions.

There are problems and limitations with web applications, especially when it comes to performance, security, and browser limitations. The biggest limitation with a web application is the lack of offline support. Additionally, user interface functionality is quite poor; things like drag and drop support is very hard or even impossible to do. Web applications also consume a lot of server resources and bandwidth because things have to be done with a round trip to the server, followed by a waiting period. Applications that require print support are limited to "print screen" with hardly any formatting control. There are some plugins and ActiveX controls that help to alleviate these problems, but they tend to suffer from the same deployment problems that a lot of the desktop applications have. The ideal solution would be to find a balance between web and desktop application deployment.

There have been some past attempts to remove these burdens from configuration and deployment managers, but no single solution has presented itself that could solve all the problems. Aside from traditional deployment methods like MSI packages, the initial release of the .NET 1.0 Framework provided the ability to launch applications directly from a web site such as http://localhost/application.exe (also known as href-exes), but this method usually required security policy changes on the client, which meant that an MSI package had to be run first. This method does not support the idea of an offline mode.

Recently, a couple of managed libraries were made available that aided in the updating of application versions. Both the Updater Application Block (UAB) and Jamie Cool's AppUpdater libraries support the ability to download new versions of a product to the desktop, eliminating the security and performance concerns of href-exes. The downloaded applications are stored on the local disk, so offline mode was supported.

Version 2.0 of the Microsoft Visual Studio .NET and the Microsoft .NET Framework provide a new technology called ClickOnce, which allows us to develop desktop applications that are deployed using a safe, system-controlled and secure installation process, and are updated automatically from a centralized server location. This is all made possible because .NET applications are designed for application isolation and zero-impact deployment (also known as xcopy deployment).

This chapter will cover the creation, deployment, launching, and updating of a ClickOnce application using the Visual Studio 2005 IDE. ClickOnce deployment can be done manually by copying the files, the application manifest, and the deployment manifest to the deployment location, but the manual creation of the two manifest files is beyond the scope of this text.

Note

The .NET Framework SDK includes a tool called MAGE (Manifest Generator and Editor) that pro-vides both a UI and a command line interface that can create and manipulate the manifest files that power ClickOnce.

ClickOnce and MSI Comparison

While ClickOnce solves many deployment problems plaguing the software world right now, it is by no means a "silver bullet" for every deployment scenario. There will be times when ClickOnce deployment will not suffice, and it would be more beneficial to use MSI or xcopy deployment instead. The intent of this section is to educate you on the differences between ClickOnce and MSI deployment so that you can determine which solution will support the needs of your project.

Both ClickOnce and MSI have a dependency on a runtime that must be installed on the user's machine before installation can begin. ClickOnce requires the .NET 2.0 Framework in order to run. This can be installed with an old-fashioned boot-strapper. MSI files have an MSI runtime that must also be installed, although all current versions of Windows come preinstalled with this runtime. Again, this run-time could be installed with an old-fashioned bootstrapper.

The need for user input is very small with a ClickOnce deployment. Two clicks are needed: one click on the hyperlink to launch the installer, and another click on the confirmation dialog. The remainder of the installation is a progress bar. This can be a good thing, but personalization and customization of the install process are very limited. MSI files generally have wizard pages that can support many differ-ent types of user input. MSI files can be run in a `BasicUI` mode that functions in a fashion quite similar to ClickOnce.

ClickOnce can only install an application per-user. Per-machine installations are impossible, so multiple users will result in multiple copies of the software on the machine. MSI files can install on a per-machine basis. ClickOnce is also very restrictive with the installation directory. Files will always be installed to the My Applications folder within the My Documents folder. MSI files can install to any directory specified. You cannot modify the target computer with a ClickOnce install, whereas an MSI file can access the registry and other parts of the machine.

At this point, you are probably thinking, "What's so great about ClickOnce if MSI files provide more functionality and features?"

First, ClickOnce deployment takes advantage of application isolation, meaning that the installed applications are isolated from other applications and the operating system itself. This protects the user from the infamous "DLL Hell." MSI installers replace files and manipulate the registry, which can cause all sorts of problems.

MSI files cannot check for newer versions of the software without the help of additional tools. ClickOnce installers have this functionality built right into the runtime.

Updates are pushed to users when they request the deployment manifest for the application. MSI files do not support this functionality, although they can integrate pretty well with management and deployment tools such as SMS and Active Directory.

Hopefully I did not scare everyone away by pointing out the limitations of ClickOnce. Overall, ClickOnce is an excellent deployment solution, and it solves many problems that MSI installers cannot overcome.

Creating the Application

Before we can start discussing ClickOnce deployment, we need to build an application that we can work with. The simplest C# Windows Forms project will do, such as the one shown in Figure 44.1 that has a single button displaying a "Push Me!" message box.

At this stage when we have a completed product ready, a separate MSI project is normally created to deploy the files, while Visual Studio 2005 integrates ClickOnce deployment right into the IDE for the project.

Figure 44.1
Example application used for deployment.

Publishing the Application

At this stage when we have a completed product ready, a separate MSI project is normally created to deploy the files. Visual Studio 2005 integrates ClickOnce deployment right into the IDE for the project. Build your solution so that all the related binaries are compiled and select the Publish <Application Name> option from the Build menu, as shown in Figure 44.2.

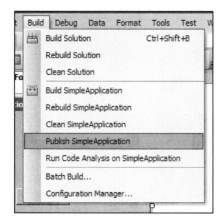

Figure 44.2
Menu option to configure ClickOnce deployment.

The first screen of the publishing wizard, as shown in Figure 44.3, asks where you would like the application to be deployed. This location can be any HTTP 1.1 web server, ftp server, a file path on the local disk, or a file path on a network drive.

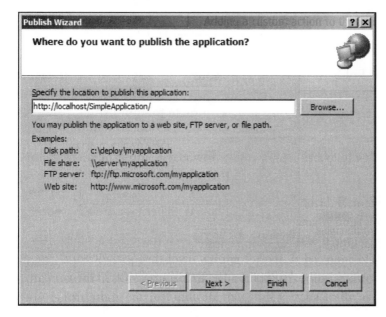

Figure 44.3
Wizard page that prompts for the deployment path.

The next wizard screen, as shown in Figure 44.4, asks whether the application will be available offline. If the application is available offline, a local cached copy of it will be installed so that the last version requested from the online data store will be launched. Keep in mind that the cached copy can not be the latest version, but typically this deployment method is used in situations where it is acceptable to have a slightly older version of the application at certain times. The cached copy is launched via the shortcut in the Start Menu if offline mode is available; otherwise, the application is only available by accessing the data store path.

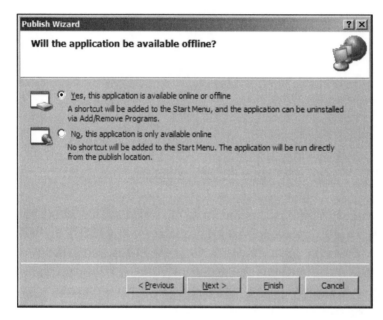

Figure 44.4
Wizard page that prompts for the deployment mode.

The final screen of the Publishing Wizard, as shown in Figure 44.5, describes where the application will be published. No additional configuration is required at this stage, so you can click the Finish button to complete the publishing process.

After the publishing process has completed, you will be redirected to a generated web page, as shown in Figure 44.6, which contains a button that can execute the ClickOnce installer. This page has the name of the application, the current version, and the name of the publisher. Notice that the publisher field is blank. This will be addressed later in this chapter.

If you mouse over the Install button, you should notice that the link is pointing to an application manifest (http://localhost/SimpleApplication/SimpleApplication.application, in this example). This is really the only link you need to give your users to launch the application. Launching the application will be covered later in this chapter.

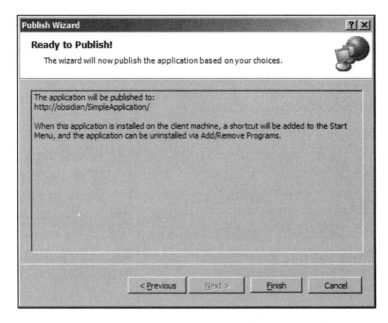

Figure 44.5 Final wizard page that informs you that the publishing is complete.

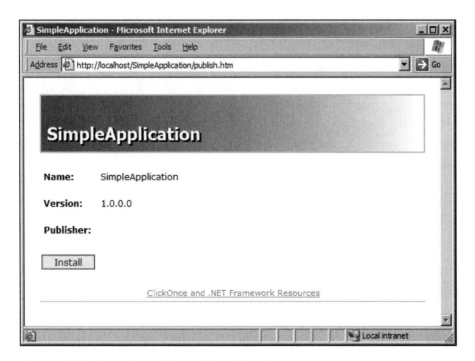

Figure 44.6 Screenshot of the web-based installer page.

The application is now deployable, so we can move on to discussing how to go about launching the application, configuration deployment settings, and pushing updates.

Launching the Application

The application can be launched by navigating to the application manifest file in the top-level folder of the deployment location. For this example, the path would be http://localhost/SimpleApplication/SimpleApplication.application.

Before the application can launch, the ClickOnce runtime must first determine if the prerequisites are installed, and then determine if the application itself is installed. The application is launched if both checks are successful; otherwise, an installer dialog is presented that will install the application along with the necessary prerequisites. The runtime checks are performed while displaying the progress dialog shown in Figure 44.7.

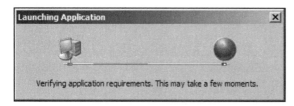

Figure 44.7
Progress dialog shown during web-based launching.

Because this is the first time the application is launched, you will be prompted with an installation dialog like the one shown in Figure 44.8. This trust dialog will describe any warnings that are a result of the security settings for the application and the installer. One warning in particular is that the publisher is unknown, but this warning is very easy to fix and will be covered later on, in the deployment configuration section.

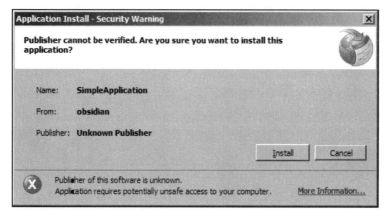

Figure 44.8
Trust dialog during application installation.

Click on the More Information... link to view additional information about the security settings for the installer. Figure 44.9 shows this.

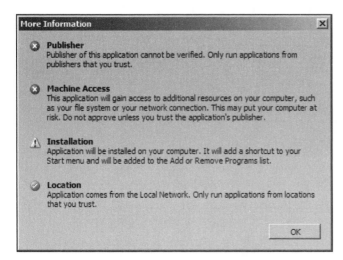

Figure 44.9
More information about the trust dialog.

Start the installation process by clicking the Install button on the trust dialog, and the application will start to be deployed. This is shown in Figure 44.10.

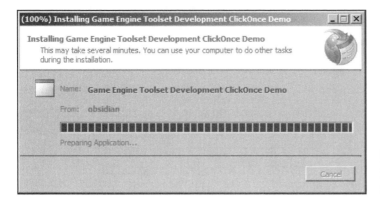

Figure 44.10
Installation dialog for a ClickOnce deployment.

The application is now installed, so all subsequent requests for the application manifest will result in the application being launched.

With installation and launching covered, it is time to show how to customize the deployment manifest for your application using the Visual Studio 2005 IDE.

Deployment Configuration

As discussed earlier, the ClickOnce deployment engine is driven by manifest files that are essentially XML documents. These documents contain various properties and settings that ClickOnce uses to deploy your application with a certain degree of intelligence. These files can be created by hand, but the focus of this topic is on using ClickOnce with Visual Studio integration.

There are a variety of settings that are accessible through the Publish property page under project properties. This property page is shown in Figure 44.11.

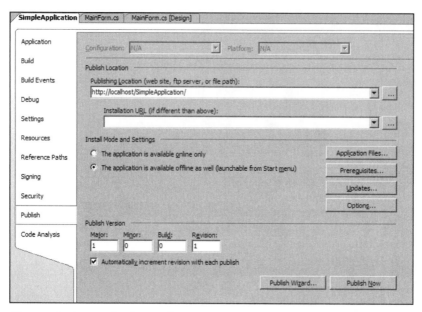

Figure 44.11 Application configuration page for ClickOnce deployment.

By clicking on the Options… button, you will be able to set publishing settings through the Publish Options dialog. This dialog, as shown in Figure 44.12, lets you specify the publisher, product name, support information, and various deployment settings, depending on your deployment strategy. It is a good thing to set this information so that fewer warnings appear in the trust dialog when a user installs the application.

Large applications typically have external dependencies on libraries or components that must be installed prior to using the application. Most notably, the .NET framework itself is required to run any managed applications. Thankfully, Visual Studio offers an excellent bootstrapper utility that will install the prerequisites before allowing ClickOnce to install the application. All of this happens behind the scenes during an installation and is configured through the dialog that is accessed by clicking on the Prerequisites… button. Figure 44.13 shows the bootstrapper configuration screen.

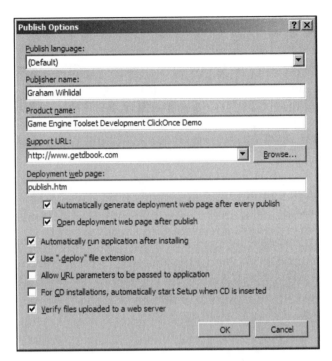

Figure 44.12
Publishing options screen
for ClickOnce.

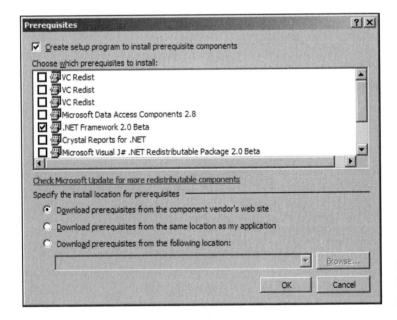

Figure 44.13
Bootstrapper configuration
screen for ClickOnce.

The bootstrapper supports custom prerequisites, but the one downside is that these prerequisites cannot be updated by ClickOnce.

Pushing Application Updates

A great feature of ClickOnce deployment is the ability to push new versions of a product to its users from a centralized location. Applying updates using ClickOnce is extremely easy, and there are also a few deployment settings that can be specified, depending on how you want your updates to be given to the users. Some users really dislike having updates installed automatically, so if appropriate, you can tell ClickOnce to prompt the users if they wish to install the new updates. You can also enforce certain minimum versions on the users so that every user has at least a certain version.

Figure 44.14 shows the configuration screen for application updates. This screen is accessed by clicking on the Updates... button, and is used to specify the versioning strategy used by ClickOnce.

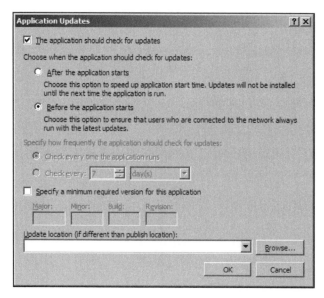

Figure 44.14
Application update configuration screen for ClickOnce.

After you make changes to the application, all you need to do is republish the application, and the new version will be available to users the next time they request the deployment manifest.

Try making a new noticeable change to our simple application, like the one shown in Figure 44.15, and republish the application.

With the new update available, navigate to the publish.htm page that is automatically generated by ClickOnce. Remember that we specified the publisher information, so there is much more information on this page than before. Figure 44.16 shows the updated web page.

Figure 44.15
Screenshot of the version 1.0.0.1 changes
to our application.

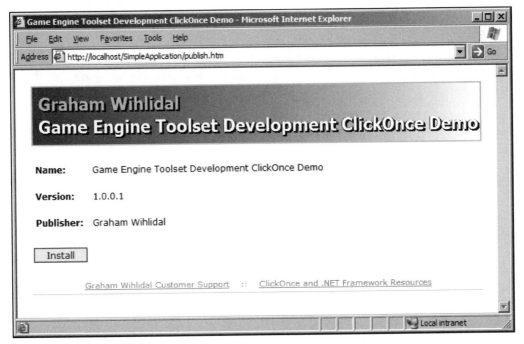

Figure 44.16 Screenshot of the republished web install screen.

Clicking the Install button will apply the new updates and launch the application.

Programmatically Handling Updates

ClickOnce supports a variety of features that generally meet the requirements of application updating, but times do arise where you want programmatic control over how and when updates occur. ClickOnce exposes a programmatic API that allows you to manually check for updates and apply them. This functionality is available in the System.Deployment.Application namespace and has a variety of features, depending on the need of the custom solution.

The following code shows the easiest way to programmatically check for updates and synchronously deploy them, but keep in mind that there is much more flexibility in the ClickOnce API than what is shown here.

```
try
{
    ApplicationDeployment updater = ApplicationDeployment.CurrentDeployment;

    UpdateCheckInfo updateInfo = updater.CheckForDetailedUpdate();

    if (updateInfo.UpdateAvailable)
    {
        string message1 = "A newer version of this application is available. ";
        string message2 = "Do you want to update the application now?";

        if (MessageBox.Show(message1 + message2,
                        "ClickOnce Demo Updater",
                        MessageBoxButtons.YesNo)
                    == DialogResult.Yes)
        {
            updater.Update();
            MessageBox.Show("Please shutdown and restart the " +
                        "application to start using the new version.");
        }
    }
}
catch (DeploymentException exception)
{
    MessageBox.Show(exception.Message);
}
```

When a new version is available and the update is downloaded, the new application files are placed in the appropriate folder named after the version. The shortcut to the application is then pointed at the new folder, which requires shutting down the application and restarting to take advantage of the changes.

A major advantage of ClickOnce deployment is that the application can be kept unaware of ClickOnce because there is no need to inherit from base classes or implement interfaces. However, it is comforting to know that support is there when you need programmatic control over ClickOnce for your deployment strategy.

Conclusion

In this chapter, you learned about ClickOnce deployment, and how it can quickly be used to deploy software on user machines, along with a versioning strategy that can keep the software up to date.

Code access security is beyond the scope of this chapter, so there was not much discussion around security permissions with ClickOnce applications. This functionality does exist in the publishing system, and there are some great tools that you can take advantage of to make your life easier.

As mentioned earlier, ClickOnce deployment is a great deployment solution, but it is not always the method you want for every situation. But for situations where you want application isolation, ease of use, offline mode, and reliable versioning, ClickOnce is a solution you can place your trust in.

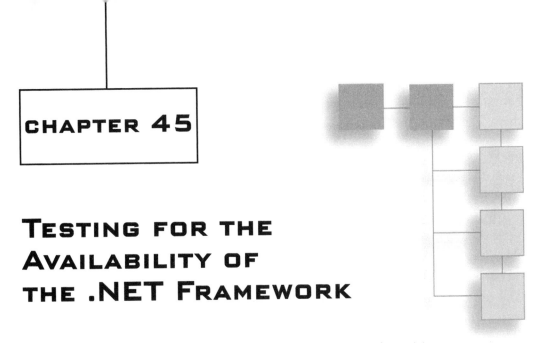

CHAPTER 45

TESTING FOR THE AVAILABILITY OF THE .NET FRAMEWORK

The only way to learn a new programming language is by writing programs in it.

Dennis Ritchie

Managed applications on the .NET platform have access to a wealth of features and prebuilt functionality, dramatically decreasing development time. Deploying .NET applications is also extremely simple, provided the required runtime is present. Managed applications have a dependency on the Common Language Runtime and the class framework assemblies, and will not function without them. Deploying these applications generally entails that you check to see if the operating system has the .NET runtime and, if not, install it. Some installation packagers have bootstrapper utilities that can automate this process for you, but generally you are on your own.

One solution is to take the manual approach by attempting to run the application. If it does not load, you obviously require the .NET runtime. This approach is not a clean way to handle deployment.

Another solution is to check the Win32 registry for entries, keys like:

```
HKEY_LOCAL_MACHINE\Microsoft\.NETFramework\policy\v1.1
HKEY_LOCAL_MACHINE\Microsoft\.NETFramework\policy\v2.0
```

While checking the registry will work in many situations, there are some cases where the installation folder has been renamed or a service pack has been applied that will not be reflected with these registry keys.

In this chapter, I present a solution that can determine the list of Common Language Runtimes that are correctly installed and allow enumeration through them. The solution will also account for service packs and renamed folder locations.

Note

The large segments of source code have been removed from this chapter and are available on the Companion Web site in order to fit this chapter into the book. Please refer to the source code of the example in order to clarify any implementation questions.

The Solution

The code in this section forms the solution for this chapter. The code compiles into a static library that can be reused across multiple projects.

Note

The full source code for the solution is available on the Companion Web site.

We do not want a dependency on `mscoree`, so we use `LoadLibrary` and `GetProcAddress` in order to use the needed functions. The prototype for `FSGetRequestedRuntimeInfo` is also copied directly into the source code so that we do not have a dependency on the header file for `mscoree`.

```
typedef HRESULT (__stdcall *FPGetRequestedRuntimeInfo)
                         (LPCWSTR exe,
                          LPCWSTR versionPtr,
                          LPCWSTR configurationFile,
                          DWORD startupFlags,
                          DWORD runtimeInfoFlags,
                          LPWSTR directory,
                          DWORD directoryLength,
                          DWORD *directoryLengthPtr,
                          LPWSTR version,
                          DWORD buffer,
                          DWORD* length);
```

The constructor for the version check class first determines whether the .NET framework is installed (in any shape or form); then it determines the base installation path for the .NET framework.

Note

The source code for the constructor is available on the Companion Web site.

The following method is used to find out where the .NET framework base installation path is. This is done by checking the Win32 registry for the following key:

`HKEY_LOCAL_MACHINE\SOFTWARE\Microsoft\.NETFramework\InstallRoot`

This method caches the installation path as well, so that multiple version checks do not need to reexecute the code to search the registry.

```
BOOL CLRVersionCheck::GetInstallationBasePath(TCHAR* basePath, DWORD bufferSize)
{
```

Note

The source code for this method is available on the Companion Web site.

```
}
```

The following method returns a list of CLR versions after querying the .NET framework base installation path.

```
size_t CLRVersionCheck::EnumerateVersions(std::vector<std::string>& versionList)
{
```

Note

The source code for this method is available on the Companion Web site.

```
}
```

The following method enumerates the directories located in the .NET framework base installation path. It is important to note that not all of these entries will be valid CLR versions, because `EnumerateVersions()` will handle the filtering and validation.

```
size_t CLRVersionCheck::EnumerateVersionDirectories(std::vector<std::string>&
                                                    versionList)
{
```

Note

The source code for this method is available on the Companion Web site.

```
}
```

The following method is used to determine whether a CLR version is actually valid and active within the operating system. This method is given a version number, and the GetRequestedRuntimeInfo() method of mscoree is used to validate it.

```
BOOL CLRVersionCheck::IsVersionAvailable(LPCWSTR frameworkVersion)
{
```

Note

The source code for this method is available on the Companion Web site.

```
}
```

Example Usage

Using the version check library is very easy. To start, link to the static library file (.lib) and include the library header (CLRVersionCheckLib.hpp).

The following code shows a simple console application that enumerates a list of available .NET framework versions and displays the results.

```
#include "stdafx.h"
#include <conio.h>

int _tmain(int argc, _TCHAR* argv[])
{
```

Note

The source code for this method is available on the Companion Web site.

Figure 45.1 shows the console application in action.

Figure 45.1 Screenshot of the console example in action.

Conclusion

This chapter discussed how to determine which versions of the .NET framework are installed on an operating system, and that they are valid and active. There are a couple ways to approach this problem, and each method has viable pros and cons. This method may require more code than simply checking the registry for the policy entries, but you can be guaranteed that the version list returned from the library only contains valid and active CLR versions. This technique is extremely useful for application deployment strategies, though there are other reasons for using this solution as well.

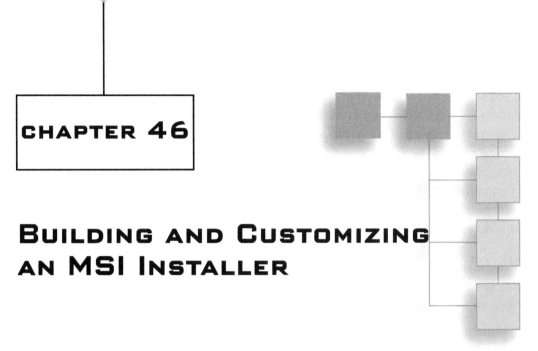

CHAPTER 46

BUILDING AND CUSTOMIZING AN MSI INSTALLER

The fantastic element that explains the appeal of dungeon-clearing games to many programmers is neither the fire-breathing monsters nor the milky skinned, semi-clad sirens; it is the experience of carrying out a task from start to finish without user requirements changing.

Thomas L. Holaday

Many years ago, installing applications was as easy as copying an executable to a floppy disk and either copying it to a user's computer or running it directly off the disk. Computers and software development have advanced to an era where complex logic and tasks can be evaluated and performed, but this advancement has introduced a new magnitude of installation complexity. Instead of a single executable, we now have to install hundreds of files, and even installations spanning multiple machines in the case of distributed architectures. Some applications even depend on the registration of shared dependencies and components like COM objects, MDAC, or the .NET Framework. Some applications have a lot of complex dependencies on shared components, which many times results in the deployment nightmare known as "DLL Hell."

A number of deployment strategies and technologies have been developed to try and address these concerns. Each approach has a place, because some approaches are better at deploying certain applications than others. A common approach, and a relatively straightforward one, is XCOPY deployment. This method of deployment is most suitable for .NET applications, because assemblies almost never rely on registry entries created during installation. Deploying an application with XCOPY deployment entails copying the relevant assemblies to the client computer. These applications can launch immediately because of the self-describing nature of .NET assemblies. Assemblies contain all the information necessary to load themselves, along with locating and loading all required dependencies. The XCOPY approach is known as zero-impact deployment because the target computer will not break with varying configurations of the registry or component. You can also uninstall the application simply by deleting the relevant files without worrying about any negative side effects. XCOPY deployment is ideal for situations where the application is relatively self-contained and can be executed manually. Other situations invite an alternative approach.

For situations that require a more robust deployment solution, Windows Installer is the best choice. Windows Installer technology produces installer files with .msi and .exe extensions that execute an installation process that installs files to specific location, and performs system configuration and registration, and does so through a user interface that is simple enough for most users to understand. By wrapping a complex installation into a user-friendly process, you reduce the total cost of ownership (TCO) by allowing the users to correctly install and configure your applications. Windows Installer can even provide a mechanism to repair corrupted installations if the need arises, making maintenance and support easier than ever. Corrupted installations using the XCOPY approach require that you manually replace the bad files or the application in its entirety. Windows Installer also provides an automatic rollback feature, ensuring that all installed files are cleanly uninstalled if an installation fails. This feature goes one step further by bringing the machine back to the state it was in before the installation was initiated.

Visual Studio Installer (VSI) is a technology integrated into Visual Studio 2005 that utilizes the Windows Installer engine. Because MSI installers depend on the existence of the Windows Installer engine, this dependency can also be installed by VSI before installation continues.

Note

The MSI format resembles a database structure, where setup information is stored along with compressed data files.

In addition to utilizing the Windows Installer engine and manipulating the Windows file system, Visual Studio Installer also provides a number of additional features to support complex installations. Installers can read and write keys within the Windows registry, including an automated mechanism to register both COM components and .NET components (within the Global Assembly Cache). Launch conditions can be used to ensure that all requirements are satisfied before installation can continue. Launch conditions can check information like the user and computer name, operating system, presence of the .NET Common Language Runtime, and if a registry entry or another application exists. Installers can also prompt the user for different pieces of information, allowing for a customizable installation process. Custom setup programs or scripts can also be initiated when the installation completes successfully.

Note

A third deployment approach, covered in Chapter 44, "Deployment and Versioning with ClickOnce," describes a new technology introduced by Microsoft in .NET 2.0. I recommend that you read this chapter if you are concerned about automatic updates, smart client installation, and isolation under a least privilege account. For robust installations, I recommend that you stick with Windows Installer.

This chapter will cover how to create and configure a Visual Studio Installer, along with showing how to develop custom installer actions for any fancy tasks your application needs to perform during installation.

Creating a Setup Project

Visual Studio 2005 provides five types of project templates that can be used to handle the setup and deployment of .NET applications. These templates are available from the same New Project menu that you create new applications from. Figure 46.1 shows the New Project dialog for the deployment project templates.

The Setup Project template is used to create a Windows Installer for your applications. This is the project type that will be covered in this chapter.

The Web Setup Project template is used to create a Windows Installer that can install a web application to a virtual directory on a web server.

The Merge Module Project template is used to package shared files and components into a module that can be shared between multiple setup projects. Merge modules are only installed during an installation if the files in the merge module have not yet been installed on the target machine.

The Setup Wizard template is a wizard that helps guide you through the creation of one of the project templates.

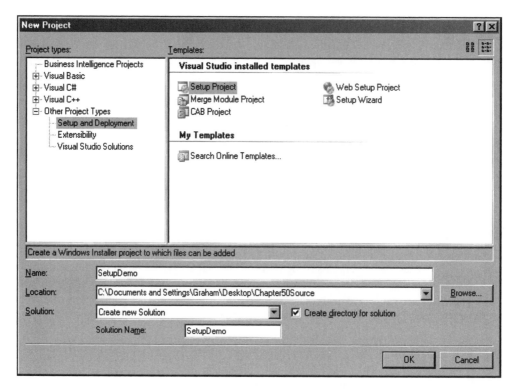

Figure 46.1 Project types for deployment in Visual Studio 2005.

The Cab Project template is used to package files without any installation logic. This project type is generally used to package files into a single file that can be deployed onto a web server, so that web browsers can download these components onto their local machines before installation.

We will start off with an existing Windows Forms application and solution that will be named SimpleApp. Create a new project in this solution with the Setup Project template. You will see the new project added to the current solution, as shown in Figure 46.2.

Figure 46.2
New setup project added to current solution.

With our new deployment project, we need to include the compiled executable from SimpleApp into the installer. This can be done by right-clicking on the setup project and selecting Project Output from the Add menu. A dialog will be presented, like the one shown in Figure 46.3, that prompts you to select what output you want to package with the installer. Select the primary output option; this will package the built assembly.

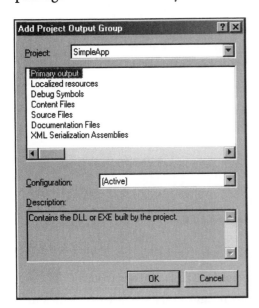

Figure 46.3
Dialog prompting for the type
of project output to add.

As it stands right now, you can build the setup project to produce an installer for the SimpleApp project, but we will press on to configuration and customization.

Project Configuration

There are all sorts of customizations that can be done on the installer, but the first area to customize is the properties section for the project. Figure 48.4 shows the properties section for the SetupDemo project that can be accessed by right-clicking on the setup project and selecting Properties. There are a number of properties that you can set; you can see what each property is for by clicking in one of the property fields and reading the description that appears on the bottom panel.

Once you have tweaked the project properties, you can move on to the various editors that are available for the installer. The editors are available through the View menu when you right-click on the setup project.

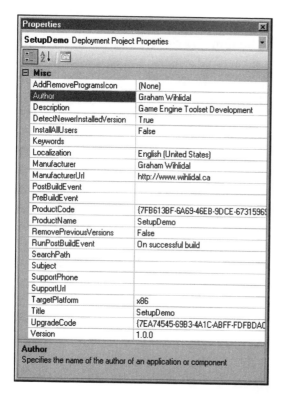

Figure 46.4
Properties for the SetupDemo deployment project.

The first editor to cover is the file system editor that allows you to add files and shortcuts to the installer, such as Start menu items. Figure 46.5 shows the file system editor. By default you are presented with three special folders: Application Folder, User's Desktop, and User's Programs Menu. All the executables, libraries, text files, images, and all other supporting files needed by your application must reside in the Application Folder. This folder can contain any number of files or directories in any hierarchy that you want. You can also create shortcuts to files or executables in the User's Desktop and User's Programs Menu folders. Additional special folders can be created by right-clicking on the parent file system node and selecting Add Special Folder.

Note

Visual Studio Installer reads project dependencies, so you do not need to add components or system files to your installer, except for ones that cannot be read from the source project, such as databases.

For our installer, we want to create a shortcut to the `SimpleApp` application on the desktop. Navigate into the User's Desktop folder, right-click, and select Create New Shortcut. This action is shown in Figure 46.5.

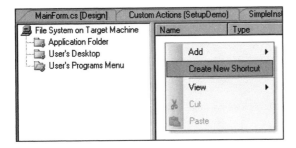

Figure 46.5
File system editor; creating a new shortcut.

We need to specify where the file within our installation package is located so that a shortcut can be created. Navigate to the Application Folder, select the primary output from the SimpleApp project, and click OK (as shown in Figure 46.6). Doing so will create a shortcut to the SimpleApp executable on the user's desktop after installation has completed.

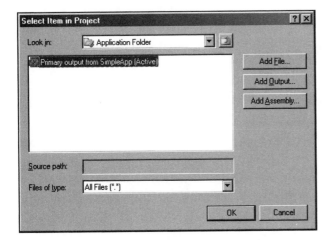

Figure 46.6
Selecting a file to create
a desktop shortcut to.

You can see the new shortcut we just created show up in the file system editor, as shown in Figure 46.7.

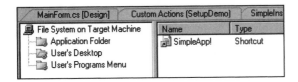

Figure 46.7
Newly created shortcut shown
in file system editor.

The next editor we can use is the file types editor, which is used to associate file extensions with an application. This editor allows you to register file extensions so that you do not have to worry about this step programmatically when you launch your application for the first time. The file types editor is shown in Figure 46.8.

Figure 46.8
Screenshot of the file types editor.

The Name property is used to describe the file type within the file types editor. The Command property specifies what application is launched when this file type is opened from the file system. The Description property is just what it says, a description of the file type within the file types editor. The Extensions property is the most important because it describes which extensions are associated with this file type registration. The Icon property is used to specify which icon is given to applications sporting the registered extensions. Finally, the MIME property is used to describe which mime type is associated with the file mapping. A file mapping has actions (Open is the action used in this example) which represent verbs that are passed into the opening arguments along with the file path so that the application can handle the file appropriately.

Another useful editor is the registry editor that allows you to manipulate registry entries on the target computer. This editor can add entries into the Windows registry from directly within the installer.

To add a key, simply right-click on the node you want to create under and select New>Key. You can add values such as strings, environment strings, binary values, and DWORDs.

Caution

Beware of what you manipulate within the Windows registry; this can be very dangerous. Make sure you give your keys a distinct grouping and naming.

The registry editor is shown in Figure 46.9.

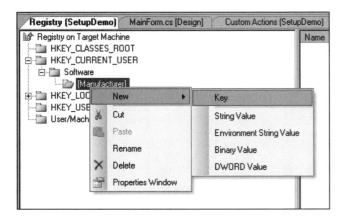

Figure 46.9
Screenshot of the registry editor.

One of the key features of Windows Installer is the ability to display user-friendly interfaces that make deployment easier and more appealing to the average user. By default, you are given a standard template for how the user interface looks and flows, but this can all be modified through the user interface editor, as shown in Figure 46.10. The user interface editor configures the dialogs that are shown during the installation, and it can add new dialogs like user registration.

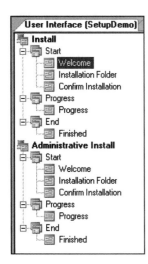

Figure 46.10
Screenshot of the user interface editor.

Finally, the launch conditions editor is used to specify the requirements that must be satisfied in order for your application to be installed on the target computer. Searches can be executed against the file system, registry, or previously installed applications to validate that certain dependencies exist (outside of dependencies that the installer automatically picks up on). By default, all .NET installations have a requirement that the .NET Framework be installed. This condition ensures that you have everything installed correctly to run .NET applications, and if not, a bootstrapper can be configured to install the .NET Framework before your installation is continued. Figure 46.11 shows the launch conditions editor.

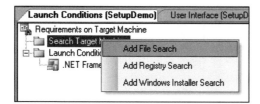

Figure 46.11
Screenshot of the launch conditions editor.

Deployment Configuration

With project configuration taken care of, we can move on to deployment configuration. Start by opening the Configuration Manager dialog by right-clicking on the setup project and selecting Properties, and then clicking on the Configuration Manager button in the top-right corner of the property page. This dialog allows you to manage multiple build configurations, each with a different group of settings. By default, the Setup Project template creates a configuration for Debug and a configuration for Release. The Debug mode creates debugging symbols that make runtime debugging a lot easier, except this mode is not optimized for performance. The Release mode is the opposite; debugging symbols are not created, and the code is optimized for performance. Be sure to change your active solution configuration to Release mode before you begin deploying your application. The Configuration Manager dialog is shown in Figure 46.12.

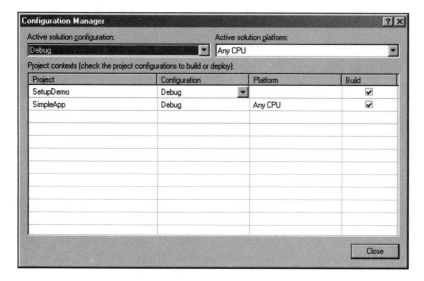

Figure 46.12
Configuration Manager dialog within Visual Studio 2005.

The files in your deployment project can be packaged in a selection of ways. The first format is to store loose uncompressed files, which basically means that no compression takes place and the files are stored as they are. This is an ideal approach because installation speed is important to you. Having uncompressed files takes a lot less time to install rather than having decompression operations that have to happen before files can be installed. This solution is ideal for local computer or network environments where you are not concerned with bandwidth or download issues. The next approach is to store your files in the setup file, which means that your files are compressed and stored within the MSI file. This approach is great for situations where you are concerned with network traffic or user competence; the fewer files you can give users with limited technical ability, the better. Lastly, you can store your files in Cabinet files (.cab). Basically, files are stored in external Cabinet files that are referenced by entries in the MSI file. At runtime, the installer uses these entries to decompress and install the Cabinet files. Cabinet files are stored alongside the MSI file in the same directory. This solution is ideal for web deployments or deployments that require interchangeable components for a variety of configurations.

You have the option of tweaking the compression level to favor different scenarios. You can select Optimized for Speed, Optimized for Size, or None. Optimizing for Speed means that files are roughly compressed, resulting in faster compression, sacrificing a reduction with the amount of compression applied. Optimizing for Size means that a more intensive compression algorithm is used to shrink the files as much as possible, resulting in an excellent level of compression at the cost of additional performance overhead. Lastly, selecting None for the compression mode will result in files being stored uncompressed within a package (if applicable). You can use this mode with a setup file if you want a fast install with a small number of files to work with.

Figure 46.13 shows the property page for the setup project configuration.

Many applications rely on the existence of shared components or frameworks before installation can occur. A solid example of this relationship is the installation and usage of any .NET application. Client machines must have the .NET runtime and supporting framework installed, or .NET applications cannot execute. Visual Studio Installer has a mechanism known as a *bootstrapper* that executes and completes successfully before actual installation occurs. This bootstrapper can be configured to make sure that certain key dependencies exist, and to offer methods to acquire these dependencies if they are not found. Visual Studio Installer requires Windows Installer 1.5 to be installed on the target computer in order to function. Windows XP was the first operating system that came bundled with Windows

Installer 1.5. Earlier operating systems required that you package a bootstrapper with your installer to account for the older or nonexistent versions. Including the bootstrapper increases your installer size by roughly 3MB. You can specify the Web bootstrapper, which means that the bootstrapper can be downloaded from the Internet if needed. The benefit of this approach is that the bootstrapper does not have to be packaged with the installer, thereby reducing the overall size of the installation package. The bootstrapper is accessed by clicking on the Prerequisites button in the setup project configuration page, and you will be presented with the dialog shown in Figure 46.14.

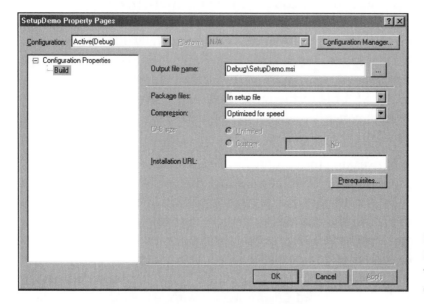

Figure 46.13
Property page for the setup project configuration.

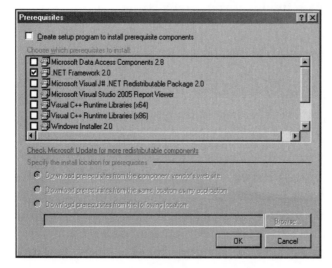

Figure 46.14
Dialog to configure the installation bootstrapper.

Custom Installer Actions

Using the boilerplate setup templates is fine and dandy, but applications with any sort of complexity often require that custom steps be performed during installation, such as the creation of databases, publishing of reports, user personalization, product license key evaluation, and so forth. These steps can be performed through the use of custom installation actions, which are code classes that you can compile within your solution, and then point the installation process at them. To start, we will add a new item to the application project, as shown in Figure 46.15.

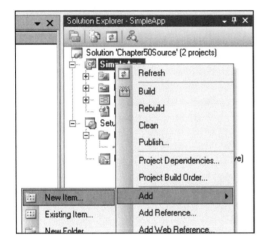

Figure 46.15
Adding a new Project Item.

The item we are adding is an Installer Class (shown in Figure 46.16), which is a class that is decorated for processing by the Visual Studio Installer. This class inherits from Installer, which exists in the System.Configuration.Install namespace.

This class provides four methods (Install, Commit, Rollback, and Uninstall), which can be overridden to run custom functionality at the appropriate state in the installer. The example provided with this chapter simply displays a message box in the constructor; although in a real world implementation you would override the four methods appropriately.

Note

The four override methods of Installer are not always called on the same instance of the class. Therefore, it is important that each method can run independently of the other methods or class instances in terms of data persistence and state.

Figure 46.17 shows the simple Installer class implementation provided with the example for this chapter.

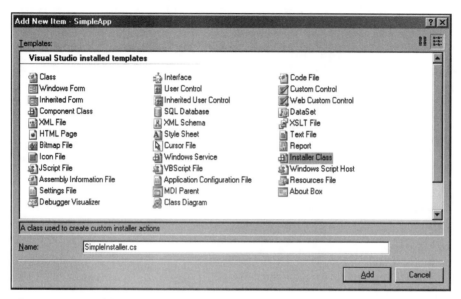

Figure 46.16 Adding a new Installer Class item.

```
 1  using System;
 2  using System.Collections.Generic;
 3  using System.ComponentModel;
 4  using System.Configuration.Install;
 5  using System.Windows.Forms;
 6
 7  namespace Chapter50Source
 8  {
 9      [RunInstaller(true)]
10      public partial class SimpleInstaller : Installer
11      {
12          public SimpleInstaller()
13          {
14              InitializeComponent();
15              MessageBox.Show("This is where you run custom install functionality!");
16          }
17      }
18  }
```

Figure 46.17 Simple Installer class implementation.

With our simple custom installer logic built, we need to link it into the setup project. This is done through the custom actions editor, which is available from the View context menu item where the other editors are located (as shown in Figure 46.18).

The custom actions editor contains groupings for the four methods of the Installer class. We are just going to add an action for the Install state, which can be done by right-clicking on the Install node and selecting Add Custom Action... as shown in Figure 46.19.

You will be prompted with a dialog that will ask you to select where the custom installer class resides. Since we just added the class to the main application, you can navigate into the Application Folder and select the primary output. This is shown in Figure 46.20.

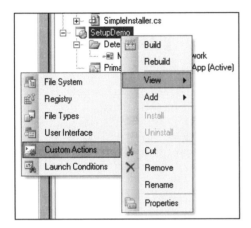

Figure 46.18
Accessing the custom actions editor.

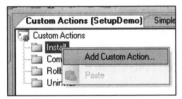

Figure 46.19
Adding a custom action to the Install node.

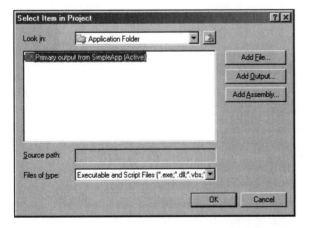

Figure 46.20
Selecting the primary output as
a source for the installer class.

The custom action is now linked into the installer and ready to fire when installation is initiated.

Deploying the Installer

You can build the installer by right-clicking on the setup project and selecting build. The bin directory of the setup project on the file system now contains the MSI and exe files, along with any supporting files used by the installer. This whole directory can be zipped up and distributed for users to run. Figure 46.21 shows the welcome screen shown to users running our new installer.

During installation, our custom installer action will execute and display the message box, as shown in Figure 46.22.

Figure 46.21
Welcome screen shown
to users for SetupDemo.

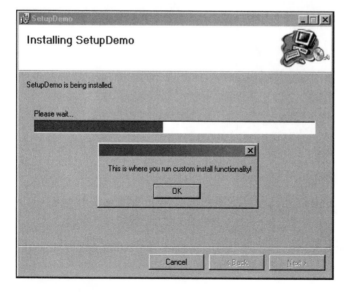

Figure 46.22
Custom installer action
firing during installation.

Conclusion

This chapter discussed the need for deployment strategies and technologies that reduce the total cost of ownership, and some approaches with .NET application deployment. The bulk of the chapter focused on a walkthrough of the construction of a fairly simple MSI setup project sporting a custom installer action. Visual Studio Installer can be leveraged to provide professional-looking installation packages that perform a lot of complex installation and registration activities behind the scenes, enabling users with limited technical ability to install your software.

Although this chapter only covered the rudiments of Visual Studio Installer, you should now have enough of a foundation to pursue additional information if necessary on harnessing the robust functionality of MSI packages and the Windows Installer engine.

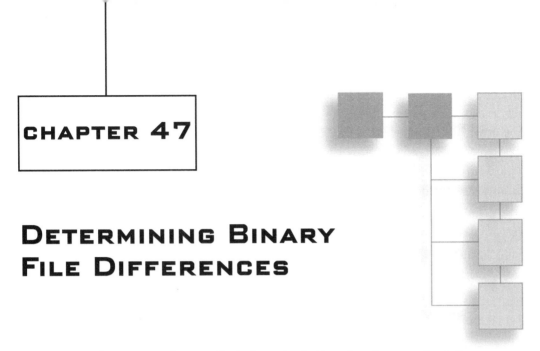

CHAPTER 47

DETERMINING BINARY FILE DIFFERENCES

A complex system that works is invariably found to have evolved from a simple system that worked... . A complex system designed from scratch never works and cannot be patched up to make it work. You have to start over with a working simple system.

John Gall, from *Systemantics: How Systems Really Work and How They Fail*

In the wonderful world of software development and deployment, products are generally never released error-free. Even in the rare instance that a product is rolled out without any internal bugs, issues appear from different hardware and operating system configurations on the end user's computer. Whether the issues are related to security vulnerabilities, application instability, or even a feature that was not feasible to implement in an earlier version, software generally requires at least a couple of revisions to keep the people using the software happy and interested in the product. This chapter will discuss one particular method of updating older versions in a manner suitable for environments requiring a small memory or hard drive footprint.

Deployment is a very important topic to address in software development. If a product you have deployed requires an important update, how will the existing people using your software receive it? The most popular medium for transferring data is the Internet, and most auto-update engines utilize it to send new versions to users. One problem with the Internet is that with such a wide demographic of users, not everyone has a great connection speed and transfer rate.

Imagine you have a 30 MB data file included with an initial release of your product, and in the next update 200 KB is modified. Would it be feasible to have everyone download the new data file? Such a large file would take a long time to download on a dial-up connection, especially when only a small fraction of the original data was modified. A better method would be to transmit only the bytes that changed, and merge them into the existing data file.

An ideal solution would be a utility that could take an old and a new version of a file, generate a list of differences, and offer a method to both apply and deploy the data changes to users.

To start, we need an algorithm that can determine a list of differences between two arbitrary sets of data that are sequentially similar, and do so in a manner that can transform the old dataset as efficiently as possible.

Note

The large segments of source code are available on the Companion Web site. Please refer to the source code of the example in order to clarify any implementation questions.

What Is Levenshtein Distance?

Devised in 1965 by a Russian scientist named Vladimir Levenshtein, Levenshtein distance (LD) is an algorithm designed to measure the similarity between two strings. The metric is also known as edit distance by people who cannot pronounce "Levenshtein," and it is a measure of the smallest number of deletions, substitutions, and insertions required to transform one string into another, which we will refer to as source (s) and target (t), respectively. An edit is either deleting a character, substituting one character for another, or inserting a character.

Levenshtein distance is a [theta](m x n) algorithm, where m and n are the lengths of the strings, that computes the edit distance in time proportional to the length of the source times the length of the target. The greater the edit distance, the more differences are present between the two strings.

Given:

```
(s) = "Apple"
(t) = "Apple"
LD(s, t) = 0 because both s and t are identical.

(s) = "Apple"
```

```
(t) = "Apples"
LD(s, t) = 1 because one insertion is required to transform s into t.

(s) = "Apple"
(t) = "Ape"
LD(s, t) = 2 because one substitution and deletion are required to transform s
into t.
```

This algorithm has been used in DNA analysis, plagiarism detection, speech recognition, document versioning systems, and spell checking. Levenshtein distance is also known as a generalization of Hamming distance, where only substitutions are handled and both strings are of equal length.

One of the biggest drawbacks to the Levenshtein distance is the expensive memory requirements of the algorithm. While the traditional matrix-based approach is extremely precise, it is only practical to use on small datasets. As soon as the algorithm is used on a large dataset, the exorbitant amount of memory and comparisons quickly rules out the traditional Levenshtein implementation for our purposes. For example, 50,000 bytes compared to a similar dataset will result in around 2.5 billion comparisons, and roughly 250 MB of memory.

Using Levenshtein distance would not completely satisfy our requirements, although the algorithm definitely influenced the solution I'm presenting in this chapter. The full source code will not be discussed in this chapter in order to make the text easier to follow, but the Companion Web site has the full source with comments. The only methods discussed in this chapter are extracted from the core logic of the differencing engine. Please refer to the source code for a stronger understanding of the implementation itself.

Generating a Difference List

The main processing component of the differencing engine is the logic that compares two source buffers and outputs a sequence of transformations that can transform source data into target data. The following methods in this section compose the majority of the central logic of the engine provided with this chapter.

The following method is roughly the starting point for building the difference list. A PatchOperation object is passed in that holds the source and target data buffers. This method initializes a few public properties and fires the PatchOperation off to the ProcessRange method. Later on, the PatchOperation is passed into BuildDifferencesList that finalizes all the difference states into the transformation sequence.

```
private static PatchOperation Process(PatchOperation operation)
{
```

N o t e

The source code for this method is available on the Companion Web site.

```
}
```

The following method processes a range of data in the source and target buffers to pull out any similarities in the data. This method mainly tries to find data that does not change between the source and target buffers to reduce the overall data size of the transformation sequence.

```
private static void ProcessRange(PatchOperation operation,
                                 int targetStart,
                                 int targetEnd,
                                 int sourceStart,
                                 int sourceEnd)
{
```

N o t e

The source code for this method is available on the Companion Web site.

```
}
```

The following method performs the actual extraction of match data within a specified range.

```
private static void GetLongestSourceMatch(PatchOperation operation,
                                          PatchState state,
                                          int targetStart,
                                          int targetEnd,
                                          int sourceStart,
                                          int sourceEnd)
{
```

N o t e

The source code for this method is available on the Companion Web site.

```
}
```

The following method compares the specified ranges in the source and target buffers to determine the length of a match.

```
private static int GetSourceMatchLength(PatchOperation operation,
                                        int target,
                                        int source,
                                        int maxLength)
{
```

Note

The source code for this method is available on the Companion Web site.

```
}
```

The following method builds the `PatchDifference` list based on the results in the `PatchOperation` object.

```
private static List<PatchDifference> BuildDifferencesList(PatchOperation operation)
{
```

Note

The source code for this method is available on the Companion Web site.

```
}
```

The following method accepts the results of the sequence compilation and builds differencing objects that will eventually be serialized into the XML transform document.

```
private static bool RecordDifference(List<PatchDifference> result,
                                     int targetStart,
                                     int targetEnd,
                                     int sourceStart,
                                     int sourceEnd)
{
```

Note

The source code for this method is available on the Companion Web site.

```
}
```

Transforming Data Using a Difference List

Once a listing of all the differences between the two datasets is generated, there are a couple more steps we must take in order to have all the data required to perform a transformation.

We must first extract the modified bytes from the new dataset and store them with the difference list. In order to store the data, we must alter the `PatchDifference` object to include an array of bytes specific to the type of change that will be performed.

There will obviously be no data needed for the NoChange and Delete difference types.

A new function will be added to loop through the difference list and extract the modified bytes, storing them in each PatchDifference object. This function is described in the following code:

```
public static PatchDifferenceData[] BuildDifferenceData(PatchOperation operation)
{
```

Note

The source code for this method is available on the Companion Web site.

```
}
```

The preceding function loops through the difference list, and for insertion and substitution types, specifies the data associated with the change. We are left with an array of PatchDifference objects containing the data related to the change. At this point, the array can be easily serialized into an XML document for an external system to use, or we can go one step further and build a complete patching engine. The example provided with this chapter shows how to do both methods.

In order to successfully transform the old file using the difference data, a particular sequence of changes must be used. You must remember that the slightest error when transforming the old data will corrupt the file and make it generally unusable. The first change to do is substitution because it does not require any bytes to be added or removed from the source data, only a direct byte swap.

You want to loop through the difference list once for each difference type. First, loop and process all the substitution types. Remember that the PatchDifference object contains the target index in the resultant data, and the data to copy.

After substitution, the next difference type to process is deletion of data. Because the algorithm does not take other deletion changes into consideration, the data offsets are incorrect after the first deletion. To solve this, we must define a simple offset counter that is incremented by the number of bytes removed each time a deletion occurs. This offset is subtracted from the offset specified in the difference list so that the correct data is deleted and no buffer overflow occurs.

Lastly, the insertion type is processed to allocate memory for new data being copied into the resultant buffer. The first step is to allocate a block of memory at the correct index, with the size specified by the PatchDifference object. Once the memory exists, the insertion data can be safely copied over.

`System.Collections.Generic.List<byte>` is an excellent choice to store the resultant data because it has many methods that allow for inserting and deleting a range of elements at a specific index.

The functions in the following code illustrate the process described in the preceding text for transforming data using the difference list.

```
public byte[] MergeDifferences(PatchDifferenceData[] differenceData)
{
```

Note

The source code for this method is available on the Companion Web site.

```
}
```

```
private List<byte> MergeDifferencePass(PatchDifferenceData[] differenceData,
                                       List<byte> result,
                                       PatchDifferenceType type)
{
```

Note

The source code for this method is available on the Companion Web site.

```
}
```

After applying the preceding changes, the old data should have been correctly transformed into the new data. The Companion Web site shows an example XML document of how a transformation sequence can look.

Thoughts for Usability and Deployment

A major fault with the algorithm discussed occurs when the source and target files are hardly similar, and very few duplicate byte sequences are found. This leads to many recursion and comparison calls. This algorithm works great on datasets that have a lot of similarities because large sequential patterns allow us to ignore processing them, but this is very slow in the opposite situation.

One method of preventing this issue is to make sure that both files selected are modifications of each other. This is hard to detect when building a patch, but after the patch is created, you can add in a pretty decent failsafe.

In Chapter 19, "Implementing a Checksum to Protect Data Integrity," an algorithm was discussed that generated a number based on the byte values in a memory buffer. This value can be used to detect file corruption and tampering. The same technique can also be used to be certain the file we are trying to patch is the correct one.

A checksum can be generated based on the source file and then serialized into the difference list. When a file is selected to be patched, you can generate a checksum for it, and only patch the file if the generated checksum matches the value saved in the difference list.

Employing this method of file verification solves a couple of issues. The obvious reason is to stop users from patching the wrong files, thus preventing the algorithm flaw discussed previously. Another benefit of using a checksum is that any files transmitted over the Internet can be verified for integrity.

Aside from source file verification, a reliable distribution system must also be in place so that users have access to the latest patch files for the software product. As previously discussed, an excellent transport medium for software updates is the Internet. A front end could query for the latest version, download the latest patch, and apply it to an older version of the product.

Compression could also be used on the binary data, which would be a great enhancement to the patching system because the resultant data size would be decreased even more. .NET 2.0 introduced the `System.IO.Compression` namespace that can accomplish this.

Lastly, another consideration for update generation is the modular structure of your software. For example, if your software has external modules or assemblies that are linked into the application at runtime, any updates specific to that library can be issued in a patch specific to just that file. If you have any modules of code that will change quite often, a general rule of thumb would be to place them in an external library and run updates against that file alone.

Conclusion

Aside from building your own patch generator, some third-party tools are readily available to do the job for you as well. Microsoft InstallShield is one of these tools that will automatically build an update between two versions of data and offer a method of transitioning between them. Another excellent deployment tool introduced with .NET 2.0 is ClickOnce; be sure to check it out.

Why would you want to make your own? Having your own patch creation and deployment system offers a lot of flexibility, and allows you to build your own front-end and deployment process that users will access. There are also no licensing fees involved since no third-party software is required.

The accessibility and deployment of software updates is an important aspect of software development, especially in regards to publicly available tools. If a program flaw causes the tool to produce corrupt game content, the program is useless until it has been updated to produce correct data. By employing a system similar to the one discussed in this chapter, users will be able to update a tool without losing precious development time.

INDEX

N